38. *The A to Z of Jainism* by Kristi L. Wiley, 2009.
39. *The A to Z of the Inuit* by Pamela K. Stern, 2009.
40. *The A to Z of Early North America* by Cameron B. Wesson, 2009.
41. *The A to Z of the Enlightenment* by Harvey Chisick, 2009.
42. *The A to Z Methodism* by Charles Yrigoyen Jr. and Susan E. Warrick, 2009.
43. *The A to Z of the Seventh-day Adventists* by Gary Land, 2009.
44. *The A to Z of Sufism* by John Renard, 2009.
45. *The A to Z of Sikhism* by William Hewat McLeod, 2009.
46. *The A to Z Fantasy Literature* by Brian Stableford, 2009.
47. *The A to Z of the Discovery and Exploration of the Pacific Islands* by Max Quanchi and John Robson, 2009.
48. *The A to Z of Australian and New Zealand Cinema* by Albert Moran and Errol Vieth, 2009.
49. *The A to Z of African-American Television* by Kathleen Fearn-Banks, 2009.
50. *The A to Z of American Radio Soap Operas* by Jim Cox, 2009.
51. *The A to Z of the Old South* by William L. Richter, 2009.
52. *The A to Z of the Discovery and Exploration of the Northwest Passage* by Alan Day, 2009.
53. *The A to Z of the Druzes* by Samy S. Swayd, 2009.
54. *The A to Z of the Welfare State* by Bent Greve, 2009.
55. *The A to Z of the War of 1812* by Robert Malcomson, 2009.
56. *The A to Z of Feminist Philosophy* by Catherine Villanueva Gardner, 2009.
57. *The A to Z of the Early American Republic* by Richard Buel Jr., 2009.
58. *The A to Z of the Russo-Japanese War* by Rotem Kowner, 2009.
59. *The A to Z of Anglicanism* by Colin Buchanan, 2009.
60. *The A to Z of Scandinavian Literature and Theater* by Jan Sjåvik, 2009.
61. *The A to Z of the Peoples of the Southeast Asian Massif* by Jean Michaud, 2009.
62. *The A to Z of Judaism* by Norman Solomon, 2009.
63. *The A to Z of the Berbers (Imazighen)* by Hsain Ilahiane, 2009.
64. *The A to Z of British Radio* by Seán Street, 2009.
65. *The A to Z of The Salvation Army* by Major John G. Merritt, 2009.
66. *The A to Z of the Arab-Israeli Conflict* by P. R. Kumaraswamy, 2009.
67. *The A to Z of the Jacksonian Era and Manifest Destiny* by Terry Corps, 2009.
68. *The A to Z of Socialism* by Peter Lamb and James C. Docherty, 2009.
69. *The A to Z of Marxism* by David Walker and Daniel Gray, 2009.
70. *The A to Z of the Bahá'í Faith* by Hugh C. Adamson, 2009.
71. *The A to Z of Postmodernist Literature and Theater* by Fran Mason, 2009.
72. *The A to Z of Australian Radio and Television* by Albert Moran and Chris Keating, 2009.
73. *The A to Z of the Lesbian Liberation Movement: Still the Rage* by JoAnne Myers, 2009.
74. *The A to Z of the United States–Mexican War* by Edward R. Moseley and Paul C. Clark, 2009.
75. *The A to Z of World War I* by Ian V. Hogg, 2009.
76. *The A to Z of World War II: The War Against Japan* by Ann Sharp Wells, 2009.
77. *The A to Z of Witchcraft* by Michael D. Bailey, 2009.

78. *The A to Z of British Intelligence* by Nigel West, 2009.
79. *The A to Z of United States Intelligence* by Michael A. Turner, 2009.
80. *The A to Z of the League of Nations* by Anique H. M. van Ginneken, 2009.
81. *The A to Z of Israeli Intelligence* by Ephraim Kahana, 2009.
82. *The A to Z of the European Union* by Joaquín Roy and Aimee Kanner, 2009.
83. *The A to Z of the Chinese Cultural Revolution* by Guo Jian, Yongyi Song, and Yuan Zhou, 2009.
84. *The A to Z of African American Cinema* by S. Torriano Berry and Venise T. Berry, 2009.
85. *The A to Z of Japanese Business* by Stuart D. B. Picken, 2009.
86. *The A to Z of the Reagan–Bush Era* by Richard S. Conley, 2009.
87. *The A to Z of Human Rights and Humanitarian Organizations* by Robert F. Gorman and Edward S. Mihalkanin, 2009.
88. *The A to Z of French Cinema* by Dayna Oscherwitz and MaryEllen Higgins, 2009.
89. *The A to Z of the Puritans* by Charles Pastoor and Galen K. Johnson, 2009.
90. *The A to Z of Nuclear, Biological and Chemical Warfare* by Benjamin C. Garrett and John Hart, 2009.
91. *The A to Z of the Green Movement* by Miranda Schreurs and Elim Papadakis, 2009.
92. *The A to Z of the Kennedy–Johnson Era* by Richard Dean Burns and Joseph M. Siracusa, 2009.
93. *The A to Z of Renaissance Art* by Lilian H. Zirpolo, 2009.
94. *The A to Z of the Broadway Musical* by William A. Everett and Paul R. Laird, 2009.
95. *The A to Z of the Northern Ireland Conflict* by Gordon Gillespie, 2009.
96. *The A to Z of the Fashion Industry* by Francesca Sterlacci and Joanne Arbuckle, 2009.
97. *The A to Z of American Theater: Modernism* by James Fisher and Felicia Hardison Londré, 2009.
98. *The A to Z of Civil Wars in Africa* by Guy Arnold, 2009.
99. *The A to Z of the Nixon–Ford Era* by Mitchell K. Hall, 2009.
100. *The A to Z of Horror Cinema* by Peter Hutchings, 2009.
101. *The A to Z of Westerns in Cinema* by Paul Varner, 2009.
102. *The A to Z of Zionism* by Rafael Medoff and Chaim I. Waxman, 2009.
103. *The A to Z of the Roosevelt–Truman Era* by Neil A. Wynn, 2009.
104. *The A to Z of Jehovah's Witnesses* by George D. Chryssides, 2009.
105. *The A to Z of Native American Movements* by Todd Leahy and Raymond Wilson, 2009.
106. *The A to Z of the Shakers* by Stephen J. Paterwic, 2009.
107. *The A to Z of the Coptic Church* by Gawdat Gabra, 2009.
108. *The A to Z of Architecture* by Allison Lee Palmer, 2009.
109. *The A to Z of Italian Cinema* by Gino Moliterno, 2009.
110. *The A to Z of Mormonism* by Davis Bitton and Thomas G. Alexander, 2009.
111. *The A to Z of African American Theater* by Anthony D. Hill with Douglas Q. Barnett, 2009.

112. *The A to Z of NATO and Other International Security Organizations* by Marco Rimanelli, 2009.
113. *The A to Z of the Eisenhower Era* by Burton I. Kaufman and Diane Kaufman, 2009.
114. *The A to Z of Sexspionage* by Nigel West, 2009.
115. *The A to Z of Environmentalism* by Peter Dauvergne, 2009.
116. *The A to Z of the Petroleum Industry* by M. S. Vassiliou, 2009.
117. *The A to Z of Journalism* by Ross Eaman, 2009.
118. *The A to Z of the Gilded Age* by T. Adams Upchurch, 2009.
119. *The A to Z of the Progressive Era* by Catherine Cocks, Peter C. Holloran, and Alan Lessoff, 2009.
120. *The A to Z of Middle Eastern Intelligence* by Ephraim Kahana and Muhammad Suwaed, 2009.
121. *The A to Z of the Baptists* William H. Brackney, 2009.
122. *The A to Z of Homosexuality* by Brent L. Pickett, 2009.
123. *The A to Z of Islam, Second Edition* by Ludwig W. Adamec, 2009.
124. *The A to Z of Buddhism* by Carl Olson, 2009.
125. *The A to Z of United States–Russian/Soviet Relations* by Norman E. Saul, 2010.
126. *The A to Z of United States–Africa Relations* by Robert Anthony Waters Jr., 2010.
127. *The A to Z of United States–China Relations* by Robert Sutter, 2010.
128. *The A to Z of U.S. Diplomacy since the Cold War* by Tom Lansford, 2010.
129. *The A to Z of United States–Japan Relations* by John Van Sant, Peter Mauch, and Yoneyuki Sugita, 2010.
130. *The A to Z of United States–Latin American Relations* by Joseph Smith, 2010.
131. *The A to Z of United States–Middle East Relations* by Peter L. Hahn, 2010.
132. *The A to Z of United States–Southeast Asia Relations* by Donald E. Weatherbee, 2010.
133. *The A to Z of U.S. Diplomacy from the Civil War to World War I* by Kenneth J. Blume, 2010.
134. *The A to Z of International Law* by Boleslaw A. Boczek, 2010.
135. *The A to Z of the Gypsies (Romanies)* by Donald Kenrick, 2010.
136. *The A to Z of the Tamils* by Vijaya Ramaswamy, 2010.
137. *The A to Z of Women in Sub-Saharan Africa* by Kathleen Sheldon, 2010.
138. *The A to Z of Ancient and Medieval Nubia* by Richard A. Lobban Jr., 2010.
139. *The A to Z of Ancient Israel* by Niels Peter Lemche, 2010.
140. *The A to Z of Ancient Mesoamerica* by Joel W. Palka, 2010.
141. *The A to Z of Ancient Southeast Asia* by John N. Miksic, 2010.
142. *The A to Z of the Hittites* by Charles Burney, 2010.
143. *The A to Z of Medieval Russia* by Lawrence N. Langer, 2010.
144. *The A to Z of the Napoleonic Era* by George F. Nafziger, 2010.
145. *The A to Z of Ancient Egypt* by Morris L. Bierbrier, 2010.
146. *The A to Z of Ancient India* by Kumkum Roy, 2010.
147. *The A to Z of Ancient South America* by Martin Giesso, 2010.

148. *The A to Z of Medieval China* by Victor Cunrui Xiong, 2010.
149. *The A to Z of Medieval India* by Iqtidar Alam Khan, 2010.
150. *The A to Z of Mesopotamia* by Gwendolyn Leick, 2010.
151. *The A to Z of the Mongol World Empire* by Paul D. Buell, 2010.
152. *The A to Z of the Ottoman Empire* by Selcuk Aksin Somel, 2010.
153. *The A to Z of Pre-Colonial Africa* by Robert O. Collins, 2010.
154. *The A to Z of Aesthetics* by Dabney Townsend, 2010.
155. *The A to Z of Descartes and Cartesian Philosophy* by Roger Ariew, Dennis Des Chene, Douglas M. Jesseph, Tad M. Schmaltz, and Theo Verbeek, 2010.
156. *The A to Z of Heidegger's Philosophy* by Alfred Denker, 2010.
157. *The A to Z of Kierkegaard's Philosophy* by Julia Watkin, 2010.
158. *The A to Z of Ancient Greek Philosophy* by Anthony Preus, 2010.
159. *The A to Z of Bertrand Russell's Philosophy* by Rosalind Carey and John Ongley, 2010.
160. *The A to Z of Epistemology* by Ralph Baergen, 2010.
161. *The A to Z of Ethics* by Harry J. Gensler and Earl W. Spurgin, 2010.
162. *The A to Z of Existentialism* by Stephen Michelman, 2010.
163. *The A to Z of Hegelian Philosophy* by John W. Burbidge, 2010.
164. *The A to Z of the Holiness Movement* by William Kostlevy, 2010.
165. *The A to Z of Hume's Philosophy* by Kenneth R. Merrill, 2010.
166. *The A to Z of Husserl's Philosophy* by John J. Drummond, 2010.
167. *The A to Z of Kant and Kantianism* by Helmut Holzhey and Vilem Mudroch, 2010.
168. *The A to Z of Leibniz's Philosophy* by Stuart Brown and N. J. Fox, 2010.
169. *The A to Z of Logic* by Harry J. Gensler, 2010.
170. *The A to Z of Medieval Philosophy and Theology* by Stephen F. Brown and Juan Carlos Flores, 2010.
171. *The A to Z of Nietzscheanism* by Carol Diethe, 2010.
172. *The A to Z of the Non-Aligned Movement and Third World* by Guy Arnold, 2010.
173. *The A to Z of Shamanism* by Graham Harvey and Robert J. Wallis, 2010.
174. *The A to Z of Organized Labor* by James C. Docherty, 2010.
175. *The A to Z of the Orthodox Church* by Michael Prokurat, Michael D. Peterson, and Alexander Golitzin, 2010.
176. *The A to Z of Prophets in Islam and Judaism* by Scott B. Noegel and Brannon M. Wheeler, 2010.
177. *The A to Z of Schopenhauer's Philosophy* by David E. Cartwright, 2010.
178. *The A to Z of Wittgenstein's Philosophy* by Duncan Richter, 2010.
179. *The A to Z of Hong Kong Cinema* by Lisa Odham Stokes, 2010.
180. *The A to Z of Japanese Traditional Theatre* by Samuel L. Leiter, 2010.
181. *The A to Z of Lesbian Literature* by Meredith Miller, 2010.
182. *The A to Z of Chinese Theater* by Tan Ye, 2010.
183. *The A to Z of German Cinema* by Robert C. Reimer and Carol J. Reimer, 2010.
184. *The A to Z of German Theater* by William Grange, 2010.

185. *The A to Z of Irish Cinema* by Roderick Flynn and Patrick Brereton, 2010.
186. *The A to Z of Modern Chinese Literature* by Li-hua Ying, 2010.
187. *The A to Z of Modern Japanese Literature and Theater* by J. Scott Miller, 2010.
188. *The A to Z of Old-Time Radio* by Robert C. Reinehr and Jon D. Swartz, 2010.
189. *The A to Z of Polish Cinema* by Marek Haltof, 2010.
190. *The A to Z of Postwar German Literature* by William Grange, 2010.
191. *The A to Z of Russian and Soviet Cinema* by Peter Rollberg, 2010.
192. *The A to Z of Russian Theater* by Laurence Senelick, 2010.
193. *The A to Z of Sacred Music* by Joseph P. Swain, 2010.
194. *The A to Z of Animation and Cartoons* by Nichola Dobson, 2010.
195. *The A to Z of Afghan Wars, Revolutions, and Insurgencies* by Ludwig W. Adamec, 2010.
196. *The A to Z of Ancient Egyptian Warfare* by Robert G. Morkot, 2010.
197. *The A to Z of the British and Irish Civil Wars 1637–1660* by Martyn Bennett, 2010.
198. *The A to Z of the Chinese Civil War* by Edwin Pak-wah Leung, 2010.
199. *The A to Z of Ancient Greek Warfare* by Iain Spence, 2010.
200. *The A to Z of the Anglo–Boer War* by Fransjohan Pretorius, 2010.
201. *The A to Z of the Crimean War* by Guy Arnold, 2010.
202. *The A to Z of the Zulu Wars* by John Laband, 2010.
203. *The A to Z of the Wars of the French Revolution* by Steven T. Ross, 2010.
204. *The A to Z of the Hong Kong SAR and the Macao SAR* by Ming K. Chan and Shiu-hing Lo, 2010.
205. *The A to Z of Australia* by James C. Docherty, 2010.
206. *The A to Z of Burma (Myanmar)* by Donald M. Seekins, 2010.
207. *The A to Z of the Gulf Arab States* by Malcolm C. Peck, 2010.
208. *The A to Z of India* by Surjit Mansingh, 2010.
209. *The A to Z of Iran* by John H. Lorentz, 2010.
210. *The A to Z of Israel* by Bernard Reich and David H. Goldberg, 2010.
211. *The A to Z of Laos* by Martin Stuart-Fox, 2010.
212. *The A to Z of Malaysia* by Ooi Keat Gin, 2010.
213. *The A to Z of Modern China (1800–1949)* by James Z. Gao, 2010.
214. *The A to Z of the Philippines* by Artemio R. Guillermo and May Kyi Win, 2010.
215. *The A to Z of Taiwan (Republic of China)* by John F. Copper, 2010.
216. *The A to Z of the People's Republic of China* by Lawrence R. Sullivan, 2010.
217. *The A to Z of Vietnam* by Bruce M. Lockhart and William J. Duiker, 2010.
218. *The A to Z of Bosnia and Herzegovina* by Ante Cuvalo, 2010.
219. *The A to Z of Modern Greece* by Dimitris Keridis, 2010.
220. *The A to Z of Austria* by Paula Sutter Fichtner, 2010.
221. *The A to Z of Belarus* by Vitali Silitski and Jan Zaprudnik, 2010.
222. *The A to Z of Belgium* by Robert Stallaerts, 2010.
223. *The A to Z of Bulgaria* by Raymond Detrez, 2010.

224. *The A to Z of Contemporary Germany* by Derek Lewis with Ulrike Zitzlsperger, 2010.
225. *The A to Z of the Contemporary United Kingdom* by Kenneth J. Panton and Keith A. Cowlard, 2010.
226. *The A to Z of Denmark* by Alastair H. Thomas, 2010.
227. *The A to Z of France* by Gino Raymond, 2010.
228. *The A to Z of Georgia* by Alexander Mikaberidze, 2010.
229. *The A to Z of Iceland* by Gudmundur Halfdanarson, 2010.
230. *The A to Z of Latvia* by Andrejs Plakans, 2010.
231. *The A to Z of Modern Italy* by Mark F. Gilbert and K. Robert Nilsson, 2010.
232. *The A to Z of Moldova* by Andrei Brezianu and Vlad Spânu, 2010.
233. *The A to Z of the Netherlands* by Joop W. Koopmans and Arend H. Huussen Jr., 2010.
234. *The A to Z of Norway* by Jan Sjåvik, 2010.
235. *The A to Z of the Republic of Macedonia* by Dimitar Bechev, 2010.
236. *The A to Z of Slovakia* by Stanislav J. Kirschbaum, 2010.
237. *The A to Z of Slovenia* by Leopoldina Plut-Pregelj and Carole Rogel, 2010.
238. *The A to Z of Spain* by Angel Smith, 2010.
239. *The A to Z of Sweden* by Irene Scobbie, 2010.
240. *The A to Z of Turkey* by Metin Heper and Nur Bilge Criss, 2010.
241. *The A to Z of Ukraine* by Zenon E. Kohut, Bohdan Y. Nebesio, and Myroslav Yurkevich, 2010.
242. *The A to Z of Mexico* by Marvin Alisky, 2010.
243. *The A to Z of U.S. Diplomacy from World War I through World War II* by Martin Folly and Niall Palmer, 2010.
244. *The A to Z of Spanish Cinema* by Alberto Mira, 2010.
245. *The A to Z of the Reformation and Counter-Reformation* by Michael Mullett, 2010.

The A to Z of Irish Cinema

Roderick Flynn
Patrick Brereton

The A to Z Guide Series, No. 185

The Scarecrow Press, Inc.
Lanham • Toronto • Plymouth, UK
2010

Published by Scarecrow Press, Inc.
A wholly owned subsidiary of
The Rowman & Littlefield Publishing Group, Inc.
4501 Forbes Boulevard, Suite 200, Lanham, Maryland 20706
http://www.scarecrowpress.com

Estover Road, Plymouth PL6 7PY, United Kingdom

British Library Cataloguing in Publication Information Available

Library of Congress Cataloging-in-Publication Data

The hardback version of this book was cataloged by the Library of Congress
as follows:

Flynn, Roderick.
  Historical dictionary of Irish cinema / Roderick Flynn, Patrick Brereton.
    p. cm. — (Historical dictionaries of literature and the arts ; no. 17)
  Includes bibliographical references.
    1. Motion pictures—Ireland—Dictionaries. I. Brereton, Pat. II. Title.
PN1993.5.I85F695 2007
791.430941503—dc22   2007004289

ISBN 978-0-8108-7613-2 (pbk. : alk. paper)

Contents

Editor's Foreword

For a relatively small country, Ireland has an impressively large and dynamic film industry. This might very well not be the case, however, had it not been for the efforts of countless actors, directors, entrepreneurs, and—more recently—politicians. There has always been an Irish passion for cinema (as there has been a passion for literature and theater), but the recent expansion might not have happened had the state not intervened to make Ireland an attractive and lucrative production location. The result has been not only more but often better films, and a shift from provincial subjects to those that are more universal in nature and thus able to attract larger box-office receipts and foreign audiences.

This progression in Irish cinema is related first in a chronology and introduction, which trace over a century of history; a dictionary, with several hundred entries on the pioneers and current leaders in the industry, actors and directors, authors, distributors and exhibitors, schools and arts centers, government bodies and legislation, and above all the films and recurrent themes; and a bibliography, to enable interested readers to further explore any areas of particular interest. *The A to Z of Irish Cinema* is an excellent place to start and to come back to periodically for further information.

Patrick (Pat) Brereton and Roderick (Roddy) Flynn are two specialists on Irish cinema who were born and educated largely in Ireland. At present, both are employed by the Dublin City University's School of Communications, where Dr. Brereton is a lecturer in film and media studies and chair of the bachelor's program in multimedia, and Dr. Flynn is a lecturer and chair of the master's program in film and television. Both have written extensively not only on Irish cinema but also on cinema more broadly. A reference book like this was a new venture for them, but they have achieved a wonderful result—a useful tool for their students and others, both at home and abroad.

Jon Woronoff
Series Editor

Preface

This book's objective is to allow readers with different levels of familiarity to gain a multifaceted and comprehensive understanding of Irish cinema. We have proceeded on the assumption that some readers will be familiar only with large-scale international productions made in and about Ireland and that some will be entirely unfamiliar with indigenous (and in particular more recent) filmmaking and filmmakers in Ireland.

With that established, our core consideration in determining what to include and exclude has been influenced by our central assumption of what constitutes the film form. We have adopted the commonsense definition of "a film": a cinematic form that has dominated global screens since World War I: live-action, fictional, feature-length films (usually originating in Southern California but not included—for obvious reasons—in this volume). Thus we have sought to catalogue instances of this form emerging from Ireland since the turn of the 20th century. Given that indigenous production did not begin to occur on a regular basis until the 1980s (and even then with sporadic gaps), the total output of Irish filmmakers is still quite modest, perhaps no more than 200 feature films in total. Consequently, we have attempted to be fairly exhaustive in our coverage. Recognizing that many readers will associate a number of "foreign" films with Ireland, we also discuss American, British, and French films shot in Ireland in an attempt to situate indigenous films within a wider cultural context.

Our stress on fiction film, however, means that documentary film and animation receive less attention. Although most of what little indigenous production that occurred in Ireland before 1970 was nonfiction, the documentary form has subsequently migrated largely to television and thus falls outside the scope of this book. In the case of feature-length animation, Ireland has produced relatively little, compared to live-action films. Nonetheless, we include substantial discussion of the work of documentarists such as Robert Flaherty, Louis Marcus, George Morrison, and John T. Davis, as well as the institutions that commissioned their work. Similarly, the book discusses the attempts at establishing an industrial-scale animation sector in the 1980s and the success of more artisan-scale production of animation since then.

We have also grappled with the question of what constitutes specifically *Irish* film. To begin, we worked within an impossibly zealous definition: anything produced in Ireland by an Irish director with an Irish story. This meant, for example, that we could discuss more or less any film supported by the Irish Film Board since the 1980s. However, even that approach presented problems—how would we deal with a film such as *How Harry Became a Tree*, a Film Board–supported film directed by a Serb and based on a Chinese folk tale (albeit set in Ireland)? Clearly we needed a broader definition to account for films that have helped define how Ireland and the Irish are understood by filmmakers outside Ireland and also by audiences in Ireland and elsewhere.

Thus our broader definition includes mainly American and British pictures such as *The Quiet Man* and *Ryan's Daughter* (although it also encompasses *The Purple Taxi* for a Francophone audience) that have defined the acceptable limits of how things Irish may be represented not merely for subsequent foreign filmmakers working in Ireland, but arguably, even for Irish directors working in Ireland.

At the other extreme any attempt to treat of all films that represent Ireland in an encyclopaedic fashion must perforce be doomed to failure. In his *Irish Filmography*, Kevin Rockett attempted simply to list all filmed fictional representations of Ireland and the Irish and came up with over 2,000 titles. We have concentrated on only the major overseas representations.

We use a final framing device to determine what to include: the fact (already pointed to) that Irish cinematic texts are the products of an industry that has been, like so many other culture industries across the globe, alternately ignored and supported by the Irish state. In short, in this volume, film is simultaneously treated as a textual form and a commercial product. In part this dual cultural analysis–political economy approach reflects that of the institution where we both have worked for the past decade, the School of Communications at Dublin City University. However, it also acknowledges the inescapable truth that very few film industries on the planet would exist were it not for state support and the efforts of those who have lobbied successive governments for such support. Thus, this volume gives as much consideration to institutions such as the Irish Film Board and the Irish Film Institute and to political figures such as Michael D. Higgins and Sean Lemass as it does to directors such as Jim Sheridan and Neil Jordan.

As a final caveat we should stress that the assessments offered of various filmmakers and their films herein are historically contingent. The vast majority of those referred to in this book are still active and it may not be possible to deliver absolutely definitive verdicts on their careers for some years to come.

Acknowledgments

We must acknowledge those individuals who were most generous in facilitating the research work undertaken for this book. In no particularly order we would like to thank Ruth Barton at University College Dublin, Kevin Rockett at Trinity College, Tony Tracy of University College Galway, Louise Ryan at the Irish Film Board, Sunniva O'Flynn and the librarians at the Irish Film Institute, Julie Allen of the Dublin City University Library, the staff of the National Archives, David McLoughlin of Screen Producers Ireland, and Morgan O'Sullivan of World 2000.

Over the years our work has been informed by that undertaken by our students, especially at a postgraduate level. However, we would like to particularly acknowledge a debt to the dissertation work of Maeve Connolly, Díóg O'Connell, Nicholas Fennell, Niamh McCole, Trevor Curran, and Eimear O'Kane.

Roddy Flynn would also like to acknowledge the financial support made available by the Research Advisory Panel at Dublin City University, which facilitated this work by providing a fellowship for the year 2005.

Our thanks also to our editor at Scarecrow Press, Jon Woronoff, and assistant editor April Snider.

Finally, we would both like to thank our families, without whom none of this would be possible or worthwhile. Much love and thanks to Ciara, Angela, Robert, Rita, Conor, Romy, and Ava.

Acronyms and Abbreviations

ABC	Associated British Cinemas
AIFM	Association of Independent Filmmakers
AIP	Association of Independent Producers
BAFTA	British Academy Film and Television Arts Awards
BBC	British Broadcasting Corporation
BES	Business Expansion Scheme
BFI	British Film Institute
CRC	Cultural Relations Committee
DFVC	Derry Film and Video Co-operative
DIT	Dublin Institute of Technology
EFDO	European Film Distribution Office
EU	European Union
FCOI	Film Company of Ireland
FIFS	Federation of Irish Film Societies
FII	Film Institute of Ireland
FMI	Film Makers Ireland
FTC	Fair Trade Commission
GAA	Gaelic Athletic Association
IBEC	Irish Business and Employers Confederation
ICC	Industrial Credit Corporation
ICTU	Irish Congress of Trade Unions
IDA	Industrial Development Authority
IFC	Irish Film Centre
IFCB	Irish Film Centre Building Ltd.
IFFC	Irish Film Finance Corporation
IFI	Irish Film Institute
IFS	Irish Film Society
IFT	Irish Film Theatre
IFTA	Irish Film & Television Academy

IPP	Irish Parliamentary Party
IPU	Independent Production Unit (RTÉ).
IRA	Irish Republican Army
ITGWU	Irish Transport and General Worker's Union
ITN	Independent Television News
MoMA	Museum of Modern Art (New York)
NCAD	National College of Art and Design
NFII	National Film Institute of Ireland
NFSI	National Film Studios of Ireland
NIFTC	Northern Ireland Film and Television Commission
PIRA	Provisional Irish Republican Army
PWC	PriceWaterhouseCoopers
RADA	Royal Academy of Dramatic Arts
RIA	Royal Irish Academy
RIC	Royal Irish Constabulary
RTÉ	Radio Telefís Éireann (Irish TV broadcaster)
RUC	Royal Ulster Constabulary
SPI	Screen Producers Ireland
TD	Teachta Daila [MP]
TVS	Television South (UK broadcaster)
UCD	University College Dublin
UCI	United Cinemas International
UIP	United International Pictures
UPA	United Productions of America
UVF	Ulster Volunteer Force

Chronology

1896 The first public cinema screening takes place at Dan Lowrey's Star of Erin Ballroom (now the Olympia Theater) on Dublin's Dame Street as an element of a variety performance.

1897 The earliest known moving picture footage in Ireland is shot by a Lumière cameraman on Dublin's O'Connell Street.

1889 Belfast doctor Robert A. Mitchell becomes the first (recorded) Irish person to film in Ireland, taking as his subject the Bangor Yacht Race.

1909 The first cinema in Ireland built to show films—the Volta— opens on Mary Street in Dublin. James Joyce is the first manager of the cinema.

1909 The Cinematograph Act passes in the British Parliament in London. This act allows local councils across the United Kingdom and Ireland to censor the screening of films in cinemas operating under council jurisdiction.

1910 The Kalem Company becomes the first Hollywood production company to cross the Atlantic for the express purpose of shooting on location, around the Lakes of Killarney in County Kerry.

1914 World War I commences.

1916 The Easter Rising breaks out and is put down within a fortnight by the British Army. James Mark Sullivan establishes the Film Company of Ireland.

1917 Norman Whitten establishes the General Film Supply Company in Dublin, the first regular newsreel supply service.

1918 World War I comes to a close.

1918   The Film Company of Ireland releases *Knocknagow*.

1920   *Willy Reilly and His Colleen Bawn*, the last feature produced by the Film Company of Ireland, is released.

1922   The Irish Free State established.

1923   Despite the ongoing Civil War, Dáil Eireann replaces the existing 1909 Cinematograph Act with a new Film Censorship Act. This places control over film censorship in the hands of a single film censor with responsibility for the entire Irish Free State. The first film censor, James Montgomery, is appointed.

1926   The state approves production of *Ireland*, the first government information film. The film (produced by the ad agency McConnell-Hartley) is first screened in 1929. Isaac Eppel's *Irish Destiny* is released.

1929   Savoy Cinema, in Dublin, opens with the premiere of *Ireland*.

1930   The Dublin Amateur Film Society is established.

1932   A Fianna Fáil government led by Eamon de Valera takes power. Sean Lemass is appointed minister for industry and commerce, a position he will hold intermittently until 1958.

1934   *Man of Aran* is shot by Robert Flaherty in the Aran Islands off the west coast of Ireland.

1935   The Theatre Royal, a 4,000-seat theater, opens in Dublin's Hawkins Street.

1936   A papal encyclical on mass media is published.

1936   *The Dawn*, the first full-length fiction film produced and shot in Ireland, goes on release. The Irish Film Society is established by — among others — Liam O'Leary and Eddie Toner.

1937   Father Richard Devane, leader of 1920s campaign against "evil literature," lobbies Eamon de Valera to establish a state inquiry into the role of cinema in Irish national life.

1938   Sean Lemass establishes the Inter-Departmental Committee on the Film Industry.

1939   World War II (termed "The Emergency" in Ireland) commences. The Emergency Powers Order permits the censor to ban films on the grounds that they might undermine Irish neutrality.

1940   A new film censor, Richard Hayes, is appointed.

1942   The Inter-Departmental Committee submits its report to Lemass, who shelves it until the close of war.

1943   The National Film Institute of Ireland is formed under the auspices of Archbishop John Charles McQuaid.

1945   Laurence Olivier films *Henry V* in neutral Ireland; he is unable to do so in the United Kingdom because of wartime conditions.

1946   Lemass submits proposals to the cabinet for a national film studio. The cabinet rejects the proposals. *A Nation Once Again*, the first of the films funded by the National Film Institute, is released.

1948   After 16 uninterrupted years in government, Fianna Fáil loses an election to a Fine Gael–led coalition.

1951   *The Quiet Man* is released. The Arts Council of Ireland is established, but film is excluded from its remit. The Fianna Fáil party is returned to power.

1953   Gael Linn is established to promote use of the Irish language in the media.

1954   Fianna Fáil loses a general election and is replaced by a Fine Gael–led coalition government.

1956   The Cork Film Festival (the first of its kind in Ireland) runs for the first time with support from the Irish Tourist Board. Gael Linn launches the first Irish-language newsreel service, *Amharc Eireann* [A View of Ireland].

1957   Four Provinces releases *Rising of the Moon*, directed by John Ford. Fianna Fáil wins the general election from the coalition opposition.

1958   Lemass formally opens Ardmore Studios in Bray, County Wicklow.

1959   Gael Linn releases *Mise Éire*.

1960   The Industrial Credit Corporation establishes the Irish Film Finance Corporation.

1963   Francis Ford Coppola shoots a debut feature for Roger Corman in Ireland, in part at Ardmore Studios.

1967   Jack Lynch visits the set of John Huston's *Sinful Davy* at Ardmore. The government appoints Huston to head an inquiry into the film industry in Ireland.

1968   The *Report of the Film Industry Committee* is published, which recommends establishment of the Irish Film Board to fund indigenous and overseas filmmaking in Ireland.

1969   *Ryan's Daughter* is shot on the Dingle Peninsula in County Kerry.

1970   The Film Bill is introduced to the Dáil based on the findings of a report by the Film Industry Committee However, the bill is shelved due to a political crisis involving illegal gunrunning, which became known as "the Arms Crisis," to protect nationalists in the North.

1973   A Fine Gael–Labour coalition enters government. Radio Telefís Éireann (RTÉ) purchases Ardmore Studios on instructions from the minister for industry and commerce, Justin Keating. The Arts Council remit is extended to include film.

1975   Ardmore is reestablished as the National Film Studios of Ireland. Bob Quinn's first film, *Caoineadh Airt Ui Laoire* [Lament for Art O'Leary], is released.

1977   Fianna Fáil wins the general election. The Restrictive Practices Commission investigates allegations of discrimination in Dublin cinema release patterns. This leads to an informal agreement to quicken the release time for suburban cinemas. The Arts Council sets up the Irish Film Theatre (IFT), which begins screenings in the Sugar Company Cinema, Earlsfort Terrace, Dublin. The Arts Council launches the Film Script Awards. The Federation of Irish Film Societies is established. Minister for industry and commerce Desmond O'Malley commissions a report on the running of the National Film Studios of Ireland. Joe Comerford's *Down the Corner* is released.

1981   The Film Board Bill becomes law, and the Irish Film Board is established. Pat Murphy's first feature, *Maeve*, is released.

1982   The state places the Ardmore, which is losing money, into receivership. The Film Board funds Neil Jordan's first feature, *Angel*.

1984   The IFT closes due to an economic crisis driven by reduced audiences. Pat O'Connor's first feature, *Cal*, is released.

1987   A Fianna Fáil–Progressive Democrat coalition wins the general election. Citing the national economic crisis, the government suspends operation of the Film Board. Section 35 of the Finance Act is introduced, and the European Union MEDIA project begins its pilot phase.

1989   Jim Sheridan's first feature, *My Left Foot*, is released.

1990   The European Union's MEDIA '95 program begins. Thaddeus O'Sullivan's first feature, *December Bride*, is released.

1991   Daniel Day-Lewis and Brenda Fricker win Best Actor and Best Supporting Actress Oscars for their respective roles in *My Left Foot*. The international vehicle *Far and Away* is shot in County Kerry.

1992   **June:** A report on the indigenous audiovisual production industry (*The Coopers and Lybrand Report*) is published. **December:** Ireland joins Eurimages. A report of the special working group on the film production industry is published. The independent television production sector report (*The FMI Report*) is published. A new Fianna Fáil–Labour coalition government comes to power and creates a new Department of Arts, Culture and the Gaeltacht. Labour TD Michael D. Higgins becomes the new department's first minister. One feature film is made in Ireland.

1993   Neil Jordan wins the Best Original Screenplay Oscar for *The Crying Game*. Soon after, Michael D. Higgins reestablishes the Film Board. Rod Stoneman is appointed chief executive of the Film Board. Section 35 is radically altered to encourage greater private investment in filmmaking. Sixteen features are made in Ireland.

1994   *Braveheart* is shot in the Curragh in County Kildare and at Ardmore Studios. *In the Name of the Father* is released. The Fianna Fáil–Labour coalition collapses and is replaced by a Fine

Gael–Labour–Democratic Left coalition. Michael D. Higgins remains minister for arts, culture and the Gaeltacht.

1995 The first Indecon report (*A Strategy for Success Based on Economic Realities*) is published.

1996 The Irish Screen Commission is established.

1996 *Michael Collins* is released and becomes very successful at home.

1997 *The Butcher Boy* is released. A Fianna Fáil–Progressive Democrat coalition wins a general election. Síle de Valera is appointed minister for arts, culture and the Gaeltacht.

1998 The second Indecon report (*Supporting the Effective Continued Development of the Irish Film Sector*) is published.

1999 *The Strategic Development of the Irish Film and Television Industry 2000–2010 (The Kilkenny Report)* is published.

2002 John O'Donoghue becomes minister for arts and sport.

2003 The PriceWaterhouseCoopers Review of Section 481 is published.

2004 Mark Woods, the Film Board chief, resigns.

2005 Simon Perry, the new Film Board chief, is appointed.

2007 Sheamus Brennan becomes minister for arts and sport.

Introduction

Making definitive statements about when a particular national film industry began is bound to be problematic. In the case of Ireland, the issue is made even more complex by the fact that when cinema technology emerged in the 1890s, Ireland did not exist—at least not as an internationally recognized independent state. Official cultural histories in the 20th century would argue that the Irish nation (i.e., the people and culture) had been in existence for centuries (if not millennia), but the political institution of the Irish nation-state did not come into existence until the Westminster Parliament passed the Government of Ireland Act in 1921. One way or the other, filmmaking activity commenced within the Irish element of what was then the United Kingdom of Great Britain and Ireland within two years of the Lumière Brothers' invention of the cinematograph in 1896. Indeed, the first known moving pictures of Ireland—shots of O'Connell Street in Dublin—were recorded by a Lumière cameraman in 1897. A year later in 1898, a Belfast doctor, Robert A. Mitchell, became the first Irishman to shoot a film within Ireland, capturing documentary footage of a yacht race.

However, in contrast to many other European nations, which developed substantial filmmaking infrastructures during the early 1900s, regular filmmaking activity did not develop in Ireland until the second decade of the 20th century. This is not to suggest that Ireland was entirely unexposed to cinema. The first public screening took place in 1896 in Dan Lowrey's Star of Erin theater, and public exhibition developed rapidly throughout the rest of that decade and into the new century. For the most part, however, screenings were elements of music hall variety shows, or they took place as part of the performances of itinerant showmen touring towns and villages outside Ireland's main cities. It was not until 1909 that the first permanent cinema—the Volta—opened in Dublin's Mary Street.

When even a modicum of regular production activity began, it was driven by interests external to Ireland: a pattern that would be repeated for most of the twentieth century. Key among the early production companies working in Ireland was the Kalem Company, one of the most successful Hollywood-based production companies of the era. Kalem's first trip to Ireland is widely regarded as the first example of a transoceanic Hollywood production shoot. Led by director Sidney Olcott, "the Kalems" arrived in Killarney, County Kerry, in 1910 and over the course of the next four years shot some 70 stories in Ireland. The marketing for all of them made much of the shooting locations. The films were made primarily with a diasporic audience in the United States in mind, rather than being targeted at an indigenous Irish audience. Olcott thus established a tradition in which cinematic representations of Irish affairs and events shown to the wider world did not come from within Ireland but were constructed from without.

Tellingly, when native-born Irish came to produce films in Ireland, they were often émigrés returning from America (even Olcott's parents came from Cork). In 1914 Walter MacNamara returned to Ireland to make *Ireland, a Nation*, which recounted political events in Ireland from Grattan's parliament in 1780 to Robert Emmet's 1803 rebellion. Two years later Killarney-born James Mark Sullivan, a successful lawyer in the United States, returned to Ireland to establish the Film Company of Ireland. This was the first professional indigenous production company and produced several significant features before the end of the decade, including *Knocknagow* (1918) and *Willy Reilly and His Colleen Bawn* (1920). However, Sullivan returned to America in 1920, and, as a result, there was no production company creating indigenous fiction operating in Ireland by the time the Irish Free State was established in 1922.

The absence of such a company indirectly contributed to the atmosphere in which the new state debated and passed its first piece of cinema-related legislation. In July 1923, while a civil war raged between those in favor of and those against the treaty with the United Kingdom that had ended the War of Independence, those on the protreaty side who constituted the de facto government of Ireland found time to pass a Censorship of Films Act, the only piece of Irish legislation directly related to film until the 1970s. When the construction of indigenous representations seemed impossible, censorship equipped the nascent state with another tool for determining the "official" view of Ireland by strictly determining the range of representations available to the Irish cinema-going public. That highly conservative official view was actively informed by a Christian ethos and led to the banning or cutting of some 11,000 films by 1980.

Films were made in the 1920s but in a sporadic fashion: Norman Whitten, who had established a newsreel company in the second decade of the 20th century, produced three comedy features in 1922, all of which featured Jimmy O'Dea. Isaac Eppel wrote and produced *Irish Destiny* in 1926, but neither Whitten nor Eppel produced any further features. The 1930s saw a similar pattern: Playwright Denis Johnston directed a silent adaptation of a Frank O'Connor short story, "Guests of the Nation," in 1935, and a year later Killarney garage owner Tom Cooper premiered the result of two years of work in the form of *The Dawn*, a remarkably accomplished drama about the War of Independence. In 1938 Jimmy O'Dea starred in *Blarney*, a comedy produced by his own O'D Productions vehicle, but again neither Johnston, Cooper, nor O'Dea remained involved in cinema production in the long term.

In the meantime, some of the most popular representations of Ireland were produced in Hollywood or by British producers. In 1936, John Ford made the first of his Irish-themed talkies, choosing Liam O'Flaherty's novel *The Informer* as his source material. (The novel had previously been shot in 1929 as a silent by American director Arthur Riordan working in the United Kingdom.) However, although Ford's film proved very popular with Irish audiences, even it was eclipsed by the success of *Man of Aran*, a British-produced "documentary" made two years earlier by Robert Flaherty. The mythic tone of the film and its stress on a frugal, self-sufficient way of living chimed with the political vision of then taoiseach Eamon de Valera, arguably much more so than the one government-sponsored film made up that point: *Ireland* (1929), essentially a travelogue film made for distribution to Irish embassies overseas. *Man of Aran* was also warmly received overseas, where it was easily associated with Flaherty's previous works on "primitive" societies, *Nanook of the North* (1922) and *Moana* (1926). Therefore, it arguably had a powerful influence on subsequent representations of Ireland and the Irish: Although on the face of it David Lean's film *Ryan's Daughter* (1969) may appear a very different film from *Man of Aran*, both are informed by a similar set of assumptions about the primitive relationship between the Irish people, the land, and the elements.

That such control of international representations of Ireland lay in the hands of individuals outside Ireland, especially those in the U.S. and British film industries, did not go unnoted within Ireland. The late 1930s saw the beginnings of a debate about the role of cinema in Irish life, reflected in the 1936 establishment of the Irish Film Society. The society sought to expose at least some people to images other than those Hollywood productions the Irish censor deemed safe for public consumption. In 1937, a Jesuit priest, Father Richard Devane, called on de Valera to establish a public inquiry into how cinema might be used to promote national ideals rather than simply being treated as a threat to the moral fabric of the country. However, then minister for industry and commerce Sean Lemass hijacked the resulting inquiry, which concerned itself mainly with questions of how to go about establishing a commercially viable film industry in Ireland, a question to which it concluded there was no convincing answer. The inquiry did indirectly lead the state to partially fund the operations of National Film Institute of Ireland, established under the auspices of the Catholic Church in 1943 and the closest thing to a state film body till the 1980s.

Nonetheless the involvement of Lemass and the Department of Industry and Commerce proved to be important for subsequent Irish film policy: Until the 1990s film was tacitly regarded by the state as an industrial undertaking rather than a cultural one, and policy was formulated accordingly. Postwar film policy was focused on attracting large-scale overseas productions to film in Ireland more than it was concerned with the development of an indigenous production sector. Thus although politicians acknowledged that the representation of Ireland as a primitive backwater in films such as *The Quiet Man* (1951) was regrettable, such deleterious imagery was to be tolerated if the film had a positive economic impact through providing casual employment, increasing tourist numbers, or even increasing Irish whiskey sales.

This thinking was brought to its logical conclusion in the establishment of Ardmore Studios in 1957. Although nominally undertaken by private capital, it subsequently emerged that most of the capital used to build the studio had been provided by two agencies of the Department of Industry and Commerce, where Sean Lemass was still minister. Lemass had submitted plans to the cabinet for a state-funded studio as early as 1946 but was thwarted by the Department of Finance, which expressed reservations about investing state money in an infrastructure designed to accommodate the needs of foreign production companies rather than the more modest requirement of any putative domestic producers.

Although it was clearly understood that financing the establishment of Ardmore would gradually and indirectly facilitate the development of an indigenous production sector, in point of fact, the studios failed spectacularly to accomplish this goal. A policy designed to ensure that productions filmed at the studios had access to British government funding for film production effectively ensured that Irish personnel were largely excluded from working on productions at Ardmore. In any case, almost from their inception, the studios found it difficult to secure a constant supply of clients and spent much of the 1960s and 1970s teetering on the brink of financial collapse.

Nonetheless, Ardmore's existence did encourage more filmmakers from overseas to create movies in Ireland than had been the case before. In 1967, the noted Hollywood director John Huston, who by that point had lived in Ireland for more than a decade, convinced then taoiseach Jack Lynch of the potential to create not just the conditions for more filmmaking in Ireland but for an Irish film industry. Lynch appointed Huston to head a 24-member committee to study the question; it published its report (*The Report of the Film Industry Committee*) in 1968. Unusually, the committee argued that the development of an indigenous production sector was of such cultural importance that the state should fund small-scale domestic production through the establishment of a national film board. Even more unusually, then minister for industry and commerce George Colley accepted these recommendations without demur and arranged for the drawing up of a bill to put them into effect.

The Film Bill of 1970 received only a first reading in the Irish parliament, however. An entirely unrelated domestic political scandal led to a cabinet reshuffle, and the Film Bill was first temporarily sidelined, then entirely mothballed after a new administration came into power in 1973. Film production continued but relied almost exclusively on overseas productions using Ardmore as a location.

Despite the absence of a film board, the mid-1970s witnessed some moves toward the establishment of at least a semipermanent indigenous production capacity. From the early 1970s an increasingly number of commercials for Irish products destined for Irish television were shot in Ireland, and the prospect of some kind of regular work for film crews began to emerge. The 1973 Arts Act extended the remit of the Arts Council to include film, and in 1977 former Radio Telefís Éireann (RTÉ) director Bob Quinn completed *Poitín*, his first feature, with the proceeds of the first Arts Council Film Script award. Other recipients of Arts Council funding in this period included Kieran Hickey, Joe Comerford, Cathal Black, and Pat Murphy, a group regarded in aggregate as constituting the "first wave" of indigenous Irish filmmakers in the late 1970s and early 1980s.

State policy with regard to film still focused on Ardmore, however. In 1973, Radio Telefís Éireann acquired the studios (then in receivership) on behalf of then minister for industry and commerce Justin Keating. Two years later, Keating established the National Film Studios of Ireland at Ardmore, under the chairmanship of British director (but resident of Ireland) John Boorman, himself a major client of the studios. In effect, then, Ardmore became a state-run film studio, and substantial sums were invested in the upgrading of the facility. Despite this Ardmore continued to be affected by the difficulties that had plagued it in the 1960s—the failure to secure regular clients. The state's insistence on making support of Ardmore the main element of national film policy increasingly became a source of tension for emerging independent filmmakers, who argued that the money put into Ardmore could be better utilized by funding a film board.

Matters came to a head in the late 1970s after another minister for industry and commerce, Des O'Malley, appointed a private consultancy to investigate the running of the studios. The resulting report largely supported the views of the independent filmmaking sector, which was by now more or less permanently lobbying for the establish of a board. Finally, in 1979, O'Malley published the Film Board Bill, arguing that the board should have the freedom to support a mix of international and indigenous projects. Despite attempts to alter this in parliamentary debates, the final text of the 1980 Film Board Act required only that the board consider the need to reflect national culture in allotting its funds.

Nonetheless, during its first six years of operation, the Film Board did in fact concentrate on domestic projects. Indeed, from a political perspective it might be argued that it did so to an extent that affected its continuing existence. In addition to a range of shorts, documentaries, and experimental works, the board partially funded 10 feature films between 1981 and 1987. Even the most populist of these features were characterized by native casts and a focus on issues that were intensely local. They were also critically well received and generated a small academic publishing industry concerned with their significance as moments in the development of a national cinema. For the most part, however, they were not commercially successfully, a point that would prove critical in the economically depressed days of the mid-1980s. In 1987, when 50,000 Irish people were emigrating each year and with unemployment rates reaching 20 percent, a newly elected government introduced swinging cuts in public expenditure. While health, education, and social welfare were all subject to cuts, even the tiny sum granted annually to the Irish Film Board came in for scrutiny. When the board was established in 1980, it had been optimistically assumed that returns from previous film investments would obviate the need to fund the board on an ongoing basis. In practice this never happened, and the new government decided to suspend the operations of the board, rather than—as they saw it—continuing to pour money away.

To mitigate the situation, the state pointed to the establishment of a new European Union program—simply called MEDIA—to develop the European audiovisual sector, which was anticipated to provide some revenues for Irish filmmakers. In addition attention was drawn to Section 35 of that year's Finance Act, which allowed companies to write off investments in film production against tax. Taken together these initiatives would, the government was confident, more than compensate for the loss of the Film Board.

There was some truth in this, but MEDIA was expressly prohibited from funding production, whereas Section 35, at least in its early years, was generally considered too unwieldy to attract many investors. As a result, production levels gradually declined to a point in the early 1990s where virtually no feature film activity took place. Ironically, however, when viewed in terms of their impact on the direction the industry took later, it was during this hiatus that two of the most significant Irish films were made. In 1989, former theater director Jim Sheridan directed *My Left Foot*, which in contrast to the more culturally specific films produced under the first Film Board was a classic populist text in the Hollywood mold. The film was well received in Ireland but initially enjoyed only modest box office success. Released in the United States, however, it was nominated for five Oscars, including Best Director and Best Film, a remarkable achievement for a debutante director. Although the film lost out to Oliver Stone and *Driving Miss Daisy*, respectively, in those two categories, Daniel Day-Lewis, who played Christy, and Brenda Fricker, who played his mother, won the Best Actor and Best Supporting Actress categories. Rereleased in Ireland, the film became a massive hit and took $14 million in the United States, a significant multiple of its production cost. In the process *My Left Foot* created a template that other Irish producers in the 1990s and the early years of the 21st century would attempt to emulate: the local story with universal appeal.

Four years later director Neil Jordan's *The Crying Game* was nominated for six Oscars, and Jordan himself won in the Best Screenplay category. On the face of it, this came from a different mold from the one that had produced *My Left Foot*: *The Crying Game* explored national and gender politics in a manner that occasionally conflated the two. However, it did so within a thriller format, complete with a stunning midstory twist that was compelling for any audience.

Not surprisingly, both filmmakers quickly found themselves working within a Hollywood context, although Sheridan (until his most recent picture) used the opportunity to tell exclusively Irish stories, while Jordan mixed fare like *Interview with the Vampire* and *In Dreams* with *Michael Collins* and *The Butcher Boy*. Nonetheless their career paths arguably suggested that the ultimate objective for the Irish industry might be to operate as an offshoot of Hollywood.

In the background of these Oscar successes, moves were underway to address the gap left by the suspension of the Film Board. In summer 1992, two major reports on the future of the Irish audiovisual sector were published under the auspices of Film Makers Ireland, a lobby group for independent producers, and the Irish Film Centre Building Ltd. in association with the Industrial Development Authority. These in turn fed into the deliberations of a committee appointed by then taoiseach Albert Reynolds on film policy. The significance of these reports lay in their terms of reference: Reflecting the economic realities of the day the reports all stressed the economic importance of developing the film industry, particularly as it affected employment. Consequently, their recommendations tended to focus on two areas: fine-tuning tax incentives for film investment and direct state subvention of production.

There was one final element affecting film policy developments. An election in autumn 1992 produced an unusual coalition of the populist Fianna Fáil Party together with the social democratic Labour Party. One of the representatives of the latter, Michael D. Higgins, was made minister at a new department, Arts, Culture and the Gaeltacht (the Irish-speaking regions of Ireland). A sociologist by training and artist by inclination, Higgins was an unusual member of the cabinet. However, he proved a most effective politician, exploiting opportunities such as the wave of euphoria following Neil Jordan's Oscar success to reestablish the Irish Film Board and encourage the expansion of Section 35.

The impact of these changes on the film landscape in Ireland is difficult to overstate. While, the first Film Board supported 10 features over six years, since 1993, the second has funded the development of more than 500 pictures and the production of over 100. Similarly between 1993 and 2003, over €640 million was raised for film production via the Section 35 (later redesignated Section 481) tax break. In short, in the space of less than half a decade Ireland went from having no film industry to speak of to being the fastest-growing audiovisual producer in the European Union. Furthermore, the fact that Section 35/481 was available to any production using Ireland as a location drew in a number of high-profile, large-budget overseas productions, starting with *Braveheart* in 1994, and later including *Saving Private Ryan*, *Reign of Fire*, and the most recent big screen version of *King Arthur*.

Such an expansion in activity has not been without its growing pains. The first wave of indigenous Irish film in the 1970s and 1980s came out of a radical arts-based platform that endorsed a cultural agenda of encouraging the Irish to speak to themselves and placed relatively little stress on the commercial imperative (and thus the need to address other "outsider" audiences). This introspective rationale was of course used to justify investments in the arts generally. The films produced by the new generation of filmmakers in the post–1993 period, however, have been criticized as less concerned with exploring the conventional tropes of Irish identity—particularly religion, politics, the "troubles," family, and repressive sexuality—and have become more preoccupied with an urban milieu of post–Celtic Tiger affluence speaking to a more universal popular culture.

References to universality also draw attention to another debate stimulated by the recent expansion in production activity: Does the more recent output of the Irish production sector even constitute Irish film? A strict definition would doubtless demand that an Irish film be shot and set in Ireland with an Irish cast, that it be made by an Irish crew, and that it be funded with Irish money. (Purists might mischievously add that the language should be Irish rather than English.) Were such criteria to be enforced, this would indeed be a slim volume: It might perhaps include Tom Cooper's *The Dawn*, those films commissioned by the various state bodies over the decades, and the early work of Bob Quinn, Cathal Black, and Joe Comerford, but little else. The sheer cost of making films has meant that overseas money has long played a key role in funding production in Ireland, with all the implications (story and cast, for example) that come with "foreign" money. Furthermore, definitions of what "foreign" means have long been blurred in Ireland by Ireland's de facto status as an Anglophone country with a long history of emigration (and thus a population dispersed to the four corners of the earth). It has long been the case that filmed stories about the Irish and Ireland have emerged from a variety of national film cultures and in particular from the United States. Even the first sustained efforts at fiction filmmaking that actually took place within Ireland were driven by a Hollywood-based outfit, the Kalem Company.

The film industry in the Republic of Ireland certainly has much in common with film industries in other European countries and reflects continuing attempts to create a national cinema market. However, a major difference from other European states is that English is Ireland's majority language, as it is in the British industry. This has resulted in the paradox that, while Ireland likes to position itself as a European country with a mainland European culture, its most obvious sources of finance and target audiences are American and British, and while the latter may be geographically European, culturally and economically Ireland has refused to embrace a pan-European identity. (Politicians and others now speak of the "Boston versus Berlin" polarization.)

Much ideologically based criticism assumes that American cinema automatically represents a form of cultural imperialism that thwarts the development of indigenous culture. In recent years this criticism has found an echo in the suggestion that recent economic prosperity in

Ireland has come at the cost of increased global homogenization and that the more cosmopolitan, universal scope of recent indigenous films has simply been the cinematic symptom of that. However, on a more positive note, other critics have questioned the foundational and insular markers of Irish identity forged by Catholic nationalism and the Gaelic revival and valorize the growing influence of a more universal, global, and in particular *American* popular culture on the country as both positive and liberating.

For decades it was fashionable to deride "Oirish" productions such as John Ford's *The Quiet Man* on the basis that they painted impossibly romantic pictures of Irish life. Yet as modern Ireland comes to terms with the impact of decades (or even centuries) of emigration, the representations offered by the hyphenated Irish are increasingly accepted as offering legitimate perspectives (among many more) on Ireland and Irishness.

THE DICTIONARY

– A –

ABBEY THEATRE. The Abbey has been strongly associated with all the great literary figures of the Gaelic revival at the start of the 20th century, particularly W. B. Yeats and J. M. Synge, who actively sought inspiration from the West, and was regarded as the purest embodiment of Irish identity and individuality. Yeats helped found the Irish Literary Theatre and The Abbey with Lady Gregory (1899), and the resultant literary renaissance produced plays like *The Countess Cathleen* (1899), *Diarmuid and Grainne* (1901), and *Cathleen Ni Houlihan* (1902), which according to some critics mythologize a feminized form of Irish nationalism. Synge's plays, especially *Riders to the Sea* (1902) and *The Playboy of the Western World* (1907), also helped mark a new independent Irish identity. While this provoked much controversy—the latter film glorified violence—it also endorsed a heightened romantic sensibility, which has been carried over into classic films like **Man of Aran** and **The Quiet Man**. A Dublin working-class sensibility was brilliantly captured by the plays of Brendan Behan, such as *The Borstal Boy* (1967), *The Plough and the Stars* (1926), and *Juno and the Paycock* (1924), which were translated into film by **John Ford** and Peter Sheridan.

Furthermore, the central importance of the Abbey actors can be seen in the large number of them working in the new media industry. Their theatrical skills and unique style have marked many Irish American films over time. As early as 1916, the **Film Company of Ireland**'s productions were drawing heavily on the Abbey's resources: J. M. Kerrigan (later to become a Hollywood character actor) and Fred O'Donovan both made their film debuts in the com-

1

pany's *O'Neil of the Glen* (which Kerrigan also directed). Subsequently well-known actors like **Noel Purcell, Jimmy O'Dea**, and **Cyril Cusack** have built long careers in film together with their theatrical work, alongside many fine contemporary actors including **Niall Toibin, Donal McCann**, and **Colm Meaney**, to mention a few, who honed their craft in the Abbey and in Dublin theater generally during their formative acting years.

Given the absence of any sustained indigenous production activity until the 1980s, the Abbey was also long identified as a potential basis for a domestic film industry. In 1937 the Abbey Theatre submitted a memo to the Department of Finance seeking £20,000 from the state via the Trade Loan Guarantee Act with a view to obtaining a matching £20,000 offered by the Milton Shubert Organization, then one of the biggest theatrical groups in New York. This money was to be used to equip a studio in Dublin for film productions, to be made under the artistic control of the Abbey Theatre, which would also provide the subjects and actors. The American group would advise on apparatus and technical services. Although the department's refusal to countenance such a loan meant that nothing came of the 1937 proposal, a very similar idea would later underpin the establishment of **Ardmore Studios**. In 1957 **Louis Elliman** produced a 55-minute made-for-TV version of George Shiel's Abbey play *Professor Tim*. The film, which was directed by **Emmet Dalton**, was produced under the auspices of Dublin Film and Television Productions Ltd., of which Elliman and Dalton were directors. Crucially, however, the two were joined on the board of a sister company—Dublin Film Productions Management Ltd.—by Ernest Blythe, then chairman of the Abbey.

The relationship between these two companies (and Blythe's presence on the board of the latter) was explained by the fact that *Tim* was designed to test the potential of the American market. If the film took off in the United States, then the two companies would collaborate to produce film versions of a further 26 to 39 Abbey plays. Dublin Film Productions Management Ltd. would deal with the question of rights for the Abbey plays, and Dublin Films and TV Productions Ltd. would actually shoot them.

Tim led to a deal with RKO Teleradio in New York to produce a series of Abbey plays as made-for-TV movies, and this apparent guarantee of work was the basis upon which Ardmore's construction was predicated. Although the RKO deal apparently fell through within a few years, Abbey stage productions did constitute a sizeable number of the films made at Ardmore in its first five years of operation, including the first film shot at Ardmore, an adaptation of Walter Macken's *Home Is the Hero* (1958); another George Shiel play, *The New Gossoon*, released as *Sally's Irish Rogue* (1958); and Hugh Leonard's *The Big Birthday*, released in the United Kingdom as *Broth of a Boy* (1959).

***ABOUT ADAM* (1999).** The Hollywood-style romantic comedy *About Adam*, directed by **Gerry Stembridge**, introduces the eponymous hero (played by Stuart Townsend) as a dark but spirited young man capable of casting a spell over any woman (or indeed man) he encounters. Having become engaged to Lucy Owens (Kate Hudson), he then precedes to bed most of her family, a rake's progress that—unusually—the film presents not from a moralistic perspective but rather as a series of comic interludes. What is most striking about *About Adam*, however, is not the story or even the casting (Kate Hudson's presence is clearly the result of the influence of Miramax, one of the film's producers) but the uncredited star of the movie: Dublin itself. The *Variety* review of the film noted that the film conveyed "a very different impression of contemporary Dublin from that imparted in most Irish films" (Levy, 2000). Stembridge goes out of his way to portray Dublin not as a seedy, grime- and crime-filled dystopia but a modern, urbane, cosmopolitan European capital peopled by middle-class characters living in an upper-middle-class bohemian milieu of classic cars and expensive apartments.

In effect then, *About Adam* constitutes a rare example of post–Celtic Tiger cinema, set as it is in breezy, self-confident, and prosperous Ireland. It was the subject of some academic criticism for its alleged "non-Irishness" and lack of identifiable place marks, together with its very open attitude to sexuality that was quite a change from the religious intolerance of previous decades. The light tone and casting helped the film receive extremely wide distribution, by Irish standards; the film was released in—among other locations—the United States, Chile, Mexico, Argentina, Australia, and Spain. However, although the film performed well in Ireland, taking in £660,000, it disappointed elsewhere: In the United States, for example, it was limited to an 11-print release, which ended after three weeks with just $160,000 earned.

ACADEMY AWARDS. Given the lack of continuity of production until the 1980s, Irish success at the awards ceremony of the Academy of Motion Picture Arts and Sciences has been limited. Belfast-born actress Greer Garson won Best Actress for *Mrs. Miniver* in 1942, and **Barry Fitzgerald** won the Best Actor award for *Going My Way* in 1944. In more recent years, set designer **Josie MacAvin** won an award for her work on *Out of Africa* (1985) (her third nomination), and Hollywood-based but Irish-born makeup artist Michelle Burke won two Oscars for her work on *Quest for Fire* (1981) and *Bram Stoker's Dracula* (1992). Finally, in 2002, the Academy awarded **Peter O'Toole** an honorary Oscar for providing "cinema history with some of its most memorable characters" (Academy of Motion Pictures Arts and Sciences, 2003).

Normally we would not pay much serious attention to an award ceremony as bland as the Oscars in a tome such as this, but the perceived importance of the winning of Oscars at key moments has had an important political impact on film policy in Ireland. From the 1950s to the 1970s, the nominations for short films and documentaries by talents as diverse as Hilton Edwards (for *Return to Glennascaul*), **Patrick Carey**, and **Louis Marcus** consistently demonstrated what directors could achieve even in the absence of a proper infrastructure for filmmaking. The respective successes of Daniel Day-Lewis and **Brenda Fricker** in the Best Actor and Best Supporting Actress categories, for their performances in **Jim Sheridan**'s *My Left Foot*, led to calls for the revival of the **Irish Film Board**. (When then taoiseach Charles Haughey praised the makers of the "Irish Film," it was pointed out that the film had been made possible—that is, funded—largely by a British Television Company.)

However, it was another Irish success three years later that would have the single greatest impact. **Neil Jordan**'s *The Crying Game* was nominated for six Oscars at the March 1993 ceremony. As the night proceeded, it appeared that the film was destined to win nothing, losing out in the first five of its six categories. However, in the last—the Original Screenplay category, for which Jordan himself was nominated—it won. The effect at home was dramatic and immediate.

Within 24 hours, minister for arts, culture and the Gaeltacht **Michael D. Higgins** announced the reinstatement of the **Irish Film Board**, effective immediately. Furthermore, several months later, the **Section 35** tax incentive was radically altered, leading to a huge increase in the level of funding available for films made in Ireland.

Linking these changes to the Oscars does not suggest that such decisions would not otherwise have been taken but that they created a political opportunity, which the minister exploited to the fullest possible extent.

ACCELERATOR **(1999).** Directed by Vinny Murphy, the film follows Johnny T. (Stuart Sinclair Blyth) on the run from paramilitary vigilantes because of his "antisocial" behavior. In Dublin he meets Whacker (Gavin Kelty), who challenges him to a car race from Belfast to the Papal Cross in the Phoenix Park in Dublin, a distance of about 100 miles, for a bursary of IR £1200, aided and abetted by contributions from other gang members who also want to get in on the action. The resultant episodic road movie narrative involves a number of young gang members as they pair off and journey up North to steal cars in Belfast. This new generation actively ignore the politics of the North, but as their convoy of stolen cars drives toward the border, they meet army checkpoints—with dramatic consequences. Although made for a relatively low budget, the high-octane pace of the film worked well with working-class audiences in Dublin, who appeared to have closely identified with the protagonists.

ACCESS CINEMAS. See IRISH FILM SOCIETY.

ADAM AND PAUL **(2004).** The film, directed by Lenny Abrahamson, is structured around a day in the life of two heroin addicts constantly teetering on the edge of oblivion. The film makes much of the language of the doped-up junkie, which is by turns pathetic and blackly comic, and is strongly reminiscent of Samuel Beckett's *Waiting for Godot*. This is augmented by the filmmakers' visual humor, which perversely echoes the classic comic film duo Laurel and Hardy. Yet, at the same time, the serious subject matter is not made light of, and the film's success is ensured by the powerful acting of Mark O'Halloran (who also wrote the screenplay) as Adam, who is more grounded, older, and better resourced than his sidekick, Paul, played by Tom Jordan Murphy, who is more naive, spaced-out, and hopelessly accident prone.

The narrative follows the two flaneurs as they find themselves in various parts of Dublin, capturing their colloquial syntax and portraying their bleak existence for a mainstream viewing public, while maintaining a tight balance between alienating voyeurism and sentimental identification. This strategy is reinforced by regular use of wide shots, filmed with great skill by lighting cameraman James Mather, that take in the magnitude of the Dublin scenery and strengthen the portrayal of the characters' fruitless existence. On separate occasions the two antiheroes are dwarfed by the Dollymount Strand chimneys, the Ballymun flats, statues on O'Connell Street, and the Liffey Bridge, which are not in themselves valorized as identifiable markers of the city. As their story follows various engaging comic and other gags and incidental meetings, their journey's pain and ecstasy ends as it began.

The film performed extremely well on the European festival circuit. It belatedly followed the short and critically acclaimed silent calling card *3 Joes* (1991), and the director has served the intervening time well in the advertising industry and shows great promise for the future.

***AGNES BROWNE* (1999).** Based on Brendan Carroll's comic novel *The Mammy*, the film version is intended as an amusing portrayal of a large inner-city Dublin family during the 1960s. Angelica Huston (daughter of **John Huston**) stars (and also directs) as the eponymous heroine, a street trader and a widow with seven children who finds romance in the unlikely shape of Pierre, a French baker (Arno Chevrier). Extensive reference is made to the comic patter of the famous female traders in Dublin, who remain a cultural and tourist representation of solid working-class values. However, it is often difficult to empathize with the protagonist, who works in a vegetable stall.

***AILSA* (1994).** *Ailsa* is an adaptation of a short story by writer Joe O'Connor; it is directed by **Paddy Breathnach**. Starring Brendan Coyle and Andrea Irvine, the film charts the descent of its protagonist

(Miles) into voyeuristic obsession with a neighbor in his apartment block. Miles's day job involves manually writing up genealogies for Irish Americans and tracing their identities. His growing obsession is expressed through a rather understated voice-over that explores the slow disintegration of an obsessive male who is unable or unwilling to find meaning in his own life. The single-focus film uses very effective lighting and interior sets to evoke the claustrophobia and artificiality of the living quarters. The film is particularly notable for its cinematography, which self-consciously strives to give the film a "European" art-house look. *Ailsa* won the Euskal Media Prize at the 1994 San Sebastian Film Festival for Best First Film, and the proceeds were used by director Breathnach and producer **Ed Guiney** to partially fund, respectively, *I Went Down* and *Guiltrip*.

ALL SOULS' DAY **(1997).** Featuring **Eva Birthistle**, Declan Conlon, and Jayne Snow, the film was loosely inspired by Oscar Wilde's "Ballad of Reading Gaol," and in particular the line "each man kills the thing he loves." However, as another quote from Wilde placed at the start of the film—"All life is a limitation"—suggests, writer and director **Alan Gilsenan** is also exploring notions of subjectivity, particularly with regard to how we construct meaning and relate stories. In a curious twist on the trope that informs films like *Citizen Kane* (1941) and *Rashomon* (1950), *All Souls' Day* suggests not that no two people have the same perspective on the same events but that the story recounted by a narrator is not necessarily the same story heard by an audience.The film proceeds to explore this idea in an elliptical fashion and is given a dreamlike quality by the use of a variety of formats, including video, Super 8, and 16 mm. This is a rare excursion into avant-gardism for 1990s Irish cinema.

AMERICAN WOMAN (THE CLOSER YOU GET) **(2000).** A group of Irish lads are bored and dissatisfied with the local women in their small town. Led by fashion-conscious butcher Ian, they decide to pool their resources and put an advertisement in an American newspaper inviting American women to their local town dance in the hope of attracting potential new partners. The local women, including Ian's assistant Siobhan, decide to retaliate in their own way. Characterized as a sweet and charming romantic farce from the producers of *The*

Full Monty (1997) and starring Ian Hart, **Sean McGinley**, Cathleen Bradley, Niamh Cusack, and **Ruth McCabe**, the film (directed by Aileen Richie) was critically regarded as overly contrived and performed poorly at the box office.

AMERICAN-IRISH FILMS. Since the success of **Kalem** films about Ireland, Hollywood has remained preoccupied by the Irish diaspora as the primary focus for Irish-based film. The film historian Kevin Rockett affirms that much Irish representation is focused on policemen, gangsters, sports heroes (especially boxers, as in **John Ford**'s seminal *The Quiet Man*), and politicians (who are often corrupt).

Early representations of the Irish in U.S. cinema (i.e., in the period from 1891 through the second decade of the 1900s) tended to reflect a preassimilated vision of the Irish that echoed the rather crude—not to say racist—representations offered by mid-19th century U.K. publications such as *Punch*. Charles Musser notes that "Paddy" and "Bridget" were stock characters in early cinema. Stereotypically represented as inordinately stupid, their roles invariably involved misinterpreting simple instructions with "hilarious" results such as in Edwin S. Porter's 1903 *The Finish of Bridget McKean*.

However by the 1920s as the Irish increasingly integrated into the higher echelons of American society, such representations had largely disappeared. Nonetheless some critics speak of a continuing preoccupation with "Irish American" identity with some going so far as to suggest that "white Irish" representations create a more acceptable face for multicultural America. Certainly the Irish remain one of the most frequently portrayed ethnic minorities on film. Historically the broad appeal of Irish American stories in the 1930s and the 1940s lay primarily in their ability to present the Irish as representative of a broader ethnic vision of America. The cultural rehabilitation of Irish America began in the most unlikely of all film genres: the gangster film. Notable historical examples include the films of James Cagney, who is the best-known Irish American tough guy on film. The aforementioned *The Public Enemy*, directed by William Wellman, tells the story of the rise and fall of an Irish American gangster Tommy Powers from 1909. Critics singled out Cagney as the model of a new type of popular hero, at once distinctly Irish yet also representative of a broader urban America. Cagney found even greater expression of this phenomenon in the 1938 film *Angels with Dirty Faces*. The Catholic dimension of Irish American culture was always a primary badge of identity and became even more pronounced during the war years, peaking with Bing Crosby's Father O'Malley films, *Going My Way* (1944) and *The Bells of St. Mary's* (1945). Of course tough-talking gangsters and realistic yet kindly priests were not the only Hollywood Irish stereotypes; others included saintly, suffering mothers, dashing adventurers, and beautiful colleens. For a period too after World War II, as the United States enjoyed a sustained period of prosperity and the earliest beginnings of mass air transit, Irish American cinema took a nostalgic turn as by-now second- and third-generation audiences looked to the kind of romanticized depictions of "the old country" offered by films like **Darby O'Gill and the Little People** (1959) and, most famously, John Ford's *The Quiet Man* (1952). Such representations catering to Irish diasporic audiences continued to cater to them as late as the 1990s with, for example, **Far and Away** (1992), a historical evocation of the plight of Irish emigrants played with too much panache by Nicole Kidman and Tom Cruise, and the more "authentic" Irish American experience in **This Is My Father**.

However, it has been a male, criminal sensibility that has remained at the forefront of representations of Irishness over recent decades with films like Phil Joanou's *State of Grace* (1990) with its depictions of internecine strife within the Irish American community (here represented by Sean Penn, Gary Oldman, and Ed Harris). In the same year the Coen Brothers' *Miller's Crossing* (1990), which also focused on Irish gangsters, this time played by Tom Reagan (Gabriel Byrne) trying to prevent a gang war being started by Irish boss Leo O'Bannon (Albert Finney). (Indeed such representations are so commonsensical that it seemed only natural that virtually all the beat cops in Brian de Palma's *The Untouchables* (1987) should be coded as Irish.)

Alongside Sam Mendes's adaptation of *The Road to Perdition* (2003), the most successful recent foray into Irish gangster territory is Martin Scorsese's *The Departed* (2006), which won Best Picture and Best Director at the Oscars. This tale of Boston Irish gangsters and police (played, respectively, by Jack Nicholson and Martin Sheen alongside Leonardo DiCaprio) remakes the 2002 Hong Kong thriller *Infernal Affairs* and echoes Scorsese's classic Italian gangster films. However, this was not Scorsese's first attempt to engage with the place of the Irish in his native land. *Gangs of New York* (2002), dealing with Irish gangs at the end of the 19th century, made for an interesting companion piece with his earlier take on that period: his 1993 adaptation of Edith Wharton's *The Age of Innocence*. (Indeed arguably Scorsese touched on Irish America much earlier through the character of Jimmy Doyle in 1977's *New York, New York*. Doyle was played by Robert de Niro, a quintessentially Italian actor who nonetheless also played Irish gangster Jimmy Conway in another Scorses picture, *Goodfellas*, in 1990.)

There are other, more upbeat, aspects to the representation of Irish America in contemporary cinema, although they are arguably just as stereotypical. *Titanic* (1997), *The Devil's Own* (1997), and *Blown Away* (1994), which feature Irish or Irish American characters, all include virtually interchangeable interludes of the Irish "at play" drinking, making music, and dancing at various functions. Invariably such films also depict the more melancholic (if not alcoholic) flip side to Irish American drinking culture: There is a clear lineage running through Paul Newman's shabby lawyer Frank Galvin in *The Verdict* (1982), Jack Nicholson's dipsomaniac Francis Phelan in *Ironweed* (1987), and Brian Cox's portrayal of James Brogan (father to Edward Norton's Monty) in *25th Hour* (2001).

Indeed although *25th Hour*'s Irish American protagonist offers yet another criminal representation, it is unusual in that it offers a depiction of the more middle-class element of that culture. In a similar vein, Irish American actor-director Edward Burns has, since his 1995 debut *The Brothers McMullen*, sought to do for Irish America what Woody Allen spent four decades doing for Jewish America. In a series of films—*She's the One* (1996), *Sidewalks of New York* (2001), *Ash Wednesday* (2002), and *The Groomsmen* (2006)—he has suggested that it is possible to foreground Irish American characters without necessarily turning their ethnicity into the central theme of the film.

ANGELA MOONEY DIES AGAIN **(1996).** The film stars Mia Farrow (daughter of **Maureen O'Sullivan**) and **Brendan Gleeson** and also features Irish comics Pat Shortt, Jon Kenny, and Tommy Tiernan. Directed by **Tommy McArdle**, the film could be described as a farcical comedy that uses attempted suicide to get some laughs.

Gleeson plays a bespectacled husband attempting to placate his "mad" wife, Angela (Mia Farrow), and prevent her public attempts at suicide, which are apparently designed to "wake up the natives," whom she considers sheeplike in their acceptance of religion and early forms of global capitalism (the latter exemplified by the buyout of the local creamery by a big American corporation).

Flashbacks reveal her passionate love affair with outsider John Malone, who apparently loved swimming in the nude and wading in the local boghole. The rejection of their relationship by the community and her family apparently explains her psychological imbalance. But even Gleeson is unable to contain, much less understand, his wife, or for that matter his role in this undercooked narrative.

Nevertheless the film provides an interesting study of mental illness—albeit tinged with romantic excess and spectacle—within a small-minded rural Irish environment where boredom is frequently alleviated by spontaneous outbursts of bacchanalian indulgence. As the celebrations to commemorate the takeover of the creamery reach a climax, the new American owner (**Patrick Bergin**) is revealed as Angela's former lover, who has apparently forgotten those events of his youth. As he flies off in his helicopter, he remarks to his pilot how they are a strange people. Meanwhile down below Angela is being carted off to the hospital again in an ambulance: In a strangely downbeat conclusion to the otherwise comic proceedings, it appears that this time she has succeeded in performing her "final act."

ANGELA'S ASHES (2000). Based on the internationally successful autobiography by the Irish American Frank McCourt, the film version of *Angela's Ashes* is directed by **Alan Parker** and stars non-Irish actors Robert Carlyle and Emily Watson. Born in abject poverty, Frank's father was an unemployable alcoholic. The film revels in presenting the utterly miserable conditions McCourt grew up in, including the death of siblings through malnutrition. It engendered much criticism in Limerick for its relentlessly negative portrayal of the city, where it appears to rain without cease. However, Frank retained the belief throughout his childhood that a better life could be found. This story appealed to the huge diasporic Irish community in America who were forced to emigrate during very hard times and seek to validate this memory, which is at odds with the wealthy Celtic Tiger reality of today.

ANIMATION. Considering that Ireland is hardly noted internationally as an animation center, it is striking that for a period in the late 1980s, it was home to the largest animation company in the world outside Disney's Hollywood operation. There were some animation antecedents before the arrival of industrial-scale operations. In 1964 Gunther Wolf came to Ireland and set up a studio producing animated TV commercials. He was followed in the early 1970s by Harry Hess, a former UPA animator who had worked on classics such as *Mister Magoo*, and by Jimmy Murakami, who arrived in Ireland in 1970 to work as art director on **Roger Corman**'s *The Red Baron* (1971). Hess established his own studio and in 1973 became a lecturer at the National College of Art and Design (NCAD), where he oversaw the production (with **Radio Telefís Éireann**) of an award-winning short animation, *Pinpoint*. Murakami also set up a studio, Murakami Films, to produce live-action and animated commercials, although he punctuated this by occasional feature work, including working as director on Corman's classic *Battle Beyond the Stars* (1981).

Inevitably the confluence of activity contributed to the emergence of indigenous talent. Aidan Hickey (1942–) trained at NCAD before completing a postgrad film course in London. On returning to Ireland in the early 1970s he made his first film for RTÉ, *An Saol ag Dul Thart*, and subsequently produced—with RTÉ's encouragement—a series called *The Magic Piano*, which was sold to 16 countries. Other Irish animators from the 1970s and early 1980s included Steve Woods, who trained under Harry Hess, and Tim Booth, who began his career in London in the early 1970s before returning to Ireland and working with Murakami Films.

However, on the whole prior to 1985, the animation sector in Ireland was little more than a cottage industry. In that year the Industrial Development Authority (IDA), recognizing that animation was a labor-intensive growth industry, offered an attractive package of incentives (grant aid and support along with a special 10 percent rate of corporation tax) to U.S. animation studios considering establishing themselves outside America. The impact was immediate, leading to the establishment of two major companies, Sullivan Bluth and Emerald City, and subsequently Murakami Wolf.

Born in 1939, Don Bluth had worked as an apprentice at Walt Disney Studios from 1955, returning there as a full-fledged animator in 1971. He worked on a series of Disney animations such as *Robin Hood*, *Winnie the Pooh*, and *The Rescuers* before leaving Disney again in 1979 with two colleagues to set up an independent animation studio.

This studio produced only one feature—*The Secret of NIMH* (1982)—but attracted the attention of Steven Spielberg, who secured funding from Universal for Bluth to produce his next picture, *An American Tail* (1986). Bluth also partnered with Morris Sullivan, a millionaire former financial consultant, who recognized that for Bluth to compete on the global market he needed to locate outside the United States where labor costs were lower. This coincided with IDA policy and, in 1985, Sullivan Bluth was established, first in North County, Dublin, then at a fully equipped studio near the Phoenix Park.

Emerald City was a subsidiary of the New York–based D. L. Taffner company, which in contrast to Sullivan Bluth, who adopted the classical Disney feature format, produced hour-long versions of classic stories such as *Oliver Twist* and *Phantom of the Opera* for American television. Finally, in 1989, Jimmy Murakami established a Dublin subsidiary of the Los Angeles firm he had established with Fred Wolf. Murakami had spent the early 1980s working with the London-based animation company TVC on adaptations of Raymond Briggs's work, *The Snowman* (1982) and *When the Wind Blows* (1986). Murakami Wolf concentrated on television production, securing the contract for the highly successful *Teenage Mutant Ninja Turtles* series.

At its peak, the animation sector was the jewel in the IDA's crown. From virtually nothing in 1985, the animation sector employed over 500 people (one-third of all persons working in the Irish audiovisual industry at that time) as of December 1991, including both freelance and permanent employees. Also a by-product of the development of the animation industry was a growth in training courses at Ballyfermot College in Dublin, which was initially set up in conjunction with

Sullivan Bluth. It became a very Hollywood-style conveyor-belt animation course, which left room for the development of a more art-based course at the Dun Laoghaire Institute of Art and Technology, with both feeding directly into this burgeoning area of media production.

Publicly, too, there was a perception of success—*An American Tail* was a massive box office hit, and Sullivan Bluth followed it with the high-profile *Land before Time* (1988) and *All Dogs Go to Heaven* (1989). There was also a burgeoning indigenous sector. By 1991, companies such as Animedia Teo (where Steve Woods worked), Quinn Films, Tim Furnee's Moving Still Animated, and Aidan Hickey's Grafliks, though all operating on a much smaller scale, promised continuity of production.

However, 1991 also marked a dramatic turning point. Emerald City shut down, with the loss of 50 jobs, while Murakami Wolf cut the number of employees from 130 to 30 after it failed to secure consistent follow-up work on completion of the *Turtles* series. Eventually Murakami and Wolf went their separate ways, although both continued to work in Ireland. Indeed, Fred Wolf Films continued to employ over 30 people to produce the cartoon series *Budgie, The Little Helicopter*, based on four children's books written by former duchess of York Sarah Ferguson. In 2000 the firm finally shut down, although it continues to operate in Los Angeles.

Sullivan Bluth lasted longer than most, although financial head Marcus Sullivan left the company in the late 1980s, and the company went through several incarnations (including a 1992 liquidation) before emerging in 1993 as Don Bluth Ltd. However, in April 1994, Don Bluth returned to America (taking many of the creative staff he originally brought over from the United States with him) when he was offered the chance to head up the new 20th Century Fox animation division (ironically at the time the Irish company was indirectly owned by Rupert Murdoch's News Corporation, which also owned Fox). Although several companies (among them **Merlin Films**, which held a 10 percent stake in the company) expressed an interest in acquiring the Irish studios, they finally closed with the loss of 300 jobs in 1995. Animedia Teo also shut down in this period.

The sudden decline was prompted by a number of factors. As early as 1986, the minister for finance at the time had removed one of the tax incentives (relating to limited partnerships) that had attracted Sullivan Bluth in the first place. However, although animation had appealed to the IDA because it appeared to offer—in contrast to live-action work—the promise of full-time, permanent employment, in fact the animation sector proved as transient as the rest of the audiovisual sector: Projects appeared irregularly, and workers were sourced on a per project basis. Thus, much of the industry worldwide was freelance, and Ireland was no exception to this. Second, geographically, Ireland was peripheral to the core of an industry located in California. Finally, and probably most importantly, there is the inherent logic in the animation process. Animation is a mass-production process (particularly for television, which does not require the same standard of animation as the cinema). Each second of animation requires 24 individual drawings, so a 20-minute program like the *Turtles* requires up to 15,000 drawings. Yet there is no need for the animators themselves to produce each drawing. The creative part of the process (writing scripts, recording soundtracks, designing the characters, and producing detailed storyboards) can be done in Ireland, while the more mechanical and time-consuming inking and painting is farmed out. While the IDA envisaged the labor-intensive part of the process going on in Ireland (and indeed Murakami Wolf did carry out the entire process in Ireland for the first two years of its operation), it proved too expensive, leading to much of it being completed in the Far East, in countries like the Philippines, Korea, Singapore, and Taiwan.

The burst bubble left behind a skilled and determined workforce, however, which constituted the basis for the modern Irish animation sector. Monster Productions, for example, acquired some of Sullivan Bluth's equipment and helped service films like *Space Jam* (1996), the Bluth-directed *Anastasia* (1997), and more recently animation for Madonna's videos, although the bulk of their work is for commercials. A year before Bluth Studios closed, German producer Ralph Christians established Magma Films, which, although doing live-action work, has enjoyed most of its successes with animation series, such as *Loggerheads* and *Norman Normal*, for the European market. Terraglyph was set up in Dublin in 1995 and has become Ireland's largest permanent studio, employing up to 45 employees at the peak of production. Their first feature, *Carnivale* (1999), was released internationally and has won a number of awards. Subsequent features include *Help! I'm a Fish* (2001) and *Duck Ugly* (2002).

However, the bulk of Irish animation companies now do their work in the commercials sector rather than producing feature-length fiction. The key difficulty for the Irish animation sector is the same facing its live-action counterpart: Since American animation dominates world screens, how can Irish animation find a unique voice, much less a globally successful one? It has been suggested that smaller companies like BrownBag Films, which made the highly successful (and Oscar-nominated) *Give Up Yer Aul Sins* (2002), have succeeded by making a virtue of the local specificity of their work coupled with the strategic use of new technology, affording them a competitive edge. Certainly it is notable that pioneers like Aidan Hickey (who received an Irish Film Award in 2004) and Steve Woods, who have long produced recognizably indigenous work, weathered the storm of the early 1990s and continued to run their own companies. Both have directed productions for BrownBag Films.

ANNE DEVLIN **(1984).** Directed by **Pat Murphy**, this historical period drama deals with the Irish rebel Robert Emmet (Bosco Hogan) as he plots the rising of 1803. However, rather than focusing on the rebellion, as is conventional, the film concentrates on the romantic female in his life and the struggle she has to support his political activities. In effect, the film portrays the military struggle for Irish freedom as paralleled by a struggle for female emancipation, most overtly in the scenes in which a British Army officer interrogates Anne about Emmet. The central performance by **Brid Brennan** is phenomenal, as she appears in almost every scene and dramatizes a wide range of emotions. The cultural critic Luke Gibbons speaks of her silence, passivity, and endurance in the face of torture as a calculated act of resistance (Rockett, Gibbons, and Hill, 1988, 248). Female agency is far from passive in this compelling mixture of melodramatic and republican revisionism.

ARDMORE STUDIOS. Ardmore Studios is the only for-hire facility in Ireland capable of accommodating full-scale feature film production. As of 2005 the studio complex, located in Bray, County Wicklow, consisted of five sound stages, plus wardrobe, props, and administrative offices. Several facilities companies are also housed on the Ardmore site.

Nominally established as a private company by impresario **Louis Elliman** and producer **Emmet Dalton** in 1958, the studios were in fact bankrolled by the state from their inception, as a means of drawing filmmaking activity to Ireland. From the outset the studios found it difficult to attract a steady throughput of work, and despite support mechanisms like the **Irish Film Finance Corporation** it was in financial difficulties throughout the 1960s. Sold into private ownership by the Industrial Credit Corporation (a state bank) in 1964, the studio went into receivership three times between 1958 and 1972. See also LEMASS, SEAN.

In 1973, on the instruction of the minister for industry and commerce, Radio Telefís Éireann purchased the studios at a cost of IR £500,000 "in the belief that this was an essential prerequisite to the development of the film industry in Ireland" (Reynolds, 1982). Used for two years as a base to service productions of commercials and filmed documentaries, in 1975 the Department of Industry and Commerce established a state-sponsored body—the National Film Studios of Ireland (NFSI)—to run Ardmore Studios. Chaired by director John Boorman, and run by Sheamus Smith (later film censor), the NFSI invested substantial sums of money in upgrading the studios, as well as marketing them to overseas producers. To facilitate this, between 1975 and 1982 the state advanced grants of £1.5 million to the company. Despite this the NFSI failed to secure a steady supply of work. This fact, together with the lack of a proper capital structure, which resulted in heavy interest payments, saw the studios incur losses of around £500,000 per annum before grants. In its last year of operation (1981/2) the board of the NFSI projected losses of approximately £780,000, and the company already owed the commercial banks some £2 million. Thus in May 1982 the minister for industry and commerce, Albert Reynolds, announced the closure of the studios.

The Dáil resolution closing the studios required that the purchaser should use them "exclusively for the purpose of Film Studios or otherwise for the business of film making or similar or related activities for three years following the close of sale" (Bruton, 1985). Such a stipulation made the studios difficult to sell. Eventually SIPRA Ardmore did buy the studios in July 1984 but went bankrupt before the studios could be reopened. Then in 1986 Mary Tyler Moore Productions, together with **Morgan O'Sullivan**'s Tara Productions, and NADCorp (the state-owed venture capital company) took control of the studios. After an investment of IR £1.2 million to refurbish the studios and build a fourth sound stage, the complex reopened as MTM Ardmore. MTM used the studios to shoot several episodes of their detective series *Remington Steele* starring **Pierce Brosnan.** In 1988 MTM was taken over by TVS, an independent British broadcaster. Then in 1990 the promoters (who included rock band U2's manager Paul McGuinness and accountant Ossie Kilkenny) of what would become Ireland's first privately owned television station (**TV3**) acquired the Tara and TVS stakes, leaving NADCorp with a 32 percent share in the studio.

This final ownership change coincided with the most successful period in the studio's history. Since the upturn in filmmaking activity in 1993, Ardmore's books have been consistently in the black, as the studio played host to indigenous productions and such large-scale undertakings as *Braveheart, Reign of Fire* (2002), and the most recent Jerry Bruckheimer filming of the *King Arthur* myth.

ART SCHOOL INFLUENCE. The student protests that spread to Ireland in 1969 directly influenced the work of **Joe Comerford**, **Pat Murphy**, and **Thaddeus O'Sullivan**, who trained in art schools. Their highly political art-house filmmaking was explicitly concerned with exploring different methods of visual representation, an approach that was prevalent during this period and can be compared with similar art movements in Great Britain and Europe. More experimental art-house filmmakers, who were less concerned with producing conventional narratives and more preoccupied with experiments in formal installations, included artists like **Vivienne Dick**.

ARTS COUNCIL. Established by the Arts Act of 1951, the Arts Council initially had little impact on film culture in Ireland mainly because of the decision to define the arts exclusively as painting, sculpture, architecture, music, the drama, literature, design in industry and the fine arts, and applied arts generally. Some indication as to why film was excluded can be gleaned from then taoiseach John A. Costello's introduction to the Arts Bill, which contrasted "real art" with "the shoddy meretricious products of modern entertainment industry" (among which he specifically included film).

However, a second Arts Act in 1973 broadened the council's responsibilities to include film. The council did not immediately make film awards (although ironically it did make a drama award of £1,000 to a young **Jim Sheridan** in 1973) but first consulted with the **National Film Studios of Ireland**, the **National Film Institute**, the **Irish Film Society**, and the organizers of the Cork Film **Festival** with a view to identifying gaps in film support. The result of these discussions was a decision to initially support low-budget production and the use of film in education. In 1975, **Cathal Black**, **Joe Comerford**, and **Bob Quinn** all received small (less than £1,000) awards to allow them to develop scripts. Education was dealt with through an initially small grant to the National Film Institute. In 1976, the council's literature and film officer, **David Collins**, organized a fortnight of European films, the success of which led to the establishment of the **Irish Film Theatre** as a subsidiary of the Arts Council and implicitly added exhibition support to the council's responsibilities. Similarly, when the Federation of **Irish Film Societies** was established in 1977, the council offered sufficient funding to allow the federation to employ full-time staff to cope with the rapid growth in membership. Finally, in 1980 the council took over the funding of the Cork Festival Film from Bord Fáilte [Irish Tourist Board] and subsequently provided funding to the Dublin and Galway festivals as well.

In 1977, the council instituted a script award worth £6,000, which was supplemented with £5,000 from **Radio Telefís Éireann** (RTÉ) and the promise of technical and equipment assistance from the National Film Studios of Ireland. Early recipients included Bob Quinn for *Poitín*, **Kieran Hickey** for *Exposure*, and Joe Comerford for *Travellers*. However, in 1982, RTÉ, citing financial difficulties, announced that it could no longer support the awards (by now worth £55,000). Although a one-off deal between the council, RTÉ, and the **Irish Film Board** ensured that that year's recipient (**Pat Murphy** for *Anne Devlin*) eventually received her full award, the council conceded that future awards would be significantly smaller.

The arrival of the Irish Film Board in 1981 had in any case raised questions about the council's future role with regard to film. Following a review of its cinema policy the council's 1983 annual report declared its ongoing commitment to supporting exhibition, access to equipment, the encouragement of educational services, and "the maintenance of the status of artist for the film-maker" (Arts Council, 1984). To support production, the council broadened the scope of its awards to more experimental work emphasizing film as a visual art. Typical of this was the 1985 award to Bob Quinn for a feature-length silent film scored by avant-garde composer Roger Doyle. (The project—then titled *End as a Gander*—would eventually emerge as *Budawanny*.)

With the suspension of the Film Board in 1987, the council was again forced to reconsider film policy. Initially the council sought an increase in grant-in-aid from the state to allow it to increase its script award funding in lieu of the Film Board's activities. In point of fact, however, the overall council budget was cut in 1987, and this was reflected in a decline in current expenditure on film. Nonetheless the Arts Council continued to support feature development and short film production throughout the hiatus in the Film Board's activities, and the more prominent role of the council in supporting film was reflected in the appointment in 1989 of the council's first dedicated film officer.

As a latecomer to the Arts Council's remit it was perhaps unsurprising that for much of the 1970s and 1980s film received only a tiny portion of the total council budget. In 1975 the total value of film grants was £2,900, just over 2 percent of the council's total grant budget. Although the £104,000 granted to film a decade later was a vast increase in numerical terms, it amounted to a slight decrease as a percentage of the overall Arts Council budget. This changed somewhat in the wake of the **Irish Film Institute**'s (IFI) mid-1980s announcement of its intention to pursue the establishment of an **Irish Film Centre.**

The council had supported the IFI since 1975 but substantially increased the level of funding to that organization after its dramatic reinvention in 1979. By 1994, the grant of £330,000 to the IFI was the third-largest grant made by the council to a single organization.

Despite this, the council came in for criticism from filmmakers in the 1990s for the lack of clarity in its film role, especially after the reestablishment of the Film Board in 1993. In 1997 the council commissioned Erika King Associates to ascertain the views of the film community and to outline future avenues for the council. The recommendations of that report (and the *Developing Cultural Cinema in Ireland* report that followed it in 2001) found their practical expression in the council's 2004 action plan, which prioritized three areas for support: the production of experimental and innovative work of high artistic ambition, improving access to international platforms for Irish filmmakers and their work, and in general terms improving the environment for exhibiting cultural cinema in Ireland through supporting the development of a regional network of art-house cinemas, enhancing the film work of regional arts centers, and developing audiences through film education initiatives.

ASSOCIATION OF INDEPENDENT FILM-MAKERS. *See* SCREEN PRODUCERS IRELAND.

ASSOCIATION OF INDEPENDENT PRODUCERS. *See* SCREEN PRODUCERS IRELAND.

ATTRACTA **(1983).** This was considered by many to have been **Kieran Hickey**'s most ambitious undertaking, based on a screen version of William Trevor's short story of the same name and adapted by the author. The veteran stage and screen actress Wendy Hiller, who won an Oscar for her performance in *Separate Tables*, was signed up to play the role of the spinster teacher who visits the grave of a Belfast victim of violence, evoking memories of her own. The strong supporting cast includes Kate Thompson, **John Kavanagh**, and Deirdre Donnelly.

– B –

THE BARGAIN SHOP **(1992).** The film tells the story of Billy (**Garrett Keogh**), who embraces the new commercialized Dublin by trashing his antique shop in favor of a franchised bargain basement enterprise. The story, directed by **Johnny Gogan**, could be read as an allegory around the nascent Irish film industry and its need to craft its unique voice rather than nakedly pursuing commercial goals by "giving the public what they want." This is expressed by several characters in the film who fight a rearguard action against the inevitability of "regeneration and progress" that have no meaning or real worth beyond promoting the sale of cheap, mass-produced imports.

The specifics of the somewhat underdeveloped narrative include a conspiracy to siphon money to a corrupt planning official to allow extensive rezoning for a massive and lucrative high-rise project orchestrated by Jim (**Brendan Gleeson**), the sharp-suited and golf-playing businessman who pulls the strings from his rooftop office. The attempt to save the bargain shop and the neighborhood is complicated by a growing romantic attachment between Billy's new assistant, Maria (**Emer McCourt**), and Packy (Stuart Graham), who pontificates on the "**troubles**." This subplot appears at odds with the main narrative. Nevertheless the ending of the film, as the shop front is pulled down, remains enticingly enigmatic.

BARRY LYNDON (**1975**). This stylish, picaresque, historical costume drama is based on the novel by William Makepeace Thackeray and is heavily influenced by the painters of the period, as exemplified by the dreamy cinematography of John Ascott, who won four creative **Academy Awards**. The blurb for the narrative teases: How does an Irish lad without prospects become part of the 18th-century English nobility? Although many find Ryan O'Neill's imitation of an Irish accent somewhat flawed, O'Neill, in the title role of Redmond Barry, is surrounded by a strong cast of Irish and British actors as the story moves from Ireland to Europe and the Seven Years' War. Barry is an Irish rogue who falls in love with Nora, who is already in a match with an English officer. Fearful of losing a "good match" for their daughter, however, her family tricks Barry into fleeing his home, inadvertently sending him on a series of adventures that help him to ascend socially to eventually become—for a period at least—an established member of the French aristocracy.

Film lore has it that the shoot in the Waterford area was a very secret affair, with cult director Stanley Kubrick overseeing every aspect of the production and being a very hard taskmaster. He is said to have rewritten his screenplay constantly, often while shooting took place, and take after take was made of various scenes. Consequently, however, the viewer is treated to the beauty of several exterior battle scenes, which are choreographed using natural light that puts many contemporary special effects–driven epic battle films to shame. The film's leisurely pace coupled with a length of over three hours and a requirement that the viewer carefully follow the narrative's many twists and turns contributed to its box office failure. Nevertheless, the film remains one of the late and great Stanley Kubrick's lesser-known cinematic treasures.

BEAUFORT. This is a small village near Killarney in County Kerry, where the **Kalem Company** came to make their first films in Ireland. In early cinema productions good natural light was essential because of the limitations of film stock and the lack of effective artificial light (incidentally a key driver in the American film industry's early move from the East Coast of America to Hollywood). **Sidney Olcott** made up to 70 successful features and shorts over four summer visits to Ireland, using the unique landscape of lakes and mountains and tapping into Irish republican history and traditions. Unfortunately, because of its distance from the capital and for other social and economic reasons, the area has lost favor of late as a location for filming, notwithstanding some notable exceptions. Filmmakers now prefer the more accessible Wicklow near Dublin and the nearby main production facilities at **Ardmore Studios**.

BECKETT, SAMUEL (1906–1989). Famed as an experimental Irish playwright and novelist, Beckett won the Nobel Prize for Literature in 1969. His classic plays, including *Waiting for Godot*, were highly influenced by slapstick film comedy from Charlie Chaplin to Laural and Hardy. This style of acting and repetitive storyline has been reapplied in numerous films, most recently in ***Adam and Paul*** (2004). Beckett's own direct foray into the medium with *Film* (1965), starring Buster Keaton, is an artistic experiment; the no-dialogue script was published by Faber and Faber (1972) in its first English edition.

In 1999 and 2000, Michael Colgan, the highly regarded Irish theater producer, coordinated a major project initiated by **Radio Telefís Éireann (RTÉ)** and **Channel 4** to film all 19 of Beckett's plays.

Though some purists described this as a sacrilege, the producers wanted to interpret the plays and hopefully broaden their appeal beyond the more rarefied highbrow theatrical experience, using advantages of film like the close-up and more natural speech patterns that are more difficult to reproduce for audiences in large auditoriums. Over 11 hours of drama were filmed in a year, at a cost of around €5 million, by some of the best international film directors around, including local heroes **Neil Jordan** and **Damien O'Donnell**. The adaptations include *Play*, director Anthony Minghella; *Happy Days*, director Patricia Rozema; *Krapp's Last Tape*, director Atom Egoyan; *Not I*, director Neil Jordan; *Catastrophe*, director David Mamet; *What Where*, director Damien O'Donnell; *Act with Words*, director Karel Reisz; and *Rough for Theatre II*, director Katie Mitchel.

BERGIN, PATRICK (1951–). Bergin was born in Dublin, the middle child in a family of five (older brother Emmet is a noted television actor). His father was a member of the Labour Party and was a senator during the 1950s. He studied English and drama at university and for a brief period worked as a teacher in London. While in London, he established his own theater company, initially working offstage but increasingly as an actor. His appearance in a short produced under the auspices of the National Film and Television School in England led him into screen acting. This in turn led to roles opposite **Gabriel Byrne** in *The Courier* and also in television miniseries *Act of Betrayal* (1988) and *Taffin* (1988).

By the early 1990s he was rapidly becoming Ireland's best-known international actor. Following a lead role as Victorian explorer Richard Burton opposite **Fiona Shaw** in Bob Rafelson's *Mountains of the Moon* (1990), he appeared opposite Julia Roberts in the stylish thriller *Sleeping with the Enemy* (1991), playing her psychotic husband. The film was a major hit and remains his best-known role. A series of lead roles in film and television productions followed: *Robin Hood* (1991), *Patriot Games* (1992), and *Map of the Human Heart* (1993).

Since then his star power has somewhat waned. He has found a niche playing Victorian characters, such as Victor Frankenstein in *Frankenstein* (1992), a police inspector hunting Jack the Ripper in *The Ripper* (1997), and the lead role in an adaptation of Arthur Co-nan Doyle's *The Lost World* (1998). He is also, by his own admission, on the list when Hollywood goes casting for psychopathic bad guys. However, these tend to be smaller-scale productions, and increasingly he works in television. Thus, although clearly it is not difficult for him to secure such roles, his most interesting recent work has been in Irish cinema. He appeared in *Angela Mooney Dies Again* in 1996, played the key detective role in *When the Sky Falls*, and portrayed an Irish Republican Army (IRA) member in *Silent Grace*. Most recently Bergin took on the demanding role of the Citizen in *Bloom*, the partial adaptation of Joyce's *Ulysses*. He has also recently returned to the stage in Dublin, playing the role of Edward Carson opposite Adrian Dunbar's Oscar Wilde in a revival of Ulick O'Connor's *A Trinity of Two*.

BEST (2000). Cowritten by director **Mary McGuckian** and her partner **John Lynch**, who is arguably miscast in the lead role of George Best, possibly the greatest footballer Ireland (or the world, according to many experts) ever produced. The film traces Best's failure to fulfil his early promise and his decline into alcoholism (which contributed to his death in December 2005). The film was marketed with the telling tag line, "With the world at your feet, what is there left to tackle?" However, it offers little insight into questions such as why Best lost his high-flying career with Manchester United to alcoholism. Nevertheless—and revealingly—George Best himself was apparently quite happy with this early portrayal of him both on and off the pitch.

BIRTHISTLE, EVA (1974–). Birthistle is unusual among Irish actresses in that the vast bulk of her experience is on-screen rather than onstage, where previously she has made only a handful of appearances. A native of Bray, County Wicklow, she moved with her family to Derry when she was 14, where, though raised a Catholic, she attended a mainly Protestant school. From there she went on to study at the Gaiety School of Acting in Dublin. On graduating she took on a number of film roles before achieving domestic stardom through a stint in the rural soap *Glenroe*. She left the security of the soap after less than two years, a decision justified by her subsequent success.

Birthistle has been fortunate to secure a variety of leading roles from the outset of her career. Her debut in **Alan Gilsenan**'s *All Souls' Day*, as a mentally disturbed young woman with an even more psychotic boyfriend, was a minor tour de force. This was followed by major roles in *Drinking Crude*, *Saltwater*, *Timbuktu* (again with Gilsenan), and **Neil Jordan**'s *Breakfast on Pluto*.

Since 2000 in particular she has become a fixture in one-off roles in a variety of mainstream British television dramas, including *Silent Witness*, *Holby City*, and both retellings of the Bloody Sunday story (*Sunday* and *Bloody Sunday*). In 2004 she was awarded an Irish Film and Television award for her role in Ken Loach's *Ae Fond Kiss* and was named a Shooting Star by the European Film Academy.

THE BISHOP'S STORY **(1993).** The relationship between *The Bishop's Story* and **Bob Quinn**'s earlier film *Budawanny* is difficult to explain. *Budawanny* (literally "priest's penis") relates the tale of a parish priest (**Donal McCann**) on the western seaboard who has a relationship with a woman (Maggie Fegan) he may or may not have known previously in London. She becomes pregnant, and the priest confesses his impending fatherhood to his flock ("Soon you will have another reason to call me father") but seeks to stay on as parish priest. The woman, unwilling to be cast in the role of a Magdalene on the island, departs suddenly for the mainland, leaving the priest to confront his loss of faith.

The Bishop's Story (which Quinn has described as the finished version of the story) retells this story, using most of the footage from *Budawanny* but adding new material: The priest, now promoted to an atheistic bishop (McCann, reprising his earlier role behind a thick beard), offers his own retrospective and highly cynical narration of the tale to a younger priest. This effectively replaces the commentary from *Budawanny* delivered by the priest's bishop (Peadar Lamb), an interior monologue that is interspersed with the narrative of the film. Both narration and commentary in the two films serve the same purpose, however, expressing a conviction that the Church's real function is social rather than spiritual, the theocracy acting more as a bureaucracy.

There are other changes besides different narrators, however. *Budawanny* was shot in black and white without sound: in effect a silent

movie with only very occasional recourse to intertitles. These strictures, although prompted by a limited budget rather than deliberate
intent, suited some of the themes of *Budawanny* admirably; the backdrop against which the story unfolds—Irish rural culture and the economic problems faced by the Gaeltacht areas—occasionally comes to
the foreground over the central narrative. In fact the grainy feel of the
footage recalls nothing as much as Robert Flaherty's ***Man of Aran***,
which shares these thematic concerns. This served to give *Budawanny* a uniquely Gaelic appearance: The frugality of the people
and the barren quality of the landscape were reflected by the absence
of Hollywood-style sweeping camera shots and special effects. It also
made it a fascinating experiment in moviemaking. Denied the facility of sound to recount the tale, Quinn risked reliance on older cinematic codes including music, montage, and so on and succeeded in
communicating some extraordinarily complex ideas and sentiments.
The Bishop's Story takes the *Budawanny* footage and sepia-tints it,
emphasizing its status as a memory. It also partly revoices it: Ghostly
disembodied voices emerge from an aural gloom when characters
speak, the echoes again emphasizing the operation of memory.

Indeed, sound plays a crucial role in both films through the pre-
dominance of Roger Doyle's largely electronic score. Music was one
of the driving forces of *Budawanny*, a virtually silent film, directing
the audiences' attention as efficiently as a pointing hand: Moods were
created, conflicts expressed via sweeping soundscapes and clashing
melodies. In *The Bishop's Story* the same soundtrack is used to similar effect, although the failure to update the score's electronic in-
strumentation simply serves to date the film.

BLACK, CATHAL (1953–). Born in Dublin, Cathal Black grew up in
Phibsboro, on the northside, where as a child he encountered a local
myth of a man with a movie camera setting off explosions up by the
Royal Canal for a war movie he was making. Intrigued, Black began
to explore filmmaking and even before leaving school at 16 was ex-
perimenting with Standard 8 film. This led to his joining **Radio
Telifís Éireann**, where he was employed as a cameraman. Finding
this too restricting he left after 16 months, at which point he met **Joe
Comerford**, with whom he collaborated on *Withdrawal*, a stark look
at the culture of heroin use in Dublin.

One of the earliest recipients of **Arts Council** funding, Black made his solo debut in 1976 with *Wheels*, a 20-minute adaptation of a somber John McGahern short story, "Nightlines." The story follows a boy who returns to his parents' small farm only to escape again to the city to flee their suffocating expectations. In interviews Black has described the film as similar to his own relationship with his father, who disapproved of Black's decision to leave a safe job in **Radio Telefís Éireann** for the insecurities of working in film.

His first widely seen short, *Our Boys* (1981), is a powerful examination of the abuse of students by the Christian Brothers. It uses archival footage of the 1932 Eucharistic Congress in Dublin and was made shortly after the visit of Pope John Paul II to Ireland. Because of its controversial subject matter, it was not aired by the national broadcaster (RTÉ) until 1994. The film was considered ahead of its time in Ireland for its use of the drama documentary format, mixing footage of interviews with former Christian Brother pupils with dramatizations of the treatment meted out to them.

Pigs (1984) was Black's first feature-length film and used an arthouse, Brechtian style to evoke the grim situation of squatters in a large decaying Georgian house in Dublin. A very early and provocative example of contemporary urban issues that social realism dealt with, the representation was a long way from the usual romantic evocation of rural Ireland on film.

With the closure of the **Irish Film Board** in 1987, Black found himself unable to secure sufficient funding to allow him to continue directing, and he became a lecturer on film production at the College of Commerce (later Dublin Institute of Technology) in Rathmines. In interview, he has stated that the enforced sabbatical from filming shaped the way he would subsequently approach film, making him more patient and allowing him to imbue his work with a hitherto unavailable sensitivity (Browne, 1996).

This is reflected in Black's more recent works such as the well-received *Korea* (again based on a short story by John McGahern). *Love and Rage* (1998) stars Greta Scacchi as a wealthy liberal Scottish woman who owns a small house on Achill Island at the end of the 19th century and begins an affair with her newly employed manager, James (Daniel Craig). Soon she feels that his motives are questionable, and she worries about possible violence to her person, so she has him fired. A somewhat conventional tale of violence and revenge follows. The film has had very mixed reviews.

BLACK, DONALD TAYLOR (1951–). His first **documentary**, *At the Cinema Palace: Liam O'Leary* (1983), is a profile of one of the best-known Irish film historians and archivists. Throughout his career Black has concentrated primarily on TV documentaries, and he has also directed in the theater. Most recently he directed the British Film Institute (BFI) Century of Cinema series on Irish cinema, *Ireland: Ourselves Alone?* (1995), written by film historian **Kevin Rockett**. Currently he is head of film and media studies at the Institute of Art, Design and Technology (IADT), Dun Laoghaire, Dublin.

***BLOODY SUNDAY* (2002).** Both this version directed by Paul Greengrass and another interpretation, *Sunday* (2000), directed by Charles McDougall (which attracted less popular attention), were made for the 30th anniversary of the awful events of 1972 that were a major turn for the worse in the "**troubles**." Writer-director Paul Greengrass, following in the tradition of gritty British realism, attempts to capture the "fly on the wall" reality of a day in the life of the Northern "troubles" when the British Army shot 13 people on a march to protest the introduction to Northern Ireland of internment without trial. It won the Golden Bear award at the Berlin Film Festival and the World Cinema award at the Sundance Film Festival. Critics highlight how the confusion, fear, chaos, and hatred engendered by the conflict are well dramatized.

"Bloody Sunday" marked a watershed in the civil rights organization in Northern Ireland, which was influenced by Martin Luther King in America and the peaceful revolution headed by Gandhi in India. The film is about remembering the past with a view to facilitating the healing process 25 years after the "men of violence" on all sides took center stage. Incidentally, the title that became popular parlance for the horror of the day was also the title of another film directed by John Schlesinger, *Sunday Bloody Sunday* (1971), which was showing in Derry when *Bloody Sunday* was filmed, as displayed in the opening scene.

The drama-documentary used ex-soldiers, even paratroopers, who knew how to perform their role, alongside some of the actual families who were affected by the original atrocity. Filmed at a cost of $5 million, it was shot in Dublin's Ballymun high-rise estate, which accurately replicated the actual northern estate. The movie cuts rapidly between scenes involving a number of major characters, most particularly Protestant member of Parliament Ivan Cooper (**James Nesbitt**), who is leading the march. Other characters include a 17-year-old Gerry Donaghy (Declan Duddy), who was previously arrested for rioting, and Major General Ford (Tim Pigott-Smith) who tells Brigadier MacLellan (Nicholas Farrell) what to do on the day. And it is from their various perspectives that we see the events of the day unfold. Although the film is careful to avoid slavish subscription to any one of the various theories about who was ultimately responsible for the killings, the filmmakers leave no doubt as to the culpability of the soldiers and their commanders.

BLOOM **(2003).** Starring **Stephen Rea**, Angeline Ball, and **Hugh O'Conor**, this personal project by Sean Walsh explores James Joyce's renowned and complex novel *Ulysses* and steers the viewer through many of the key episodes to make it more accessible, while retaining some of its cross-references and nonlinear appeal. In particular the long night sequence (*Circe*) is creatively presented and allows Stephen Rea to display his full range of acting skills. The film begins and ends with the formal literary device of stream-of-consciousness to get inside the mind of Molly Bloom, the main character. Although lacking in overall polish and probably the finesse of **John Huston**'s *The Dead*, for example, this is a useful interpretation, following the only other attempt, by **Joseph Strick**.

BLOW DRY **(2001).** Set in a small Yorkshire town where the national hairdressing championship is about to begin, the locals have little inkling of the big noise the event will make. As one would expect in such a comic genre piece directed by **Paddy Breathnach**, there is a lot of intrigue, scheming competition, and poor sportsmanship displayed as the contestants fight against each other.

BOGWOMAN **(1997).** This is a poignant tale following the experiences of Maureen (Rachel Dowling), a young unmarried mother from an island off Donegal who moves across the border to Derry at the close of the 1950s to marry boyfriend Barry (Peter Mullan). The story, directed by Tom Collins, uses Maureen's perspective—that of a Catholic living in Derry's Bogside—to trace the seeds of the "**troubles**" as they developed during the 1960s.

BOORMAN, JOHN (1933–). Born in London, Boorman lived through the Blitz (an experience that would later inform his 1987 film *Hope and Glory*). He joined Independent Television News (ITN) in 1955 and became an editor before moving to a commercial station, Southern Television, in 1957 as an editor-director. In 1961 he moved to work with the BBC, producing and directing a series of well-received documentaries that gathered good ratings, and the ambitious one-off drama *The Quarry*, a thinly veiled first outing for Boorman's King Arthur obsession. This led to an offer to direct a film featuring the popular band the Dave Clark Five. The resulting *Catch Us If You Can* (1965) launched Boorman's feature career, although it wasn't till the release of the nihilistic *Point Blank* (1967) that his star really began to rise. He has subsequently remained one of Britain's most interesting directors, working on a diverse range of material from *Deliverance* (1972) and *Zardoz* (1973) to *Hope and Glory* (1985) and—finally achieving a lifetime ambition to film the Arthur legend—*Excalibur* (1981).

However, he has also been a key figure in the Irish film industry for several decades. While editing *Leo the Last* (1969) at **Ardmore Studios**, he and his wife fell in love with the Wicklow countryside and decided to buy a holiday cottage. The former rectory they purchased in Annamoe, County Wicklow, became their home. Although Boorman's marriage subsequently ended, he has continued to live in Annamoe ever since, and its surroundings were the setting for his 1991 television meditation, *I Dreamt I Woke Up*. He has subsequently shot many of his films in Ireland, regardless of their nominal location, and over the past three decades he has been **Ardmore Studios'** most consistent customer. *Deliverance* was edited at Ardmore, *Zardoz* was shot there (and on location in the Wicklow Mountains), and the studios were used for models shots and the editing of *Exorcist II: The Heretic* (1976).

Given this, Boorman was the obvious choice as chairman when the studios reopened as the **National Film Studios of Ireland** in 1975.

However, although he was not involved with the day-to-day operation of the studios (except when renting them to make films), his association with them did not endear him to independent Irish filmmakers. Ever since **Louis Marcus**'s seminal 1967 articles on the irrelevance of Ardmore to a putative indigenous industry, Irish filmmakers tended to regard the studios as part of the problem of a misguided state film policy rather than an element of the solution.

This simmering resentment came to the surface as a result of Boorman's mentoring of **Neil Jordan**. Boorman encountered Jordan via the latter's 1976 short story collection *Nights in Tunisia*. Noting the visual quality of Jordan's writing, Boorman invited him to collaborate on a never-filmed screenplay, *Broken Dream*. Boorman subsequently gave Jordan his first directorial experience, a documentary on the making of Boorman's 1981 production of *Excalibur*.

Excalibur was notable in itself, in part because it was the largest production shot in Ireland since ***Ryan's Daughter***, but also because of the opportunity it afforded a whole generation of Irish actors: **Gabriel Byrne, Liam Neeson,** and **Ciarán Hinds** all made their feature debuts in the film. With *Excalibur* complete, Boorman was immediately appointed to the newly formed **Irish Film Board** and began working as executive producer on Jordan's first feature, *Angel*, a condition of **Channel 4**'s agreement to finance the film. However, when the Film Board was still only partially appointed, and it awarded a substantial proportion of its initial budget to *Angel*, Boorman was accused by the **Association of Independent Producers** (AIP) of having abused his position on the board. For his part, Boorman argued that he hadn't been present when the decision was made but that it was in any case the correct decision. The AIP conceded that even a full board might have made the same decision but argued that the appearance of the decision remained problematic.

The lasting bitterness engendered by the *Angel* controversy clearly altered Boorman's level of engagement with domestic film politics. The National Film Studios of Ireland were disbanded in April 1982, and Boorman resigned from the Film Board in the same month. Perhaps coincidentally, his use of Ardmore also declined in the 1980s. *The Emerald Forest* (1985) and *Hope and Glory* (1987) were both shot outside Ireland.

However, at the start of the 1990s, Boorman appears to have reengaged with Ireland. He cofounded **Merlin Films** in 1989 and in 1998 made a triumphant return to form with a film that won the Cannes Film Festival award, *The General*, remarkably his first fiction film explicitly set in Ireland, but one that clearly reflected his three decades of living within Irish society. Now in his 70s, he continues to work on large-scale productions, and where possible he continues to use Irish technicians and locations. A glance down the crew list of *The Tailor of Panama* (2001), starring **Pierce Brosnan**, reveals a myriad of Irish names in senior crew positions, and though the film is set in South America, parts of it were shot in Ireland. Similarly, though *Country of My Skull* (2004) was shot in South Africa, the cinematographer was **Seamus Deasy**, by now Boorman's cameraman of choice.

***BORSTAL BOY* (2000).** Screen adaptation of Brendan Behan's famous stage play and directed by Peter, the brother of **Jim Sheridan**, who had long planned a biopic on the playwright. The film follows 16-year-old Behan's (played by Shawn Hatosy) experiences in a British jail after he was arrested for Republican (IRA) political activities in Liverpool during World War II. While in prison he reconsiders his Republican beliefs, or at least the methods he has hitherto assumed were necessary to achieve Republican goals.

***THE BOXER* (1997).** Having previously offered one political reading of the Northern Ireland "**troubles**" with his drama on British injustice, *In the Name of the Father*, Jim Sheridan here tries to demonstrate the need for creating an alternative to political violence. Danny Flynn (Daniel Day-Lewis) emerges from prison after serving 14 years for carrying out a Provisional Irish Republican Army (PIRA) operation, where he came to a recognition of the limits of political violence. He seeks to create a new family and community based on tolerance and reconciliation using the sport of boxing as a way to unify sectarian communities. Fighting by the (British) Queensbury rules is signaled as the only road to creating a new nonsectarian community. In contrast to this ethical stance, his old IRA commander, Harry (**Gerard McSorley**), wants him to continue with them.

Issues are further complicated by the still smoldering fires of romance between Danny and Maggie (Emily Watson), daughter of the
IRA chief of staff (played with aplomb by Brian Cox). Maggie is a
prisoner's wife: Though estranged from her IRA-member husband,
the rules of republican community make it impossible for her to be
seen to be involved with another man. The issue comes to a head
when Maggie's son, furious at the prospect of his mother being taken
away from him, burns down the boxing gym Danny has established
with his old coach (Ken Stott). A police murder follows, and the
support of official authorities for the nonsectarian boxing club sparks
riots—the political grass-roots community is not ready yet to support
an impartial police force following years of division. But, of course,
in the end a narrative resolution is found as the "bad apple" is disposed of and the newly created family can eventually "come home."
    The film most clearly references Elia Kazan's *On the Waterfront*
(1954), with both films concerning aged boxers who have been compromised in the past, with much of the narrative and characterization
echoed in Sheridan's film. The maxim spoken by Father Barry at the
end of Kazan's classic sums up: "You have lost the battle, but you
have a chance to win the war."

***THE BOY FROM MERCURY* (1996).** When the film was released in
theaters in Ireland, it earned the paltry sum of IR £6,457 at the box
office. Yet when it was screened on Irish television, over 468,000 or
45 percent of the audience share watched director **Martin Duffy**'s
children's parable, which probably says something about audiences'
strategic decisions about attending Irish films at the cinema. Like
many classic children's narratives, the story follows conventional
Hollywood rules of emotional identification and development and
applies some very effective magic realist techniques to correspond
with the boy's feelings of alienation, which are finally relieved when
his big brother takes him under his wing and protects him from bul-
lies, doubling as an alternative father figure.

BRADY, ORLA (1961–). Raised on Dame Street in Dublin, where her
family owned a successful public house, she studied acting in Paris.
On returning to Dublin she secured the role of Adela in the *House of
Bernarda Alba* at the Gate Theatre. Her early career was almost ex-

clusively onstage, where she built an enviable body in work from playwrights as diverse as Anton Chekhov and J. M. Synge. Her shift to the screen came relatively recently. In 1993 Brady moved to London (where she maintains a home) and has found herself in constant demand in British television drama serials ever since, often cast in roles as strong-willed, intelligent, and not necessarily Irish women. Typical of these was her Cathy in a London Weekend Television adaptation of *Wuthering Heights*.

Brady has appeared in few films, but those she has made have been striking. She debuted in **Mary McGuckian**'s *Words upon the Window Pane* as the strongly independent Hester van Homrigh, who was mistress to writer Jonathan Swift. A four-year film hiatus was followed by her commanding lead role in *A Love Divided* as a Protestant wife (again based on an actual person) married to a Catholic man who refused to bow to the social convention of 1950s Ireland that the children of such mixed marriages should be raised as Catholics. The role won enthusiastic reviews and secured her the Best Actress award at the Monte Carlo International Television Festival.

Despite this success Brady has subsequently worked mainly in television. She appeared in an adaptation of Nabokov's *The Luzhin Defence* (2000) and the little-seen Czech film *Fogbound* (2002). Back in Ireland she played a Republican prisoner in Maeve Murphy's *Silent Grace*, a film with an intriguing premise but unfortunately released at a point when the IRA ceasefire made such stories difficult to sell at the box office. More recently she has played the lead role character of Maureen Boland in Radio Telefís Éireann's (RTÉ) hit dramas *Proof* and *Proof II*. In 2003 she married Los Angeles–based photographer Nick Brandt and now divides her time between both sides of the Atlantic.

BRAVEHEART (1995). Considering that the narrative of Mel Gibson's multi-Oscar-winning epic traces the life and death of a 13th-century Scottish folk hero, *Braveheart* is not an obvious candidate for inclusion in this book. However, from a political economy perspective, it occupies a significant symbolic place in the development of the Irish film industry since the 1990s.

The $70 million film was jointly financed by 20th Century Fox and Paramount and was to have been shot over 16 weeks on location in

Scotland. However, the filmmakers faced the logistical difficulty of securing sufficient extras in Scotland for the massive battle scenes that constitute the dramatic high point of the film. The executive producer on *Braveheart*, Steve McEveety, contacted Irish producer **Morgan O'Sullivan** to ask if Ireland would be a more flexible location. O'Sullivan in turn went to the Department of Arts, Culture and the Gaeltacht, which was sufficiently enthused by the project to send an assistant principal officer to O'Sullivan's next meeting with the producers in London. At that meeting it was apparent that not only were the producers promised access to **Section 35** funding but also to 1,600 reservist soldiers as extras (reportedly for a nominal cost). These were to be housed in the Curragh army base, which was adjacent to a potential location for shooting the battle scenes.

As a consequence the film's Scottish shoot was shortened to 5 weeks with the remaining 11 shifting to Ireland, 6 at **Ardmore Studios** and 5 on various Irish locations. In Great Britain opposition politicians lamented the loss of the film, criticizing the Conservative government for failing to match Ireland's filmmaking incentives. In Ireland, however, the arrival of the film, coming just a year after the reestablishment of the **Irish Film Board** and the radical changes to Section 35, appeared to suggest that a Hollywood-scale industry was a real possibility.

However, the major significance of the shift was the clear demonstration of the lengths to which the Irish state was willing to go to attract large-scale audiovisual productions to Ireland. Mel Gibson reported that the decision to move to Ireland was based on purely creative factors, but in addition to literally having a small army placed at its disposal, the production was able to raise $10 million via Section 35, then the most substantial use of that tax break in a single film. The message was not lost on overseas producers, who, in the wake of the *Braveheart* production, queued up to use Ireland as a location.

BREAKFAST ON PLUTO (2005). **Neil Jordan**'s second adaptation of a Patrick McCabe novel—the first being *The Butcher Boy*, which by all accounts is more lighthearted and episodic in its narrative trajectory. The film displays a roll call of well-known Irish actors caricaturing Irish stereotypes, in many cases with great humorous effect.

Liam Neeson—reprising his seminal role in *Lamb* at the start of his career—plays the father in both the biological and spiritual senses. Fathering what turns out to be a colorful transvestite son, Patrick (Kitten) (**Cillian Murphy**), the priest has to deal with the consequences after the mother leaves the baby at his door before departing for England.

The story follows Kitten's journey to find his mother (and himself) and his encounters with various larger-than-life characters along the way. These include Billy Rock (Gavin Friday) and his Mohawks band (which he briefly joins, to the consternation of the confused band members), Silky String (Bryan Ferry), a homicidal seducer, Bertie (**Stephen Rea**), an eccentric magician, and John-Joe (**Brendan Gleeson**), an Irish emigrant dressed up in a "Wombles" costume at a kiddies' fairground. The setting of the story—in a border town—ensures that the "troubles" remain a constant presence, but Jordan has been at pains to stress that this is not a film about politics but rather addresses the question of how an individual can preserve his own identity when powerful competing ideologies seek to win followers. Kitten does this by remaining an eternal optimist in the tradition of Voltaire's *Candide*. Thus although Republican sympathies are called upon, Kitten remains aloof from it all. When he is implicated in an Irish Republican Army (IRA) attack in London, his optimism renders his interrogation strangely comic and ensures that the narrative remains at a surreal level.

Eventually, if most unusually in the "sins of the father"–fixated Irish narrative, Kitten and his father are reconciled, and the priest "does the right thing" by supporting his transvestite son and an unwed but pregnant friend, in spite of violent local opposition.

The story is carried by a marvelous performance by Cillian Murphy and is characterized by constant use of 1970s music and sugary pop songs that reflect Kitten's rose-tinted perspective on the world and ensure that nostalgia for the period is maintained at all times. Incidentally, Irish Film Board provided much of the funding, and hopefully it will become a financial success for all concerned.

BREATHNACH, PADDY (1964–). Along with a new generation of Irish filmmakers, including Gerry Stembridge and Vinny Murphy, Breathnach is heavily influenced by mainstream American cinema and much less preoccupied with conventional markers of Irish identity or progressive avant-garde styles. Yet, surprisingly, he learned his craft while working on several films of Joe Comerford and Bob Quinn, who remain preoccupied with formal experimentation and the interrogation of Irish political identity.

Having made a strong impact with his "long short" *A Stone in the Heart*, Breathnach's first feature as a director was *Ailsa*, but it was with *I Went Down* (1997), his revisionist comic gangster genre piece, that he made a mark for himself as a uniquely Irish talent and gained a strong following. His subsequent comic feature *Blow Dry* (2001) was filmed in Britain and explores the "comic" world of hairdressing but lacks the sure tone of his previous attempts. His most recent film, *Man About Dog* (2004), was a solid commercial success, becoming the 10th most successful film released in 2004 and grossing over €2 million at the box office, but was dismissed by many critics as no more than a risible, lighthearted romp that draws on the supposed cultural importance of dogs in Irish society. Other critics have argued that Breathnach has not delivered on his earlier promise, but it would appear that there is an element of intellectual snobbery built into such criticism, which infers that Irish films ought to have "serious ideas" embedded in their structure and at the same time not replicate a Hollywood generic model. At a minimum *Man About Dog* clearly demonstrates that Breathnach is very comfortable with the basic skill of telling a story, a talent that is not necessarily shared by all Irish directors.

BRENNAN, BRID (1955–). A *New York Times* article from 1992 musing on who was likely to win that year's Tony for Best Feature Actress noted that although three actresses had been nominated from Brian Friel's *Dancing at Lughnasa*, Brid Brennan, who played "the sister with the sad face who did the knitting" (Witchel, 1992), had the best chance. Brennan duly went on to win the award and won an Irish Film & Television Academy Award for Best Actress when she reprised the role of Agnes in **Pat O'Connor**'s film version of *Lughnasa* (having previously appeared in O'Connor's *Ballroom of Romance* a decade and a half earlier).

Brennan's intense, drawn features marked her as someone to watch from her earliest screen roles. Originally from Belfast, she made a brief debut in *Excalibur* before securing the more eye-catching role of Roisin in Pat Murphy's feminist experiment *Maeve*. Between 1982 and 1984 she appeared in Graham Reid's *Billy* trilogy on the British Broadcasting Corporation (BBC) opposite the young Kenneth Branagh, touchingly attempting to hold her family together after her mother's death from cancer. This was immediately followed by what remains her outstanding screen role as the eponymous protagonist in *Anne Devlin*. Her performance in that film was simply astonishing: Appearing in virtually every frame, she created a character who was far more than a footnote in the narrative of her better-known employer, the historical Irish rebel Robert Emmet.

She has subsequently established herself as a versatile player on the film screen and has become a familiar face to British audiences through a series of memorable one-off roles in television crime dramas. Although most of her Irish work tends to be in the theater, she also starred in *Words upon a Window Pane*, *Trojan Eddie*, and *Felicia's Journey*.

BROKEN HARVEST (1994). Structurally similar to *This Is My Father* (both frame stories from 1950s Ireland with a contemporary American setting), *Broken Harvest*, from director Maurice O'Callaghan, traces the impact on family and community of a feud between Art O'Leary (Colin Lane) and Josie Lane (Niall Buggy), two farmers who had taken opposite sides in the Irish Civil War and who had also fought for the love of Catherine (now Art's wife, played by Marian Quinn). The film was a labor of love for director-producer-writer Maurice O'Callaghan, who spent the best part of a decade making the picture and raising the £1.25 million budget.

BROSNAN, PIERCE (1953–). Although born in Navan, County Meath, he and his mother moved to Putney, London, in 1964, after his father abandoned the family. He quickly adopted a cockney accent to fit in at school, a fact that subsequently allowed him to play Irish and English roles with equal facility. Although initially working as a commercial artist (Brosnan still paints in his spare time), he enrolled at a drama school in 1973 and appeared in several West End productions. In 1979 he moved to screen acting, securing lead billing in his first role in *Murphy's Stroke* for Thames Television. He made an eye-catching, if brief, appearance as an Irish Republican Army (IRA) member in the classic gangster film *The Long Good Friday* (1980) before securing another lead in an American television miniseries, *The Mannions of America*, which followed a family of 19th-century Irish emigrants to America. He followed this with the key role in the long-running television series *Remington Steel* in 1982, which indelibly established his suave star persona.

Brosnan was famously courted by 007 producer Albert Broccoli for the role of James Bond when Roger Moore retired after *A View to a Kill* (1985), but, equally famously, Mary Tyler Moore Productions refused to allow him to break his Steele contract. Incidentally his wife, Cassandra Harris (formerly married to **Richard Harris**'s brother Dermot), had previously appeared in the Bond film *For Your Eyes Only* (1981). Brosnan was bitterly disappointed, especially after *Remington Steele* was canceled the following year (1987).

For a period, Brosnan seemed condemned to spend the rest of his career in B movies and television series. (He later returned to Ireland in 1988 to make the poorly received *Taffin*, costarring another former Bond girl, Alison Doody.) In 1991 his wife died of cancer, leaving him to look after her two children from her first marriage and the son they had together. However, in the early 1990s his career began to pick up with *The Lawnmower Man* (1992), loosely based on a Stephen King short story. This was an unexpected hit, and he demonstrated an unexpected gift for self-deprecating comedy in *Mrs. Doubtfire* (1993). However, his career was transformed in 1995 when he received a second shot at the role of Bond, after Timothy Dalton's two 007 films had underperformed. In *Goldeneye* (1995) Brosnan reinvigorated the role and the coffers of Metro Goldwin Mayer (MGM) that financed it. Three further Bond outings followed, each more successful than the last: *Tomorrow Never Dies* (1997), *The World Is Not Enough* (1999), and *Die Another Day* (2002).

Mindful of the fate of previous former Bonds, he interspersed his secret agent outings with roles in a variety of genres—eccentric scientist in the postmodern comedy *Mars Attacks* (1997), geologist hero in ecothriller *Dante's Peak* (1997), and fur trapper turned conservationist in Richard Attenborough's *Grey Owl* (1999). His most successful non-Bond outings during this period—*The Thomas Crown Affair* (1999) and the **John Boorman**–directed *The Tailor of Panama*

(2001)—suggested that the public was most at home with him in the Bond persona.

He went one stage further in ensuring the longevity of his career by turning producer and establishing the production company **Irish Dreamtime** in 1996. In part as a consequence, in the the last decade he has turned in an increasing number of Irish roles: While it's hard to regard his appearance in *The Nephew* as anything more than a ploy to market the film, his performance in *Evelyn*, as a father in 1950s Ireland attempting to reclaim his children from the care of the state, suggested a thespian potential rarely displayed in previous work. He lost the Bond role in 2005, apparently due to disputes with the producers over money, but, if anything, the period since has been his busiest yet.

THE BROTHER'S MCMULLEN (1995). Accurately described by critics as a "Catholic Woody Allen" movie, the film directed by Edward Burns captures the angst and religious guilt of a second-generation Irish family living in America. Although they feel no hint of nostalgia or romanticism toward Ireland and the homeland, their urban and very modern troubles are shaped by their distant Irish roots. The success of the film in America and elsewhere points to the potential for such stories to speak to a large population of second- and third-generation diasporic Irish. The focus of familial conflict begins, as in many classic Irish narratives, at the father's funeral, when the mother announces she is going to leave immediately, having gotten married in the first place because she was pregnant. This revelation draws her children together in various ways as they work through their complicated relationships and find innovative ways to resolve their conflicts and learn to accept the new reality of their lives.

BUDAWANNY (1986). Director **Bob Quinn's** take on Irish **Catholicism** is unusual in that—in contrast to films such as *The Magdalene Sisters* and *Song for a Raggy Boy*—it offers a sympathetic discussion of religion in Ireland from the perspective of a priest, rather than that of the victim of Church authority. The film opens with the bishop (Peadar Lamb) trying to dictate a letter to his ex-priest (**Donal Mc-Cann**), and the narrative is framed around flashbacks of the actual story, which is told from the bishop's point of view. Interspersed with the black-and-white and subtitled flashbacks are the bishop's comments on the need for religion and his job to make it "work"—a long way from the more authoritarian monologue of a bishop in charge of his flock. Luke Gibbons (Rockett, Gibbons, and Hill, 1988) affirms that there are two narrative styles at work: The "realist" sections attempt to act as a framing "master" narrative that controls the stylistic excesses of the melodramatic silent sequences. This stylistic conflict exemplifies a struggle between the bureaucratic modern Church and the more popular—albeit pagan—religion of the islanders.

We witness a woman attempting suicide and ending up in the priest's house, where she later finds a useful role as his housekeeper. The inevitability of the story rings true as their relationship develops and is all but accepted by the local community. *See* also *THE BISHOP'S STORY*.

BUSINESS EXPANSION SCHEME (BES). In 1984 the Fine Gael–Labour government introduced a scheme to encourage private capital to invest in small-scale business enterprises. Investors were allowed to subtract from taxable income any investment (up to a maximum of £25,000 per annum) in a manufacturing business (this included a number of service industries such as filmmaking) on condition that they maintained the investment for at least five years. An individual was not permitted to make more than £75,000 in BES investments in his or her lifetime. Although not explicitly targeted at film, at least two film production companies used the scheme between 1984 and 1990. The most notable example of this was **Strongbow Films**, which was originally set up purely to take advantage of the scheme and which raised £900,000 for *Eat the Peach* from BES investors in 1986 alone.

The scheme was not used more often by film companies because of the £25,000 per annum limit. At a time when even a low-budget feature cost in the region of £500,000, raising funds based on this scheme alone required a substantial selling effort on the part of producers. Furthermore, given that film projects—which were considered inherently high risk by investors—were competing with other less-risky areas for BES investment, film producers found it difficult to find willing BES investors. This was particularly true after *Eat the*

Peach recorded an official loss of £750,000 for its 273 BES share-holders despite having performed well in local markets. Thus the ***Coopers and Lybrand Report*** found that between 1987 and 1991, 10 projects had raised just £1.18 million between them through the BES. In the longer term the BES scheme was significant because it paved the way for the introduction of the **Section 35** incentive, which even in its original 1987 form was regarded as a dramatic improvement on the BES scheme with all of its strictures.

***THE BUTCHER BOY* (1998).** Neil Jordan's acclaimed masterpiece from the novel of the same name by Pat McCabe has become a major critical success, with much academic analysis given over to the film. The story focuses on Francie Brady (Eamonn Owens), a boy who we soon begin to suspect is a paranoid schizophrenic, living in an extremely dysfunctional family. The film oscillates between mystical nostalgia for a rural past and a futuristic vision of American mass culture. The story is framed against the geopolitics of the Cold War and the pervasive fear of nuclear catastrophe. Francie takes his cue from the media, which in itself offers a critique of the various moral panics of the time, especially with the impact of mass media and religious spectacle on morality and cultural identity. At one stage Francie imagines that he is Richard Kimble from the long-running television series *The Fugitive*, and at another he has a vision of the Virgin Mary. Jordan's casting of controversial iconic Irish singer **Sinead O'Connor** as the Mother of God serves to question conventional religious worship while exploring its psychic potency. Some critics have even pointed out how the image of Mary playing a harp outside Francie's model Irish cottage represents an attack on Eamon de Valera, the political leader and architect of the 1937 constitution who was a strong believer in maintaining close ties between Irish politics and **Catholicism**, and promulgated the idealized patriarchal notion of a "comely Irish maiden" needing protection from the vagaries of sexual promiscuity and modernity generally.

While the film enjoyed a good critical reception, placing it as one of the great Irish and even European films, it has not been as commercially successful as it perhaps ought to have been, possibly because of its difficult subject matter.

BYRNE, GABRIEL (1950–). One of six children born into a Dublin family, Byrne was educated by the Christian Brothers. He trained as a priest in England but left before taking Holy Orders and went to college at University College Dublin before becoming a secondary teacher. Although he began working with the Dublin Shakespearian Society in 1974 and also worked at the Project Theater during **Jim Sheridan**'s tenure, it wasn't until 1979 that he turned professional. His first television appearances were in the Irish rural soap *The Riordans* and its successor, *Bracken*, in which he played the eponymous farmer. Early film roles included those in **Thaddeus O'Sullivan**'s *On a Paving Stone Mounted* (1978), *The Outsider* (1979), and *Excalibur* (1981).

He subsequently appeared in numerous Hollywood and European art-house films. The earliest of these raised some doubts about his wisdom in choosing roles, an apparent failing that has plagued him ever since. After appearing in a number of less-memorable films like *Reflection* (1983) and *Hannah K* (1983), he eventually starred in the superbly taut political thriller *Defence of the Realm* (1985) as a journalist out of his depth in the murky world of state secrets. Then followed roles in Ken Russell's *Gothic* (1986), as well as nonmainstream film roles in *Julia and Julia* (1987), *Siesta* (1987), and *A Soldier's Tale* (1988).

He moved to America and made a major international impact in the Coen Brothers' 1990 film *Miller's Crossing*. His role as Tom Reagan, the infinitely cynical advisor to Albert Finney's Irish gangster boss, was tailor-made for Byrne's world-weary star persona. Other major roles in big-budget films followed: *Point of No Return* (1993), *Smilla's Sense of Snow* (1997), and more recently the remake of *Assault on Precinct 13* (2005). However, the quality of the films has remained variable: *The Usual Suspects* (1995), Jim Jarmusch's *Dead Man* (1995), and David Cronenberg's *Spider* (2002) were all well received. Most of the rest had a poor reception.

It is enormously to his credit, however, that he has remained closely allied to the Irish film industry both as an actor and more unusually as a producer via his own company, Plurabelle Films. He lent star power to *The Courier* in 1988, acted in and coproduced *Into the West* (costarring his then wife Ellen Barkin) in 1992, then appeared in at least one Irish film a year between 1994 and 1998: *All Things*

Bright and Beautiful (1994), **Frankie Starlight** (1995), **The Last of the High Kings** (1996), *Draíocht* ["Magic"] (1996), **This Is the Sea** (1997), and *The Brylcreem Boys* (1998). Indeed, he even wrote the screenplay for *Draoicht*, an Irish-language drama (directed by his former partner 'Aine O'Connor) and had a hand in the script for *The Last of the High Kings*. That list might have been longer still: He was scheduled to play an Irish Republican Army (IRA) prison leader in *In the Name of the Father* (1993) but fell out with Jim Sheridan, although he retained an executive producer credit on the film. He also sat on the **Irish Film Board** for a number of years in the 1990s.

In more recent years he has branched out into other media; for example, he received a Tony nomination for his performance in the 2000 Broadway revival of Eugene O'Neill's *A Moon for the Misbegotten*, and in the same year he was executive producer and starred in the short-lived sitcom *Madigan Men*.

– C –

CAL **(1984).** Based on a novel by Bernard McLaverty and set in Northern Ireland during the 1980s, the film explores the emotional trauma of a young man, Cal (**John Lynch**), who is not fully committed to the political struggle and the Provisional Irish Republican Army (PIRA), and a widow (Helen Mirren), who was a casualty of the **"troubles."** **Pat O'Connor**, the director, was criticized for placing personal emotions in the foreground, above and beyond the specific political situation in the North; nevertheless the film was very well received, with Mirren winning Best Actress award at the Cannes Film Festival.

CAREY, PATRICK (?–1994). Though largely unacknowledged at the time of his death in 1994, in the 1960s and 1970s Patrick Carey's short film works were considered among the high points of Irish cultural life. The son of a Gate actress and a founder of the **Irish Film Society**, Carey emigrated to England in the 1940s, where he trained as a cameraman and discovered a gift for nature photography. He then went to Canada, where he worked for that country's National Film Board. In the early 1960s he returned to Ireland, and in 1965 he was commissioned by the **Cultural Relations Committee** (CRC) to make a documentary to celebrate the centenary of W. B. Yeats's birth. *Yeats Country* went on to win the Golden Bear at Berlin, an **Academy Award** nomination, and other international prizes.

Further commissions from the CRC, **Radio Telifís Éireann (RTÉ)**, Bord Fáilte, the Department of Lands, and Roinn na Gaeltachta led Carey to direct and shoot a series of well-received shorts including *Errigal*, *Waves*, and *Oisín* (for which he received a second Oscar nomination in 1970). **Louis Marcus** has written of Carey's work in this period that it demonstrated a unique chemistry between his personal sensibility and the Irish countryside. For Marcus, Carey presented Ireland as a land of clouds and mist, of threatening woods, of looming mountains and dark fields occasionally caressed by a passing band of sunlight (Marcus, 1994). This was in stark contrast to representation offered by John Ford in *The Quiet Man*.

By the mid 1960s Carey was also frequently employed by international directors—including Fred Zinneman on *A Man for All Seasons* (1966)—seeking to exploit his ability to convey this atmospheric sense of the countryside. Indeed, by the end of that decade his stature at home was such that he was invited to become a member of the **Huston Committee.** However, when the Film Board Bill that emerged from that committee's report was sidelined in the early 1970s, Carey returned to Canada, where he worked and lived until his death.

It might also be argued that the kind of films Patrick Carey made was falling out of favor by the end of the 1960s. With the disappearance of the supporting short in cinema programs and—until Michael Moore's more recent polemical work—the shift of the documentary form to television, Carey's lyrical shorts found it harder and harder to find a home onscreen.

CARNEY, JOHN, AND TOM HALL. Although primarily known in Ireland for their hit comedy-drama series *Bachelor's Walk*, which ran for three years from 2001 (and which was also directed by Kieran Carney, brother of John), the pair have also been behind some of the most interesting low-budget work produced in Ireland in the last decade.

Neither Carney nor Hall had much training in film before embarking on their first film, a road movie entitled *The Edge of the World*.

Tom Hall had studied at the National Film School in Dun Laoire for just six months before leaving. Carney, by contrast, spent the early 1990s in The Frames, a popular local band (whose lead singer, Glenn Hansard, had been a member of *The Commitments* cast). The Frames experience proved educational; however, it was Carney's exposure to shooting on video while making promos for the band that encouraged him to link up with Hall in 1995 to make their own films.

Although *The Edge of the World* was never completed, the experience of shooting it (on Super VHS) proved vital for subsequent work. Their actual feature debut—*November Afternoon*—premiered at the 1996 Cork Film Festival, where it created something of a sensation. Made with a crew of two (Carney and Hall) and a cast of four, the film cost virtually nothing to produce, beyond hire of studio space. Beautifully shot on video on black and white, the finished film—with its jazz-inflected score, composed by Carney—was reminiscent of a John Cassavetes film. Much of the polished appearance was due to the postproduction on the film, which the **Irish Film Board** funded after Carney and Hall showed them a trailer of the completed shoot and which allowed them to screen the film on 35 mm film.

The low-budget approach was not simply an aesthetic choice. As their later work would show, it allowed them a freedom to explore territory—incest in the case of *November Afternoon*—in a manner that might have been difficult to finance using traditional funding models. Their next production, *Just in Time*, a 50-minute one-off drama made as part of **Radio Telifís Éireann**'s short-lived *Real Time* drama slot, was equally warmly received, with a subject matter—middle-class, middle-aged angst—that was more palatable to prime-time audiences. Once again it was characterized by sumptuous lighting and a script that realistically captured the natural rhythms of contemporary speech.

If Carney and Hall had followed the normal career trajectory for most Irish filmmakers after *Just in Time*, they would have proceeded to make a mid-budget feature. Instead they returned to the low-budget approach of *November Afternoon* to make *Park*, which they shot on digital video for a few thousand Irish pounds. Again using minimal crew and cast, in *Park* they dealt with another taboo subject—the sexual abuse of minors. The result was less visually dramatic than their debut, but the budgetary freedom afforded by the format allowed the filmmakers to concentrate on the two lead performances, creating an unsettling tale of the encounter between a park-keeper and a girl apparently skipping school.

Carney worked alone on his next film, *On the Edge*, starring **Cillian Murphy** and produced (under the title *The Smiling Suicide Club*) by **Hell's Kitchen** with finance from Universal Pictures. Perhaps predictably it is more conventional than the films the pair made, although the decision to examine yet another Irish taboo—young male suicide—set it apart. Carney himself was on record as being unhappy with the final cut of the film, feeling that Universal's vision of the film (they wanted a teen movie, and Carney wanted an adult movie about young people) did not coincide with his. The result did not satisfy either party, and the film was not widely released.

Since then Carney and Hall have worked mainly in television on the aforementioned *Bachelor's Walk* and more recently *The Last Furlong*. The pair also shot another unreleased film in 2003 entitled *Zonad*, starring Cillian Murphy as an alien who arrives in an Irish village intent on drinking and hitting it off with the local women. Its production—it was also shot on digital video—suggests that Carney and Hall are not in a hurry to return to the strictures of large budgets.

CASSIDY, ELAINE (1980–). Cassidy grew up in Kilcoole, County Wicklow, near the set of now defunct Irish soap *Glenroe*, a fact that encouraged her to consider acting as a career in later life. She first appeared onscreen in Geraldine Creed's short *The Stranger within Me*. Two years later Creed cast her again opposite Angie Dickinson and Gina Moxley in *The Sun, the Moon and the Stars*. In 1998 she was simultaneously offered a recurring role in *Glenroe* and the lead in Atom Egoyan's film adaptation of *Felicia's Journey*. Opting for the latter (although she did appear in five episodes of the soap) proved a wise choice. She was a revelation as Felicia, the pregnant teenager abandoned by her boyfriend who falls prey to the sinister schemes of Bob Hoskins's quiet psychopath.

Subsequent casting has played upon the innocence of the Felicia character to varying effect. Cassidy was (literally) muted but eye-catching in the international hit *The Others* (2001) and managed the feat of appearing simultaneously otherworldly and grounded as Runt in Kirsten Sheridan's *Disco Pigs*, where she more than held her own opposite **Cillian Murphy**'s scene-stealing performance as the slowly disintegrating Pig. Since *Disco Pigs* her best work has been on television, where she again played the innocent as Hitler's niece in *Uncle Adolf*, and as Maud, the only apparently innocent character in Irish director Aisling Walsh's adaptation of Sarah Waters's novel *Fingersmith*. Still very young, she offers the rare (for an Irish actress) prospect of a major international career.

CATEGORIZING IRISH FILM. In *Ten Years After: The Irish Film Board 1993–2003*, a book published to mark a decade of the board's existence, feature films produced in this period are divided into the following categories: Childhood (6), Rites of Passage/Coming of Age (14), Family/Adult Relationships (27), Politics/History (17), Urban Ireland/Crime (19), and Migration (9). The dominant trend of mainstream classical narrative films remains a preoccupation with the theme of love and relationships. The category titled Family/Adult Relationships has 10 more examples than Politics/History, for example. This can be read as a confirmation that the second wave of film production is less concerned with politics, history, and identity than its more radical predecessor. Or alternatively it can signal the mainstreaming of Irish cinema as it becomes more influenced by external global forces of world cinema than by its national legacy.

Nevertheless, as with all generalizations, there remains conflicting evidence about this move toward more postmodern, global ahistorical filmmaking. While notable examples, such as *About Adam*, *When Brendan Met Trudy*, and *The Most Fertile Man in Ireland*, flesh out this move away from traditional preoccupations, other equally successful narratives, including *Dancing at Lughnasa*, *The Magdalene Sisters*, and *Agnes Browne*, remain concerned with nostalgic Irish history and its various hidden traumas. Hence it is difficult to categorize clear trends in filmmaking with much certainty.

CATHOLICISM. The 1923 Censorship Act was initiated by the first censor, James Montgomery, and specified extremely stringent measures to ensure that Roman Catholic doctrine was followed to the letter of the law. An incident in 1923 in Drumcollogher, County Limerick, illustrates the historically discredited attitude toward cinema. After a showing of the bible epic *The Ten Commandments*, a fire broke out, claiming 48 lives. The fire was caused by the inflammable film stock, which posed a continuous threat of combustion. Commenting on the awful incident, the bishop of Killaloe apparently cautioned that this wretched cinema craze was bound to end in a disaster sooner or later.

In June 1936, Pope Pius XI articulated his growing concern with the fast-spreading influence of cinema in an encyclical entitled *"Vigilanti Cura" on Motion Pictures*, advising on the potential of the medium for good as well as evil. In the 1940s Archbishop John McQuaid set about implementing the edict with the establishment of the **National Film Institute** (NFI) in 1943. He gave £250 toward the cost of three projectors and suitable film, and the institute was subsequently instrumental in promoting film for educational purposes.

In the classic Irish films *The Quiet Man*, *Odd Man Out*, and even *Ryan's Daughter* representations of the clergy were certainly favorable, validating the great reverence in which the people held the Church. Like other Catholic countries such as Italy, the Church was closely linked with legitimating the censorship of film that continued for decades. Surprisingly, it took a long time for expressions of anticlericism to become a feature of Irish film as displayed most disturbingly in **Cathal Black**'s *Our Boys* (1981) or more recently in *The Magdalene Sisters* (2002) and *Song for a Raggy Boy* (2003). Cultural historians have traced this move toward a postreligious contemporary phase within Irish culture to the numerous scandals around violence toward schoolchildren and fears that pedophiles are being condoned and harbored by Church authorities. The creation of "moral panics" around the pernicious influence of film, which the Church used so often to legitimate the crude censorship of film, have of late been used by the media against the erstwhile hegemonic moral authority of the Catholic Church in Ireland and elsewhere.

Religious extremism has of course also been considered a primal historical cause of the **"troubles"** in the North between tribal Protestant and Catholic sects. However, as in *Odd Man Out* and more recent films and documentaries—like those of **John T. Davis** in the North and **Alan Gilsenan** in the South, for example—representations of Irish Catholicism and Protestantism are much more complicated and fleshed out than it would appear in conventional stereotypical representations of religious agency.

CENSORSHIP. It has long been a source of wry amusement that in July 1923, amid the smoke of civil war, Dáil Eireann found time to pass the Censorship of Films Act, which until the introduction of the Irish Film Board Act at the close of the 1970s had the unique distinction of being the only piece of Irish legislation directly related to film. The introduction of the legislation was all the more surprising given that the new state had inherited the British Cinematograph Act of 1909, which already permitted local councils to act as censors over material screened within their jurisdictions.

Arguably, however, the civil war created an atmosphere in which the act became inevitable. Kevin O'Higgins, the minister who introduced the act, while conceding that cinema could not be blamed for "*all* our present troubles" (O'Higgins, 1923), could not help mischievously speculating whether Eamon de Valera was "addicted to frequenting cinemas when he was young" (O'Higgins, 1923). Arguably the act was also designed to equip the nascent state with another tool for determining the "official" view of Ireland. That view—which would prevail until the 1960s—was captured in one of the contributions to the parliamentary debate on the 1923 act from Professor William Magennis, who would subsequently become the first chairman of the Films Appeal Board:

> Purity of mind and sanity of outlook upon life were long ago regarded as characteristic of our people. The loose views and the vile lowering of values that belong to other races and other peoples were being forced upon our people through the popularity of the cinematograph. (Magennis, 1923)

This highly conservative **Catholic** ethos actively informed the framing of the act. O'Higgins had been prompted to bring it forward after receiving a deputation made up of the Irish Vigilance Association, the Priests' Social Guild, and representatives from the Catholic, Episcopalian, and Presbyterian Churches. Consequently, the act laid down guidelines for the censor requiring that films should be banned if they were "indecent, obscene or blasphemous." Furthermore, the membership of the Appeals Board provided for by the act included senior members of both Catholic and Protestant clergy for the first 40 years of the act's operation.

Thus from 1924 to 1965 films dealing with (or even mentioning) illegitimacy, divorce, abortion, contraception, and in the postwar years rape and homosexuality were excluded from Irish cinemas: 11,000 films were cut or banned by 1980. Furthermore, despite the specific provision in the 1923 act for a limited certificate allowing some films to be screened in "the presence of certain classes of persons," by 1945 no censor had exercised it. Both the censors and Appeals Board felt that the labeling of a film with a limited certificate "would arouse unhealthy curiosity" (Boland, 1945).

Thus every film passed received a universal certificate (equivalent to the U or General certificate). Even after they were first introduced, they were used sparingly. Furthermore, while it may have appeared that cutting was better than banning because it allowed the film to be shown, this did not always hold true. Otto Preminger's 1959 film *Anatomy of a Murder* is a courtroom drama dealing with an alleged rape and features a key scene presenting forensic evidence. When presented by its distributor for certification in Ireland, however, the censor cut all references to the rape and forensic evidence, rendering the film meaningless: The character on trial was clearly accused of something, but what?

The only screenings exempt from these controls were those undertaken by the **Irish Film Society** from 1936. From its inception, the society argued that since its screenings were for members only, they were effectively private and thus fell outside the purview of the act. In effect, then, the society established a precedent whereby films screened in club conditions did not require prior certification by the Irish censor. (Various film **festivals** and more permanent art-house venues that emerged from the 1950s would subsequently use this precedent.) That the Department of Justice permitted the precedent arguably reflected a class prejudice, which was exhibited in a tolerance of viewings of uncensored films by those members of society equipped with sufficient cultural capital to inoculate them against the "vile values" referred to by Professor Magennis.

The close of the 1950s, however, saw massive change sweep through the country. Traditional restrictions, imposed by the introspective economic and moral protectionism operating in Irish society, loosened, fuelled by the economic crisis of the 1950s and the obvious failure of social and economic policies of the previous decades.

At the same time a new generation of journalists, born after independence and equipped with a more international outlook, came to the fore. Events such as the lifting of the *Lady Chatterley* ban in Britain in 1960 led to a questioning of traditional precepts and to wider social debate on this side of the Irish Sea.

Simultaneously, Irish distributors and exhibitors began to apply pressure to relax censorship: The availability of product was now restricted by both censorship and the decline in the output of American studios. This coincided with the appointment of Brian Lenihan as minister for justice in October 1964. Sympathetic to the distributors and exhibitors (and facing a press barrage over the banning of Henry Hathaway's *Of Human Bondage*, which had been made in Ireland, and by the demand to cut Stanley Kubrick's *Dr. Strangelove*), Lenihan in January 1965 appointed an entirely new Appeals Board (the previous chairman, J. T. O'Farrell, had been a member for over 40 years). The new board had a specific brief: start issuing limited certificates (i.e., certificates limiting entry to specified age groups). Hitherto the Censorship of Publications Appeals Board had largely rubberstamped the censors' decisions. After 1965 the incumbent censor, Dr. Christy Macken, continued to issue bans, but increasingly the board began to overturn them: 29 of the 42 films banned by Macken in 1965 were subsequently passed by the board, albeit with cuts and limited certificates. After 18 months of this Macken began to issue a greater number of limited certificates, although he continued banning substantial numbers of films outright. The board for its part continued overturning the majority of these bans. Finally, in 1972, Macken was replaced by Dermot Breen, then director of the Cork Film Festival, whose appointment was regarded as completing the liberalizing process. The first film censor who actually had a background in film, Breen consolidated the Appeal Boards policy: Although he did continue to ban films, he did so at a greatly reduced rate, so that the Appeals Board had less and less work to do. Indeed, Breen was regarded as so liberal—at least in relation to his predecessor—that it was argued that the Appeals Board would now have to "catch up" with him.

Breen remained censor until 1978, when former **Radio Telefís Éireann (RTÉ)** presenter Frank Hall replaced him and largely maintained Breen's approach. However, when Hall retired in 1986, his replacement became the first overtly liberal (as opposed to *relatively* liberal) holder of the post. Like Dermot Breen, Sheamus Smith also had a background in film, having acted as chief executive of the National Film Studios of Ireland at **Ardmore Studios**. Between 1986 and 2003, Smith would ban outright only 10 films released to theaters, although these included *Showgirls* (1995), *From Dusk till Dawn* (1995), and *Natural Born Killers* (1994). The last of these caused a minor furor, however, when, in the wake of Smith's refusal to certify it, the **Irish Film Centre** (IFC) announced plans to screen the film on an open-ended run. The IFC assumed that since the screenings were limited to members, they would be covered under the club screenings "rule." However, the unusually open-ended nature of the run left the **Irish Film Institute** (IFI), which operated the cinemas, open to Smith's criticism that the screenings were prompted more by commercial than cultural considerations. Smith drew the attention of the Department of Justice to the screenings, which in turn threatened to issue an injunction against the Irish Film Institute if the film were screened. Faced with the threat of a spell in prison, the IFI board met three hours before the first scheduled screening of *Natural Born Killers* and decided to pull the film. The incident was significant in that it indicated that the same paternalistic rationale that had informed the "gentleman's agreement" permitting limited access to uncertified material in the 1930s was still in place 60 years later.

For the most part, however, Smith brought a new degree of sensitivity to the post, especially with regard to the traditionally complex field of certifying art-house material. The passing of Peter Greenaway's brilliant but grotesque *The Cook, the Thief, His Wife and Her Lover* (1989) without any cuts represented something of a breakthrough, a recognition that it was aimed at a particular audience segment (a fact made explicit by its exhibition at Dublin's **Light House** Cinema).

Smith retired in 2003, to be replaced by John Kelleher, a former **Radio Telefís Éireann (RTÉ)** and feature films producer (including *Eat the Peach*). As the first actual filmmaker appointed to the position, Kelleher has gone out of his way to be more responsive to public opinion. This has led to the (unprecedented) publication of censorship decisions and an enunciation of the general principles informing the work of the censor and his staff, among which is the view that adults should be free, within the law, to choose what they wish to view. In effect, then, Kelleher has begun to redefine the role of the office, acting less as a censor and more as a classifier of material.

CHANNEL 4. Channel 4 began broadcasting in the United Kingdom in 1982, having been set up as an indirect result of the recommendations of a government-commissioned report on the allocation of a fourth channel. The *Annan Report* concluded that rather than simply handing the channel over to the existing British broadcasters, the fourth channel should be run independently with an explicit remit to address niche audiences hitherto ignored by the other terrestrial broadcasters, the British Broadcasting Corporation (BBC) and Independent Television (ITV). In practice Channel 4 came under the financial umbrella of ITV (which funded the channel in return for the right to sell advertising around Channel 4's programs) but retained editorial independence. Channel 4 adopted a publisher-broadcaster organizational model, whereby it commissioned a substantial proportion of its programs from independent producers. As part of its remit the new channel was to address the programming needs of ethnic minorities within Great Britain. Although this was not immediately obvious at the time, this would prove a massive boon to film and television makers within Ireland.

By the early 1980s there were approximately 1.5 million people of Irish extraction living in the United Kingdom, nearly 2 percent of the population. In effect the Irish constituted an ethnic minority. In addition Jeremy Isaacs, the channel's chief executive from 1982 until 1989, had a previously demonstrated interest in Ireland, having already produced *Ireland: A Television History*. In March 1982 (eight months before Channel 4's first broadcast), Isaacs informed an audience at the Third Celtic Film and Television Festival in Wexford that he planned to include Irish sports and politics as part of the channel's weekly schedule. In practice those particular nonfiction programs failed to materialize, although in June 1986 the channel did commission eight documentaries on contemporary Ireland under the collective title of "The Irish Reel." From its inception, however, the channel was a major cofunder, with **Radio Telefís Éireann (RTÉ)**, of Irish-themed television drama, partially financing series such as *The Year of the French*, the **Little Bird**–produced *The Irish RM*, *Caught in a Free State*, and **Strongbow**'s *When Reason Sleeps*.

The channel was also a key source of funds for feature films. Often credited with single-handedly reviving the British film industry in the 1980s (indeed for a period it *was* the British film industry), the channel's Film on Four Strand would prove a crucial source of funding for Irish film. The first Irish filmmaker to benefit from Channel 4's largesse was **Neil Jordan**, whose debut feature, *Angel*, was funded (to the tune of £800,000) largely by Channel 4. (The Jordan association would continue with the director's subsequent *The Company of Wolves*, **The Miracle**, and **The Crying Game**, the last of which was one of its most successful at the box office, taking $62 million in the United States.) The remainder of *Angel's* budget— £100,000—came from the **Irish Film Board**, and this funding partnership continued throughout the existence of the first Film Board: **The Outcasts**, *The Country Girls*, **Eat the Peach**, **Budawanny**, **Reefer and the Model**, and **The Courier** were all cofunded by Channel 4 and the board. Indeed given the complaint by the Film Board's first chairman, **John Boorman**, that the money given to the board (around £500,000 per annum) was insufficient to make "half of one decent film" (Dwyer, 1997), it is arguable that very few of the board projects would have come to fruition in the absence of Channel 4 Films.

Channel 4's support of Irish cinema during this period was not limited to Film Board projects, however. Under a policy of supporting workshop production in the regions, Channel 4 funded both the **Derry Film and Video Collective** (and the collective's only feature production *Hush-a-Bye Baby*) and Belfast Independent Video.

In 1988, however, Isaacs stood down as chief executive and was replaced by former BBC director of programs Michael Grade. Perceived as more commercially minded than his predecessor, Grade's tenure saw Irish television drama and documentary commissions dry up. However, Channel 4 Films continued to invest in Irish features through the 1990s; these included *Trojan Eddie*, *Dancing at Lughnasa*, and *Southpaw*. In 1998, Channel 4 Films was rebranded FilmFour and continued as a production and distribution entity. However, in 2000 and 2001 the company posted losses of £3 million and £5.4 million, respectively. Although these were not of themselves unsustainable losses, they highlighted a structural weakness in the company, namely the absence of a long-term relationship with one of the major U.S. studios, which had allowed other smaller operators like Miramax and Working Title to sustain occasional losses. In July 2002, then, FilmFour was effectively wound up. Channel 4 has subsequently continued to invest in film production but at much more modest investment levels. From the perspective of Irish filmmakers the arrival of alternative funding sources in the 1990s—the Irish Film Board, **Section 481**, and RTÉ—has meant that FilmFour's demise has not had the catastrophic effect that it would have had it taken place in the 1980s. Nonetheless, it has closed one obvious avenue of commercial funding for Irish film.

CHAOS **(2001).** Directed by Geraldine Creed, the film recounts the bizarre story of a killer, who happens to also be a biker, on a journey as he leaves his life to join an eclectic band of traveling performers on a tour of postapocalyptic Europe. In addition to its Irish shoot the story was also filmed in Germany and Lanzarote and stars Jason Barry, Lindsey Harris, and Tommy O'Neill (who also wrote the script).

CIRCLE OF FRIENDS **(1995).** Based on a best-selling Maeve Binchy novel, the film opens in a small village in 1950s Ireland. Three friends, Benny (Minnie Driver), Nan (Saffron Burrows), and Eve (Geraldine O'Dawe) are confirmed together and pledge everlasting friendship, but shortly afterward, Nan and her family move away. Half a decade later, however, the three are reunited at university in Dublin. Nan's years living in Dublin have given her a veneer of sophistication compared to her friends—Eve is an orphan being raised by nuns, and Benny must return home to her village every night.

At college, Benny meets Jack (Chris O'Donnell), a medical student and college rugby star. At a party hosted by Eve, Benny and Jack begin a frustratingly chaste relationship. Benny's parents, however, are determined that she will marry the repulsive Sean, who works in her father's business. When her father suddenly dies, Benny is forced to leave college and work in the shop with Sean, whose advances she attempts to ward off. Meanwhile Nan meets the local Protestant landlord Simon Westward (Colin Firth) for illicit assignations in Eve's cottage. When she becomes pregnant, however, Westward dumps her. Desperate, Nan seduces Benny's boyfriend Jack, who is drunk, and then informs him that he is the father of her baby. Unhappily he agrees to stand by her, and they become engaged, thus breaking Benny's heart.

From this opening synopsis it is not hard to see why *Circle of Friends* was easily the most successful film funded by the Irish Film Board in the early 1990s. Its adherence to a familiar narrative structure and its soft primitive depiction of Ireland doubtless contributed to its $24 million performance at the American box office and the $4.5 million it took in the United Kingdom. However, given filmmaker **Pat O'Connor**'s pedigree it was an enormous disappointment. Most depressing are the film's Victorian values: Nan, who sleeps with the local landlord, becomes the "bad girl" willing to betray her best friend to get a husband. Meanwhile Benny, who retains her chastity for most of the film, is rewarded for her (as it turns out) temporary virtue. Nan is last seen leaving for a boat to England and is never heard of again, while Benny not only gets her man but also turns out to be a successful writer.

Disappointing too is the film's crude John Hinde postcard–styled representation of Ireland of the 1950s. Although the film stops short of showing flame-haired children with turf-carrying donkeys, virtually every shot looks like it received Tourist Board (**Bord Fáilte**) approval: glistening streams, neat villages arranged around a picturesque green, and so on. Occasionally, this is technically impressive: The film's signature establishing shot for University College Dublin (ironically, actually Trinity College shot from the Dublin Castle end of Dame Street) looks like contemporary footage. But for the most part it only serves to underline the good-girls-go-to-heaven, bad-girls-don't, fantasy element of the narrative itself. The Michael Kamen score, drenched in horrendous saccharine Irish-styled melodies, does nothing to counter the effect of the visuals.

The saving grace of the film lies in some of the performances, especially that of Minnie Driver, who lent the character an intelligence not evident in Andrew Davies's script. This role as the outwardly tough but inwardly vulnerable Benny proved a career breakthrough for her. Inevitably, however, given the absence of Irish actors in lead roles, audiences were subjected to cringe-worthy attempts at local accents, some so bad as to obscure the dialogue. Chief among the culprits was Chris O'Donnell, clearly chosen to give the film international appeal, but always looking more like an American high school jock than what in the 1950s would have been a rare creature in Ireland—a university student.

CLASH OF THE ASH **(1987).** Scripted and directed by Fergus Tighe, who later scripted *2by4*, the drama incorporates an effective rite-of-passage debut that ties in with a series of Irish films that can loosely be described as "Leaving Certificate" films. Starring Vinny Murphy, Alan Devlin, and **Gina Moxley**, the story focuses on a young man who has to decide what he wants to do with his life in a small rural Cork environment, where most of the excitement is played out on the hurling pitch. Naturally he craves the excitement of distant shores, while at the same time he is frightened of the unknown, which all forms of **emigration** entail. This gentle story captures the social reality of the period and regional place, remaining a memorable first outing for Tighe.

COLLINS, DAVID. *See* IRISH FILM THEATRE; SAMSON FILMS; STRONGBOW FILMS.

COMERFORD, JOE (1949–). One of the leading lights of the radical tendency that briefly flourished within Irish cinema of the 1970s and 1980s, Comerford first made an impact with a series of short experimental films, including *Waterbag* (1974) and *Withdrawal* (1984). His first short (60 minutes) feature, *Down the Corner* (1977), made with the assistance of the British Film Institute (BFI) and Dublin's Ballyfermot Community Workshop, examined working-class poverty. His next feature, *Traveller* (1981), dealt with Ireland's indigenous "others," the Travelling community, and was based on a script developed with **Neil Jordan**, who was reportedly very unhappy with the finished film. Comerford was one of the last recipients of funding from the first **Irish Film Board**, which partially financed his next feature, *Reefer and the Model* (1988). This much later film dealt with smugglers in Connemara, County Galway, who get mixed up with the Irish Republican Army (IRA). His most recent film, *High Boot Benny* (1993), is situated in the North as the peace process begins to take off, but for some critics the film remains overly confusing and insubstantial.

Indeed, it might generally be argued that watching Joe Comerford's work is rarely an easy task. It is often deliberately antirealist, and concern for a linear narrative is absent (when his films are synopsized, the story must frequently be inferred). In fact, to try to understand Comerford's work by looking at the story is almost to miss the point. His films often proceed as a series of vignettes, where scenes bear scant relation to those immediately following or preceding them. Ironically, his films suggest a filmmaker who mistrusts the power of image and narrative. For example in *Reefer and the Model* one woman refuses to have her photograph taken by the local photographer on the grounds that in her honeymoon photos "I looked happy in them and I wasn't." The antirealism is often evident too in the characters themselves, frequently larger than life with a romantic past; they are given to cryptic dialogue delivered in a deliberately over-the-top manner.

A cynic might suggest that Comerford simply does not understand the medium. It is also possible to believe the obverse: that Comerford understands cinema so well that he is attempting to make it do something totally new, to invent a new cinema language.

THE COMMITMENTS (1991). Based on the best-selling book by **Roddy Doyle**, the film version directed by **Alan Parker** includes a cast of young unknown actors in the story of the rise and fall of a working-class Dublin blues band. The narrative structure conforms to classic Hollywood preoccupations with the dream of success, and the characters themselves are also preoccupied by American cultural influences. Jimmy Rabitte (Robert Arkins) has a vision to bring soul music to Dublin and ends up managing a most successful young band, importing an aging guru saxophonist, Joe the Lips (Johnny Murphy).

Parker, a northern British film director (who also directed *Angela's Ashes*), has been criticized for taking on local indigenous stories and overuniversalizing them so that they will appeal to mass audiences. The oft-repeated tag line in the film—"They had nothing, but they were willing to risk it all"—legitimates the band's domestication of black American blues by styling working-class youths from the north side of Dublin as "blacks of Ireland." As the critic Lance Pettitt perceptively notices, the deep schism between Dublin's working class and the huge hinterland and rural community, dramatized in Doyle's novel, is carefully avoided to maintain a universal audience (Pettitt, 2000, 126–127). This very successful feel-good movie of struggle in adversity with a strong sense of local identity through a young unknown cast, and Doyle's effective use of the vernacular, has helped put Irish working-class characterization on the world map.

CONAMARA (2000). Starring Andreas Schmidt and Garret Keogh, among others, the film directed by Eoin Moore explores everyday life in a remote part of County Galway. Maria's simple life with her husband and daughter is thrown into disarray when an old flame from Germany arrives and a new business venture begins, forcing her to make major choices about her future path in life.

CONCORDE ANOIS TEORANTA. *See* CORMAN, ROGER.

CONROY, JACK. Conroy originally entered the film industry in the early 1970s working as a gaffer (electrical supervisor) on a number of **Ardmore**-based projects, including Robert Altman's *Images* (1972) and John Boorman's *Zardoz* (1974). In 1984, however, he made the switch to camera operator, initially working on adaptations of Frederick Forsyth novels. The international and Oscar success of *My Left Foot*, on which he worked as a cinematographer, brought his work to the attention of the wider world, and although he has worked on Irish projects, such as *The Field*, *The Playboys*, and *Gold in the Streets*, since the mid-1990s he has increasingly worked in the United States. Much of this work has been on made-for-television projects such as **Terry George**'s adaptation of Neil Sheehan's book on Vietnam, *A Bright Shining Lie* (1998), and Dennis Quaid's 1998 directorial debut *Everything That Rises*. However, he has also worked on theatrical releases like Sam Shepard's *Silent Tongue* (1994) and *Homeward Bound II* (1996).

CONROY, RÚAIDHRÍ (1979–). Rúaidhrí made his acting debut at the age of eight in an **Abbey Theatre** production of *The Field* in which his father—Brendan Conroy—was also appearing. When in 1996 he appeared in *The Van* as Kevin, the role of his sister, Diane, was played by Neilí Conry, Rúaidhrí's real-life sister. (The entire family dynasty has yet to appear together in a single screen production, however.)

Rúaidhrí made his film debut in 1990 in **Pat O'Connor**'s *The Dawning* before appearing in *Hear My Song* the following year. He followed that with what remains his best-known role—that of Tito in *Into the West*, in which his portrayal displayed streetwise savvy and affecting vulnerability in equal parts. On the strength of this, he was offered what is arguably his most accomplished screen role, that of the bruised but sensitive Conrad, a student at a special needs school, in the British film *Clockwork Mice* (1995). He followed this with another warmly received lead role in *Moondance*, offering a skilled depiction of the turmoil of adolescent sexuality.

Since then much of his work has been onstage rather than onscreen, although in addition to Irish films such as *Nothing Personal* and *When the Sky Falls* he appeared in the British supernatural thriller *Deathwatch* (2002), with **Hugh O'Conor,** and the Hollywood wartime legal drama *Hart's War* (2002), which also featured **Colin Farrell**. On the stage, however, he has received critical plaudits, most particularly for Martin McDonagh's *The Cripple of Inishmaan*, which is set on the Aran Islands during the filming of Robert Flaherty's *Man of Aran*. When the original London production of the play moved to New York, only Conroy, who played the lead role, remained with the show. More recently, he and McDonagh collaborated on the latter's first foray into film, the short *Six Shooter*, which in addition to winning awards at the Foyle, Cork, and British Independent Film Festivals secured the Oscar for Best Short Film in 2006 and in which Conroy takes one of the two lead roles opposite **Brendan Gleeson.**

COOPER, TOM. *See THE DAWN*; HIBERNIA FILMS.

COOPERS AND LYBRAND REPORT. In 1991, the Industrial Development Authority (IDA) together with Temple Bar Properties, the state agency charged with developing the capital's Temple Bar area into a Left Bank for Dublin, asked the Irish Film Centre Building Ltd. (IFCB), the body created by the **Arts Council** to oversee the redevelopment of what would become the **Irish Film Centre**, to produce a report on the Irish Film Industry with a view to identifying opportunities for creating film-related jobs in the Temple Bar area and Ireland in general. The IFCB in turn commissioned the international accounting firm Coopers and Lybrand to develop an Irish strategy focused on job creation and to recommend specific initiatives to put that strategy into effect. The bulk of the research was carried out by independent producer (and later **TV3** commissioning editor) Jane Gogan.

When the resulting report (officially titled the *Report on Indigenous Audiovisual Production Industry* but colloquially referred to as the *Coopers and Lybrand Report*) was published in June 1992, it was immediately identified as marking a sea change in Irish film lobbying in that it granted equal emphasis to audiovisual production as an artistic and industrial (read "job-creating") undertaking. It would subsequently become an influential point of reference for the dramatic changes in Irish film policy inaugurated by **Michael D. Higgins** in 1993.

Given its length (the summary, conclusions, and recommendation chapter alone runs to 29 pages), no summary could possibly do justice to its content. However, the report considered every conceivable aspect of audiovisual production, from feature films, through corporate video, to **animation**. It argued that the demand for audiovisual content within the European market was likely to substantially increase in the coming decade, presenting lucrative windows of opportunity for those countries positioned to avail of them.

In this respect, however, the report criticized previous Irish approaches to developing and positioning the industry. The comments made about the **Irish Film Board**'s activities from 1981 to 1987 are indicative of this critique. Although it praised the training and development that came about as a result of the board's activities, the report nonetheless noted that the board's decision to focus on low-budget production with indigenous casts meant that the resulting films lacked international appeal. By definition, then, the report concluded that the board's funding decisions were not driven by commercial considerations. The report went on to argue that this difficulty was exacerbated by an absence of understanding and contacts for the distribution and sales of film in the international marketplace.

Not surprisingly, therefore, the report's core observation was the need for the sector to become much more market driven, and to this end it made a series of recommendations relating to training, marketing, and finance. With regard to training it recommended greater communication between the audiovisual sector and third-level institutions, with a view to better relating curricula to real-world employment opportunities. The report also noted that a focus on achieving production had meant that Irish producers were underemphasizing the marketing of their pictures and suggested that the Irish Trade Board might adopt a greater role in that respect. However, it was the section on finance that perhaps reveals the most about the philosophy underlying the report. Rather than focusing primarily on how to fund individual films, the report consistently referred to the need to aid the development of production companies capable of securing funding in the international marketplace. Thus the report identified the Industrial Development Authority as the key body in driving the future development of the sector rather than—as might have been expected—pushing for the reestablishment of the Film Board. In stressing the need to actively promote Ireland as a location for offshore production, the report also referred to the IDA.

Where the report did directly address making production finance available, it concentrated on the role of the Arts Council and fiscal incentives. It praised the Arts Council's role in supporting short films and low budgets, which it considered important from a cultural, educational, and training perspective. However, in discussing mainstream film production, it pointed to the limitations of the **Business Expansion Scheme** (especially for individual as opposed to corporate investors) and recommended adjusting **Section 35** to compensate for these.

It concluded by stressing the need for "joined-up" policymaking, a reference to the approach up to that time of spreading policymaking across a range of state bodies. Crucially, however, the arguments throughout the report for film industry support were couched—the status of film as a cultural undertaking notwithstanding—in hard-nosed financial language. The report clearly suggested that the increased state investment in the sector would be more than compensated for by increases in the return to the exchequer from income and other forms of taxation. Taken together with the approaches discussed in the *Film Makers Ireland Report* and *The Report of the Taoiseach's Special Working Group on the Film Industry*, which were published in the same period, the commercial approach implicit in the *Coopers and Lybrand Report* would inform film policymaking through the 1990s.

CORMAN, ROGER (1926–). A renowned schlock-horror B movie maker, Corman was involved with filmmaking in Ireland for over five decades. In 1963 he allowed his then apprentice Francis Ford Coppola to leave the set of Corman's *The Young Racers* in England to go to Ireland, where Coppola shot his debut picture, *Dementia 13* (1963) on a budget of less than $50,000. Seven years later, Corman himself followed Coppola to Ireland to direct his take on the Red Baron story, *Von Richthofen and Brown* (aka *The Red Baron*, 1971).

However, Corman's place in Irish cinema history is cemented by his setting up in 1995 of Concorde Anois Teoranta, a small-scale studio facility in Tully, County Galway, as an offshoot to his New Horizon Pictures operation in Santa Monica, California. Although attracted partly by the potential availability of **Section 35** funding, Corman was actively courted by Udarás na Gaeltachta, the state authority with responsibility for developing industry in the Gaeltacht (Irish-speaking) regions of Ireland. Udarás would eventually provide around £1 million to help establish the Corman operation. This wooing of Corman fitted with **Michael D. Higgins**'s general "western strategy," which attempted to decentralize audiovisual production from its east coast (and mainly) Dublin orientation. Thus the negotiations were facilitated on the part of the state by the active intervention of both Higgins and then minister for enterprise and employment Ruairí Quinn. Irish producer **Kieran Corrigan** acted as an intermediary for Corman and subsequently became a director of the film production company associated with the studio.

Inevitably the venture raised concerns about its possible linguistic impact in one of the strongest remaining Irish-speaking areas, but these were apparently allayed by assurances that the highest number possible of people employed at the studios would be Udarás-trained Irish speakers.

In cultural terms, the contribution of the studios to Irish cinema has been negligible. Although Corman did expresses an interest in producing a version of Joyce's *Portrait of the Artist as a Young Man*, and in developing a film on the life of Charles Stewart Parnell, the only nod to the local thus far is the awful *A Very Unlucky Leprechaun*. The half dozen pictures produced each year are typically exploitation films intended for the straight-to-video market, as suggested by titles like *Criminal Affairs*, *Detonator*, and *Bloodfist VIII: Trained to Kill*.

Two years after the studios arrived, the local Galway Film Fleadh [festival] decided to screen the first Irish-directed feature completed by Concorde, *Criminal Affairs*, prompting a minor furor. Questions were raised about the wisdom of allowing Udarás and Section 35 funding to support the production of films featuring rape, murder, and what were generally regarded as some pretty tacky sex scenes. Udarás responded by pointing out that they had funded some 20 film and television companies in the previous decade but did not feel they had a role in making editorial decisions about the kinds of films the companies they supported should make.

Given this, the real contribution of the studios to Irish cinema is industrial. Corman promised to employ 60 to 70 people once the studios were in full swing, 90 percent of whom would be local. Although in practice those who have worked at the studios have expressed dissatisfaction over low wages, long hours, and poor training opportunities, the Connemara facility has nonetheless provided otherwise unimaginable opportunities for young Irish filmmakers to experience filmmaking at first hand. Furthermore, the studios have arguably created a partial alternative to Dublin-Ardmore-centered filmmaking, which sees the vast bulk of films shot within a 40-mile radius of **Ardmore Studios**, in Bray, County Wicklow.

CORRIGAN, KIERAN. *See* MERLIN FILMS.

COUNTRY **(2000).** Like Kevin Liddy's earlier short film *Horse*, the story revolves around a young child and the secrets of his family. Twelve-year-old Jack Murphy (Dean Pritchard) lives with his widowed father, Frank (Des Cave), and his brother, Con (Gary Lydon), in the rural Ireland of the 1970s. Frank, an ex-alcoholic, may or not have been responsible for the death of his wife, Bridget, and consequently lives a broken life laced with regret. When Jack's Uncle Jimmy (Peter Dix) dies of a heart attack, his Aunt Miriam (Lisa Harrow) returns for the funeral and stays on indefinitely, acting as a catalyst for the healing of emotional familial wounds. She advises Con and his girlfriend Sarah (Marcella Plunkett) to make positive changes in their lives and lightens Jack's existence by opening him up to possibilities outside his limited patriarchal world. However, a vicious rape results in the girl having to emigrate as local Travellers are scapegoated for the crime.

While the story has been criticized for a stereotypical evocation of rural stultification, internecine conflict, and miscommunication, this does not detract from the elemental truth of the narrative, which is beautifully visualized through lingering shots of the evocative landscape of the West.

THE COURIER (1987). An early attempt, supported by the first **Irish Film Board** and Palace Pictures, to make a home-grown genre thriller, which is let down by a somewhat incoherent conclusion. Scripted by Frank Deasy and directed by Joe Lee, the plot follows motorcycle courier Mark (Padraig O'Loinsigh), who discovers that his employer, Val (**Gabriel Byrne**), uses his courier business as a front for a drug ring, and that he (Mark) has unwittingly been delivering heroin around Dublin. The soundtrack was noted for its use of a range of Dublin-based bands on the cusp of international success.

COWBOYS AND ANGELS (2003). David Gleeson's love of film was instilled by his father, who ran a small cinema in Cappamore, County Limerick. The film, Gleeson's first as director, eschews the usual negative stereotype of Limerick, avoiding images of the city as a crime capital with gang feuds and stabbings. Starring Michael Leagh and Allen Leech, it tells the story of Shane, a lost and lonely and very untrendy 20-year-old civil servant from the country who encounters the impossibly camp Vincent when the two find themselves sharing a flat. As Shane is introduced to Vincent's demimonde, a fish-out-of-water narrative emerges, and Shane finds his life transformed. With more than its fair share of plot contrivances, the story is sometimes difficult to accept, particularly when it detours into Dublin and drug running for dramatic effect. Nevertheless, for such a low-budget Irish film, it received good distribution and relatively favorable reviews.

CRUSHPROOF (1997). Paul Tickell, a British director, was once in training for the Catholic priesthood and received his film training courtesy of the British Broadcasting Corporation (BBC) documentary series. Fittingly, then, *Crushproof* can be identified with the emergence of a subgenre of recent British films dealing with disaffected youth. The narrative delivers a tale of loyalty and honor, taking as its central characters Dublin "pony kids" (children and teenagers from a background of poverty who devote their lives to acquiring nonthoroughbred ponies and horses) and bringing all the attendant mythology of the Hollywood Western such a story seems to demand. When the central character, Neal, celebrates his release from a Dublin prison with his "ponykid" gang (i.e., those who ride horses), he tells them,

> The knackers were refugees from Cromwell. We're the old tribe, the Bedouins. We're the Tuatha [mythical Irish tribe] of the North. We've got the warrior blood. They'll never crush us cos we're crushproof. Thousands of years old we are. The Industrial Revolution's just a blip on my bleedin' screen.

However, with a screenplay by Californian writer James Mathers, a Scottish director, and a production team that came from the United Kingdom, the Netherlands, Ireland, and Germany, perhaps it is fair to assume that the film's central themes should be seen as applying not to Ireland specifically, but to a mythical land of adolescent fantasies and male bonding that knows no national boundaries.

Shot in Dublin and County Wicklow over eight weeks in the summer of 1997, the film opens with a montage of images of classic urban decay, including continuous low-angle shots of high concrete walls, children dwarfed by the concrete structure of the pillar in the Phoenix Park, a wide shot of a posse of horses crossing a bridge over a dual carriageway suddenly eclipsed by modernity, and a train passing in the foreground. Also featured in the sequence are shots of shrines and churches, perhaps suggesting an Ireland still under the yoke of **Catholic** control. It is less visually compelling for many critics than *Accelerator*, though there is a similar use of music and fast editing, particularly in scenes of violence and conflict. It is clear from the opening sequence that the filmmakers were keen to emphasize location over the individual, in contrast to the film adaptations of **Roddy Doyle**'s Barrytown trilogy, which were criticized for not always delivering authentic imagery of Dublin.

THE CRYING GAME **(1992). Neil Jordan**'s films are frequently pre-occupied with the crossing and blurring of boundaries between countries, for example Ireland and Britain in *Angel* and ***Michael Collins***. *The Crying Game* by contrast was critically and commercially acclaimed for its blurring of gender politics. Jody, a black British Army soldier serving in Northern Ireland, is lured into an IRA kidnapping. He befriends one of his captors, Fergus, an IRA man increasingly disillusioned with the "armed struggle," and shows him pictures of his black girlfriend. The relationship is suddenly terminated by a British Army ambush on the IRA hideout, during which Jody is accidentally killed. Fergus escapes to London, where under an assumed name he finds Dil, Jody's girlfriend, and they strike up first a friendship, then a romance. However, when Fergus sees Dil naked for the first time, the camera pans down "her" body to rest briefly on male genitalia. Shocked, Fergus lashes out, fleeing Dil's apartment. Nevertheless Fergus gradually comes to terms with Dil's sexuality, and a reconciliation is effected. However, Fergus's former IRA colleagues come back into his life, insisting that Fergus participate in an assassination.

Given the background of its lead character, *The Crying Game* could hardly avoid being a political film, but it goes way beyond the narrow confines of the politics of nationhood. The decision to set the opening scenes in the North foregrounds such politics, but ultimately Irish partition comes to represent far more fundamental divisions and differences in gender, race, and sexual preference.

The film constructs these divisions along an oppressor-oppressed axis. Jody initially represents the oppressor—both a British Army soldier, regarded by the IRA as an invader, and a heterosexual male who is in a position to be kidnapped only because he attempts to ravish a female member of the IRA cell. Yet the film tacitly argues not merely that such roles are quite fluid but that they are artificially constructed. Jody the oppressor, for example, is simultaneously the oppressed: a black man sent to "the only place in the world where they still call you nigger to your face." The fluidity and artificiality of such roles is even more evident in the relationship between Fergus and Dil. Initially, Fergus, a white, apparently heterosexual male relates to Dil as a black, heterosexual female. Although little physically changes about Dil during the film, in the wake of the revelation about Dil's sexuality, Fergus's perception of him/her immediately shifts to that of a homosexual male (an earlier comment from Jody about his own sexual organs—"It's only a piece of meat"—takes on a new resonance in this scene). Jordan has been criticized for his "rabbit-out-of-the-box" approach to this scene, but given that the viewer is likely to bring the same prejudices and preconceptions to the film that the characters show, the surprise is arguably essential not merely to shock people out of their passive consumption of the narrative but simply to draw attention to the ongoing process we all engage in of making unconscious assumptions and readings in understanding the people we meet.

The oppressive forces in the film are represented by the British Army and the IRA. Thus oppression itself is identified as organizational in origin. Jody argues with Fergus that it's not in the nature of terrorists (and by extension the Irish) to release hostages, but crucially, he excepts Fergus from this generalization, conceding the primacy of individual humanity over the demands of the organization. Yet at a wider level the film identifies society at large as an oppressive force, imposing norms in relation to gender roles, sexuality, and race. There is even an indirect commentary on the role of Hollywood —as part of society at large—in reinforcing norms. Director Jordan draws attention to and subverts the "male gaze" of Hollywood's representation of women that renders them objects for the (implicitly male) spectator to watch. Dil, first seen in a photograph, immediately becomes an object not just for the cinema audience but also for the characters within the diegesis of the film. After the narrative bombshell that she is a he, however, the filmic representation of Dil changes: Voyeuristic, lingering full-body shots are dropped in favor of close-ups.

Given the construction of society as the oppressive force, Fergus, existing outside society (both society at large and the smaller IRA infrastructure) and unconstrained by the dogmatic pursuit of ideology that dictates the actions of his IRA colleagues, is increasingly motivated by his essential humanity and compassion. Jody and Dil are similarly situated; their color and sexuality in a frequently racist and conformist society position them in society but not of it. Acceptance of one's essential humanity, overcoming the barriers of the artificial constraints imposed by society, represents the goal for the lead characters in *The Crying Game*. Jody and Dil ("I can't help what I am") have already achieved this before the narrative starts. Thus the story of the film is Fergus's journey to that goal, a journey prompted by his internal struggle with the contrasting directions of IRA orders and his own compassion, and ending with his acceptance of his feelings for Dil.

In the end, Jordan seems to say that love can conquer all divisions, be they along lines of race, gender, nationality, or sexual preference. This may appear overly simplistic: Clearly the differences at the heart of *The Crying Game*—genitalia, skin color, and so on—are real and cannot be reasoned out of existence. The point *The Crying Game* makes, however, is that the effect of these differences on how we relate to one another is socially constructed and artificial and ultimately can be overcome.

CULTURAL RELATIONS COMMITTEE (CRC). In January 1949, Clann Na Poblachta minister for external (foreign) affairs Sean MacBride established an advisory Cultural Relations Committee to carry out, or to give financial support to, Irish cultural projects of a high artistic standard with a view to enhancing Ireland's image and reputation overseas. The committee would assess applications for funding on their artistic and cultural merits and consider the views of Irish embassy staff in the country for which an event was proposed before making recommendations. Although this was not overtly stated at first, in deciding on the activities to be assisted the committee would also assess their potential to promote tourism and foreign direct investment. In contrast to most governmental committees, the CRC was not, for the most part, made up of civil servants but rather of influential figures within the indigenous arts sector.

In its first year of existence the committee received £2,600 to defray the cost of a wide range of cultural activities. In his first Dáil speech on the committee, in August 1949, MacBride referred to a long-term scheme to build up a library of short documentary films on Irish life and activity. That scheme bore its first fruit with the CRC-commissioned *W. B. Yeats—A Tribute*, produced by the **National Film Institute of Ireland**. The committee continued to commission documentaries through the 1950s and 1960s, perhaps most notably with **Patrick Carey**'s *Yeats Country*, which was nominated for an **Academy Award** in 1966. Not all of these documentaries immediately saw the light of day, however. In 1951 the committee commissioned **Liam O'Leary** (himself a committee member) to make *Portrait of Dublin*. However, by the time the film was completed, a new Fianna Fáil administration was in power and effectively quashed the film.

By the 1970s, the committee had effectively ceased commissioning new filmed work, although it did occasionally fund activities that might indirectly lead to filmmaking activity such as travel to and from Ireland. For the most part, however, from the 1970s on its film activities were limited to assisting screenings of Irish films at overseas festivals. This was somewhat formalized in 1993 when then minister for foreign affairs Dick Spring announced that the committee was engaged in an ongoing program, in cooperation with the **Irish Film Institute**, to purchase outright prints of Irish films with a view to making them available for screening at festivals abroad.

Indeed, as the 1990s progressed, increasing doubts were raised about the wisdom of placing responsibility for promoting Irish culture overseas in the hands of Foreign Affairs, especially given the obvious potential for overlap with the activities of the **Arts Council**. In 2003, therefore, that year's Arts Act placed responsibility for the CRC in the hands of the Department of Arts (although Foreign Affairs continuity was maintained through the ongoing presence of a senior civil servant from that department on the committee). This was followed in 2005 by the decision to replace the committee with Culture Ireland, a new national agency charged with establishing a strategic plan for the international promotion of Irish art and culture. It was anticipated that it would spend its initial €2 million budget on grants to Irish artists and arts organizations for overseas activity and for the funding and facilitation of Irish participation at international arts events.

Considering that the **Irish Film Archive**'s festival work ("Green Screen") had been financially supported by the Cultural Relations Committee for several years, it was appropriate that the Irish Film Institute's director Mark Mulqueen was among the first set of members. One of the first decisions undertaken by the agency was to support the Archive's *Reel Ireland* package of Irish film that was to be made available to noncommercial exhibitors throughout 2005 and 2006.

CUNNINGHAM, LIAM (1962–). Born in the North Wall area of Dublin, he trained as an electrician and worked for several years with the Electricity Supply Board (ESB). After a three-year stint working on rural electrification schemes in Zimbabwe, he returned to Dublin in 1987 looking for a change of career. He joined an acting school, and his professional stage debut quickly followed with the lead role in a production of Dermot Bolger's *Lament for Arthur Cleary*. (He would later reprise the role in a television version of the play.) From there he went to work with the Passion Machine theater group, at the same time as **Brendan Gleeson**, although the two never appeared in a production together. He then moved to London, working first at the Royal Court and then with the Royal Shakespeare Company for 18 months.

This brought him to the attention of British Television. He received a Best Actor nomination from the Royal Television Academy in 1995 for a one-off role in the psychological drama *Cracker*, and he has continued to alternate between television and film work ever since. In 1994 he appeared in *War of the Buttons*, a Warner Brothers' film shot in Ireland, which won him a further leading role in a 1995 feature adaptation of Frances Hodgson Burnett's *A Little Princess* and brought him to the attention of American audiences. Roles in Jerry Zucker's *First Knight* (1995) and *RKO 281* (1999), in which he played famed Hollywood cinematographer Gregg Toland, followed.

In the late 1990s he enjoyed an unusual degree of exposure in Ireland. In addition to leading roles in the critically acclaimed *Sweety Barrett* (1999) and *A Love Divided* (1999), he also starred in the **Radio Telefís Éireann**–British Broadcasting Corporation coproduction *Falling for a Dancer* (1998), set on the Beara Peninsula in Cork. By 2000 Cunningham had a well-established presence in Ireland and Britain, and though based in Dublin, he has effortlessly shifted back and forth across the Irish Sea, appearing in a number of British Television series (especially detective shows such as *Messiah* and *Prime Suspect*) and a number of films shot in Ireland, including *The Abduction Club* (2002), ***Breakfast on Pluto***, and, most recently, Ken Loach's *The Wind That Shakes the Barley* (2006).

CUSACK, CYRIL (1910–1993). One of a handful of Irish actors with an international reputation in the 1960s, Cusack was also famed for his ability to underplay his roles (and indeed to steal scenes). He was born in Kenya, where his father, James Cusack, was a police sergeant. His mother was a vaudeville actress, and when his parents separated while he was still a young child, Cusack's mother brought him back to England, where she worked in theater. Soon afterward she and her new partner, Breffni O'Rourke, moved to Ireland to join O'Brien and Ireland Players, a touring company. So when he was just seven, Cusack made his stage and film debuts in the play *East Lynne* and the film ***Knocknagow***.

Cusack continued to appear on stage while attending the Dominican College in Newbridge and University College Dublin, where he considered becoming a barrister before leaving without a degree to join the **Abbey** in 1932. He was an almost constant presence on the Abbey's boards until 1945, although he also made occasional appearances at the Gate Theatre and on the London stage, including a performance as Christy Mahon in J. M. Synge's *The Playboy of the Western World*.

He made a number of appearances in British films from 1935, including a key role in Carol Reed's ***Odd Man Out***. From the late 1940s in particular he became a staple in British films made and set in Ireland, including *Jacqueline* (1956), *The Rising of the Moon* (1957), ***Shake Hands with the Devil***, and *A Terrible Beauty* (1960). He used the income from this work to establish his own touring theater company, and between 1947 and 1960 he brought plays by George Bernard Shaw, Shakespeare, and Franz Kafka to stages in Dublin, Paris, and New York.

By the mid-1960s he was an increasingly recognizable character actor in international cinema, with roles in Martin Ritt's *The Spy Who Came in from the Cold* (which used Dublin as a double for East Berlin in 1966), Francois Truffaut's *Fahrenheit 451* (1966), and Fred Zinneman's *The Day of the Jackal* (1973). These roles were interspersed with appearances in less-memorable films, including a sequence of Italian productions between 1971 and 1976 with lurid titles such as *Hired to Kill* (1972), *Run, Run Joe* (1974), and *Street War* (1976).

Throughout this period he remained keenly engaged with theater work. In addition to his own company, he briefly managed the Gaiety Theatre after the war and in 1956 brought a highly controversial production of Sean O'Casey's *The Bishop's Bonfire* to the same theater. He also returned to the Abbey, both as a shareholder and—from 1965—as one of the directors. And of course he continued acting onstage, drawing critical acclaim for performances in works by Anton Chekhov, Brian Friel, Sean O'Casey, and William Shakespeare.

Cusack was at the cutting edge of the nascent film industry in the late 1970s, taking the lead role in **Bob Quinn**'s *Poitín*, his first in an indigenous film since *Knocknagow* in 1917. The role perfectly captured Cusack's most commonly utilized onscreen persona: a vague, almost fey exterior that masked a ruthless cunning and steely determination to secure his objectives. When his character of the poitín maker is threatened by the louts played by **Donal McCann** and **Niall Toibin,** he exacts a cold, merciless revenge.

Despite his age, his screen work did not tail off in the 1980s. He made three more appearances in Irish features: *The Outcasts* (1982), a cameo in Jim Sheridan's *My Left Foot*, and in *Far and Away*, his penultimate performance. He also reached a new domestic audience through television, in **Radio Telefís Éireann**'s (RTÉ) major drama series *Strumpet City* (1980), and **Pat O'Connor**'s *The Ballroom of Romance* (1982), and in a recurring role in RTÉ's rural soap *Glenroe*. His stage work also seemed unabated: He gave a memorable performance in a 1987 production of Oscar Wilde's *John Bull's Other Island* and in a 1990 production of Chekhov's *Three Sisters*, in which three of his daughters—Sinead, Niamh, and Sorcha—played the three sisters. (In 1989 he appeared onscreen with his son-in-law, Jeremy Irons—husband of Sinead—and his grandson, Samuel Irons, in a television version of Roald Dahl's *Danny, the Champion of the World*.)

Cusack passed away in October 1993; he had suffered from motor neurone disease but never retired. Although not a member of a political party, he was avowedly republican in his leanings and was a champion of the Irish language. He was also a writer of some note—he was a published poet, adapted Kafka's *The Trial* for the stage, and wrote his own play, *Tar Éis an Aifreann* [*After the Mass*]. Finally, although he never completed his studies at UCD, in 1977 the National University of Ireland (of which UCD is a component college) awarded him an honorary doctorate, as did Trinity College, Dublin in 1980.

– D –

DALTON, EMMETT (1898–1978). Although primarily of interest in this book for his later career as a film producer, Emmet Dalton's early experiences offer ample material for any screenwriter looking to recount a "boy's own"–style story. (Indeed it is arguable that he at least partially inspired two screen roles, in **Neil Jordan**'s *Michael Collins* and, as discussed below, in *This Other Eden*.) Though born in Massachusetts, he was raised in Ireland. After leaving school in Dublin in 1915, Dalton joined the British Army, went to the front in France, won a Military Cross for bravery, and was promoted to major while still in his teens.

When the first (preindependence) Dáil was established in 1919, Dalton returned to Ireland and joined the Irish Volunteers, the force that would become the Irish Army after 1922. He was a high-ranking officer during the War of Independence and became a close aide and friend to Michael Collins. Among his escapades in this period was an extraordinary attempt to free volunteer general Sean MacEoin from Mountjoy Jail: Dalton led a team of volunteers, wearing their old British Army uniforms, to the prison in a stolen army vehicle and presented the governor with fake papers for MacEoin's transfer. The ruse worked until the governor rang Dublin Castle, the seat of British authority in Ireland, for confirmation of the release, at which point Dalton and his men had to fight their way out of the prison.

After the treaty establishing the Irish Free State was signed, Dalton sided with the protreaty forces and was promoted to general of the Free State Army with particular responsibility for prosecuting the antirepublic campaign in the Cork region. Consequently, he was with Michael Collins when the latter was assassinated in an ambush at Béal na Bláth, and Collins literally died in his arms.

However, although most historians agree that had Collins's driver heeded Dalton's instruction to burst through the roadblock that set up the ambush, Collins would have lived, Dalton came under suspicion for having assassinated Collins himself (largely because the bullet that killed Collins struck the back of his head—a fact generally ascribed to a ricochet bullet). In November 1922, apparently devastated by Collins's death, he resigned his commission and for a short while acted as clerk of the Senate. However, he also left this post and emigrated from Ireland with his wife.

His return to Ireland came through an entirely different path. In 1942, he entered the film business working first with Paramount and then the Samuel Goldwyn Company before becoming an independent producer in 1955 and establishing Emmet Dalton Productions. At this point Dalton began to negotiate with Abbey chairman Ernest Blythe (with whom Dalton had a long relationship dating from Blythe's position in the Free State's first cabinet) with a view to producing filmed adaptations of Abbey plays. At approximately the same time Dalton contacted **Louis Elliman**, and all three men became directors of Dublin Theatre and Television Productions, which produced the first of the projected Abbey adaptations, *Professor Tim*, for American television. When the distributors of *Tim*, RKO, offered Dalton a deal to produce 12 pictures in a single year, Dalton and Elliman decided to proceed with plans to build **Ardmore Studios.**

Once the studios were built, Emmet Dalton Productions became a key early client. Between 1958 and 1962, the company would make 7 films there. These included four Abbey adaptations—*Sally's Irish Rogue*, *Home Is the Hero*, *The Big Birthday*, and ***This Other Eden***— and 3 further pictures financed by the **Irish Film Finance Corporation** (IFFC): *The Devil's Agent*, *Middle of Nowhere*, and *Lies My Father Told Me*. (It should be noted that Dalton had been instrumental in convincing the Industrial Credit Corporation to establish the IFFC.)

Of all these pictures, *This Other Eden* is perhaps the most interesting both intrinsically and in terms of how it related to Dalton's past. Based on a 1953 play from Louis D'Alton, the prologue sequence set during the War of Independence clearly paralleled Dalton's Civil War experiences. The sequence depicts a senior Irish Republican Army (IRA) officer driving to meet a British agent to discuss peace terms. When the officer is shot (by Black and Tans), the friend who accompanied him, Devereux, is suspected of his betrayal. The film then moves forward to the 1950s, when Devereux—now living an obscure existence as the editor of a local newspaper—has adopted an ambiguous attitude toward the treatment of the past "glories" of the War of Independence and the manner in which his erstwhile comrade is commemorated. While it is not clear that Louis D'Alton was explicitly basing his play on Dalton's life, the similarities may have accounted for Dalton's decision to film the play.

By the time Ardmore went into receivership in 1963, Dalton was 65, and his involvement with production appears to have come to a close. When he died in 1978, the *Irish Times* described him as "a man of history when Ireland was making history" ("Death of General Emmet Dalton," 1978). Yet the attendance at his funeral suggested that Civil War rivalries were not entirely a thing of the past: Despite his former senior military status, not one member of the Fianna Fáil cabinet attended his interment.

DANCING AT LUGHNASA (1998). The film version directed by **Pat O'Connor** of Brian Friel's famous play has an all-star cast including Meryl Streep as the eldest of the Mundy sisters, a schoolteacher who can barely afford to feed her siblings (played by Kathy Burke, Catherine McCormack, Kathy Bates, Sophie Thompson, and **Brid Brennan**, reprising her Tony Award–winning role on Broadway). **Michael Gambon** also appears as their returning brother, Jack. He was a priest in Uganda for the previous 25 years and has assimilated pagan rituals and apparently has become alienated from his Catholic faith. Various economic and other hardships befall the sisters as they try to find love and manage their frugal existence. However, when a radio is installed in their home, the sisters find it possible to express passions denied any other outlet by the conservative society they live in. At the pre-Christian, midsummer festival of Lughnasa, the sisters are unified in a spontaneous dance of unrestrained joy.

The Lughnasa dance was very much the high point of the highly successful stage version, but onscreen the dance sequence does not have the same impact, especially when it is followed by the narrator's brief but glum account of the fates that subsequently befell the sisters. In no small part as a consequence, reviews of the film were muted in their praise, describing it as an efficient transposition of the source material but little more.

DARBY O'GILL AND THE LITTLE PEOPLE (1959). Albert Sharpe, **Jimmy O'Dea**, Sean Connery (with an Irish brogue), and Jack McGowran star in this farcical comedy, directed by Robert Stevenson, about a character who falls into a water hole, only to be rescued by leprechauns (Irish fairy folk), who grant him three wishes. Walt Disney had wanted to make an "Oirish story" for children for a long time and even traveled to Ireland to research the project. Described by some critics as a charming film, filled with warmth, tenderness, love, drama, and betrayal, the crudeness of its use of Irish stereotypes induces cringing in contemporary Irish audiences. However, it has long been welcomed by its target audience: second- or third-generation Irish Americans.

DAVIS, JOHN T. (1947–). Davis was born in Belfast, studied in the College of Art, works out of his own studio, and has become one of the most innovative documentary filmmakers in Ireland today. He jointly directed the experimental feminist fictional *Maeve* (1982) along with **Pat Murphy**. Drawing on his love of music he initiated his documentary career with *Shell Shock Rock* (1978), which dealt with the Northern punk music scene. In addition to music he has remained fascinated with Americana and has made several documentaries in the United States, including *Route 66* (1985), which explores how forgotten communities fared along the famous road that linked the East and West but became a relative backwater as new high-speed motorways were built, bypassing many of the smaller towns.

In *Power in the Blood* (1989), broadcast on the British Broadcasting Corporation (BBC) and made for the Arena arts slot, Davis displays his visual storytelling powers aided by the stunning cinematography of Sé Merry. In the opening scenes we meet evangelical country and western singer Vernon Oxford. Soon he travels from his American homeland to try and save the souls of the people of Northern Ireland. The documentary journey includes a highly charged treatise on the power of religion to affect people's lives.

Davis was unable to film one scene near the end inside the Long Kesh prison, where Vernon's loyalist friend is imprisoned. So Vernon performs a concert for the prison warders, who are members of a country and western fan club. In a scene outside the clubhouse some of the members (in full cowboy costume) let off steam by displaying their shooting skills. Given that these individuals are agents of a state that ostensibly maintained the "repressive state apparatus" of the troubled Northern Irish state, the scene ranks as one of the most incongruous representations of the Protestant community in this period.

Davis's insider point of view and frequently poetic examination of the potency of the Bible Belt as extended to Northern Ireland continues in *Dust on the Bible* (1989). After a fallow period he made *Uncle Jack* (1996), which is a nostalgic portrait of his uncle, the cinema architect John McBride Neil, who designed many of Ulster's most spectacular cinemas. The director's poetic stylization and lyrical valorization of the local Northern Irish as part of a wider global identity has helped ensure that his documentaries have universal appeal. Unfortunately, a disastrous fire at his home greatly affected his filmmaking career. But he bounced back much later with *Travellers* (2000), which he codirected with photographer Alen MacWeeney, whose 1960s photographs of Ireland's travelling community provided the inspiration for Davis to film the people and places recorded 30 years before. Most recently he directed *A House Divided* (2003), which is a film portrait of the members of the Northern Irish Assembly intended for display in government buildings.

***THE DAWN* (1936).** Produced by **Hibernia Films**, *The Dawn* is a key historical artifact in Irish cinema history, arguably the most significant "Irish" film in the 50 years preceding **Neil Jordan**'s *Angel*. It is a remarkable film not because of its narrative or the quality of the acting but simply for the fact that it was made at all. Between 1933 and 1936, Killarney garage owner Tom Cooper and 250 locals—none of whom had any previous experience in filmmaking beyond attending the local cinema—assembled an ambitious feature-length film set during the Irish War of Independence. All filming was done on a single camera with a fixed focal length, while virtually every other piece of equipment—lighting, microphone booms, editing facilities, and so on—was built from scratch. A local chemist acted as a film laboratory.

The story commences in 1866, when Brian Malone, a member of the Fenian Brotherhood (a nationalist underground group), is wrongly accused of betraying his comrades to the British. Flash forward to 1919, when his grandson (also called Brian Malone) is a member of the local Irish Republican Army (IRA) fighting column. His brother Billy, however, refuses to participate in these activities, bringing disgrace to the family.

With the onset of the War of Independence against the British, members of the column raise doubts about Brian's trustworthiness, citing his grandfather's apparent disloyalty, and they vote to exclude him from their activities. Furious, Brian changes sides and joins the British-run police force in Ireland, the Royal Irish Constabulary (RIC). Inevitably, he is ostracized by his family and his girlfriend, Eileen.

As the War of Independence grows more savage, the British introduce a new paramilitary force—the Black and Tans—to quell the Irish insurgency. As an RIC officer, Brian finds himself part of a Black and Tan raid on Eileen's home, increasing her enmity toward him. Meanwhile the IRA column (led by Eileen's father, Dan), use information from their mysterious intelligence officer to unmask a British spy in their midst. Turning the leak to their advantage, they send a false report to British intelligence to lure the Black and Tans into an ambush.

Unaware of the trap but disgusted by the methods of the Black and Tans, Brian deserts just before the ambush. In the aftermath, however, Brian's brother Billy Malone is shot dead by the local RIC. Brian's and Billy's father accuses the IRA of the murder, but it emerges that Billy was the column's intelligence officer, responsible for its success up to this time. John Malone is comforted by the news that his son died for Ireland.

Given the level of amateurism, *The Dawn* is a remarkably accomplished piece of work. Despite a lack of formal training, director Cooper had clearly internalized the rules of cinema language. Indeed, the use of montage implies an awareness and understanding of the formalism of 1920s Soviet cinema. Only the occasional clumsy edit or sound dubbing undermines the otherwise seamless production quality. Where amateurism does show, however, is in the acting, which clearly owes much to a theatrical rather than cinematic tradition. Nonetheless, *The Dawn* is never less than entertaining— Cooper was not above throwing the odd song or comedic interlude into the mix to keep the action going. This doubtless contributed to the warm reception the film received from contemporary Irish audiences and critics who (prematurely) hailed the film as releasing Irish cinemagoers from the bondage of Hollywood.

The film's representation of the War of Independence was very much influenced by the prevailing Irish political orthodoxy of the period in which it was made. The portrayal of IRA activities is, to say the least, romanticized: IRA members are depicted as overgrown boy scouts lounging in fields while awaiting orders for the next attack. They are to a man "good sorts"—captured prisoners face not a beating but civilized treatment. The Black and Tans, by contrast, are caricatures, their commanding officer rarely without a drink in his hand, laughing gleefully when IRA prisoners are shot without trial.

The film also appears to criticize the political settlement of 1922: The IRA is clearly established as seeking not simply an independent Ireland but a republic. One of the IRA characters argues that they want only to be left alone and not to have anything to do with Britain. When Billy Malone dies, his father, John, stresses that the fight must go on, to the implied ultimate goal of an Irish republic. The film does not merely criticize the treaty of 1922 implicitly but arguably also justifies the Civil War that followed it. The film sidesteps an explicit consideration of such issues, however, by being limited to the 1919 period. Given this, *The Dawn* is indicative of the ambiguous attitude toward the whole 1916–1923 period that prevailed in the Ireland of the 1930s, just as Neil Jordan's **Michael Collins** displayed the more conciliatory attitude of the 1990s.

THE DAWNING (1988). Set in the South during the summer of 1920, the film was directed by Robert Knights. Eighteen-year-old Nancy (Rebecca Pidgeon) lives with her once wealthy Aunt Mary (Jean Simmons) and her grandfather (Trevor Howard) in a fading Georgian house by the sea. As in most conventional historical dramas, there is romantic intrigue: Nancy thinks she is in love with the very proper Harry, a family friend, who is, however, captivated by Nancy's neighbor Maeve. The story line frames the current political conflict. A stranger (Anthony Hopkins) is hiding out in their beach hut. At first Nancy thinks it might be her long-lost father, and she visits him daily. But when he shows off a gun, she withdraws from him but decides to keep his presence a secret. After 12 British soldiers are shot at the local races, her secret is exposed, and dreadful consequences follow as the gunman on the run is shot several times, in spite of surrendering to the army. The film explores revenge, a controversial shoot-to-kill policy that has bedeviled Irish conflicts, and the romantic representation of rebel heroes, all well-worn tropes in films using the backdrop of the Irish "troubles."

THE DEAD (1987). Closely adapted from the famous short story from *Dubliners* by James Joyce, the film version is a fitting swan song for a major Hollywood director and Irish citizen **John Huston**. The film stars his daughter, Angelica Huston, **Donal McCann**, Helena Carroll, Cathleen Delaney, Ingrid Craigie, and Rachael Dowling and was scripted by another of Huston's family, his son, Tony. The story recounts the New Year's celebration in Dublin 1904 of two spinster sisters, Aunt Julia and Kate, along with their niece Mary Jane, as they welcome middle-class guests into their home for an evening of culture and music. Their main concern is that their friend Freddy does not arrive too drunk. Among the attendees are their nephew, Gabriel Conroy (McCann), and his wife, Gretta (Huston). Conroy feels superior to the other guests, preferring European culture and holidays, for example, to the more primitive, as he sees it, West of Ireland.

During the festivities his wife becomes listless as the well-known ballad "The Lass of Aughrim" is sung. Later in their hotel room, she tells Gabriel that it reminded her of a young man whom she loved years earlier in Galway, where she was born and reared. He was very ill but came out to see her in the rain to display his love for her. Later she heard how he died soon afterward. Joyce's famous closing ends with a realization of how Gabriel had never loved like this, as a blanket of snow connecting everything in its reach falls over the landscape.

The film version functions very effectively as an ensemble piece, closely adapting the nuanced exposition of the short story, and thankfully avoids attempting to open out with exterior shots, with the exception of the very effective and lyrical use of snow at the end of the film.

DEAD BODIES (2003). Low-budget (shot on high-definition video) genre thriller from first-time screenwriter Derek Landy and director Robert Quinn (also his first feature). The efficiently made story traces protagonist Tommy's (Andrew Scott) efforts to hide the body of his inadvertently killed girlfriend, and to hide the fact of her death from his new love (Kelly Reilly), all while being pursued by local police (led by **Sean McGinley**) and a corrupt politician (**Gerard McSorley**).

DEASY, SEAMUS (1947–). Now an internationally recognized director of photography, Seamus Deasy made his first short film—*The Island*—in 1966 when he was still only 19, and he has subsequently worked in a wide range of genres and types of films. During the 1970s and 1980s he was **Bob Quinn**'s cameraman of choice, working on *Poitín* and *Budawanny* (and the revamp of *Budawanny*, *The Bishop's Story*). He also collaborated twice with **Bill Miskelly**, on *The Schooner* and *The End of the World Man*.

Deasy's most critically acclaimed output, however, has come about as a result of his work with **John Boorman**. Having shot *Two Nudes Bathing* for Boorman in 1995, Deasy was the logical choice to shoot Boorman's biopic *The General*, about Dublin criminal Martin Cahill. The film was nominated for a series of awards, and Boorman won Best Director at Cannes in 1998. However, virtually every review of the film also singled out Deasy's luscious black-and-white cinematography. *The Observer*'s veteran critic Philip French even compared Deasy's high-contrast images to the work of photographer Bill Brandt. This was ironic since the film was actually shot on color stock and color desaturated in postproduction.

The film cemented Deasy's reputation, however, and in 2003 Boorman used him as director of photography on *In My Country*. Although poorly received, the film was significant because it was shot not in Ireland but in South Africa. Boorman could have chosen any cinematographer but selected Deasy. Similarly when Karel Reisz and Michael Lindsay-Hogg came to Ireland to shoot *Act without Words* and *Waiting for Godot*, respectively (both 2000), as part of the series of Samuel Beckett adaptations undertaken by **Parallel Productions** and the Gate Theatre, both chose Deasy as director of photography. So too did Barry Levinson when he shot *An Everlasting Piece* in the same year.

Although still based in Ireland and most recently lensing Pearse Elliott's *The Mighty Celt*, he is also increasingly in demand for U.S. television productions; he acted as director of photography on the historical drama *Benedict Arnold: A Question of Honor* (2003) and the political thriller *The Grid* (2004). In 2005, the Galway Film Fleadh hosted a tribute to Deasy's four decades of work.

DECEMBER BRIDE (1990). This beautiful re-creation of a historical rural Protestant community focuses on Sarah (Saskia Reeves), who lives with two brothers (**Donal McCann** and **Ciarán Hinds**), one of whom fathers a child with her, although she refuses to name which. Many critics suggest that the painterly style is reminiscent of a European tradition, following in the footsteps of Karl Dreyer and Robert Bresson, with **Thaddeus O'Sullivan**'s perfectionist eye for detail and the power of color to capture the mood of a scene.

The film is a very well regarded art-house drama from the original novel by Sam Hanna Bell published in 1951; the term *December Bride* refers somewhat pejoratively to a woman who marries late in life, and the film deals very sensitively with contemporary public debates over maternity and sexual politics in Ireland during the period. The evocation of place through careful cinematography ensures that the film has a high-quality tone throughout. The director spoke of how he wanted to position the film in a Northern European context, visually and culturally, to try to produce the feel of a deep Presbyterian religious outlook, which is prevalent in such areas.

DERRY FILM AND VIDEO CO-OPERATIVE (DFVC). The DFVC was established in 1984 as the first independent film and video workshop in the northwest of Ireland. From its inception the workshop received annually reviewed grants from **Channel 4**, as part of its policy of supporting workshop production in regional areas of the United Kingdom. The establishment of the group was driven by a desire to allow the people of Derry to make programs that reflected their own perceptions of the reality of Derry life as a means of countering the often sensational and inaccurate representations offered by visiting film crews.

The group's first project was Derry Video News, followed by a series of documentaries on strip-searching and British Army involvement in urban planning. These projects reflected the group's nationalist perspective. They were followed by the co-op's most ambitious documentary, *Mother Ireland*, in which director Anne Crilly explored a range of female images that had historically been used to represent

Ireland, with a view to understanding how those emerged and what their ideological impact might be. In the course of the documentary, Crilly interviewed several women from a republican background, including then active Irish Republican Army (IRA) member Mairead Farrell.

This in turn led to the documentary being banned in the Republic of Ireland under Section 31 of the Broadcasting Act, which allowed the minister for communications to prohibit any program carrying interviews with members of "subversive" organizations. Furthermore, despite having funded the production in the first place, Channel 4 also refused to screen the film. The decision was a preview of changes to British legislation requiring broadcasters to refrain from carrying direct statements by members of proscribed organizations (including the IRA).

After producing *Mother Ireland*, the group shifted to a subject informed by a different kind of politics, which grew out of a drama workshop on sex and sexuality organized for Derry teenagers. The result was **Hush-a-Bye Baby**, directed by *Mother Ireland*'s producer Margo Harkin.

Although the co-op ceased to exist in the 1990s, a report commissioned by the group and published in February 1988 has had a lasting impact on the environment for filmmaking in Northern Ireland. The *Fast Forward Report*, written by Sara Mackie, offered a detailed assessment of the critical state of audiovisual funding in the North. Given that between the British Film Institute, the Arts Council of Northern Ireland, the European Union, and Channel 4, only the last had made any kind of significant funding available for independent filmmakers, the report recommended the establishment of a Media Council for the North, which would have responsibility for scripting, production, postproduction, education, research, and training. This recommendation was taken up a year later in the establishment of the **Northern Ireland Film Council**, initially as a body of volunteers and later with funding from the Northern Ireland Arts Council.

DIARY OF A MADMAN (1990). This was **Ronan O'Leary**'s third production in four years, and like his previous film, *Fragments of Isabella*, it was based on a stage production, this one by Dublin's Focus Theatre Group. Wheelchair-bound actor Tim McDonnell adapted

Nikolai Gogol's 1835 short story to allow himself to play the lead role of Poprishchin, a Saint Petersburg clerk who becomes obsessed with his superior's daughter and slowly descends into insanity, ultimately believing himself to be the deposed but rightful king of Spain. After receiving several awards for the stage production, McDonnell reprised the role in O'Leary's film, which received critical praise for the manner in which the director worked around the single set location.

DICK, VIVIENNE (1950–). Born in Cork, she later studied archeology and French for her degree at University College Cork. After moving to New York in 1975 she joined the Millennium Film Co-Operative and began exploring Super 8 film. She became a successful artist, with major exhibitions at the Whitney Museum and the Museum of Modern Art. Having met **Thaddeus O'Sullivan** and Bob Quinn in New York, she came back to Ireland and along with **Lelia Doolan** helped run the first film production course at the College of Commerce, Rathmines, currently part of Dublin Institute of Technology (DIT). However, finding it difficult to develop her practice, she moved to London in 1984 and later became a director of the London Filmmakers' Co-operative. Currently back in Ireland she teaches at the Galway Mayo Institute of Technology (GMIT) and continues to produce art works.

Her film and multimedia installation work, which has been highly influential, includes *Station Island* (1978; MoMA), *Beauty Becomes the Beast* (1979; IFA, MoMA), *Liberty's Booty* (1980; IFA, MoMA), *Trailer* (1983; LUX), *Like Dawn to Dust* (1983; IFA, BFI), *Images/Ireland* (1988; LUX), *New York Conversations* (1991; IFA), *A Skinny Little Man Attacked Daddy* (1994; IFA), and *Excluded by the Nature of Things* (2002).

***THE DISAPPEARANCE OF FINBAR* (1995).** The film, scripted by renowned novelist Dermot Bolger and directed by Sue Clayton, shifts from its opening urban working-class Dublin location to the immaculate snowy landscapes of Sweden when the eponymous Finbar (**Jonathan Rhys Meyers**) mysteriously disappears after falling off a Dublin motorway flyover. Having established itself as a quasi-magical-realist text, the film then follows the efforts of Danny (Luke

Griffin) to find his absent friend in Scandinavia and in the process acquire some sense of what it means to be Irish in a globalized modernity.

DISCO PIGS **(2002).** This is a provocative reworking of a play by Enda Walsh, who also scripted the film. Directed by Kirsten, daughter of **Jim Sheridan**, it features magnificent performances from leads **Cillian Murphy** and **Elaine Cassidy**. The often surreal narrative deals with two dysfunctional children—Pig and Runt—who live in their self-created world and ends with a tragic yet heightened romantic denouement. Rather than being a fully rounded social-realist exposé of a problem society that can be traced across a contemporary landscape and social environment, the film sketches a psychological study of two enigmatic and flawed individuals. *Disco Pigs* reverses the gender dynamic so that it is the female, Runt, who sets their love free by mercy-killing the troubled boy Pig in the film's dramatic ending. Such a perverse closure resonates with the very pertinent "Irish" problem of male teenage suicide and the current discourse around what some counterintuitively argue is the dominance of a feminist discourse within contemporary Ireland.

The film certainly ties in with other angst-ridden teenage and children's films like ***The Butcher Boy***, which also uses a child's perspective and point of view to drive the narrative forward. However, it may be somewhat disingenuous to dismiss the narrative trope as emblematic of a continuing preoccupation with dysfunction within the Irish family and body politic. Together with the extreme violence of the nightclub scene toward the end, the repeated mantra "Love is blue" is the only enigmatic conclusion in this romantic evocation. The film dialogue and vernacular are in a rarely heard Cork accent that was used in the play, and while this makes it somewhat difficult at times for audiences to understand, it gives voice to a major regional dialect. The majestic sea serves as a backdrop to calm and neutralize such violence, reflecting the deployment of nature in classic Irish films like ***Ryan's Daughter*** and others.

DISKIN, DERMOT. After working in the early 1990s as an assistant editor on a range of films, including ***The Commitments*** and ***Last of the High Kings***, Diskin moved to full editor status on **Temple Film**'s

The Tale of Sweety Barrett in 1998. He has worked consistently since, carving out something of a niche in low-budget feature such as *Dead Bodies*, *Goldfish Memory* (for which he received an Irish Film & Television Academy Award nomination) and *Boy Eats Girl*. However, he has also made a name for himself on larger-scale productions such as *Man About Dog* and *The Mighty Celt*.

DISTRIBUTION. This has been long identified as a key problem for Irish and most non-Hollywood production since obviously, without distribution, films cannot find an audience. As early as 1937, when a coherent policy on encouraging production in Ireland began to emerge, it was pointed out that the small scale of the Irish market meant that any hypothetical industry would ultimately have to look to the export market to become viable. The difficulty lay with the fact that in the 1930s (as today), Hollywood-based companies largely dominated global distribution. Since in the 1930s these companies were also production companies and vertically integrated, there was little hope that they would willingly distribute films made by outside production concerns based in Ireland. This stark reality was a key factor in the realignment of film policy in the postwar period, which began to examine ways to attract overseas (especially American and British) production companies to work in Ireland rather than creating an indigenous industry. *See also* LEMASS, SEAN.

In a somewhat different fashion, distribution remains a problem for the modern Irish film industry. Very few "Irish" films receive a theatrical release outside Ireland unless they are backed by an American distributor to begin with (as would usually be the case with the work of directors like **Jim Sheridan** or **Neil Jordan**). Indeed many makers of Irish films find it difficult to access cinema screens *within* Ireland. This is because the Irish distribution market remains dominated by the local offices of the American majors—UIP, 20th Century Fox, Columbia-Tristar, Warners, and Buena Vista. In theory these companies could acquire the Irish distribution rights for Irish films. In practice this tends not to happen largely because historically the Irish market has been treated as a subsidiary element of the U.K. market. Consequently, the Irish offices of the majors—with one exception —can do little independent of their London-based head offices. The one exception to the rule is Buena Vista, which on occasion has acquired rights for the more commercial Irish films, such as *I Went Down*, which received a 50-print release, comparing favorably with many Hollywood blockbusters.

There are several indigenous distribution companies, but only two of these operate on a consistent basis. One of these is Abbey Films, which is part of the **Ward Anderson** empire in Ireland. For the most part, however, Ward Anderson acts as an agent for smaller U.S. distributors rather than acquiring rights in the true sense of a distributor. The other company is Eclipse Pictures. Originally formed as Clarence Pictures, the company was established in 1993 by the Irish production company **Little Bird** to handle distribution for its films in Ireland. In addition to acting as an agent for three U.S. production companies—Icon Film Distribution, UGC Films, and Verve Pictures—Eclipse has become the first port of call for Irish producers seeking to release their films in Ireland.

DIVORCING JACK (1997). Directed by David Caffrey and starring David Thewlis, Rachael Griffiths, and Ian McIlhenney, the film humorously deals with the changing situation after an Irish Republican Army (IRA) ceasefire in Northern Ireland, while uncovering corruption at all levels. Commenting on the **"troubles"** using the format of comedy is certainly rare within Irish film and demonstrates a brave attempt in taking on the various shibboleths of Irish cultural nationalism. A wise-cracking local journalist (and self-confessed alcoholic) is unconvinced by the air of euphoria sweeping the province following the peace agreement and, aided by a manic taxi driver, a gun-toting nun, and an American journalist, he seeks to uncover corrupt dealings at the highest level in the state, while also dealing with his disenchanted wife.

DOCUMENTARY. While the dominant focus in Irish academic audiovisual production has been on fiction film, Ireland has a long tradition of documentary filmmaking, as comprehensively outlined by Harvey O'Brien in his 2004 study. The work of directors who stand out includes the seminal Robert Flaherty's poetic treatment of actuality in *Man of Aran*; it also includes films by contemporary filmmakers, such as **John T. Davis**'s insightful Northern Irish documentaries. Others include **Thaddeus O'Sullivan**'s *On a Paving Stone*

Mounted (1978), Anne Crilly's *Mother Ireland* (1988), **George Morrison**'s *Mise Éire* **[I Am Ireland]** (1959), **Liam O'Leary**'s *Portrait of Dublin* (1951), Sean O'Mordha's *Portrait of an Irish Artist* (2001), **Louis Marcus**'s *Rhapsody of a River* (1965), **Alan Gilsenan**'s *The Road to God Knows Where* (1988), and Sean O'Morda's *Samuel Beckett: Silence to Silence* (1984). Other documentaries that paint a broad picture of Irish film culture include *As Others See Us: The Movies* (1998; UTV), *Irish Cinema—Ourselves Alone* (1995; Poolbeg Productions), and *Short Story—Irish Cinema 1945–1958* (1986; BAC Films). *See also* GAEL LINN.

DOOLAN, LELIA (1935–). The career arc of Lelia Doolan neatly mirrors that of Irish cultural production since the 1960s. Born in Cork, she was schooled in a Dublin convent before studying arts at University College Dublin, where she won the Browne Gold Medal for French and German. After some postgraduate work in Berlin on Berthold Brecht, she moved into theater and journalism. These talents were combined when she joined **Radio Telefís Éireann (RTÉ)** in 1964, becoming a full-time producer-director and working on news and drama. Critically she established the long-running *Riordans* series and founded the seminal current affairs program *Seven Days*.

In 1969, when she was only 34, she became head of light entertainment at RTÉ, but her appointment was short-lived. Complaining about RTÉ programming policy, which she described as "trivial, emasculated and contrary to the national cultural spirit" (Woodworth, 1993), she resigned her post (later outlining her reasons for doing so in the book *Sit Down and Be Counted*, which she coauthored with colleagues Jack Dowling and **Bob Quinn**).

In 1971 Doolan was appointed artistic director of the **Abbey Theatre** but again departed under controversial circumstances after two years. Moving to Belfast she worked in community video and adult education and gained a PhD in social anthropology from Queen's University. From 1979 she taught media and communications (the first courses of their kind in Ireland) at the College of Commerce, Rathmines, in Dublin.

In the 1980s Doolan moved to Galway, where she founded the Galway Film Fleadh, studied homeopathy, and worked as an executive producer for the **Irish Film Board** on Fergus Tighe's *Clash of the Ash*. From 1984 to 1987 she worked to raise £1.4 million to produce **Joe Comerford**'s *Reefer and the Model*. The story of how that money was raised amply demonstrates Doolan's energy and dynamism. Having raised half the budget from RTÉ, **Channel 4**, and the Irish Film Board, she secured the rest from **Strongbow** and British-American producer Hemdale. However, both Strongbow and Hemdale subsequently withdrew their funding just before the film was due to go into production in April 1987. Undeterred Doolan flew to Hemdale's Los Angeles office, where she met company head John Daly, armed with Irish sausages and rashers. At the end of the meeting Daly agreed not merely to honor Hemdale's original commitment but also agreed to fund the completion bond for the picture. A further £25,000 resulted from persistent calls to Irish financier Tony O'Reilly, allowing the picture to go ahead.

By the start of the 1990s, Doolan was a director of the Galway Film Resource Centre and the **Irish Film Centre**, and a manager of the European Script Fund. Then, in April 1993, **Michael D. Higgins** appointed Doolan as chair of the revived Irish Film Board, a decision that was warmly welcomed by the Irish filmmaking community because she brought a mix of cultural sensitivity and financial pragmatism to the position. Doolan was regarded as an active chair continually lobbying government for increased funding for the board. When the British *Evening Standard* film critic Alexander Walker accused the board of funding nationalist propaganda (citing **Thaddeus O'Sullivan**'s *Nothing Personal* in particular), Doolan personally entered the fray, noting that the board judged projects by their artistic quality and authenticity rather than by political criteria.

In 1996, she initiated a project to acquire a touring cinema—the Cinemobile—to bring nonmainstream film to smaller towns lacking their own cinema. In May 2001 the project came to fruition, and Doolan chaired the Galway-based body that ran the Cinemobile. Meanwhile, in November she used her introduction to the Film Board's annual report to call for the establishment of a levy on cinema seats to provide a secure fund for Irish film production. In December Doolan announced that she was resigning as Film Board chair, citing a desire to pursue other interests. She remains an active figure in contemporary Irish cultural politics.

DOYLE, RODDY (1958–). Internationally successful novelist and author of film scripts and several plays, he was brought up in Kilbarrack in Dublin and taught English and geography at the secondary level for 14 years after getting his degree from University College Dublin. He continued to teach even after achieving success at his writing, and it wasn't until the publication of his fourth novel, *Paddy Clarke Ha Ha*, which won the Booker Prize in 1993, that he left teaching for his current career in full-time writing. His film scripts include **When Brendan Met Trudy** (2000) and, from his own novels, **The Van** (1996), **The Snapper** (1993), and **The Commitments** (1991), which have become famed for their Dublin vernacular. He is currently working on a film script for Liam O'Flaherty's novel *Famine*, a long-cherished project of **John Ford**'s.

DOYLE, TONY (1942–2000). Doyle grew up in County Roscommon and graduated from University College Dublin in the 1960s and spent most of his acting career working in Great Britain, cutting his teeth in many of the famous play-for-today television series in the 1960s. From his base in Britain he went on to star in many television series including *Ballykissangel*, *Between the Lines*, and the Irish rural soap *The Riordans*. Most recently he negotiated the almost impossible feat of making audiences sympathetic with a tyrannical patriarch in a television adaptation of John McGahern's novel *Amongst Women* (1997). In Irish film he was cast in central roles in films including **Eat the Peach, Circle of Friends**, and **A Love Divided**; he also performed as a veteran gangster in **I Went Down**. Known for his great professionalism, many critics consider him the epitome of the ambiguous father figure, which has remained a central trope within Irish narratives.

DRIFTWOOD (1996). Directed by **Ronan O'Leary** and also scripted by him with Richard Wearing, *Driftwood*'s narrative is remarkably similar to that of Rob Reiner's earlier classic *Misery* (1990). Sarah (Anne Brochet) finds The Man (James Spader) washed up on a beach. She brings him back to her lonely home on the shore. When he awakes, he is suffering from total memory loss, unable to recall even his name. However, it emerges that Sarah herself also suffers from mental ill health. Away from The Man, she talks to her deceased mother (Anna Massey) who—though conjured by Sarah's imagination —berates her daughter for her inability to maintain a relationship. The film is a study of obsession, with Sarah telling The Man that he has washed up on an island that is visited only once a year by a supply vessel. It later emerges that this is a ruse designed to bind him to her. Sarah's house is in fact on the mainland just a few miles from the nearest village.

Shot at **Ardmore Studios** and—ironically given the narrative—on location in the Aran Islands, the film suffered from the inevitable comparisons with *Misery*. Critics also pointed to its overly slow pacing and occasional farcical dialogue. Consequently it received a very limited and brief release in Ireland and France (as *La geôlière*) before receiving an equally limited video release.

***DRINKING CRUDE* (1997).** This low-budget debut feature from director Owen McPolin follows Paul (Andrew Scott) over his post–Leaving Certificate summer, as he decamps from his small hometown for London. Quickly finding himself homeless and penniless he is taken under the wing of likeable rogue Al (James Quarton), who offers him work cleaning oil tankers. The pair are soon joined by abused mother Karen (**Eva Birthistle**) and her baby, the four forming an unlikely family unit. The film was critically well received on its limited release, in particular for the character-driven narrative.

DUBLIN-BASED FILM. Irish cinema has always had a strong urban-rural divide in its filmmaking strategy, both thematically and practically. Much of the filmmaking makes use of the touristic uniqueness of the landscape, and hence filmmakers choose to film outside the more anonymous cities. However, with the growth of population and the gravitation toward the capital, along with filmmakers' desire to reflect real-life experience, Dublin has become the primary focal point for filmmaking. In particular many writers and directors have been drawn to the subject of urban gangsters, with *The Courier*, *Joyriders*, *The General*, *Veronica Guerin*, and others being set in the capital out of necessity and for generic accuracy.

While some critics suggest that the city is still not big enough to reflect the range of criminality and violence that are prerequisites for a Hollywood film, more social realist and working-class narratives using gangster themes are being made. Filming in Dublin greatly expanded with the success of **Roddy Doyle**'s novels, such as the well-traveled and successful *The Commitments* (1991), and more contemporary fare such as *Intermission* (2004). Meanwhile, wealthy suburban and middle-class culture has been represented through apparently placeless narratives such as *When Brendan Met Trudy* and *About Adam*, which have been both criticized and valorized for making Dublin seem like any other big city. Unfortunately, because of economies of scale and for other creative reasons, cities like Cork, Galway, Limerick, or Waterford receive very little cinematic representation. Hopefully this will change with the **Irish Film Board**'s current active policy of sponsorship of films made outside of Dublin.

DUFFNER, J. PATRICK. Duffner is a long-established film editor who was involved with **Kieran Hickey** and Sean Corcoran in B.A.C. Films from the mid-1970s. As a result he was editor on virtually all of Hickey's work, from shorts like *A Child's Voice* (1978), the long-form breakthrough *Exposure* (1978), and later films such as *Criminal Conversation* and *Attracta*. Hickey passed away in 1993, but by that point, Duffner had already broadened his range of collaborators. He was editor on both **Neil Jordan**'s debut, *Angel*, in 1982 and **Jim Sheridan**'s first film, *My Left Foot*, in 1987. He would subsequently work with both again on *Michael Collins* and *The Field*. He also edited **Thaddeus O'Sullivan**'s eye-catching debut, *The Woman Who Married Clark Gable*. Most recently, he worked on Anthony Byrne's culinary fantasy *Short Order* (2005).

DUFFY, MARTIN (1952–). Born in Dublin, he worked as a television editor at **Radio Telefís Éireann (RTÉ)** before embarking on a freelance career; he also edited Margo Harkin's *Hush-a-Bye Baby* and **Bob Quinn**'s *The Bishop's Story*. He wrote and directed *The Boy from Mercury* (1995), which though it received warm critical praise had a disappointing box office release. The story is a highly developed rite-of-passage fantasy as it lovingly re-creates 1950s Ireland. In 1998, Duffy directed *Bumblebee Flies Anyway*, returning again to themes of childhood and loss; the film unfortunately received only a cable TV release in America. In 2000 he directed *The Testimony of Taliesin Jones*, which focuses on a young boy and a missing parent.

Duffy now lives outside Ireland and remains preoccupied with making and producing appealing narratives for children of all ages.

DUNBAR, ADRIAN (1958–). The eldest of seven children born into an Enniskillen, County Fermanagh, family, Adrian Dunbar attended the local Catholic school—Saint Joseph's—before taking his first job in the local Unipork factory, where his job entailed chopping pigs' heads in half. From this inauspicious beginning he moved to become a jobbing musician, became involved in amateur dramatics, and finally ended up at the London Guildhall School of Music and Drama. Although he made his screen debut in 1984, the vast majority of his work during the 1980s was onstage, although he did appear—well down the cast—in two Irish-themed films during this period: *The Dawning* (1988) and **Jim Sheridan**'s *My Left Foot*. His first major screen role was in British Broadcasting Corporation (BBC) Northern Ireland one-off drama *The Englishman's Wife* (1990), but it was Peter Chelsom's light comedy *Hear My Song* the following year that properly established Dunbar as a leading man. The film established key elements of his screen persona: charming but often untrustworthy or even menacing. Like many Irish actors he is best known in the United Kingdom for his television work, where he is frequently cast in psychological thrillers, typically playing husbands who are not all they seem (cf. *Suspicion* [2003]).

His big-screen work has been concentrated largely in Irish films. Although he appeared in two back-to-back British gangster films in 2002 (*Shooters* and *Triggermen*), he has appeared in seven Irish feature films since *Hear My Song*. For the most part, however, he is carefully cast in supporting roles. Dunbar played the depressed farmer in *The Playboys*, the amorous son in *Widows' Peak*, and Martin Cahill's first in command in *The General*. He played an ideologically motivated IRA man in *The Crying Game*, his character acting in stark contrast to Stephen Rea's reluctant protagonist and Miranda Richardson's near-psychotic temptress. He was also well-cast in *How Harry Became a Tree* as **Colm Meaney**'s nemesis, in which he managed the near-impossible feat of remaining at least semisympathetic even though he apparently seduced the young heroine.

In 1999, George Lucas cast him in the role of Bail Organa in the first of the *Star Wars* prequels, *The Phantom Menace* (1999). Although he was limited to five or six lines in the movie, his role as stepfather to the character of Princess Leia meant that he would have played a larger role in the subsequent prequels. However, after filming Dunbar's part, Lucas cut Dunbar entirely from the film for reasons involving the plot, and American actor Jimmy Smits played the role of Organa in *Attack of the Clones* (2002) and *Revenge of the Sith* (2005). In interviews, Dunbar has been philosophical about the missed opportunity, and he has taken on more stage work than would have been the case had the *Star Wars* role led to more Hollywood work. More recently he returned to his Northern Ireland roots, playing a Catholic father opposite **Ciarán Hinds**'s Protestant father in *Mickybo and Me* (2005).

– E –

***EAT THE PEACH* (1986).** Perhaps the most overtly commercial film to be funded by the first **Irish Film Board**, *Eat the Peach*, directed by Peter Ormrod, is a tragi-comedy based on fact. It follows two men—Vinnie (Stephen Brennan) and Arthur (**Eamon Morrissey**)—who respond to the oppressiveness of their midlands existence by building a motorcycle "wall of death" (inspired by the Elvis Presley movie *Roustabout*) in the middle of a bog. For Vinnie riding the wall offers a brief escape from the everyday obligations to family and community and his humdrum existence. Like that of Icarus, however, his escape proves all too short, and—although the film ends on an optimistic note—he crashes back to earth.

Despite its commercial ambitions the film eschews the kind of classic Hollywood narrative that follows clearly drawn characters driven by explicit motivations. Stephen Brennan's performance is so low-key as to be invisible. Vinnie's motives are explained less by overt dialogue and more by shots sticking him in the middle of a flat landscape that stretches to the horizon. The film is not necessarily about individual characters but rather captures a rural Ireland frequently sidelined in cinematic representations. Some critics have even suggested that the constructed precarious spectacle of the "wall of death" the characters create echoes the nascent filmmaking experience in Ireland, as artists try to create and live out their dreams. It also works as a historical document capturing a pre–Celtic Tiger Ireland where Japanese semiconductor factories, venal politicians, smugglers, and country and western bars exist side by side.

The fact that the film presents an Ireland that a home audience could actually recognize may have contributed to its massive domestic success. Equally, its refusal to countenance a *Quiet Man–Ryan's Daughter* style of representation probably sealed its fate outside Ireland, where it failed to make an impact.

ELEMENT FILMS. Producer Ed Guiney and former production accountant Andrew Lowe established Element Films in June 2001. Guiney has been involved in film since establishing the Trinity Video Society (with Lenny Abrahamson) while studying at Trinity College in the 1980s, which led to his producing the Abrahamson-directed short *3 Joes*, which won awards at festivals in Ireland and Germany.

In 1993 Guiney established Temple Films with Stephen Bradley, initially as a television production company making primarily factual programs for **RTÉ**, UTV, and **Channel 4**. However, in 1994 Temple produced its first feature, *Ailsa*, directed by **Paddy Breathnach**, which won the Euskal Media Award at that year's San Sebastian Film Festival. From that point Guiney arguably became the most consistent producer of domestically originated cinema, including *Guiltrip* (Gerard Stembridge, 1995), *Sweety Barrett* (Stephen Bradley, 1998), *On the Edge* (John Carney, 2000), and *Disco Pigs* (Kirsten Sheridan, 2001).

The decision to transform Temple into Element was driven by an express desire to combine existing strengths in the production of new Irish work with an added focus on larger-scale European-originated material. This in turn led to the relationship with Guiney's partner at Element, Andrew Lowe. A chartered accountant by trade, Lowe was also formerly head of business affairs for the **Irish Film Board**, where his duties included negotiating and monitoring the board's investments in a wide range of feature films cofinanced with international partners. It also led to the signing of a first-look deal between Element and Kuhn and Co. (run by Michael Kuhn, former head of Polygram Films) at the Cannes Film Festival in May 2002.

Subsequent work from Element has reflected this international dimension. Element acted as Irish coproducer on the Irish-themed

Magdalene Sisters and *Omagh* (both of which won multiple awards) in addition to the most recent remake of *Lassie*. However, the company has continued to produce more "local" fare such as the comedy-horror *Boy Eats Girl* and (picking up Guiney's relationship with Lenny Abrahamson where *3 Joes* left off) *Adam and Paul* (with the Speers Company).

Through a joint venture with **Hell's Kitchen**, Element also acts as Irish coproducer on projects that originate in North America. A second joint venture with **Samson Films**—Accomplice Television—has successfully produced several drama series for **Radio Telefís Éireann (RTÉ)**.

ELLIMAN, LOUIS (1906–1965). Louis Elliman could reasonably be described as the greatest Irish theatrical impresario of the first half of the 20th century, but he was also a key figure in Irish cinema. One of 12 children born into a Dublin Jewish family, his father, Maurice, arrived in Dublin in 1900 after fleeing tsarist persecution in Latvia. Although Maurice started out as a grocer, he became involved in the cinema trade, initially by establishing a cinema-seating business on Dublin's Camden Street and later by opening his own cinema—the Theatre De Luxe—on the same street.

Louis attended the National University of Ireland and was subsequently apprenticed by his father to a chemist in South Richard Street. However, he left that position after a few years and moved to London, where he became the agent for First National Films, thus launching his entertainment career. In 1936, Maurice Elliman moved from cinema into theater, when, advised by Louis, he purchased the Gaiety Theatre (which remained in Louis's control until his death in 1965). "Mr Louis," as he became known, introduced a number of innovations to the Gaiety: He instituted the still extant Christmas pantomines, which were initially produced by **Jimmy O'Dea**'s O'D productions; established annual seasons of performances by the Dublin Grand Opera Society; and for several years invited Hilton Edwards and Micheál MacLíammóir, founders of Dublin's Gate Theatre Productions, to give spring and autumn seasons of plays.

In 1936 Louis Elliman also acquired the recently (and lavishly) rebuilt Theatre Royal on Dublin's Hatch Street, the largest theater ever built in Ireland. Acquisitions continued through the 1930s, and by the start of the 1940s the Elliman Group owned cinemas—through Amalgamated Cinemas and Irish Cinema Ltd.—in most major Irish cities and in Dublin's southern suburbs.

In 1945, however, the Rank Organization acquired a majority interest in the Elliman Group's cinema holdings, reorganizing them under the Odeon (Ireland) Ltd. brand. Elliman continued to act as managing director of the cinema chain (a position he maintained until 1963) and took a central role in the running of the flagship Theatre Royal. However, as the heyday of the theaters began to wane, Elliman's interest moved toward film production. In 1951, he executive-produced the Hilton Edwards Oscar-nominated short *Return to Glennascaul* and subsequently acted as its distributor in the United Kingdom and Ireland.

However, Elliman's ambitions went far beyond short film production. In January 1957 the *Sunday Independent* carried an interview with him in which he discussed plans to produce a 55-minute made-for-TV version of George Shiel's **Abbey Theatre** play *Professor Tim*. *Tim* was directed by **Emmet Dalton** and produced under the auspices of Dublin Film and Television Productions Ltd., of which Elliman and Dalton were directors. The two were joined by Ernest Blythe, chairman of the Abbey on the board of a sister company—Dublin Film Productions Management Ltd.

The relationship between these two companies (and Blythe's presence on the board of the latter) was based on the use of *Tim* as a pilot to test the potential of the American market. If *Tim* took off in the United States, then the two companies would collaborate to produce film versions of a further 26 to 39 Abbey plays. Dublin Film Productions Management Ltd. would deal with the question of rights for the Abbey plays, and Dublin Films and TV Productions Ltd. would actually shoot them.

Tim appears to have led to a deal with RKO Teleradio in New York to produce Abbey adaptations, and on the basis of this apparently guaranteed work, Elliman became convinced that there was a sound financial case for building a studio in Ireland. In August 1957, Elliman announced the acquisition of a site for a studio at Ardmore Place, Herbert Road, in Bray, County Dublin. At a press launch for the studios, Elliman stated that their films would all have an Irish background—either the story content or the writer would be Irish. He even suggested that Ardmore would become a miniature Hollywood. A month later, **Ardmore Studios** (Ireland) Ltd. was registered with the Companies Office and included among its principal objects the business of motion picture production.

With a budgeted construction cost of £161,000 Ardmore was a substantial financial undertaking. Although initial reports suggested that Elliman funded the studios privately, it subsequently emerged that the studios were largely funded by the Department of Industry and Commerce via the Industrial Development Authority and the Industrial Credit Corporation. Fittingly, then, it was **Sean Lemass**, the minister for industry and commerce, who conducted the official opening ceremony in May 1958.

However, the studios were not a success and ran into a series of funding and union-related difficulties. By 1963, they were placed into receivership, and any involvement Elliman might have had with them came to an abrupt conclusion. In any case ill health forced him to retire the same year. He died the following year at only 59, but his standing in Irish society was evinced by the attendance at his funeral, which included representatives of then president Eamon de Valera, then taoiseach Sean Lemass, and members of various theatrical and cinema organizations such as the Irish Cinemas Association, the **Irish Film Society**, and the Cork Film Festival.

EMIGRATION. Emigration has been a key characteristic of Irish demography and culture since the Great Famine of the 1840s, when approximately one million people left the country, primarily for Britain and America, to escape poverty. This hemorrhage of Irish people from rural areas in particular continued until the 1960s and recommenced in the 1980s for a range of economic reasons. *The Field* and other rural narratives dramatize the oft seen ritual of the "American wake," which sought to celebrate and commemorate those about to leave for America, unlikely ever to return again.

As a result of the legacy of emigration over the centuries, there is a large population of varying generations of Irish in America and throughout Britain especially. These diasporic Irish have been a focus for nostalgic filmmaking, going as far back as the **Kalem Company**, and this preoccupation has continued up to the present day. Consequently, films that appear dated and overly nostalgic for contemporary indigenous audiences—like *Angela's Ashes*, *Far and Away*, or *Waking Ned*, as well as classics like *The Quiet Man*— nevertheless struck a chord with Irish Americans, who remember Ireland for the hardship and poverty and overly stereotypical humor they left behind and possibly expect this vision of their long-lost homeland to be affirmed if not valorized.

Furthermore, the lure and appeal of America in particular remains an abiding trope within Irish literature, and many writers affirm how America was the next "parish" over from the West of Ireland. Within popular culture, for example, a whole generation of Irish males in the 1950s was brought up with the lure and appeal of the American Western, and John Wayne remains the epitome of affirmative and progressive masculinity. Playwrights like Brian Friel, for example, in *Philadelphia Here I Come*, incorporate the myth of American popular culture that represented freedom, open-mindedness, and escape from a restrictive Catholic sexuality. This appeal has been articulated in many Irish films, including even very pessimistic ones like the *Butcher Boy*, which valorizes American popular culture. More recently there has been a slow growth of American Irish diasporic films like *The Brothers McMullen*, *This Is My Father*, and *Gold in the Streets* that demonstrate the effects of emigration from the other side of the Atlantic, along with a small number of British migration stories like *Felicia's Journey*.

The economic revival of the country that began with the political policies of **Lemass** the 1960s and the recent phenomenal growth of the so-called Celtic Tiger economy have radically altered Irish migratory patterns. For the first time in the nation's history there has been a general cessation of economic-based emigration and even the beginning of a net immigration of natives and various other economic and political migrants. The future holds the prospect of more immigrant narratives as the Irish strive to integrate growing numbers of migrants from poorer countries; this echoes the long cycle of emigration of large numbers of Irish people up to this time. In the interim, Irish filmmakers dealing with immigration have focused on the often negative, indeed racist, response of some "natives" to the new arrivals. **Gerry Stembridge**'s *Bad Day at Black Rock* (2001) and **Alan Gilsenan**'s harrowing short *Zulu 9* (2001) are typical of these. *See also IN AMERICA.*

***THE END OF THE WORLD MAN* (1985).** This children's story, directed by **Bill Miskelly**, presents an ecological debate around protecting a habitat, a theme that is rare in Irish cinema. Even more remarkable, although the film is set in Northern Ireland, there are no references to the **"troubles,"** an observation that should not be that surprising but nevertheless signals how they have dominated so much representation of the province. Set in Belfast in the mid-1980s, Paula and Clara play in "the glen," a beautiful habitat of forest. But one day they happen upon a government official and discover his plans for a leisure center and car park. Horrified at such a threat to their beloved play area, they start a campaign to avert this destruction. Unfortunately, the film downplays their efforts since ultimately it is an adult who discovers that the glen has historical significance and therefore cannot be destroyed. Nonetheless, this is a well-meaning and effective children's film.

EURIMAGES. Designed to complement the support schemes offered under the European Union's **MEDIA** program, the Council of Europe established Eurimages as a pan-European film support fund in 1988. Eurimages member countries finance the fund, and the precise sum donated by an individual country is calculated based on a formula related to gross national product (GNP) and population. In contrast to the MEDIA Program, Eurimages seeks to encourage European coproduction by offering interest-free production loans. To qualify for support, a coproduction must involve at least three independent producers from the fund's member countries. In addition, Eurimages supports **distribution** of films in and from those member states outside the EU, which are thus unable to avail of distribution support from the MEDIA program. Support for **exhibition** is available under similar conditions.

Ireland became a member in 1992, a decision that coincided with the publication of the ***Coopers and Lybrand Report***, which strongly recommended Irish membership. Irish involvement—initially costed at £110,000 per annum—was originally funded jointly by the Department of the Taoiseach and **Radio Telefís Éireann (RTÉ)**. Subsequently the **Irish Film Board** paid the Irish subscription from its own resources. Irish membership was considered particularly advantageous in 1992 given the fund's stated bias toward small countries with a low audiovisual output and the fact that the refusal of the British government to join made Ireland the first English-speaking country to do so. (Great Britain did join in 1993 but pulled out again in 1997.)

Although only a handful of Irish films have received distribution support under Eurimages, the coproduction funding element of the scheme has been a major boon for Irish producers. Although Irish membership from 1992 to 2005 has cost in the region of €2 million, projects with an Irish involvement have received €9.2 million in return. Furthermore, although the list of films with Irish producers attached includes titles like *Messaggi Quasi Segreti*, the majority of the projects supported have been recognizably Irish (i.e., characterized by an Irish setting, cast, and story). Several Irish producers have used the scheme on a number of films: James Flynn of **Metropolitan Films** has partially funded three films (including *Nora*, which received over € 600,000) via the scheme; Ed Guiney's **Temple Pictures** used it for *Guiltrip and Sweety Barrett*, while **Little Bird** has used it for both feature and documentary support. Unusually, the scheme has also been very effectively used by Irish **animation** companies: Terraglyph has raised over € 1.3 million for two feature-length animations (*Help, I'm a Fish* and *Moby Dick—The Legend Returns*), while Magma succeeded in drawing down €550,000 for their *Ugly Ducking and Me* coproduction.

EVELYN **(2002).** Produced by and starring **Pierce Brosnan**, this 1950s period drama directed by Bruce Beresford is based on a true story of a carpenter suffering from alcoholism. When his wife leaves him and his children for a new life abroad, Desmond Doyle (Brosnan) is considered incapable of rearing his three children, as was legally conventional at the time, and they are put into an orphanage. The film tells of his legal battle to overturn the control of Church and state to get his three children back. The incident became a major symbolic news story at the time. According to some critics, however, the resultant film uses too many Irish stereotypes and is overly sentimental in its dramatic exposition. Nevertheless, the oldest daughter, Evelyn, is effectively played by Sophie Vavasseur and speaks up for the lack of human affection in the orphanage. Irish actors in this conventional human-interest story include Frank Kelly and Garret Keogh.

***AN EVERLASTING PIECE* (2000).** A comedy about two barbers living in Belfast in the 1980s who join up to try to design the ultimate toupee (referred to in local argot as a "piece") in the hope of making it big in the Irish market. The film portrays clashing religious beliefs and various other difficulties, and the business deal produces some humorous episodes. Starring Barry McEvoy, Brian F. O'Byrne, Anna Friel, Billy Connolly, and **Colm Meaney** and directed by Barry Levinson, the film remains overly self-conscious and somewhat sentimental at times.

***EXCALIBUR* (1981).** This adaptation of Malory's *Morte D'Arthur*, a story of the quest for the Holy Grail, has a climatic battle between Arthur and Mordred. Set in the beautiful wild scenery of County Wicklow, where the director **John Boorman** eventually secured a home, the historical epic is somewhat unfairly considered an uneven exercise in mythic fantasy. The film effectively explores a range of larger-than-life mythic heroic characters as they weave their complex story together. This early film provided essential acting experience for many Irish theater actors looking to the possibility of a career in film.

EXHIBITION. The key figure in early cinema exhibition in Ireland was unquestionably impresario Dan Lowrey, who gave the first public presentation of moving pictures in Ireland at his Star of Erin Music Hall (now the Olympia Theatre) in Dublin's Dame Street in April 1896. Although initial audiences were reportedly not overly enthusiastic about the screening, Lowrey persisted, bringing Lumière films to his Empire Variety Theatre in Belfast later the same year and Professor Jolly's cinematographe to his Palace Variety Theatre in Cork in 1897. Meanwhile Edison films were screened at the Rotunda Hall in Dublin from November 1901. Irish cinema exhibition grew rapidly, with films being screened in music halls, fairgrounds, towns, and village halls, or indeed anywhere with enough room for a traveling projectionist to set up the apparatus.

In early decades of film, all classes of Irish society enjoyed going to the cinema, but not necessarily to the same venues. **Liam O'Leary** has noted that a working-class theater such as the Dame Street Picture House could be refused permission to run films on a Sunday morning lest its patrons mix with the socially "superior" classes emerging from the nearby Quaker Meeting House in Eustace Street (L. O'Leary, 1984). (Ironically the same meetinghouse would later become the location for the Irish Film Centre.) Meanwhile, the entourage of the king's representative in Ireland might patronize James T. Jameson's screenings at the Rotunda Round Room.

Jameson would go on to become a prosperous exhibitor, operating three of the nine permanent Dublin venues by 1913: the Rotunda, the Theatre De Luxe, and the Volta Picture Theatre. The last shared its name with what was generally regarded as the first cinema built for that purpose in Ireland, the Volta, which opened in Dublin's Mary St. in December 1909. The cinema was initially managed and programmed by **James Joyce**, who had encouraged four Italian businessmen to put up the capital for the venture. However, after Joyce returned to his family in Italy, leaving the cinema in the hands of one of the Italian partners, audiences declined and the cinemas were sold at a loss to an English firm, the Provincial Theatre Company.

The number of permanent venues expanded rapidly in the 1910s and 1920s, from 150 in 1916 to 190 by 1935, and again to 220 by 1939. Not surprisingly, Dublin accounted for a disproportionate number of these: By 1939, nearly a quarter of all cinemas and a third of total national seating capacity were based in Dublin and its environs (the seating capacity reflected the prevalence of 1,000-plus seat auditoriums in the capital). However, by the 1930s virtually every town of any size had a cinema: 80 of 190 permanent establishments extant in 1935 were located in towns with a population of less than 4,000. In effect, then, cinema acquired a status parallel to that of the Church in Ireland: omnipresent and frequently attended. The 1942 *Report of the Inter-Departmental Committee on the Film Industry* estimated that those cinemas had recorded 28 million admissions in 1939, equivalent to 10 visits per annum per person.

Indeed the same report considered complaints from Dublin exhibitors that the number of cinemas in the capital had reached the saturation point and that further openings would inevitably cause existing theaters to close. Yet although the committee did not believe that the exhibition business should be an exception to the operation of the free market, it did express a concern with growing tendencies toward oligopoly in the market. These concerns were prompted by the fact that in the 1930s ownership of cinemas in the larger towns of Dublin, Cork, Waterford, and Galway was largely dominated by overseas groups, and in particular Associated British Cinemas, the flagship cinema of which—the Savoy on Dublin's O'Connell Street—had opened in 1929. However, in 1946 a duopoly structure emerged as another British Chain—Rank—took a majority interest in the Amalgamated Cinemas and Irish Cinemas Ltd., which had previously been owned by the **Elliman** family. Thus, Rank came to own some of the largest cinemas in the capital, including the Metropole, the Capitol, and the largest theater in Ireland, the Theatre Royal. Indeed Rank continued to expand throughout the 1940s, controlling 19 cinemas by 1950 (and acquiring 4 cinemas in 1949 alone).

Little came of the 1942 report's concerns, although a decade later, Rank's growing influence in particular prompted the Department of Industry and Commence to propose a new investigation of the extent to which foreign chains dominated the exhibition sector. The department was particularly concerned about the possibility that independently owned Irish exhibitors might be crowded out of the market. Once again, however, little of practical value came of the investigation.

In any case by the end of the 1950s, the first signs of decline in cinema going began to emerge. In the United States cinema attendance peaked in the immediate postwar era and declined consistently until the mid-1970s. In Ireland, a similar decline was noted, but it began a decade later. Cinema going in Ireland peaked in 1954, when 54 million admissions were recorded in the 327 cinemas operating within the republic. Within a decade (1966), however, this figure had fallen dramatically to 22 million as alternative leisure activities emerged. Inevitably this led to a rash of closures: Between 1962 and 1977, somewhere in the region of 160 to 190 cinemas closed; by 1975, there were just 184 screens operating. The number of cinemas was smaller still because those that stayed in business usually did so by subdividing their single auditoriums into multiple smaller theaters. Thus in 1969, Odeon's flagship cinema in Dublin, the Savoy, changed from a 2,000-seat-plus single-screen venue into a two-theater cinema, and then in 1975 into a three-screen cinema. (By the 1990s further subdivision had increased the number of theaters within the Savoy complex to six). Other large-scale cinemas either followed suit or, as with the 4,000-seat Theatre Royal, simply closed down. The decline in audiences continued throughout the 1970s, reaching its lowest point in 1985, when 4.5 million admissions were recorded to the 135 screens still operating in the Republic of Ireland. The effect of this decline was disproportionately felt in smaller towns—between 1962 and 1977, 47 towns saw their only cinema close.

The decline in audiences brought with it dramatic shifts in the ownership structure of Irish exhibition. In 1969 the British EMI Group bought out Associated British Cinemas, thus acquiring the two-cinema Adelphi-Carlton group in Dublin. (Though numerically small the Adelphi and Carlton were economically significant, both being based in Dublin City Centre and accounting for 4,304 seats between them.) Meanwhile, through the 1950s and 1960s, the Irish-owned **Ward Anderson** group had taken advantage of the declining value of cinemas to gradually acquire substantial holdings, first outside Dublin, then within the Dublin market, beginning with the acquisition of the Green Cinema on St. Stephen's Green in 1968. Thus by the start of the 1970s Ward Anderson was the dominant force outside Dublin, and by 1983, after acquiring Rank's remaining Dublin cinemas, was the dominant force everywhere.

So dominant was Ward Anderson that in the early 1970s a series of accusations were leveled at the group that it (along with Adelphi-Carlton Ltd. and Rank) was colluding with distributors to prevent independent cinema owners in the provinces and Dublin suburbs from accessing major releases. Eventually in 1976, the Restrictive Practices Commission investigated the structure of the industry, but although it found that provincial cinemas were indeed experiencing difficulties in accessing titles, it concluded that this was due to commercial considerations aimed at maximizing revenues from individual titles. The commission specifically stated that it found no evidence of any kind of secret agreement between Ward Anderson and film distributors operating in Ireland aimed at conferring a monopoly on the group. Nonetheless, the commission did recommend that the industry as a whole adopt a disputes resolution procedure for dealing with future problems in the **distribution** of films to cinemas across the country.

In effect, then, as of the mid-1980s, the Irish cinema market was split between Ward Anderson, the Adelphi-Carlton group, and independent cinema owners based outside Dublin city center. From the mid-1980s, however, attendances began to increase again from the 1985 low point of 4.5 million to 7 million by the end of the decade. This trend continued throughout the 1990s as Ireland recorded the highest per capita rates of cinema attendance in Europe. Much of the renaissance was due to the arrival of multiplex cinemas in 1990 (although multiplexes cannot account for the upturn prior to this date). The arrival of the multiplexes transformed the industry. Generally located in suburban locales, they offered free parking, prebooking of seats and—with a minimum of 10 screens—greater choice than any Irish cinema had previously made available. They also introduced a new cinema business model, laying as much stress on the revenues from sales of soft drinks and snacks as from ticket sales.

The first Irish multiplex was opened in Tallaght, South County Dublin, by United Cinemas International (UCI—a joint venture of Universal and Paramount), which quickly opened a second site a year later in the northern suburb of Coolock. (A third UCI opened in the western suburb of Blanchardstown in 1996.) By the mid 1990s, the Tallaght and Coolock UCIs alone accounted for 20 percent of all cinema admissions in the Republic of Ireland. Rather than competing head-on with the newcomers, Ward Anderson sought to develop greenfield sites for its own multiplexes in the Dublin suburbs of Santry and Dun Laoire, and to consolidate its provincial dominance by closing older cinemas in provincial towns and building new "miniplexes" instead.

However, the obvious attraction of the multiplex model had a devastating effect on smaller independently owned cinemas. As of 1992 there were 79 cinemas in Ireland with 189 screens. Of those 31 were single screen and only 3 cinemas had 10 or more screens. By 2000, however, only 10 single-screen cinemas remained, whereas virtually every major town in Ireland now has at least a 4-screen cinema. Furthermore, as of 2005, there were only 66 cinemas in Ireland but 329 screens. Cinema closures in this period have been concentrated in

towns with populations of less than 10,000 situated in the less economically successful border, midlands, and western counties, many
of which have only 1 cinema. (Indeed County Roscommon has no
cinema at all.) Thus although single-screen cinemas in smaller towns
still exist, they are often economically marginal and family run.
Those independent cinema owners with a long-term interest in the
business have themselves followed the multiplex route.

Despite the ongoing decline in cinema numbers, it is irrefutable
that the arrival of the multiplexes has boosted overall attendances. In
2003, 17.3 million admissions were recorded in the Republic of Ireland, nearly 4.4 per person and twice the average European attendance. The seemingly infinite potential in the market attracted a
range of new players through the 1990s, albeit largely to the Dublin
market. In 1993 the Adelphi-Carlton group (then owned by MGM)
built a city-center multiplex. This passed through several hands (including Virgin and UGC) before being bought out by a British venture capital company, the Blackstone Group, in December 2004, by
which point the cinema had been expanded to encompass 17 screens.
Prior to that, the largest cinema had been a 14-screen West Dublin
multiplex, owned by the South African chain Ster Century. This too
was sold—to a British firm, Vue Entertainment—in May 2005. And
in August of the same year another venture capital firm, Terra Firma,
bought the UCI's three Dublin cinemas.

As of 2005, smaller cinema owners still complain that they find it
difficult to access prints of films while they are still fresh. An initiative announced in April 2005 may offer some succor for the future.
Avica Technologies, a U.S. digital exhibition equipment firm, drew
up plans through its Thurles-based subsidiary, Digital Cinema Limited, to install 515 digital projectors in 105 Irish cinemas (i.e., every
cinema in the republic and Northern Ireland) by April 2006. If actually achieved, this would make Ireland the world's first entirely digital exhibition market and would obviate the need for smaller cinemas to chase distributors for prints.

EXPOSURE **(1978).** Directed by Kieran Hickey and produced by
Hickey's B.A.C. Films with funding from the **Arts Council, Radio
Telefís Éireann (RTÉ)**, and the **National Film Studios of Ireland**,
the film follows a three-man ordnance survey team from Dublin—

Dan, the leader (**T. P. McKenna**), Eugene (Niall O'Brien), and Oliver (Bosco Hogan)—as they arrive at a hotel on the west coast of Ireland, where they will spend a week mapping the area. They quickly encounter the hotel's only other guest, Caroline, a German photographer. Stuck in a remote location the four quickly establish a rapport over drinks in the bar. Both Dan and Eugene are in unhappy marriages, so it is left to bachelor Oliver to strike up a relationship with Caroline, which becomes a source of tension among the men.

When Oliver and Caroline go out one night, Dan and Eugene drunkenly break into Caroline's room and rummage about in her bags and clothing, inadvertently breaking some of her camera equipment. A shocked Caroline and Oliver walk in upon them in the midst of their rampage. Dan and Eugene sheepishly leave—followed a few moments later by Oliver. Caroline is left alone weeping. The next morning, they awake to find that she has already left the hotel.

The dearth of dramatic filmic material in Ireland of the 1970s renders any picture from the period fascinating. Yet this would be the case with *Exposure* regardless of when it was made. Its ambition belies its short running time (52 minutes) and relatively small budget, and its success owes much to the screenplay. At a time when more mainstream subjects might have claimed the attention of Irish filmmakers, director Hickey with his coscreenwriter Philip Davison offered an incisive study of the nature of Irish masculinity and Ireland's relationship to modernity.

The political rhetoric prevalent in the 1970s insisted that Ireland had become a modern nation, pointing to European Union membership, rapid industrialization, and increasing wealth, reflected in the widespread acquisition of consumer goods. *Exposure*'s ordnance survey team embodies this rather narrow definition of modernity: urban, relatively sophisticated, and equipped with high-tech mapping equipment.

However, the persistence of stifling premodern social mores in 1970s Ireland is also evident in the film. The society portrayed in *Exposure* remains openly patriarchal, demanding appropriate behavior from not just women but also men. The men are unable to discuss anything but the least sensitive subjects among themselves: Dan and Eugene's discussions of their marriages are confined to furtive conversations with their wives in the hotel's phone box. Eugene is portrayed as craving some declaration of affection from his wife, while she—apparently conditioned to believe that men do not need such reassurance—is unable or unwilling to do so.

These norms are implicitly challenged by the figure of Catherine, who represents the social consequences of pursuing precisely the kind of modernity that Ireland already identified itself with; she is cosmopolitan, sexually liberated, and independent of men. By identifying such characteristics with Catherine, however, Hickey associates them with "the other." Catherine thus unwittingly represents a test of Ireland's claim to modernity: The response of other characters to her acts as a marker of the actual extent to which they accept the full logic of modernity. Mrs. Sinnott, owner of the hotel, is immediately identified as part of the "old order": rural, elderly, actively applauding the men's heavy drinking. It is therefore not surprising when she fails the test through making her disapproval of Oliver's and Caroline's relationship quite clear.

However, the real test comes with the response of the men to Caroline. Unable to verbally express their frustration with their own marriages and their envy of Oliver's relationship with Caroline, Dan and Eugene can find an outlet only in their drunken rampage through Caroline's room. However, even Oliver, when faced with the choice of sticking to the safety of Irish society or abandoning it for the exotica represented by Caroline automatically—if shamefacedly—takes the safe option. Ultimately, then, it is ironic that Caroline's photographic assignment is to capture images of Ireland: It is precisely only images that she succeeds in capturing. The drama's closing shot is of Catherine, exposing a photograph of the men before it has time to fix on the paper: As their image is exposed, the three men fade from view.

– F –

***THE FANTASIST* (1986).** Critically lambasted on release in 1986, *The Fantasist* created that most unique of genres—the Irish sex-crime thriller. Produced by New Irish Film Productions (a company established by broadcaster Mike Murphy), and directed by Robin Hardy, best known for cult 1970s horror *The Wicker Man* (1973), the film featured a mixed international cast, including Moira Harris, Christopher Casenove, Timothy Bottoms, and **John Kavanagh**. It follows Patricia (Harris), whose university studies are financed by her rich uncle, who expects her to return to manage the family farm. However, instead of returning home after graduating, she remains in Dublin city with her flat mate Monica, where she tries to cope with her two suitors—Danny, who is married, and the increasingly eccentric Robert. Her dalliances are played out against a background of growing paranoia in the city as a psychopathic serial killer adds to his tally of victims.

***FAR AND AWAY* (1992).** Shot on 65 mm and directed by Ron Howard, the film was conceived as a vehicle for then husband and wife Tom Cruise and Nicole Kidman. Apparently inspired by the plays of 18th-century dramatist Dion Boucicault, screenwriter Bob Dolman, along with the director, created a whimsical romantic historical comedy that opens in 1890s Kerry. Though from opposite ends of the social spectrum, tenant farmer Joseph Connelly (Cruise) and aristocratic Shannon Christie (Kidman) emigrate on the same boat to America after Joseph's father is killed by unscrupulous landowners. Once in America they fall in love, and in the film's closing set piece they participate in the spectacular Oklahoma Land Rush.

Boucicault aside, the story also clearly takes *The Quiet Man* as a reference point. This is evident in the portrayal of Kerry villagers as disheveled but charming inebriates, the tourist board–esque landscape imagery, and in particular Kidman's portrayal of Shannon as a staunchly independent woman who overtly recalls **Maureen O'Hara**'s Mary Kate from the earlier film. Both films also share a romantic tone: The representation of the voyage to America as a pleasure cruise is at some remove from the actuality of 19th-century emigrant coffin ships. That said, in placing a tenant laborer and a landlord's agent (Thomas Gibson) at the center of the narrative, *Far and Away* at least hints at political, social, and cultural divisions entirely absent from *The Quiet Man*'s ecumenist vision of Irish life.

Shot in western Kerry (in many of the same locations used for ***Ryan's Daughter***) and Dublin (which doubled for 19th-century Boston), *Far and Away* was the biggest picture shot in Ireland since *Ryan's Daughter* in 1969. Although the £40 million spent by the production was welcomed by the state, it placed the sum spent on indigenous films the same year—£3.5 million—in stark relief and demonstrated the extent to which the Irish audiovisual sector then depended on overseas projects.

FARRELL, COLIN (1976–). As a teenager he was sent to the expensive Castleknock College but left before completing his Leaving Certificate. In interviews he has described himself as a confused teenager who briefly saw a psychologist and claimed that he did too many drugs at the time. Farrell initially sought to emulate his footballer father but drifted into acting instead. Following a stint in the British television drama series *Ballykissangel*, and roles in the locally produced films ***Drinking Crude*** and ***Ordinary Decent Criminal***, he was taken up by Joel Schumacher to play a young American soldier in the expressionistic *Tigerland* (2000), for which he won an award from the influential Boston Society of Film Critics. Leading roles opposite Bruce Willis and Tom Cruise quickly followed in, respectively, *Hart's War* (2002) and the Steven Spielberg–directed *Minority Report* (2002). When Joel Schumacher came to cast him again in the high-concept *Phone Booth* (2002), he had so definitively entered the ranks of A-list stars that the entire picture was marketed around him.

Farrell's meteoric rise to success has made him a major star in a relatively short time, and his film roles are certainly wide ranging, although several—including *The Recruit* (2003) and *S.W.A.T* (2003)— have been little more than vehicles designed to cash in on his sudden ascent. Reminiscent of classic Irish hell-raisers like **Richard Harris** and **Peter O'Toole**, his larger-than-life persona is effectively marketed to fan his commercial success. Typical of this was his cameo role in ***Intermission***, in the opening sequence of which he unexpectedly punches a shopgirl after initially appearing to woo her with a brash verbal charm.

In *A Home at the End of the World* (2004), based on the novel by Michael Cunningham, he plays against type as a very sensitive and sexually ambiguous youth. More recently in Oliver Stone's strange and heavily criticized historical epic *Alexander* (2005), he takes on the title role of a historical leader who is again sexually confused. In this rambling epic, which features more Irish actors than many indigenous products, Stone somehow justifies this overcasting by allegorically paralleling the power relationships between Alexander's homeland and the imperial power of Rome with the relationship between former colonies like Ireland and the colonizer, Britain.

Farrell is the most prolific and highest-paid Irish actor, yet he glibly asserts that he would gladly work for minimum wage for doing something he loves so much. The importance of his film persona is even parodied in a recent postmodern comic thriller, *Kiss, Kiss, Bang, Bang* (2005), and despite living a very public private life that entails drink, drugs, and accidental fatherhood, there's little to suggest that anything can prevent his becoming the most successful Irish star actor yet.

FEDERATION OF IRISH FILM SOCIETIES. *See* IRISH FILM SOCIETY.

FELICIA'S JOURNEY **(1999).** Based on a William Trevor novel of the same name, and directed by Atom Egoyan, the film is well served by actors Bob Hoskins and, in a revelatory performance, **Elaine Cassidy** as the innocent abroad. The slowly executed thriller follows a pregnant young Irish girl across the Irish Sea to Birmingham as—having been disowned by her father—she searches for the unborn child's father, who has abandoned her. In Birmingham she encounters Quincy, the lonely yet somewhat sinister catering manager of a big factory, who offers to help her find her former boyfriend. The northern British industrial squalor is well contrasted with the beautiful preindustrial Irish landscape, coupled with its more regressive mores, embodied in her elderly father, who insists on unconditional acceptance of his rules. Since his family had fought the British in 1916, he cannot allow his daughter to consort with a boy who does not want to stay at home and, worse, entertains the idea of joining the British Army. Felicia has to discover her identity and role in life outside such stultifying restrictions. After numerous twists the thriller resolves itself conventionally as Felicia finds a kind of modus vivendi for facing her future.

FERNDALE FILMS. *See* PEARSON, NOEL.

FESTIVALS. Film festivals began in Ireland in 1956 with the establishment of the Cork International Film Festival, which has run ever since. The Cork Festival was driven largely by the initiative of Dermot Breen, a former manager of the Palace Theatre in Cork, the city's first public relations manager, and in the mid-1970s, the official Irish film censor. Breen sold the festival as a means of drumming up tourist trade and convinced **Bord Fáilte** [Irish Tourist Board] to financially support the festival as an element of the annual An Toastál arts festival. Bord Fáilte would remain the sponsor until the 1980s, expending generous sums of money to bring over international guests, especially journalists from British newspapers, thus ensuring international coverage for the event. Unusually, Breen initiated a short film competition as part of the festival, a move his predecessors continued after Breen's death in 1978.

Cork remained the only ongoing annual festival in Ireland until the 1980s. However, with the closure of the **Irish Film Theatre** in 1985, Dublin was left without a venue for 35 mm screenings of non-mainstream material. To at least partially address the gap, journalists Michael Dwyer and Myles Dungan established the Dublin Film Festival the same year. Despite being regarded initially—even by its founders—as a stopgap measure, the first Dublin festival was extremely successful with audiences, even recording a financial surplus at the end of the first year. Consequently even when new permanent art-house venues such as the **Light House** opened in Dublin in 1988, the festival not only survived but actually thrived, arguably enjoying its most successful year in 1992, not simply in terms of audiences but also in terms of the range of guests who attended the festival. These included Oliver Stone, Krzysztof Kieslowski, Theo Angelopoulos, cinematographer Freddie Francis, documentarist Errol Morris, and composer Michael Nyman, whose band performed during the festival.

By the end of the 1990s, however, the Dublin Festival was beset by financial and staffing difficulties. The figures behind its early successes, Dwyer and Dungan, together with programmers like Martin Mahon (of Yellow Asylum) and administrators like David McLoughlin, had all amicably ended their involvement by the mid-1990s. In 1998, the festival lost its major sponsor (ACC Bank) and its main venue, the **Ward Anderson**–owned Screen Cinema. In 2001 the **Arts Council** commissioned a report on the difficulties at the festival that identified the absence of a coherent programming policy and an unworkable management structure. The report's analysis came too late to save the festival, which last ran in 2001.

However, in 2003, a new organization, the Dublin International Film Festival, picked up where the previous one had left off. Indeed, there were striking personnel overlaps between the two organizations: The new festival was programmed by Michael Dwyer and chaired by David McLoughlin, who had become a film producer (for *Dead Bodies*, among other films) in the interim. To all intents and purposes the new festival was a reinvention of the original, even down to the retention of the Surprise Film feature that had proved an unexpected hit with audiences of the original festival.

The last long-established festival operating in Ireland is the Galway Film Fleadh ("fleadh" is the Irish term for "festival"), which first ran in 1988, using the Claddagh Palace cinema as a venue. Founded by **Lelia Doolan** and Miriam Allen, the fleadh operated on a smaller scale than either the Dublin or the Cork festival, but nonetheless the fleadh found a niche in the annual festival calendar. Widely regarded as the most intimate and laid-back of the major festivals, it also introduced a quasi-professional element, running master classes and seminars on various aspects of film production and policy from its inception. Thus in 2005, festival goers could attend master classes in acting, directing, and screenwriting with, respectively, Campbell Scott, Luis Mandoki, and Paul Schrader, all guests of the fleadh. It has also been a competitive festival since its inception, initially offering prizes for best short, and later offering awards for best Irish feature.

The fleadh's status was indirectly enhanced from 1993, when the reformed **Irish Film Board** established its headquarters in Galway, and in particular when organizer Lelia Doolan became chair of the Film Board. This created an added incentive for Irish film professionals to make the journey to the west coast. In 1995, the fleadh lost its venue when the Claddagh Palace was bulldozed to make way for apartments, but the fleadh has subsequently thrived in Galway's Town Hall and Omniplex cinemas.

In addition to these, there are now an increasing number of newer festivals around the country. Dublin alone hosts festivals for gay and lesbian, French, German, Spanish, documentary, and digital cinema. There are also annual festivals in Kerry, Limerick, and Derry. All

Irish film festivals are usually financed by a mixture of sponsorship, box office income, and Arts Council funding. The last of these is particularly critical for the smaller festivals. Until 1980 Bord Fáilte had financed the only festival then in place—the Cork Festival—but from that year, responsibility for such funding was transferred to the Arts Council, which awarded the Cork festival £42,500 in its first year alone. As of 2003, the council directly grant-aided eight film festivals to the tune of € 382,000 and indirectly financed several others through funding for arts festivals with film components.

THE FIELD (1990). The late John B. Keane (1928–2002) wrote the play, which **Jim Sheridan** himself adapted and directed. For the film version the setting was changed from the play's Kerry of the 1960s to Connemara of the 1930s. (The key role of a returned emigrant from England became an American, played by Tom Berenger, to make the film more palatable commercially.) **Ray McAnally** had originally signed a contract for the main part of the Bull McCabe but then tragically died; eventually **Richard Harris** succeeded him and made the role his own.

The film opens with two men in silhouette pushing a cart over mountainous fields and unceremoniously dropping the carcass of a donkey into deep water below. They then gather seaweed in pouches to carry back up the mountains—a direct visual reference to the "hard primitivism" of Robert Flaherty's seminal *Man of Aran*—so that they can fertilize and regenerate the precious soil of the ultragreen field, which becomes the central focus of identification in the film. In the first of his many rhetorical speeches the Bull pontificates to his son, "God made the world," but "seaweed made the field."

This opening credit sequence quickly develops the central issue of the film when Tadgh (Sean Bean), playing the lethargic and unintentionally cruel son, asks his father why the widow (Francis Tomelty) does not want to sell the field. After giving the widow her rent money, Tadgh plays a cruel prank where he and a friend frighten her in secret, a ritual we later discover has continued for years. His willing accomplice is Bird Flanagan (John Hurt), in a performance that all but reprises the village idiot role by John Mills in *Ryan's Daughter*.

As in many classical rural Irish narratives, from *The Quiet Man* to *Ryan's Daughter*, the local community functions as passive recipients, waiting for things to happen, with no apparent work ethic. At the same time reminiscent of a theatrical chorus, they actively affirm the attitudes, values, and pleasures of the society by endorsing the "common law" of nature in particular and of what is right and who deserves to be demonized. When the Bull confronts the publican about the impending sale of the field (the widow having finally decided to sell it), he is warned that "outsiders" might bid for the prize possession, which in turn activates a conventional reaffirmation of colonial and national solidarity, evoking victimhood and the rise of a common enemy "who drove us to the coffin ships." Rousing the passion of the pub crowd, the Bull continues, "I drove them out" and firmly concludes, "No outsider will bid for the field." But of course an outsider, in the form of a Yank, does so and initiates awesome consequences.

Land and the struggle to own and maintain it have been a primary theme in Irish narratives for centuries. The trauma of the inflicted violence and the pathological hunger for land leave the Bull unable to cope psychologically. In an overly theatrical denouement, echoing Shakespeare's *King Lear*, he descends into madness, driving his cattle to the edge of the cliff and walking into the sea trying to control its power, following the death of his son.

THE FIFTH PROVINCE (1997). The film (directed by Frank Stapleton) playfully acknowledges Irish cinematic stereotypes and then goes on to subvert them in various ways. Timmy Sugrue (Brian F. O'Byrne) lives in a house with his mother that is reminiscent of the Bates motel in *Psycho* (1960) and dreams of being a writer. However, his writing teacher considers Timmy's work to be too self-consciously Irish and too filled with the usual Irish preoccupations and gloom to appeal to a popular audience. "No more stories about Irish mothers, priests, sexual repression and the miseries of rural life," he is warned when he attends a scriptwriters' conference, where only scripts offering more cosmopolitan and contemporary representations of Ireland are valorized. Trapped in his immediate environment but also in the expectations of his chosen profession, Timmy attempts to imagine an alternative space, free of these constraints: the eponymous fifth province. On one level a surreal farce, the film is also an appealing, well-scripted comedy that addresses a recurrent dilemma for indigenous cinemas everywhere: how to compete with the global commercialism of Hollywood.

FILM BASE. The organization was established in 1986 to provide an independent resource facility with equipment, information, training, and skills for the filmmakers in the low-budget film sector. It continues to offer practical courses in scripting, directing, and editing and facilitates the discounted hire of a wide range of advanced film and video equipment. As of 2006 Film Base had just under 1,000 members, which represents a quadrupling of the 1990 figure. Originally based in Dublin's Dame Street, it was located in the Irish Film Centre for more than a decade before moving in 2004 to a large open-plan, three-story, glass-fronted building in Temple Bar just around the corner from its old home.

From its inception Film Base was also a de facto lobbying group, on behalf of not only the low-budget film sector but at times — and in particular after the closure of the Irish Film Board in 1987 — the entire industry. Until the reestablishment of the Film Board in 1993, Film Base consistently argued for the establishment of a single state body with responsibility for all aspects of Irish film policy, including training, and its members — including Jane and **Johnny Gogan**, Anne Crilly, Liam O'Neill, and **Tiernan MacBride** — made significant contributions to the influential *Coopers and Lybrand Report*. In the same year then Film Base director **Ed Guiney** was appointed to the taoiseach's Special Working Group on the Film Production Industry.

In 1987, Film Base established a bimonthly newsletter, *FilmBase News*, initially to keep members informed about the organization's activities. However, it quickly became a full-fledged debating space devoted to the politics of film support and film culture in Ireland. Its pages were as likely to feature cultural critics like **Kevin Rockett** and Luke Gibbons debating the merits of **Joe Comerford**'s work as it was Tiernan MacBride and **Film Makers Ireland** debating the lack of state support for cinema. In 1992 the magazine was retitled *Film Ireland* to reflect the broader scope of the journal. Now a glossy but still bimonthly publication, it remains the longest-running film publication in Ireland.

In 1992, Film Base collaborated with **Radio Telefís Éireann (RTÉ)** to launch an award scheme to fund the production of short films. Subsequently, similar awards were established, including Irish-language channel TG4 awards, and in 2004 two new **documentary** awards were introduced. As the price of digital technology has dropped, the organization has increasingly broadened its ambitions: It no longer aims to simply facilitate the production of shorts but increasingly seeks to promote the production of more low-budget feature films.

FILM COMPANY OF IRELAND (FCOI). By far the most significant indigenous production company of the silent era, the Film Company of Ireland was established by returned emigrant James Mark Sullivan (whose family brought him from Killarney to America when he was a boy) in March 1916. Although its first films were lost when the company's offices were destroyed during the Easter Rising the same year, by the end of 1916, the company had produced a further nine short films.

In its early films, the company drew heavily on the **Abbey Theatre**'s thespian resources, employing J. M. Kerrigan (who also acted as director), Sara Allgood, Fred O'Donovan, and his wife, Nora Clancy. The early films (many of which were shot in Kerry) were mainly comedies and were critically and popularly well received, in small part because the films were clearly directed at a local audience.

From 1917, the company made longer pictures with more political content, most notably an adaptation of Charles J. Kickham's *Knocknagow* (1917) and William Carlton's *Willy Reilly and His Colleen Bawn* (1920), both of which used historical settings to comment on the contemporary struggle for political independence. Unfortunately, *Colleen Bawn* was also the company's last film: Already under surveillance by British authorities because of his friendship with Irish Republican Army (IRA) chief of staff Michael Collins, O'Sullivan was devastated when his wife and child died in an influenza epidemic. Heartbroken, he returned to the United States, and the company effectively folded.

FILM EDUCATION. Film and media studies emerged as a degree subject in the late 1970s at the University of Ulster in Coleraine in

Northern Ireland and in the republic in the early 1980s at Dublin City University, although colleges such as the National College of Art and Design in Dublin also offered film studies courses from the late 1970s. Most notably, **Lelia Doolan** started a very important production course in the College of Commerce, Rathmines, which was later co-opted as part of the Dublin Institute of Technology (DIT). Film studies as an academic specialty was not established until 1991 when Dublin City University (DCU) introduced a masters in film (and television), followed a year later by University College Dublin (UCD). In 2003 Trinity College Dublin (TCD) established the first undergraduate degree program in film studies in the republic. Additionally many of the colleges that developed as institutes of technology, especially the National Film School at Dun Laoghaire, offer specialist undergraduate filmmaking degree courses. Outside of Dublin many film and media courses have sprung up over the last few years in the institutes and universities in the other major cities.

At the secondary level, media and film studies as discrete subjects do not exist, and Ireland is far behind Great Britain, for example, in developing separate curricula. However, adding media and film to the English curriculum has been significant, as have encouraging and promoting film study during the students' transition year, before they begin their Leaving Certificate study.

FILM IRELAND. A mainstream film magazine produced by **Film Base** and up to recently situated in the Irish Film Centre in Dublin. The idea of the magazine began with the 1987 annual general meeting of **Film Base**, the new "low-budget" filmmaker's organization that called for a better distribution of information to a growing new membership. Its editors over the years have included **Johnny Gogan**, who was the first and who went on to make films himself. In spite of various pressures the journal has survived. More recent editors have included John Doyle, Tony Keily, Patrick Barrett, Francis Power, and Paul Power, who continued to widen the magazine's appeal; and Hugh Linehan, who went on to become a film critic and editor of the weekly entertainment section "The Ticket" with the *Irish Times*; and Ted Sheehy, who was often critical of the lack of a professional film grammar within much Irish film production. Sheehy subsequently became Ireland correspondent for *Screen International*.

FILM MAKERS IRELAND REPORT. See INDEPENDENT TELEVI-SION PRODUCTION SECTOR REPORT.

THE FILM PRODUCTION INDUSTRY IN IRELAND (*REPORT OF THE SPECIAL WORKING GROUP ON THE FILM PRO-DUCTION INDUSTRY***).** *See REPORT TO THE TAOISEACH, MR. ALBERT REYNOLDS, T. D., 24 NOLLAIG, 1992.*

FITZGERALD, BARRY (1888–1961). Two brothers, William and Arthur Shields, were born in Dublin, and the older sibling, Arthur, joined the **Abbey Theatre** in 1914, eventually leaving for Hollywood in 1939, where he had many successes, including *Drums along the Mohawk* (1939), *The Long Voyage Home* (1940), and *The Keys of the Kingdom* (1944). His brother William also joined the Abbey Players as a part-time actor while keeping his day job as a civil servant, which he held until he was over 40. Surprisingly, he continued to be billed as Ireland's greatest actor. To keep his thespian pursuits a secret from his employers, he adapted the stage name Barry Fitzpatrick. However, the story goes, a printer's error reproduced it as Barry Fitzgerald, a name he was to keep throughout his career.

In 1926, Sean O'Casey was said to have written the part of Fluther Good in *The Plough and the Stars* especially for him. In the late 1920s he made his film debut in another O'Casey role, in Alfred Hitchcock's film version of *Juno and the Paycock*. Following this, he re-created his stage role of Fluther for **John Ford**'s 1936 film version and stayed on to become one of Hollywood's finest character actors, portraying likeable Irish stereotypes from priest to comic rogue, like Father Flynn in *Going My Way* (1944) and of course the very studied and famous matchmaker Michaeleen Flynn in *The Quiet Man* (1952). He was nominated for the Best Actor and Best Supporting Actor awards for his performance in *Going My Way*—and won the Best Supporting Actor Oscar. The two brothers are buried beside each other in Deans Grange cemetery in Dublin.

FLANAGAN, FIONNULA (1941–). Born in Dublin and trained at the Abbey Theatre, she has been based in the United States since 1968, where she has maintained a remarkably consistent presence on stage and screen. She has made more than 40 guest appearances in U.S.

television dramas from *Bonanza* to *Nip/Tuck* and won an Emmy in 1976 for a supporting role in *Rich Man, Poor Man*. On stage, she is regarded as the definitive interpreter of James Joyce and received a Tony nomination in 1974 for her performance in *Ulysses in Nighttown*. She cemented her Joycean credentials with her landmark one-person show, in which she plays a series of characters—real and fictional—from Joyce's life and works. Flanagan produced a screen version of this performance in 1985 under the title *James Joyce's Women* (she had appeared some 18 years earlier in **Joseph Strick**'s adaptation of *Ulysses*). She has long been a vocal supporter of Sinn Féin and was appropriately cast as an Irish Republican Army (IRA) prisoner's mother in *Some Mother's Son* (1996). Other notable big-screen roles in recent years include *Waking Ned* (1998) and her eye-catching turn as the housekeeper in *The Others* (2001).

FLEISCHMANN, GEORGE (1912–). Born in Austria, he worked on Leni Reifenstahl's film on the Munich Olympics (*Olympiad*, 1936) and later joined the German Luftwaffe. After crash-landing during a reconnaissance mission over Ireland, he was interned for the rest of World War II. Afterward he stayed on in the country, eventually helping to set up the Hibernia Picture Company in 1951. He is credited on a second unit for **John Huston**'s *Moby Dick* and went on to make numerous documentaries on the development of Irish electricity and other public utilities.

FORD, JOHN (1894–1973). John Ford's father was an **emigrant** from Ireland, and this influence infused many of Ford's great Westerns. For example, in his Irish-made film *The Rising of the Moon* (produced in partnership with Lord **Killanin**), a poteen maker (Jack MacGowran) looks ruefully toward a ruined castle dominating the land, inhabited by an old tenant farmer (**Noel Purcell**), saying of him, "From there to a wee thatched cottage . . ." to which another observer (**Cyril Cusack**) replies, "'Tisn't the castle that makes the king." The paradox of his physical proximity to the upper classes and the social distance he always felt from them would influence Ford throughout his lifetime.

Liam O'Flaherty's 1937 novel *Famine* is dedicated to Ford himself, who always wanted to bring it to the screen but never succeeded. However, the novel clearly influenced his 1940 film *The Grapes of Wrath*, from the novel by John Steinbeck, whose maternal grandfather was also driven to emigrate from Ireland by the 1840s famine. The roots of Ford's romanticism can be traced to his love of Ireland and his fond memories of visits to the homeland. When he had several successful Hollywood films under his belt, he tested his growing power by trying to persuade reluctant studio executives to let him develop three Irish projects close to his heart: his cousin Liam O'Flaherty's 1925 novel *The Informer* (1935), Sean O'Casey's 1926 play *The Plough and the Stars* (1936), and Maurice Walsh's 1933 short story "The Quiet Man." All three projects eventually reached the screen, but each presented enormous difficulties, and Ford was unable to find backing for *The Quiet Man* until the early 1950s.

With *The Informer* he succeeded only with the intervention of an old friend, Joseph P. Kennedy (father of John F. Kennedy), who had read the book and who had formed the film studio RKO in 1928. Ford became seriously interested in filming *The Quiet Man* in 1935 and took an option on Walsh's story, which was originally published in the *Saturday Evening Post* in 1933. It is a tale of an Irish American boxer named Shawn Kelvin who returns to his native Kerry after killing a man in the ring. Shawn does his patriotic duty as a member of an Irish Republican Army (IRA) flying column during the War of Independence, but he yearns for lasting peace in "a quiet place on a hillside." Though essentially a fairy tale, Walsh's story is less lighthearted and romantic than the film Ford eventually made of it. Shawn Kelvin is a fiercer, more introverted figure than Wayne's troubled but essentially good-natured Sean Thornton.

The Rising of the Moon (1957) was produced by **Four Provinces Ltd.**, established in 1952 by Lord Killanin and Irish director **Brian Desmond Hurst**, with Ford serving as a board member. The name of the company appeared at least to imply support for the reunification of Ireland and endorsed the vision of an Irish film industry, which is dramatized at the start by explicitly addressing an American audience. The film is constructed around three unrelated stories, introduced and linked by Irish American actor Tyrone Power. The first, "The Majesty of the Law," is based on a short story of the same name by Frank O'Connor; the second, "A Minute's Wait," is based on a one-act comedy by Martin J. McHugh; and the third, "1921," is a crude version of Lady Gregory's play *The Rising of the Moon*.

Ford went on to make many more classic Hollywood movies and directed some scenes in Jack Cardiff's film biography of Sean O'-Casey, *Young Cassidy* (1965), which was completed by Cardiff when Ford became ill. As a result his Irish influences remain pervasive, and his films have ensured that Irish representations have remained in the foreground of the global film culture Industry.

FOUR PROVINCES LTD. Production company formed in 1954 by Lord **Killanin**, Tyrone Power, **John Ford**, Irish architect Michael Scott, and Irish-born director **Brian Desmond Hurst**. The company was formed to make Irish films and expressed the intention of establishing an Irish studio (pre-**Ardmore**) to be designed by Scott. For a brief period in the mid-1950s, the company promised to form the basis of an Irish film industry, having apparently secured U.S. distribution guarantees (via an arrangement with *The Quiet Man* distributor Republic Pictures) for its work. In addition, since its output would qualify as British quota films (thus securing distribution in the United Kingdom), it appeared that the development of a native film industry might result from the company's endeavors. However, although the company did produce two features—a triptych of shorts directed by John Ford, *The Rising of the Moon* (1957), and a 1964 adaptation of J. M. Synge's *The Playboy of the Western World*—it never engaged in regular production. (As an interesting footnote, the company is still in existence as a production vehicle for Redmond Morris, Killanin's son and sometime **Neil Jordan** producer.)

FRAGMENTS OF ISABELLA **(1989).** Directed by **Ronan O'Leary,** this film, like his debut, *Riders to the Sea*, is based on a stage play, in this case adapted by actress Gabrielle Reidy from the Pulitzer-nominated book by Holocaust survivor Isabella Leitner. *Fragments* was another low-budget shoot for O'Leary: Though feature length at just under 80 minutes, it was completed in a six-day, £150,000 shoot at **Ardmore Studios**. The resulting film is a stark piece of work that does not seek to disguise its stage origins. It stars Reidy, who, sitting against a black backdrop, delivers a monologue recounting Isabella's experience of the Holocaust from being forced to leave her home in

Hungary to being brought to Auschwitz, where she witnesses her mother's death, to her eventual escape while marching to Bergen-Belsen. The resulting sensitively directly film is arguably O'Leary's best-realized work—the monologue sequences are beautifully lit (by veteran cinematographer Walter Lassally) and are interspersed with documentary footage of the concentration camps.

FRANKIE STARLIGHT (1995). Based on American writer Chet Raymo's novel *The Dork of Cork*, the film version directed by Michael Lindsay-Hogg stars Matt Dillon, **Gabriel Byrne**, and Anne Parillaud. Set during World War II, it follows Bernadette, an 18-year-old French girl who escapes her war-torn homeland and has a brief liaison with an American GI, which results in her becoming pregnant before ending up in Ireland. There she falls under the paternalistic wing of married customs officer Jack Kelly (Gabriel Byrne), who looks after her until the birth of her son—a dwarf—whom he teaches about the stars and nicknames Frankie Starlight. Later Bernadette falls in love with Terry (Dillon), who brings her and Frankie to America. Unable to fit in there, however, Bernadette and Frankie return to Ireland, where Frankie matures into a successful writer.

FRICKER, BRENDA (1945–). Major health worries plagued her childhood, which surprisingly aided her acting ability. At 14 Brenda was in a major automobile accident and suffered head injuries, and at 16 she was diagnosed with tuberculosis and was back in the hospital for 18 months. In interviews, she claims that these formative setbacks trained her to keep still for long periods and certainly aided her in developing the character of the strong, stoical, silent mother, a role she portrayed a number of times. She began her acting career in Irish soaps like *Tolka Row* and the British television hospital series *Casualty*. Other television films include **Pat O'Connor**'s *The Ballroom of Romance*, but she came to international prominence through winning an Oscar for her role as Christy Brown's mother in **Jim Sheridan**'s *My Left Foot*.

Fricker has appeared in a large number of Irish as well as non-Irish films over the years, most notably playing the long-suffering older mother in Sheridan's ***The Field***, earlier roles in ***Lamb*** and ***December Bride***, and roles in ***Night Train***, ***Nora***, and ***Veronica Guerin***, among others. Overall she has had a very distinguished acting career to date and remains an important Irish character actor whose name can greatly promote a film project.

A FURTHER GESTURE **(1997).** An imprisoned Irish Republican Army (IRA) man, played by **Stephen Rea**, takes part in a violent jailbreak from the Maze prison in Belfast. Afterward when most are recaptured or killed, Rea escapes to New York and a boring dead-end job. He becomes romantically involved with the sister, Monica, of a South American kitchen porter, Tulio, but learns that both are members of a revolutionary cell dedicated to the overthrow of a dictatorship in their unnamed country. Eventually Rea takes on the job of training them in guerrilla skills.

Written by well-regarded novelist Ronan Bennett, the script, as directed by Robert Dornhelm, becomes somewhat overextended. The conspiracies mount up to a scarcely credible conclusion as the Federal Bureau of Investigation (FBI) surrounds Rea, and, somewhat reminiscent of the closure of *Odd Man Out*, Rea holds up his gun and is shot in a hail of bullets. Passersby who witness these events are informed, "It's just an Irish problem" and are encouraged to pass on and forget what they have seen.

– G –

GAEL LINN. Gael Linn was founded in 1953 by Comhdáil Náisúnta na Gaeilge [National Gaelic Congress]. The Congress had been founded in the early 1940s to coordinate the promotion of the Irish language and culture. Gael Linn was given the remit to use modern media to expand the use of Irish. It commenced film production in 1956 with the production of the *Amharc Eireann* newsreel series. Typically running to four minutes length, each fortnightly "issue" had to convey news, but— with a view to maintaining the interest of a broad-based cinema audience and rejuvenating the Irish language—also had to be entertaining. Thus an individual issue might cover fashion, church ceremonies, or sporting fixtures alongside politics.

The Irish language newsreels continued for seven years until 1964, by which time the arrival of **Radio Telefís Éireann (RTÉ)** and its news service made them superfluous. Nonetheless, the significance of the newsreels went beyond their purely informational content. *Amharc Eireann* allowed Irish audiences to witness their own way of life through native eyes for the first time since the 1910s. In the longer term, the *Amharc Eireann* material has come to constitute a visual archive of a period of massive change in Irish society and remains the most heavily used source of material from that period for contemporary **documentary** makers.

Gael Linn also sought to financially assist established and emerging Irish filmmakers. To this end it produced three major documentary films: *Mise Eire*, its 1961 sequel *Saoirse?*, which covered the period from 1917 to 1922, and, in 1966, a special commemorative film on 1916, *An Tine Bheo*.

Louis Marcus, who acted as an assistant editor on *Mise Eire*, subsequently made a series of documentaries for Gael Linn, culminating in his 1973 short, *Paistí ag Obair*, which won the Critics' Award at the Cork Film Festival, was screened in the London Film Festival, and finally received an Oscar nomination. Unfortunately, this high point coincided with the end of Gael Linn film production when Roinn na Gaeltachta withdrew the organization's annual filmmaking grant.

GALLAGHER, BRONAGH (1972–). Like **Maria Doyle Kennedy**, Northern Irish actress Gallagher came to film acting prominence with her role as Bernie McGloughlin, one of the backup singers in *The Commitments*. (Ironically more than a decade later she would release a critically applauded blues-style album.) She has maintained a presence in Irish cinema, typically playing brittle characters hiding their vulnerability behind coarse exteriors in films like *Divorcing Jack*, *The Most Fertile Man in Ireland*, and *Spin the Bottle*, but has also made small appearances in massive international hits, playing a captain in *Star Wars: Episode 1—The Phantom Menace* (1999), and earlier playing ingénue addict Trudi in Quentin Tarantino's *Pulp Fiction* (1994).

GALVIN, BRENDAN. Starting out as a runner on the U2 film *Rattle and Hum* (1988), Galvin first worked as a clapper loader—the first rung on the ladder to cinematographer—on **Pat O'Connor**'s *Fools of*

Fortune in 1990. Then he worked as cinematographer on a series of early 1990s shorts with director Geraldine Creed. He graduated to focus puller in 1995 on **Frankie Starlight** and became a camera operator on *Curdled* (1996), a low-budget thriller for which Quentin Tarantino was executive producer. In the late 1990s he worked in Germany for a period before returning to Ireland in 2000, where he worked as director of photography on two of the **Samuel Beckett** adaptations produced that year—*Rough for Theatre II* and the 45-second-long *Breath*, directed by Damien Hirst. His major breakthrough, however, came when he photographed the **John Moore**–directed Hollywood hit *Behind Enemy Lines* (2001), a job that led to further Hollywood work, including Joel Schumaker's 2003 take on the Veronica Guerin story and Moore's next blockbuster film, *Flight of the Phoenix* (2004).

GAMBON, MICHAEL (1940–). Gambon appears to be such a quintessentially English actor (he was awarded a CBE by the queen in 1992) that it may come as a surprise to find he was actually born in Dublin. Such Irish roots have eased his passage into recent Irish cinema. His parents—an army officer and a jeweler's daughter—moved to London after World War II and settled in the suburb of Camden, where he attended a Catholic school. His earliest acting experiences were in an amateur theater run by the local Communist Party office, but he turned professional in 1962, working first at the Gate Theatre in Dublin before joining the English National Theatre under the stewardship of Laurence Olivier in 1963. He worked on the stage until the late 1960s, when he began to secure one-off appearances in television dramas, especially police shows such as *Softly, Softly* and the British Broadcasting Corporation's (BBC) *Play for the Day* series. This in turn lead to a series of smaller roles in several early 1970s British horror films, before playing Irish dramatist Oscar Wilde in the 1976 film *Forbidden Passion*, his first leading role in a feature. Interestingly, he auditioned for the role of James Bond after George Lazenby's essay at the role in *O.H.M.S.S.* (1969) was considered to have been a failure. More stage and television work followed, and it was not until the mid-1980s that he developed a substantial body of feature film work.

Nonetheless, his stage and television work in this period won him great critical praise, and he won Laurence Olivier Awards in 1986 and 1988 for his roles in the stage productions of *A Chorus of Disapproval* and Arthur Miller's *A View from the Bridge*, respectively, and has been nominated for the same award on four further occasions. In 1986 he also starred in the critically acclaimed BBC production of Dennis Potter's *The Singing Detective*, for which Gambon won Best Actor awards from the British Film and Television Academy (BAFTA) and the Royal Television Society.

His breakthrough film role came in 1989 with his performance as the vulgar thief in Peter Greenaway's visually sumptuous *The Cook, The Thief, His Wife and Her Lover* (1989). This brought him to the attention of Hollywood, first in Barry Levinson's *Toys* (1992) opposite Robin Williams, then in a series of forgettable B movies. In the later half of the decade, however, as Gambon's star rose, so did the quality of his roles, and he has become a recognizable character actor on the strength of appearances in Tim Burton's *Sleepy Hollow* (1999), Michael Mann's *The Insider* (1999), and more recently Wes Anderson's *The Life Aquatic with Steve Zissou* (2004). Confirmation of his Hollywood star status came when he was chosen to succeed the late **Richard Harris** in the role of Dumbledore in the *Harry Potter* series.

His first appearance in an Irish film came in 1994, when he appeared opposite Albert Finney's Oscar Wilde–obsessed character in *A Man of No Importance*. This was followed by the role of Leonard, leader of a loyalist terror gang in **Thaddeus O'Sullivan**'s *Nothing Personal*, and then two quite different roles in **Pat O'Connor**'s *Dancing at Lughnasa* as the amiable Father Jack Mundy and as the scion of an Anglo-Irish family in Deborah Warner's adaptation of Elizabeth Bowen's novel *The Last September*. He returned to the role of gangster—albeit a less menacing one—for his most recent Irish role, that of Barreler, in **Conor McPherson**'s *The Actors*. He had previously worked with McPherson on the latter's version of Samuel Beckett's *Endgame* (2000), which was produced as part of the larger Beckett on Film project that saw all of the playwright's stage works filmed for the big screen.

THE GENERAL **(1998). John Boorman** directed **Brendan Gleeson** in a sympathetic portrayal of the real-life figure of Martin Cahill (aka

"The General"), a leading Dublin criminal who was murdered in the mid-1990s. Working from the autobiography by Dublin crime journalist Paul Williams, Boorman is at pains to put Cahill's criminality into a social context, portraying the young Cahill as the product of extreme poverty. This is tacitly recognized by Cahill's lifelong antagonist, Inspector Ned Kenny (Jon Voight), who maintains a grudging respect for the criminal even while trying to catch him.

In contrast to Thaddeus O'Sullivan's more Hollywood-style take on the same person (***Ordinary Decent Criminal***), however, there is no attempt to sanitize Cahill's character: His willingness to resort to brutal methods, for example, is vividly depicted. Furthermore, although the film celebrates Cahill's single-minded determination to live his life according to his own precepts (Cahill maintained simultaneous relationships with two women, who both lived with him, and the children by the respective relationships), he is not depicted in a heroic mode: The film's grisly conclusion amply demonstrates how badly he has underestimated the lengths to which the state and paramilitary organizations are willing to go to "remove" him.

Having shot the film in color Boorman decided to desaturate the film in postproduction, rendering the finished picture black and white. The effect is to afford the story a deeper sense of social realism and avoid what Boorman termed the prettification and romanticization of poverty. He was also at pains to distance the story from conventional gangster tropes: "We're not fucking Eye-talians" exclaims Cahill when one of his henchmen attempts to embrace him.

The film was critically regarded as a return to form for Boorman, after the disappointing performance of films like *Where the Heart Is* (1990) and *Beyond Rangoon* (1995). *The General* earned him Best Director nominations in a number of festival and critic awards, and he won Best Director at the 1998 Cannes Film Festival. Surprisingly, this was the director's first film with an overtly Irish setting, although he has lived in the country for over three decades.

***THE GENTLE GUNMAN* (1952).** Scripted by Roger McDougall from his play and produced at Ealing Studios by Michael Balcon Productions, the film features a stellar cast of John Mills, Dirk Bogarde, Elizabeth Sellers, and Gilbert Harding. Directed by Basil Dearden, it tells the story of Terry, who, after working undercover in wartime

London, reconsiders his support for the Irish Republican Army (IRA) and questions the need for violence to achieve independence. However, by adapting a position of peaceful persuasion, he is soon branded a traitor by his brother and more hard-line IRA colleagues.

GEORGE, TERRY (1952–). George was born in Northern Ireland and was interned in prison in Long Kesh for a time for suspected involvement with the republican movement. He has written and produced plays at Irish Arts Center in New York City since the late 1980s—along with **Jim Sheridan**—and combined his theatrical and prison experience by coscripting *In the Name of the Father*.

George went on to write and direct another very influential "**troubles**" film, *Some Mother's Son* (1996), which deals with republican prisoners hunger striking to gain political status. The tragic inevitability of the conflict of wills that underpinned the hunger strike and the parallel creation of republican martyrs is carried through the documentary structure of the film. At one level the hunger strike was successful; following the death of Bobby Sands and others, the prisoners got all they demanded—political status. This political reality served to counter the assertion at the start of the film by the British governor, who demanded that politically motivated violence be "criminalized" to avoid the perception that the Irish Republican Army (IRA) and their loyalist counterparts were engaged in "a war." Linguistic and other distinctions between "criminality" and "political activity" have plagued Northern Ireland and have been well articulated, if overromanticized and occluded in film generally. Violent conflicts have been used as a convenient backdrop for dramatic fiction.

George also wrote the screenplay for *Hart's War* (2002) and most recently received plaudits for *Hotel Rwanda* (2004), which he also directed. Nominated for an Oscar, it won him Best Director at the 2005 Irish film and television awards. The film is set within the turbulent violence of Rwanda following the assassination of President Habyarimana, which sparked ethnic majority Hutu extremists to begin a systematic genocide of nearly one million Tutsis and moderate Hutus. The film focuses on Paul Rusesabagina (Don Cheadle), who turns the hotel where he works into a sanctuary. Nick Nolte, playing Canadian Colonel Oliver, tells him, "You're worse than a nigger, you're African!" But of course, against all odds Rusesabagina succeeds in his quest to save many lives.

Strains of *Schindler's List* (1993) pervade the overall story structure, as the film plays on the surreal nightmarish scenario. Nobody comes to the aid of the refugees, and one man has to take a stand. Critically the movie tries too hard to get its message across, as the feel-good ending takes too long to develop. But such an important true story needs to be told, and George must receive credit for using all his creative skill to represent global realities that rarely if ever get into mainstream white-dominated filmmaking.

GILLEN, AIDAN (1968–). The youngest member of a family of six from Drumcondra, Aidan Gillen was born Aidan Murphy but later changed his name to avoid confusion with an established actor of the same name. He started acting as a child with the Dublin Youth Theatre, which used the Project Arts Centre for many of their performances. Consequently, he was exposed to productions by other companies using the same theater, such as the early work of the Rough Magic and Passion Machine companies. His film debut came at 18 with a bit part in Jack Clayton's *The Lonely Passion of Judith Hearne*, which he followed with another small part in *The Courier*.

His breakthrough role involved a return to the stage, however, when he secured a part in a London production of Wexford playwright Billy Roche's *A Handful of Stars*. After he reprised the role for a television version, British director Antonia Bird cast him in a lead role in her homelessness drama, *Safe* (1993). This was followed by a series of roles in Ireland including *Circle of Friends, Gold in the Streets*, and the key role of a hunger striker in *Some Mother's Son*.

However, in the United Kingdom he is probably still best known for his portrayal of Stuart, an abrasive yet charming and hedonistic gay man at the center of **Channel 4**'s *Queer as Folk* (1998–). Unperturbed by the risk of typecasting, Gillen embraced the role with relish and stole every scene he appeared in. Although he has followed *Folk* with a number of low-budget independent pictures since 2000, he has increasingly worked in the United States (although he lives with his wife and children in North London). Following a made-for-TV movie, *The Darkling* (2000), he has worked on Broadway, earning a Tony nomination for his role in a production of Harold Pinter's

The Caretaker. However, his highest-profile U.S. role to date—aside from a turn in the Jackie Chan vehicle *Shanghai Knights* (2003)—has been as a Baltimore city council member, Tommy Carcetti, in the hit Home Box Office (HBO) series *The Wire*. He has also managed to maintain an ongoing presence in Irish film throughout this period with a number of shorts—most notably in the well-received *Burning the Bed* (2004)—and most recently starring in Fintan Connolly's second feature, ***Trouble with Sex***.

GILLIGAN, DONAL. Much like that of **Brendan Galvin,** Gilligan's career illustrates the positive and negative sides of the post-1993 upsurge in Irish filmmaking activity. Having worked on ***Hear My Song*** as a clapper loader he made an immediate impact as a cinematographer when he photographed Stephen Bourke's awarding-winning short, set during the civil rights movements in Northern Ireland, *After '68*. He immediately followed that with another lighting cameraman job on Joe Comerford's ***High Boot Benny***.

However, although he secured work on that portion of Steven Spielberg's *Saving Private Ryan* (1998) that was shot in Wexford, he was downgraded to assistant camera operator, a common fate among Irish technicians working on both indigenous and foreign films made in Ireland. Nonetheless, like a number of other Irish cinematographers, he worked on two of the Samuel Beckett adaptations—*Rough for Theatre I* and *Endgame* (both 2000) before doing some television work on **TV3**'s *Watermelon* (2003) and BBC Northern Ireland's *Pulling Moves* (2004). He has twice been nominated for an Irish Film & Television Best Cinematography award for his work on ***Dead Bodies*** and ***Omagh***.

GILSENAN, ALAN (1962–). When he was 24 he and producer Martin Mahon set up a production company, Yellow Asylum, to preserve their creative independence. Quickly caricatured by the media as an "angry young man" of the Irish cinema, he forged a strong reputation for himself. Gilsenan's wide-ranging creative interests extended to theater with his adaptation of John Banville's *The Book of Evidence*, but on reflection he affirmed that his artistic temperament was best suited to filmmaking since, he claims, it allows him to plough his own path more easily.

The bulk of Gilsenan's filmed work has been in the documentary form, where he has focused on examining transitional periods of modern life. In *Stories from the Silence* he examined AIDS in Ireland before there was any real concern. In *Prophet Songs* he tackled the issue of disenchanted priests who left the Church. However the piece of work that garnered the greatest public attention in the 1980s was *The Road to God Knows Where*, a state of the nation piece commissioned by **Channel 4,** which perfectly captured the pessimism of 1980s Ireland and which won the Special Jury Prize at the 1989 European Film Awards.

His documentaries have also arguably informed his fiction work, which on both a visual and a narrative level are instantly recognizable as his. Visually adventurous, he intercuts between different formats — Super 8, 16 mm, and digital video — at a fierce pace in nearly all of his recent works in what might be interpreted as an attempt to offer simultaneous multiple perspectives on his stories. He is also noted for taking established narratives and placing them in new settings. Thus the soundtrack of his powerful 2001 short *Zulu 9*, which traces an illegal immigrant's entry into Ireland, is overlaid with actor Brian Cox's voice intoning Joseph Conrad's *Heart of Darkness*. Similarly, his first feature — **All Souls' Day** (1997) — overtly derives its themes from Oscar Wilde's *Ballad of Reading Gaol*.

Of Gilsenan's two features, *All Souls' Day* is the more difficult work, which even he has described as "experimental." A mother visits her daughter's murderer — and former boyfriend — in prison in an attempt to understand his actions. He begins telling the story of their relationship, and as he does so, the film stock becomes grainier, placing a temporal distance between the characters and the narrated events. His explanation for his action, however, is obtuse and vague, although it ultimately implicates the mother in his actions. She comes to the prison seeking clarification, a straightforward explanation for her loss; instead the very narrative of the film itself denies such a neat closure, hinting at the ephemerality and contingency of events.

Similar themes are present in Gilsenan's more recent feature **Timbuktu**. Although reminiscent in ways of his 1999 documentary *Julie's Journey*, which traces the story of a modern Irish woman who traveled to Japan to become a Buddhist, *Timbuktu* is based on a screenplay by screenwriter Paul Freaney. Set in Algeria (although shot in

Morocco), the oblique narrative explores the contemporary global issues within Irish identity using a very broad geographical and experimental canvas. Three childhood friends, all victims of some unspeakable childhood trauma, embark on voyages to rediscover their own identities, transforming the film into a kind of road movie, albeit one where it is never clear if the final destination has been reached or not.

Gilsenan continues to work with a broad range of issues, as most recently evidenced in his haunting evocation of a Dublin mental hospital in a television series, *Asylum* (RTÉ, 2005), which effectively dramatizes the underbelly of mental disorder in Ireland that has for so long been kept hidden from everyday society. The documentary has the patience to tell the life story of a number of inmates over a period of time, while maintaining a balance between voyeuristic observation and respect for human dignity.

When not directing Gilsenan also finds time to chair the **Irish Film Institute** and to act as a member of the **Irish Film Board**.

***GIVE UP YER AUL SINS* (2002).** This **animated** series, nominated for an Oscar, was produced by the small indigenous Irish company Brown Bag Films, itself the brainchild of director-producer Cathal Gaffney and director Darragh O'Connell. In a brilliant visual coup, Gaffney took accounts of biblical stories given by children from a poverty-stricken inner-city school, which were recorded for **Radio Telefís Éireann (RTÉ)** radio during the 1960s, and illustrated them with faux-sepia-toned cartoons. The series (which was subsequently released on VHS and DVD) has helped to promote the possibility of a small indigenous animation industry (indeed, it has raised the hitherto unconsidered possibility of an animated counterpart to national cinema: national animation), and the endearing innocence of children in these animated films remains their number-one selling point for child and adult alike. This is often the reason provided for why Disney has been so universally successful and why *Give Up Yer Aul Sins* succeeded at the box office.

GLEESON, BRENDAN (1955–). Despite having come to professional acting relatively late in life, Gleeson has become one of Ireland's best known screen actors both at home and internationally. Born in Artane

on Dublin's north side, he expressed an interest in acting from childhood, and on leaving school he and several ex-classmates started an
acting group. Around the same time he met Paul Mercier, later a key
collaborator, while attending university.

On leaving university Gleeson became a teacher, working at Bel-
camp College for a decade, where he taught English and Irish. At the
same time, however, he became a key figure in Passion Machine, a
theater group established by Paul Mercier in 1984 to produce works
reflecting contemporary Ireland. Passion Machine's work was deliberately populist and included material by Mercier himself (most of
which Gleeson appeared in), **Roddy Doyle**, and **Gerry Stembridge**.
Gleeson wrote and directed three plays for the company, including
Breaking Up and *The Birdtable*.

In 1989, at the age of 34, Gleeson quit teaching to pursue a
professional acting career. His first major role came in an **Abbey
Theatre** production of Eugene McCabe's *King of the Castle*. However, from the outset, Gleeson was able to slip between stage, television, and film roles. He secured a recurring role on *Radio Telefís
Éireann* (**RTÉ**) soap *Glenroe* and began to build up a range of
smaller roles in Irish films of the early 1990s. His most prominent
early screen role was in the television drama *The Treaty* (1990), in
which he played Michael Collins. (He would also appear in the **Neil
Jordan**'s 1996 biopic of the same character, but not in the lead
role.)

Some hint of his future success emerged when in 1994 he was cast
as William Wallace's boyhood friend Hamish Campbell in Mel Gibson's *Braveheart*, a film that brought him—however briefly—to the
attention of an American audience for the first time. He followed this
with a series of fourth- and fifth-billed appearances in *Trojan Eddie*,
Spaghetti Slow, *The Butcher Boy*, and *A Further Gesture*. (He also
received second billing opposite Mia Farrow on *Angela Mooney
Dies Again*, but the film's invisible impact at the box office did little
for Gleeson's career.) However, his seemingly inexorable rise was
accelerated by two films in 1997 and 1998, respectively, *I Went
Down*, and *The General*. He played a professional criminal in both
films, and although on paper the roles of Bunny Kelly (*I Went Down*)
and Martin Cahill were similar, he produced two entirely different
but equally eye-catching performances. The influential Boston Soci-

ety of Film Critics recognized this when they gave him the Best Actor award in 1998 for—unusually—both performances.

This led to a series of calls from Hollywood, first in horror-thriller *Lake Placid* (1999), then in *Mission Impossible II* (2000), Steven Spielberg's *Artificial Intelligence* (2001), and Martin Scorsese's *Gangs of New York* (2002). He has now become an established presence in films originating on both sides of the Atlantic, a position cemented by his role in *Cold Mountain* (2003), *Troy* (2004), and as Mad-Eye Moody in *Harry Potter and the Goblet of Fire* (2005). He has also maintained a presence—albeit a more occasional one—in Irish cinema: He appeared in Martin McDonagh's acclaimed short *Six Shooter* (2004) and Neil Jordan's *Breakfast on Pluto*, and in a neat symmetry, he played the lead in Paul Mercier's feature debut, *Studs* (2005), based on the latter's own 1986 play. Ironically it is virtually the only Mercier play from the 1980s that Gleeson did not appear in on stage.

GOGAN, JOHNNY (1963–). Born in Sussex, England, he obtained a degree in politics and history at University College Dublin, after which he wrote for the *Irish Times* on Latin American politics. He was a founding member (with his sister, Jane Gogan, and Trish McAdam) of the Ha'penny Film Club in 1985 and later became very active in **Film Base** and edited ***Film Ireland*** for a while before going on to concentrate on film writing and directing.

The Bargain Shop (1992) is a television drama that dealt with contentious issues around inner-city redevelopment and the pressures of commercialism. Gogan's next film, ***The Last Bus Home*** (1997), reflects on the hollow idealism of the Celtic Tiger economy. His most recent film, ***The Mapmaker*** (2001), set in County Fermanagh, tells the story of a cartographer who discovers more than he expected—a body buried years ago. Unfortunately the film was unsuccessful at the box office.

GOLD IN THE STREETS **(1996).** Directed by Elizabeth Gill and starring Ian Hart, **Lorraine Pilkington**, and **Aidan Gillen**, the film is unusual in that it takes as its theme a subject often ignored in contemporary Irish cinema—**emigration.** Liam, a young Irish man, arrives at a bar in New York to find that unfortunately his only contact in the city has left suddenly for fear of being caught as an illegal immigrant. Mario (James Belushi), the well-connected barman, saves the day by introducing him to another native, Des, who immediately invites him to stay in his apartment along with his friend Paddy and another cousin. Liam quickly fits into the lifestyle of working illegally by day and living it up at night. Over time, however, this nomadic existence takes its toll, most markedly at Christmas, when some of the gang go back home to Ireland, while the others—unsure if they will be able to reenter the United States if they leave—remain in New York, homesick and unsure of their future. Mario observes at one stage how depression is endemic in Ireland, which frames one of the story lines of a character who is unable to buy into the American dream, with resultant tragic consequences. This engaging character story is well observed and includes an amusing cameo role by Tom Hickey as a drunk who is still lonely in New York after being there for over 35 years.

GOLDFISH MEMORY **(2004). Flora Montgomery**, Sean Campion, Fiona Glascott, and Fiona O'Shaughnessy star in this sophisticated and well-crafted comedy of manners directed by Liz Gill that deals with lesbian and heterosexual relationships. *See also* HOMOSEXUALITY.

The title evokes the ephemerality of relationships in modern Dublin. Time-lapse photography of O'Connell Street, the Liffey bridges, and most frequently the Dublin docks as ships come in and go out punctuates the narrative, both evoking the ebb and flow of time and providing an evocative sense of place. Demarcations between work and leisure are clearly articulated, and the film demonstrates how day-job roles as teachers, students, barmen, and the like affect the characters' worldview and behavior. The tone of the sharp dialogue, delivered by a strong ensemble cast, is reminiscent of a Woody Allen script. A memorable lecherous teacher with contrived chat-up lines is typical of the characters we meet; yet, in the end, even he redeems himself by meeting the right girl and settling down. The film pushes the feel-good but also rather conservative trajectory of the story line—the teacher rediscovers his true creative voice and starts writing poetry again rather than producing sterile academic papers. The goldfish motif is continued through the many cosmopolitan spaces as the various alternative characters struggle to find love and long-term mates in the endless dance of the sexes.

***GUESTS OF THE NATION* (1935).** Based on a short story by Frank O'Connor and set during the War of Independence, this 40-minute silent film directed by Denis Johnson traces the dawning awareness of some Irish Republican Army (IRA) volunteers that two English soldiers in their custody will have to be executed (thus anticipating **Neil Jordan**'s later script for *The Crying Game*). Made on a shoestring budget in a studio constructed in a Dublin back garden, the film enjoyed the tacit support of the then Fianna Fáil government; minister for defense Frank Aitken arranged for the supply of army uniforms as costumes, and he attended the premiere at the Gate Theatre in January 1936. Director Johnston was better known as a playwright associated with the Gate Theatre, and the cast (which includes **Barry Fitzgerald** and **Cyril Cusack**) relied heavily on Gate and **Abbey** actors. The film was warmly received on its release but represented Johnson's only dalliance with screen directing.

***GUILTRIP* (1995).** The film traces a day in the life of a dysfunctional young couple and arrived at an apposite moment—in the middle of referendum on the introduction of divorce to Ireland. Directed by **Gerry Stembridge**, the film follows 24 hours in the troubled relationship between Liam (Andrew Connolly) and Tina (Jasmine Russell). Conjugal relations have ceased, and it becomes clear that the whole basis of their relationship is flawed—Liam, an army corporal, has extended the behavior of the parade ground into the domestic sphere, where an atmosphere of fear and tension prevails. Thus a subsidiary theme emerges: the contradiction between the authoritarian nature associated with the military and the behavioral norms of society at large. In short, what happens when a soldier goes home?

Stembridge's intricately structured script proceeds by comparing Tina's day and Liam's night via a series of parallel edits. During the day, quiet, nervy Tina chats or flirts with Ronnie (Peter Hanly), the hapless owner of the local electronics shop, while that night during a drinking session, the domineering Liam eyes Michelle (Michelle Houlden), who happens to be Ronnie's wife. Michelle and Ronnie's relationship also faces difficulties, Michelle clearly despising her husband's cheerful idiocy.

The use of different viewpoints in cinema often comments on the very process of representation: As one account clashes with another, so the objectivity and accuracy of both are questioned. In using this technique the film is at least reminiscent of a European art-house preoccupation with this theme and the aesthetic realism and playful debates about identity that dominate such film cultures.

GUINEY, ED. *See* ELEMENT FILMS.

– H –

H FOR HAMLET **(1993).** The film stars Vinny Murphy (who also directs), Jack Lynch, and most importantly the working-class students of Jobstown Community College, who undertake a performance of Shakesphere's *Hamlet*. On any level *H for Hamlet* is an audacious undertaking: Not only does director Murphy attempt to produce a feature film on effectively no budget, but he also does so with an almost entirely nonprofessional cast of kids who would not traditionally be regarded as candidates for exposure to such high culture. Furthermore, the approach to the material is radical: The action is transposed from the 16th-century Danish court to the contemporary urban setting of Tallaght in Dublin. The story dramatizes the power of drama to affect people's lives and learn from the experience, as is the aim of many art-based community projects.

H3 **(2001).** This film was written by Brian Campbell and Laurence McKeown, a former republican prisoner who spent over 70 days on hunger strike but survived when his mother intervened after he fell into a coma. McKeown subsequently wrote a doctoral thesis at Queens University entitled "Unrepentant Fenian Bastards: The Social Construction of an Irish Republican Prisoner Community." *H3* is a fictionalized dramatization of the events between the ending of the first aborted hunger strike in 1981 and the death of Bobby Sands. The narrative is directed by Les Blair and told from a uniquely republican perspective that unproblematically posits that the hunger strikes were a last-resort response to the British government's refusal to recognize Irish Republican Army (IRA) members as political prisoners and thus acknowledge the political realities of the day in Northern Ireland. The film prompted renewed criticism of the **Irish Film Board**'s support for overtly nationalist projects and its failure to support other perspectives on the "troubles." For its part the board responded that it could fund only those projects placed before it. In any case, the fact that the film was also supported by the **Northern Ireland Film and Television Commission** mollified some of those critics who accused the Film Board of partisanship.

HALL, TOM. *See* CARNEY, JOHN, AND TOM HALL.

***THE HALO EFFECT* (2002).** Directed by Lance Daly and starring **Stephen Rea**, Simon Delaney, Fiona O'Shaughnessy, and **Mick Lally**, *The Halo Effect* tells the story of Fatso (Lally), who is the proprietor of one of the worst restaurants in the city. The business is struggling to survive Fatso's compulsive gambling as an endless succession of loan sharks and debt collectors look for a slice of the meager profits. Nevertheless, he seems to be holding things together until circumstances greatly affect his condition. In a poker game against a local crime boss he bets his chipper, and the result causes his business to come under its biggest threat ever. The tone of the film deftly changes from comedy to violence and at times even exhibits traces of absurd drama.

HARRIS, RICHARD (1930–2002). He had a long and distinguished international acting career while remaining committed to Limerick and his homeland. On screen he was famous for his earthy Shakespearian qualities and for being a versatile, adventurous, intense, and richly talented all-round actor. Eulogies by his fellow actors, including **Peter O'Toole**, **Liam Neeson**, and **Gabriel Byrne**, spoke of him being a "horse of a man" and never a pampered dilettante. He starred in over 70 films. His most famous Irish outing remains his defining role as the Bull McCabe in **Jim Sheridan**'s *The Field*, which he made his own, taking the project on following the sudden death of **Ray McAnally**. In 1995, he also starred in *Trojan Eddie* in a powerful role as king of the Travellers. Other notable international films include *This Sporting Life* (1963), reflecting his love of rugby, *A Man Called Horse* (1972), and most recently *Gladiator* (1992). His colorful off-screen Irish persona and various scandals helped to produce maximum publicity for the films he was in rather than having any negative effect on his career. He also starred in a wide range of action adventure narratives including *Major Dundee* (1965), *Camelot* (1967), *Cromwell* (1970), *Juggernaut* (1974), *Cassandra Crossing* (1977), *Gulliver's Travels* (1977), and *Wild Geese* (1978).

HEAR MY SONG (1991). Starring American actor Ned Beatty, **Adrian Dunbar** (who also coscripted the film with director Peter Chelsom), and Tara Fitzgerald, *Hear My Song* tells the story of Micky O'Neill, a music hall owner in England desperately trying to keep his business alive. At one stage, when business is particularly bad, he books the act of a man posing as legendary Irish tenor Joseph Locke. However, his situation becomes impossible when he assaults his former girlfriend, Cathleen. Desperate to redeem himself, he sets out on a journey "back in time" in Ireland to find the real-life Joseph Locke (played with conviction by Beatty) and bring him back to sing. This effective feel-good story, which was budgeted at around $2 million, successfully echoed *Eat the Peach*'s theme of flawed ambition.

HELLO STRANGER (1992). Directed by **Ronan O'Leary**, the film tells the story of T. C. (Daniel J. Travanti), who reluctantly keeps his annual dinner date with his old school friend and now stockbroker George Claxton (Tim McDonnell). He immediately notes, however, a deterioration in George's physical and mental condition. Over the course of the meal Claxton recounts how a correspondence he began with a lonely 12-year-old girl, after finding her "message in a bottle" on a Long Island beach, has created a scandal, ruining his personal and professional life.

Based on a Truman Capote short story, the film was made on an enclosed studio set, rendering it self-consciously stagebound. Although the film suffered from *longeurs*, especially in the opening scenes, tension does build over its 60-minute duration, as it becomes clear that what Claxton insists started as a joke has taken on more sinister overtones. The film was nominated for four awards at the 1993 Monte Carlo Television Festival.

HELL'S KITCHEN. Jim Sheridan and Arthur Lappin established Hell's Kitchen in 1993 in the wake of the critical and commercial successes of Sheridan's *My Left Foot* (1989) and *The Field* (1990), both of which Lappin line-produced. For nearly a decade the company enjoyed a first-look relationship with Universal, which, although it ended in 2000, effectively underwrote the construction of one of the few Irish production companies with experience across a broad range of production types and budgets.

Before teaming up with Sheridan, Arthur Lappin worked as a theater and stage producer for 18 years and was, for a period, drama and dance officer with the Arts Council of Ireland. Lappin has acted as a fully fledged producer on all of Sheridan's feature work from *In The Name of the Father* to *The Boxer* and *In America*. However, the company is not solely a vehicle for Jim Sheridan's talents; Lappin also produced **Terry George**'s *Some Mother's Son*, Angelica Huston's *Agnes Browne*, Peter (brother of Jim) Sheridan's *Borstal Boy*, and Paul Greengrass's *Bloody Sunday*.

The company has also developed a relationship with another major Irish producer, **Element Films**, leading to collaborations on **John Carney**'s *On the Edge* and Pete Travis's *Omagh*. The partnership was formalized with the establishment of Hell's Kitchen International, which aims to build on the creative, technical, and financial experience of both companies by offering a complete production support structure to foreign production companies working in Ireland. Projects to date include **Irish Dreamtime**'s *Laws of Attraction* and the Paramount-funded remake of the 1950s U.S. sitcom *The Honeymooners*.

HENNESSY **(1975).** Produced by **Roger Corman**'s American International Pictures, directed by Don Sharp, and starring Rod Steiger, Lee Remick, and Trevor Howard, this controversial drama was denied a widespread release and was generally regarded as exploiting the Northern **"troubles"** for cheap entertainment. Hennessy is a demolition officer who has broken his links with the republican movement in a bid to leave his violent past behind him. However, when his wife and daughter are killed in an outbreak of sectarian violence, he seeks revenge through a plot to blow up the Houses of Parliament on the day of the official opening by the queen. The thriller format follows attempts by both the Irish Republican Army (IRA) and the British counterterrorist agencies to stop him carrying out his plans.

HIBERNIA FILMS, 1933. Killarney garage owner Tom Cooper established Hibernia Films in 1933 to facilitate the production of *The Dawn*. Despite that film's commercial success, the company made one only more picture, *Uncle Nick* (of which there is no known surviving copy). By the early 1940s Cooper had exhausted his interest in production and sought to sell the Hibernia Studios (built specifically for *The Dawn*) to the state as the basis of a national film studio. Cooper's general interest in cinema was sustained, however, by a move into **exhibition**: By the end of the 1940s he had acquired several theaters in Killarney, Doneraile, and Tramore.

HIBERNIA FILMS, 1945. Not to be confused with Tom Cooper's earlier production company of the same name, Hibernia Films was established in 1945 by Michael Scott (who would later become involved in **Four Provinces**), Stephen O'Flaherty, William Moylan, and cameraman **George Fleischmann**. After starting operations with a documentary on Michael Davitt, the company went on to produce the Michael Scott–directed documentary short *The Silent Order* in 1948. However, considering that the company mainly sought to produce promotional and informational films for the state at a time when the state evinced relatively little interest in such activities, it was a part-time exercise for most of the partners (with the exception of Fleischmann, whose sole stock-in-trade was camerawork). Indeed, by 1949, despite the company's having produced two further films— *Next Please* and *Voyage to Recovery* for the Department of Health and *Lifeline* for Irish Shipping—Fleischmann opted to take on a more secure line of work, supplying film for Movietone in London. The company appears to have effectively ceased operations after that point.

The most interesting member of Hibernia Films was William Moylan. A former journalist, he entered the British film industry in 1927 as cinematographer and between 1936 and 1942 was in charge of production at various studios. He also worked as film producer and adviser for both the (preindependence) Indian and (postindependence) Pakistani government. He would return to Ireland in the 1960s, establishing Munster House Productions in Bray, County Wicklow.

HICKEY, KIERAN (1936–1993). Unusually for an Irish director, Hickey studied film formally in London before returning to Dublin, where, with cameraman Sean Corcoran and editor **J. Patrick Duffner** at B.A.C. Films, he produced a series of documentaries for state agencies and films about writers such as Jonathan Swift and James Joyce. In the promotional material for a festival of Irish film (The Green on the Screen) in 1984 he made some telling comments about how "Ireland on film has always been a dream country. We countered this with no filmic output of our own. So we must not complain if what films show of us is not 'real.' This was the choice we deliberately made. Ireland left the world's screens dark when it might have painted them green." Hickey wrote several books, including *The Dublin of James Joyce's Ulysses* (Ward River Press, 1982). His filmic output, which is highly regarded for its questioning of Irish patriarchal norms and innovative style, includes *A Child's Voice*, *Exposure*, *Criminal Conversation*, and *The Rockingham Shoot*.

He debuted as a fiction director with the short *A Child's Voice* in 1978. Coscripted with film critic David Thomson (who would later eulogize Hickey as "his best friend" in Thomson's *Biographical Dictionary of Film*), the film is a gothic tale about a writer (**T. P. McKenna**) who broadcasts his Le Fanu–esque tales three nights a week but who one night finds his own fictional creation turning upon him. The film, which pays homage to classic horror films of the 1940s, received extremely positive reviews, winning a prize at the 1978 Chicago International Film Festival.

The same year saw the production of Hickey's first collaboration with screenwriter Philip Davison, *Exposure*. Funded by an Arts Council Script award, the film deals explicitly with the reaction of Irish males to "the other"—here represented by a continental female—while at the same time highlighting their sexual repression and the cultural insularity of Ireland in the late 1970s. The film tells the story of three male friends who are away from home on a job and become interested in a French photographer whom they meet. Their middle-class misogyny belies a deeply felt critique of Irish masculinity.

Hickey's next collaboration with Davison was *Criminal Conversation* (1980), which starred Emmett Bergin, Deirdre Connelly, and Garret Keogh and dealt with two apparently happy and secure professional married couples living in suburbia. But at a Christmas party during a game of Charades, the happy façade of the couples disintegrates with alacrity. Revelations of extramarital affairs serve to irrevocably break up the comfort of their normal lives. While at a formal level the piece appears more theatrical, the visualization of the conflicts is effectively handled and well regarded, dovetailing with contemporary public debates about divorce in the country.

Attracta (1983) was considered by many to have been Hickey's most ambitious undertaking, based on a screen version of William Trevor's short story of the same name and adapted by the author. The veteran stage and screen actress Wendy Hiller was signed to play the role of the spinster teacher who visits the grave of a Belfast victim of violence, evoking her own memories. The strong supporting cast includes Kate Thompson, **John Kavanagh**, and Deirdre Donnelly. Hickey also directed a well-received adaptation of John McGahern's *The Rockingham Shoot* for the BBC in 1987.

Hickey's brother Des, a noted film critic and journalist who had been instrumental in the original establishment of B.A.C. Films in the mid 1960s, died suddenly in June 1992. Sadly, barely a year later in July 1993, Hickey himself passed away; having survived open-heart surgery, he suffered an embolism and died almost immediately. The timing of his passing was doubly sad given that it coincided with the reemergence of regular production activity in Ireland, which would doubtless have afforded him new opportunities to work. David Thomson said of his death, "He was the best friend I'll ever have, and in a way I feel the movies are over now that he's gone" (Thomson, 1994, 339).

HIDDEN AGENDA **(1990).** Well-known British socialist filmmaker Ken Loach sets this conspiracy thriller in Northern Ireland. The film was scripted by his longtime writing partner, Jim Allen. When an American human rights lawyer (Brad Dourif) is assassinated in Belfast, his girlfriend (Frances McDormand) and a senior police detective (Brian Cox) try to uncover the truth. They discover that the dead lawyer held an audiotape implicating political leaders within the highest level of the British establishment in illegal acts committed in the prosecution of the war against the Irish Republican Army (IRA). Although relatively effective as a thriller, it was heavily criticized in the United Kingdom for its manipulation of political realities for entertainment, coming as it did in the wake of official intervention to prevent a similar real-life investigation by senior police officer John Stalker into the operation of a shoot-to-kill policy on the part of British forces in Northern Ireland.

HIGGINS, MICHAEL D. (1941–). Higgins is highly unusual for an Irish politician in that he is a published poet of some renown who came to politics from an academic background. As a politician he has been uniquely successful in pushing through a film arts agenda in Ireland and setting the tone for its legitimacy within government policy. Educated at University College, Galway (UCG) and in Illinois and Manchester, he became a lecturer in political science at UCG. He became a Labour Party senator in 1973 before winning his first Dáil election in 1981. He lost his seat in 1982 and returned to the Senate before successfully contesting the 1987 general election and has been a TD ever since.

Labour's spectacular success at the 1992 elections (still the party's best-ever result), was followed by long-drawn-out negotiations with Fine Gael and Fianna Fáil with a view to establishing the next administration. Part of those negotiations included creating a new ministry with responsibility for arts, culture, and the Gaeltacht, areas that had hitherto fallen within the bailiwick of the Department of Industry and Commerce and the Department of the Taoiseach. When those negotiations resulted in a Fianna Fáil–Labour coalition, "Michael D." (as he is colloquially known) was appointed minister to the new department, a decision that was hailed within filmmaking circles as promising the return of the **Irish Film Board**. However, initially Higgins was somewhat cautious, suggesting that it might be 1996 before the film support structures suggested by documents such as the *Coopers and Lybrand Report* were fully in place.

However, as a pragmatic politician, Higgins seized the political opportunity gifted to him by **Neil Jordan**'s success at the 1993 **Academy**

Awards, reestablishing the Film Board within 24 hours of that ceremony. He subsequently drove through the establishment of the Independent Production Unit at **RTÉ**, the setting up of the Irish-language television station TG4, and the creation of the **Irish Screen Commission** as a subsidiary of the Irish Film Board. He has always been a great polemicist and orator, as reflected in his assertion regarding the importance of homegrown production and media literacy and the need for Irish filmmakers to make images that actively reflect and enrich national culture.

***HIGH BOOT BENNY* (1993).** Although director **Joe Comerford** had been working on the script for *High Boot Benny* since the mid-1970s, it wasn't until the reestablishment of the **Irish Film Board** that he was able to secure the financing to actually make it. Set in an alternative school located on the site of a former British fort near the border with Northern Ireland, the highly metaphorical narrative centers on three marginalized characters who constitute a kind of family grouping: Benny (Marc O'Shea), an emotionally damaged student, is the "son" of ex-priest Manley (Alan Devlin) and the school's Protestant matron (**Frances Tomelty**).

The border setting of the school is significant; the school attempts to forge a path outside the strictures of the politics informing the activities of the British Army and loyalist and nationalist paramilitaries. Initially Benny tries to embrace the idealism of the school's mission, but when a naked body is found near the school, the entire institution is drawn into the clash between local military and paramilitary forces. Writer Martin McLoone has noted that the tragedy of the film is that Benny is unable to escape the dogmas of Northern and Southern Irish politics and ultimately finds himself in the position of having to take sides.

***HIGH SPIRITS* (1988).** In a desperate attempt to hold on to his ancestral home in Ireland, Lord Peter Plunkett and his staff conspire to market the castle as a haunted hotel. Among the first coachload of American guests are Jack and Sharon, on a second honeymoon to revive a flagging marriage. During the first night of their stay, the guests duly witness a motley crew of ghosts sweeping through the castle, but these are quickly revealed as the castle staff in costume.

Feeling cheated, the guests decide to leave en masse the next morning. At this point, however, the castle's real ghosts step in to save the castle, prompting a mass haunting and inadvertent love affairs between the dead and the living.

On its release in 1988 **Neil Jordan**'s first American-financed film came as something of a shock. After his first three films, Jordan was comfortably in the vanguard of Irish filmmakers—the early promise of *Angel* was apparently confirmed by *The Company of Wolves* and *Mona Lisa*. *High Spirits* however, attracted almost uniformly negative reviews, and together with Jordan's next film, *We're No Angels* (1989), was taken as signaling the beginning of the end of Neil Jordan's career. It was not until *The Crying Game* that *High Spirits* was reassessed as a regrettable but ultimately pardonable aberration.

That said, the film unquestionably ranks at the bottom of the Jordan canon, featuring the worst acting and dialogue of any of his films, delivered by a cast clearly chosen with an eye to the American market. U.S. stars Steve Guttenberg and Darryl Hannah are clearly unsure about where to pitch their performances. Some of the Irish cast members—**Donal McCann**, **Ray McAnally**, and in particular **Liam Neeson**—acquit themselves with more dignity, but it is nonetheless local hero **Peter O'Toole** who delivers the hammiest performance. That the dialogue came from an individual who had previously displayed such a gift for using ordinary language to explore political and emotional issues of extraordinary complexity was bewildering.

In his defense Jordan has argued that the film was completed by "the studio," which imposed a feel-good style on the picture and muted the more disturbing elements. There is some evidence within the film to support this, such as a hinted discussion on the inevitable differences between the portrayal of Ireland for tourists and the reality of its everyday existence. But this too is submerged into what becomes a tourist board–approved portrayal of Ireland. There is also ample evidence of studio interference in the editing, since at times there is no narrative, just a sequence of increasingly bizarre unconnected events, and the film lacks any meaningful sense of closure.

HINDS, CIARÁN (1953–). Ciarán Hinds was born and raised in Belfast, the youngest in a family of five children. Although his father, a doctor, hoped his son would also pursue a medical career, the young Hinds was more taken with acting, a path he was encouraged to follow by his mother, herself an amateur actress. On leaving school he entered Queens University Belfast to study law, but he left before completing the degree to train as an actor at the Royal Academy of Dramatic Arts (RADA) in London. He then spent the best part of a decade working with the renowned Citizens' Theatre in Glasgow, with occasional forays to work on stage in London, Dublin, and Belfast.

He made his film debut in 1981 in John Boorman's *Excalibur*, but it wasn't until the early 1990s that an eye-catching turn with the Royal Shakespeare Company in their globe-trotting production of *Richard III* drew him to the attention of film and television producers and provided regular screen work. He had, however, already been cast in a lead film role when he played opposite **Donal McCann** in **Thaddeus O'Sullivan**'s *December Bride*. The film made the most of Hinds's physically imposing brooding presence—something that subsequent television work would also reflect. He is frequently cast in taciturn roles that disguise inner emotional turmoil; he played Captain Wentworth in *Persuasion* (1995), Edward Rochester in *Jane Eyre* (1997), and Michael Henchard in Thomas Hardy's *The Mayor of Casterbridge* (2003). Already a well-established face on British television, by the end of the 1990s he was increasingly seen on the big screen, too. He took on a number of cameo roles in Irish films in the mid-1990s, playing the mischievous Professor Flynn in *Circle of Friends* and a fairly sympathetic Sinn Féin leader (clearly modeled on Gerry Adams) in *Some Mother's Son*, and he played the male lead opposite Julie Walters in *Titanic Town*.

However, by the late 1990s he was becoming increasingly familiar to international audiences, making appearances in Chris Menges's *The Lost Son* (1999) and Kathryn Bigelow's *The Weight of Water* and receiving third billing behind Ralph Fiennes and Cate Blanchett in Gillian Armstrong's *Oscar and Lucinda* (1997). He followed these with a brief but significant appearance in Sam Mendes's *Road to Perdition* (2002), playing an Irish American gangster before going the blockbuster route opposite Angela Jolie in *Lara Croft: The Cradle of Life* (2003). He has also worked twice with Joel Schumacher in recent years, playing another gangster (this time based on a real-life figure) in that director's take on the **Veronica Guerin** story and playing Firmin in the poorly received musical adaptation of *The Phantom of the Opera* (2004). In 2005, he made a brief return to Northern Ireland to star in *Mickybo and Me* before taking on his highest-profile role to date, that of Julius Caesar in the British Broadcasting Corporation's € 100 million drama production *Rome* (2005). Final confirmation of his international appeal appeared the same year when Steven Spielberg cast him in a lead role in *Munich* (2005) as an Israeli secret service agent ordered to assassinate Palestinian guerrillas.

HOLLYWOOD FILM SITES. Many beautiful landmarks in Ireland have been made famous by the films that use these sites, which has greatly assisted the **tourist** industry. A list of these films includes Hollywood classics like **John Huston**'s *Moby Dick* (1956), in which Youghal in County Cork doubled as the whaling port of New Bedford, Massachusetts. Classics like Robert Flaherty's *Man of Aran* (1934), set on the Aran Islands off the west coast, and British director David Lean's *Ryan's Daughter* (1970), filmed on the Dingle Peninsula in Kerry, made these places famous tourist sites. Cong, County Mayo, where *The Quiet Man* (1952) was filmed, has remained a well-trodden site ever since. More recently Trim castle in County Meath was used extensively for the historical Scottish period drama *Braveheart* (1995), and in the dramatic opening sequence of Steven Spielberg's *Saving Private Ryan* (1998), Currocloe Beach in County Wexford doubled for the beaches where the D-day landings took place in World War II. The rugged landscape of Wicklow, near the **Ardmore Studios**, has served as a backdrop for many big international film productions up to the present, which have been brought to Ireland with the assistance of **Section 35** tax breaks for film production.

HOMOSEXUALITY. Homosexuality has been an extremely taboo subject in Ireland until relatively recently owing largely to religious and cultural factors. However, since the 1960s in particular there has been a remarkable shift in attitudes. In 1993 the Criminal Law (Sexual Offences) Act granted parity before the law to homosexual citizens and introducing a common age of consent of 17 years for both heterosexual and homosexual relations. While homophobia remains a problem—it still leads to violence and other forms of discrimination—it is no longer as acceptable as it once was.

Although cinematic treatment of all forms of sexuality has been subject to severe **censorship** in Ireland until relatively recently, there has of late been some implicit and even explicit exploration of homosexuality on film in Ireland. Film shorts that foreground homophobia and its effects on teenagers growing up in Ireland include Orla Walsh's *Bent Out of Shape* (1995) and Eve Morrison's *Summertime* (1995). Feature films that deal with the topic include **Cathal Black's** highly regarded *Pigs*, which explores the life of a gay man living in a Dublin squat, and **Johnny Gogan's** *The Last Bus Home*, set during a period when homosexuality had just been decriminalized in Ireland. Capturing the mood of the 1960s, *A Man of No Importance* most notably explores the dilemma for a gay man, played by Albert Finney, who tries to come out by staging a play by Oscar Wilde—almost a synonym for homosexuality—and gets beaten up as a result.

The Crying Game, of course, represents a major breakthrough, with its famous gender twist in the narrative. It became internationally successful as a case study of homosexuality and spawned a huge international industry in gender and queer studies. Similarly, **Neil Jordan's** *Breakfast on Pluto* (2006), adapted from the novel by Pat McCabe, also foregrounds gay characters and themes.

The modest domestic success of *Cowboys and Angels* suggests that the mainstreaming of homosexuality in Irish society has been at least partially achieved, given that although one of the two protagonists is openly—in fact flamboyantly—gay, the film was received more as a youth picture than as a story about a homosexual character. Similarly, although Alan Gilsenan's *Timbuktu* is much darker in tone, the homosexuality of its leading male, although important to understanding the character's background and motivations, does not constitute the subject of the film.

Recent chick-flick and art-house lesbian films include *Goldfish Memory* and *About Adam*, where open sexual experimentation and sometimes even playful subversion of "normative" heterosexuality are used with comic effect—a long way, one might conclude, from the heavily censored society that existed in Ireland for many years. More radical and less mainstream avant-garde narratives include

2by4, which deals most explicitly with homosexuality as a lived experience rather than as a narrative device. According to critic Lance Pettitt, the film is unusual in that it disrupts any form of nostalgia about emigration, American immigration groups, and in particular liberal gay rights voices in America and Ireland (Pettitt, 1997).

***HOW HARRY BECAME A TREE* (2001).** Transposing a Chinese fable to rural post–Civil War Ireland, Serbian director Goran Paskaljevic creates a potent allegory for recent European wars as he explores the individual roots of conflict through an Irish character who opts for misery over happiness and hate over love. A refreshingly noncommercial work, the film has the courage of its convictions. The director and son of a prolific Serbian director, Paskaljevic found the roots of the story in a character who believes that a man is measured by the quality of his enemies. The director's wife helped to write the script and suggested Ireland as a setting. In the end the Sally Gap area of the Wicklow Mountains was chosen as a location, which afforded a sense of scale, space, and light and allowed the makers to create a unique visual effect on a small budget. Because of slippages in budget the film had to be shot during severe winter weather, which nevertheless helped create an interesting visual aesthetic that matched the mood of the film.

Although this very enigmatic story of a man who becomes psychologically fascinated by trees cannot fully hold the movie together, it works very well as theatrical drama, with the main actor transforming his soiled fingernails and well-worn farming hands to connect with the power and beauty of majestic trees—far removed from the plastic fantasy of *Star Trek*, where the lead actor **Colm Meaney** gained his cult following. He all but emulates the "tree huggers" through his adoration of this natural phenomenon and, much to the consternation of his son, pontificates on how "a tree can overcome all that is thrown at it." Losing all that he has, in the end he wants to be literally rooted to the landscape in a way that is reminiscent of **Richard Harris**'s role in *The Field*.

His chosen antagonist, O'Flaherty (**Adrian Dunbar**), is a publican and womanizer who cannot keep his wife happy, and a disgruntled lover ends his life. Although initially acknowledging Harry's challenge, he eventually comes to regard him as an irritant. However, the relationship becomes complicated when Harry's son (**Cillian Murphy**), an innocent who cannot overcome his father's control, seeks to marry O'Flaherty's servant, on whom O'Flaherty has been imposing his favors. As a result the son takes on the pathological jealousy of his father and wants to kill the enemy (as his deceased brother did in the Civil War). But thankfully, the ending is not like the denouement of *The Field* or the ever-present "sins of the father" motif; he kills only his dog and eventually leaves Ireland with his new wife.

Of course, in many ways this surreal narrative is augmented by the evocative cinematography, which has echoes of the recent Bosnian war and other international sites of conflict where the environment and elemental nature are of primary importance.

***HOW TO CHEAT IN THE LEAVING CERTIFICATE* (1998).** Shot in black and white, this short and underdeveloped narrative, with its sketchy character exposition, is a "slow burn" that somewhat comes alive when complications begin. Directed by Graham Jones, the film is full of amusing vignettes, which appeal primarily to local audiences who have all endured the Leaving Certificate, the exam undertaken by students exiting secondary school in Ireland. **Eamonn Morrissey**'s performance as a teacher attempting to scare his pupils into studying by shouting about how the Leaving is the most important exam in their lives, determining their future, draws knowing laughs from Irish audiences. Such pressures lead the protagonists to hatch impossibly complicated schemes to pass their exam by foul means, and the film thus humorously reflects the real psychological trauma imposed by the test upon unfortunate Irish teenagers.

HUNT, PETER. Though born in France, Hunt grew up in England before moving to Northern Ireland during World War II, where he met his wife, Iris, a nurse. After the war Hunt and his wife moved to Southern Ireland and established a sound recording studio over May's record shop on Saint Stephen's Green in Dublin. Over the course of the next two decades he would acquire an international reputation as a sound engineering expert, called on by technology companies like Nagra and EMI to advise on equipment design. Hunt's name would subsequently appear as sound editor or recordist on many of the key Irish documentaries of the 1950s and 1960s, often in conjunction with cameraman **George Fleischmann**. These included **Patrick Carey**'s *Yeats Country* (1965) and the occasional fiction piece, such as the **Academy Award**–nominated short *Return to Glennascaul* (1951). With his studio employee Gene Martin, he was also responsible for all aspects of sound recording on **Gael Linn**'s *Amharc Eireann* series.

In the later 1960s he was quietly active in lobbying for state support for the industry and was one of those who encouraged **Louis Marcus** to write his seminal 1967 *Irish Times* series critiquing contemporary Irish film policy. His expertise was not limited to film sound, however; he was responsible for theater sound on productions such as Michael MacLiammoir's *The Importance of Being Oscar* and performances of *Seán O'Riada* at the Saint Francis Xavier (SFX) Centre. His recording studios were also used for music recordings—the traditional group The Chieftains recorded their first album there in 1961 with a young **Morgan O'Sullivan** as the engineer. Hunt continued working into the 1970s before retiring to his home in Greystones, where he died in the mid-1990s.

HURST, BRIAN DESMOND (1895–1986). Hurst was born in Belfast to a Protestant working-class family and left Ireland for Canada in 1921, enrolling in art college. He continued to study art in Paris and got into a circle of French and émigré intellectuals and artists. As confirmed by film historian Ruth Barton, he was introduced to **John Ford** in 1928 (Barton, 2004). During the 1930s and 1940s he became a prolific filmmaker as a director for hire. His Irish films include *Irish Hearts* (1935), a romantic melodrama based on the novel *Night Nurse* by J. Johnson Abraham, which made some money, and an adaptation of Synge's *Riders to the Sea*, apparently financed by Gracie Fields, which did not. His next Irish venture, *Ourselves Alone*, is based on the play by Dudley Sturrock and is set during the War of Independence. He became a noted figure in the British film industry over the course of the 1940s and 1950s and is perhaps best regarded for *Scrooge*, his 1951 take on Charles Dickens's *A Christmas Carol*, featuring Alastair Sim.

His last film was an adaptation of J. M. Synge's *The Playboy of the Western World* produced by the **Four Provinces** production company and starring **Siobhan McKenna**, Gary Raymond, Elizabeth

March, and Brendan Couldwell. The film is a solid if conventional and sometimes staid fleshing out and visualization of the famous play and is arguably undermined by the casting of English actor Raymond in the lead role and that of 41-year-old Siobhan McKenna in the role of ingénue Pegeen Mike. Hurst's other films include his most successful wartime drama, *Dangerous Moonlight* (1941). His Irish films remain important for expressing, albeit from a British perspective, the need for reconciliation and for appreciating Irish identity from a broader point of view.

HUSH-A-BYE BABY (1989). Directed by Margo Harkin, this well-regarded rites-of-passage story of female sexuality in Northern Ireland offers a fascinating snapshot of the mores and beliefs of 1980s Derry. Starring **Emer McCourt, Sinead O'Connor**, Michael Liebman, Cathy Casey, and Julie Rodgers in a strong piece of ensemble acting, the story focuses on Catholic girls living through the "**troubles**" and negotiating their sexual development in an extremely patriarchal society dominated by the Catholic Church. Several contentious issues including unwanted teenage pregnancies, the Irish abortion referendum, and political debates around the "supergrass" (political informer) trials are used to frame the narrative. The girls have to live with the constant threat of political violence as they walk the streets, with armed British soldiers carrying out surveillance of their nationalist community, which is constantly under threat of attack.

Produced by the **Derry Film and Video Co-operative,** it focuses on 15-year-old Goretti (Emer McCourt), who becomes pregnant but hides this from her family and most of her friends. The film is shot in an effective social realist way except for the use of expressionism in the opening and closing sequences. The film works within the paradigms of Northern Irish identity politics and is located at the intersection of class, nation, and particularly gender: A recurrent image of the Virgin Mary reaches a nightmarish visual and aural climax as Goretti gives birth, and the story is set at a time of great upheaval in the sexual politics of Ireland.

The film's television premiere on Irish television and on **Channel 4** soon afterward attracted large audiences. Nevertheless, there was much local criticism of its apparent pro–British Army stance and "Gaelic speaking Squaddies," for example, which were perceived as unreal, along with disquiet over the portrayal of teenagers as "gormless sex fiends" (Kirkland, 1999). Such representations appear mild to contemporary audiences, and the film has led to some very provocative academic study over the years. Some illustration of the transformation of attitudes can be gleaned from *The Van* (1996), which provides a very different and affirmative representation of working-class Dublin and teenage pregnancy.

HUSTON, JOHN (1906–1987). A renowned film director and indeed actor—he received an Oscar nomination for his role in the *The Cardinal* (1963) and a Cannes nomination for *Chinatown* (1974)—Huston lived in Ireland for more than 20 years, became an Irish citizen, was a key figure in the campaign for state support for a film industry, and made four films in Ireland. Born in Nevada, Missouri, he was of part-Irish extraction, his paternal great-grandfather having left Armagh for Canada in 1840. After working as a boxer and journalist, his introduction to Hollywood came at the age of 27 when his father—actor Walter Huston—invited him to do a script polish on the film he was then working on, *A House Divided*. The production company—Universal—was happy enough with the polish to offer Huston a contract as a writer.

In 1938, after a sojourn in the United Kingdom, he moved to Warners, where his contract stipulated that he was permitted to direct a film. He chose to adapt Dashiell Hammett's *The Maltese Falcon*—against the advice of his studio, which was concerned that two previous filmed versions had flopped. Famously, however, Huston's version went on to become a film classic and instantly cemented his reputation. In 1942 he joined the army, which put his directorial talents to use as part of the Signal Corps. By the end of the war he was Major Huston. He then returned to Hollywood, directing four films between 1946 and 1948, including *The Treasure of the Sierra Madre* (1948), for which his father won a Best Actor Oscar, and *Key Largo* (1948). When his contract with Warners lapsed in 1948, he established Horizon Pictures with Sam Spiegel, for which he made *The African Queen* (1951).

Just before starting work on that film, he visited Ireland for the first time. At the invitation of the Guinness family he attended a hunt ball in the Gresham Hotel, Dublin, staged by the Galway Blazer Hunt.

This led to an introduction to fox hunting in Ireland; Huston became so enamoured with this activity that in 1953 he rented a country house near Kilcock, County Kildare, where he and his family lived for a few years before he purchased a Georgian manor house in Galway, on 100 acres of land, called Saint Clerans. Having bought the house in a state of some disrepair from the Irish Land Commission, Huston spent two years and a significant sum of money restoring it. He and his family lived there for 18 years until the early 1970s.

Two of his children later returned to Ireland to work on film projects. Tony Huston wrote the screenplay for his father's adaptation of **James Joyce**'s **"The Dead**," while Angelica, who starred in *The Dead*, also directed Brendan Carroll's *Agnes Browne* in 1996. Huston's autobiographical account of life at Saint Clerans depicts him as the squire of the manor, mixing with local gentry and actively participating in the hunt season, becoming "master" of the Galway Blazers for a decade. Despite this, and the fact that in 1964 he became an Irish citizen and received an honorary doctorate from Trinity College, Huston does not appear to have regarded himself as a native in the way that, for example, **John Ford** thought of himself. Although clearly very fond of the Irish, his references to Ireland and its people in his autobiography clearly position them as the "other."

However, in part as a consequence of his residence, Huston made a number of films in Ireland from the 1950s to the 1970s. His 1954 production of *Moby Dick* saw Youghal transformed into a 19th-century New England whaling town, although most of the location shooting took place at Fishguard in Wales. Part of *Casino Royale* (1967) (which he codirected) was shot in Glencree, County Wicklow, and the following year, he shot *Sinful Davey* (1967) in its entirety in Ireland (using **Ardmore Studios** for interiors). He also used Connemara as a location for that part of the Paul Newman thriller *The Mackintosh Man* (1973), which was set in Ireland.

While working on *Sinful Davey*, he was invited by then taoiseach Jack Lynch to head a committee investigating the possibility of establishing a film industry in Ireland. Although unhappy with the committee's unwillingness to recommend extensive state support for international projects shot in Ireland, Huston nonetheless agreed to allow the resulting *Report of the Film Industry Committee* to be published under his name, and the report is generally referred to as the *Huston Report*.

Huston sold Saint Clerans in the early 1970s, finding the maintenance of the estate, and the large staff required to run it, increasingly difficult to finance. He opted instead for the warmer climate of Puerto Vallarta in Mexico. But his connections with Ireland did not end there. After making an extraordinary range of films in the early 1980s, including the musical *Annie* (1980) and the soccer-themed war movie *Escape to Victory* (1981), his last film was the adaptation of Joyce's short story "The Dead." Although perilously ill (he directed the film from a wheelchair), he fashioned a highly regarded swan song that successfully captured the stifling atmosphere of middle-class existence in Edwardian Dublin.

More than a decade after his death, his role in Irish cinema was commemorated by the establishment of a school of digital media at University College Galway, named the Huston School of Media.

THE HUSTON REPORT. *See REPORT OF THE FILM INDUSTRY COMMITTEE.*

– I –

I COULD READ THE SKY **(1999).** Adapted from the photographic novel by Timothy O'Grady and Steve Pyke, which was published to great acclaim in 1997, it tells the story of a man living in a bed-sit in London who reminisces in fragments of memory about his life growing up in the West of Ireland and his **emigration** to Britain as a working man. Starring **Stephen Rea** and novelist Dermot Healy and directed by Nicholas Bruce, this is a formally innovative, structured film that makes extensive use of monologue and point of view framing.

I WENT DOWN **(1997).** Written by **Conor MacPherson** (and loosely based on MacPherson's play *The Good Thief*), and directed by **Paddy Breathnach**, the film was widely distributed and very successful in Ireland. It follows Git Haynes (**Peter McDonald**), who has just left prison. He had confessed to a crime that was in fact committed by his father. While he was inside, his girlfriend left him, although after his release he ends up protecting the new boyfriend—an old friend of Git's—from being attacked by hoodlums. This brings him even more problems, with various favors owed. As a result he ends up driving to Cork with Bunny Kelly (**Brendan Gleeson**)—a larger-than-life freelance criminal—with the job of finding and bringing back the loquacious Frank Grogan (Peter Caffrey). As one might expect, complications develop on the job, and a Hollywood-emulating, but still distinctively Irish, caper movie ensues.

IN AMERICA (**2002**). The healing powers of faith, hope, and even magic hold sway in **Jim Sheridan**'s loosely autobiographical crowd pleaser about a contemporary Irish family facing the adventure of a lifetime in New York City. Some critics have read the film as Sheridan's post–September 11 homage to America. Never shy about self-publicity, the director has spoken of the film's allusions and homage to James Joyce's *Ulysses*. It also refers to earlier Sheridan family history, most notably to the death of his young brother at a very young age. This autobiographical tone is amplified by the fact that Sheridan cowrote the screenplay with his daughters, Kirsten and Naomi. The film has had very mixed critical reviews that cite its oversentimentality and a sometimes confusing narrative logic. Nevertheless, it has been relatively successful at the box office.

The story is told through the eyes of two children—Christy and Ariel—who have **emigrated** with their parents. Johnny (Paddy Considine) and Sarah (Samantha Morton), have come to New York illegally to escape both a recession-hit Ireland and the recent death of one of their children. In New York, Johnny, an actor, has little luck in auditions for the theater, because he does not believe in himself enough—a theme in many Hollywood narratives. Nonetheless, he displays a quixotic tenacity, as witnessed in the scene where he drags an old air-conditioner through the center of a busy street, against the traffic, and then carries it up several flights of stairs to their very run-down and sweltering apartment, only to have it short-circuit all the fuses in the building.

A constant dilemma for all immigrants to America involves the balance between standing out and integrating, and this is neatly articulated by the symbolic use of food and language translation in this film. The Irish immigrants make colcannon, a native Irish dish, for their new black friend. Sarah tells a black visitor that the Irish name for black man is "fear gorm" (literally "blue man"), whereas "fear dubh" (literally "black man") means an evil man. Djimon Hounsou responds to this translational aside with a strange affirmation—"You really understand us." By befriending the racially coded "other," these Irish migrants also affirm their positive multicultural credentials while giving comfort to a stranger, which remains one of the tenets of Christianity and a benevolent stereotypical endorsement of Irish friendliness.

For many critics, *In America* represents the celebration of an Irish American experience and universal affirmation of the certainties and sometimes hidden strength of the family unit. Where so many Irish films from the 1970s onward ended with the disintegration of the symbolic family, Sheridan argues for its durability, a prognosis aided rather than defeated by modernity. Set in 1982, the year of the release of *E.T.*, Sheridan has said his film is about getting away from that "death culture" that is so prevalent in Ireland and expressed so repetitively in Irish literature (Sheridan, 2004).

The parents want and need to experience the American dream for themselves as much as for their two surviving children. The young girl Ariel makes three wishes that function as the narrative hook and backbone throughout the film. The first wish is to ensure safe passage through customs, when they arrive at the Canadian border to make the symbolic journey into America. The second is made in the fairground scene, when Johnny tries to win an ET doll at a stall, risking the family's rent money to this end. He irrationally believes this unnecessary risk to be a marker of their need to have "faith" in their destiny and the American mythos. Thankfully, they get their doll and later witness the film *E.T.* Ariel's final wish is designed to help her mother survive her pregnancy. Having been told by the white-coated specialists not to risk having another child, the mother reacts irrationally, like the father in the fairground—"What do they know about us?" The eventual cost of medical services to carry her pregnancy to full term reaches over $30,000, but this is paid for, as in a miracle, by the eccentric man who is triply marked as "other"—African American, AIDS victim, and artist—whom they befriend before he dies.

IN THE NAME OF THE FATHER **(1993).** Jim Sheridan's third film as a director saw him shift from the relatively small scale of *My Left Foot* and *The Field* into the realms of the blockbuster. Whereas those two films remained fairly parochial in scope, *In the Name of the Father* was at the time of its release easily the biggest film ever to come out of Ireland, not just in content but also in conception, production, and marketing.

Continuing the tradition of using material from other sources (*My Left Foot* and *The Field* were based on an autobiography and stage play, respectively), Sheridan turned to Gerry Conlon's account of his 15 years in prison, having been falsely convicted, along with three others, as one of the Guilford pub bombers in 1974. The film follows Conlon (Daniel Day-Lewis) from Belfast to London in 1974, where along with three others—Paul Hill (John Lynch), Paddy Armstrong, and Carole Richardson—he finds himself accused on circumstantial evidence of IRA membership and of carrying out the Guilford pub bombings. Traveling to England in an attempt to have Gerry released, Conlon's father, Guiseppe, and his cousins the Maguires are also arrested on suspicion of involvement in the making of the Guilford bombs. All are found guilty and sentenced to long prison terms.

Up to this point the film is essentially a searing denunciation of the English justice system in the wake of the Guilford bombings, criticizing the willingness of the police and judiciary to deliberately ignore objective evidence in the hunt for a scapegoat. However, once Conlon enters prison, the focus shifts to a study of the relationship between Gerry and Guiseppe, who share a cell. A previously strained father-son relationship—Gerry resentful of what he perceives as his father's passivity, Guiseppe bewildered by his son's rage—is forced by proximity to change. The film is an interesting companion piece to Sheridan's earlier *My Left Foot* with its focus on a mother-son relationship. Ruth Barton suggests that the main protagonist moves from rejecting all parental authority, to a brief capitulation to the British police, to his admiration for the Irish Republican Army leader Joe McAndrew (Don Baker), and eventually toward reconciliation with his own father, whose place he takes in prison after Guiseppe's very emotional demise (Barton, 2002).

The two elements—critique of British justice and the growing mutual respect between father and son—merge in the final third of the film, which brings the story into the 1980s and the developing momentum of the campaign to free the Guilford Four. Guiseppe dies in prison, steeling Gerry's resolve to lead the campaign to a successful conclusion, and encouraging him to turn to a British lawyer, Gareth Pierce (Emma Thompson), to take up the legal challenge. A courtroom finale that sees the Guilford Four released brings the film to a rousing crescendo.

On release, *In the Name of the Father* received criticism from many quarters (particularly in the United Kingdom) for its blurring of fact and fiction for dramatic effect: The film depicts the Guilford Four and the Maguire Seven being sentenced at the same trial in the same courtroom, although in fact there were two separate trials. Meanwhile, the critical middle section of the film in which Gerry and Guiseppe share a cell could never have happened since the pair were never even in the same prison. Furthermore, a scene depicting Gareth Pierce accidentally stumbling across a vital piece of evidence withheld from the defense of the Guilford Four in 1974, although dramatically effective, is again pure fiction.

Nevertheless the film powerfully drew attention to glaring inconsistencies in the case made against both the Four and the Maguires, inconsistencies that remain unresolved today. Ultimately it's difficult to avoid the conclusion that what rankles about *In the Name of the Father* is the skill with which the substantive argument inherent in the Guilford Four story is made—that not only did a major miscarriage of justice occur but that also the police and judiciary were driven more by the understandable post-Guilford baying for blood of the English press and the public than by any objective notion of the pursuit of justice. Sheridan, ably assisted by his two main male leads (Day-Lewis and Postlewaite) exposes the human consequences of the injustice, skillfully manipulating the emotions of his audience with a raging soundtrack and occasionally sublime cinematography from director of photography Peter Biziou.

INDECON REPORT. Indecon is a large economic consultancy frequently used by the Irish state to advise on a wide range of public policy issues. In 1995, the Department of Arts, Culture and the Gaeltacht commissioned Indecon to assess the contribution of the **Section 481** (then **Section 35**) tax relief to the Irish economy in general and to employment in the film industry. The department specifically wished to know whether Section 35 was the most cost-efficient means of creating a sustainable film industry.

Judging by the recommendations of the report (officially titled *A Strategy for Success Based on Economic Realities*), Indecon adopted a broad interpretation of the brief. The report made 24 specific recommendations, 9 of which in no way related to tax relief, but included the need to establish an **Irish Screen Commission**, develop postproduction facilities, and—oddly—extend artists' tax relief to film personnel who either won an award at the Cannes Film Festival or were merely nominated for an **Academy Award**.

The bulk of the recommendations, however, were focused around Section 481. Heretically, the report found that although the tax relief had undoubtedly been a contributory factor in the post-1993 increase in production activity in Ireland, the tax foregone as a result had not been recouped through increased financial activity associated with the film industry (e.g., income tax from film personnel). In short, the Section 481 tax relief was costing the exchequer approximately £5 million per annum. This went against the received wisdom that had emerged from institutions like the Audiovisual Federation of the Irish Business and Employers Confederation (IBEC), which had argued that state investment in the audiovisual sector through the Film Board and Section 481 resulted in a net gain to the economy.

The Indecon report accepted IBEC's figures but noted that it arrived at its results by calculating the aggregate impact of all audiovisual production in Ireland, not all of which availed of the tax incentive. Indecon argued that if one separated out these productions, then the economy experienced a net loss as a result of Section 481. However, having stipulated Section 481's generally positive impact, Indecon did not suggest that the tax incentive be entirely removed. Noting that "on economic criteria it would be very hard to justify continuing the incentives in their present form" (Indecon, 1995), it put forward a series of recommendations designed to ensure that the tax break made a net contribution to the economy. Key among these was the decision to reduce the level of tax write-off available to private and corporation investors from 100 percent of their investment to 80 percent.

When the findings and recommendations of the report became public after its December 1995 publication, the film industry response was extremely negative, suggesting that such changes would undermine the brief renaissance enjoyed by the sector in the previous two years. Nonetheless, faced with the report, in January 1996 the minister for finance duly altered the tax relief largely along the lines recommended by Indecon. The direct impact of the changes was hard to establish definitively: The number of investors willing to avail of Section 481 did decline, but this was an express aim of the changes, and there was little evidence to suggest that producers found it substantially harder to access such funding. There was a definitive decrease in the level of foreign activity in Ireland in the wake of the changes, but a causal link between the decline and the Section 481 alterations was harder to demonstrate, especially given the simultaneous decline in the value of the dollar vis-à-vis the punt, making it more expensive for Hollywood companies to shoot in Ireland. Nonetheless, the coincidence of the reduction in foreign activity would give pause in the future to any other suggestions that Section 481 be adjusted.

INDEPENDENT TELEVISION PRODUCTION SECTOR REPORT (FMI REPORT). Although focused on developing independent television rather than film production, the FMI report was indirectly significant for the film industry in that many of its conclusions lent weight to the case made by the Irish film industry for state support through contemporary documents like the ***Coopers and Lybrand Report*** in 1992.

Commissioned by **Film Makers Ireland** in conjunction with the Industrial Development Authority (IDA) and the Irish Trade Board, the report was researched and written by Siobhan O'Donoghue, who would subsequently head **MEDIA Desk** Ireland. The basic thrust of the report was that deregulation and new technology were transforming the European broadcasting sector, spurring enormous market growth. This would inevitably lead to **Radio Telefís Éireann**'s (RTÉ) facing increased competition for Irish audiences and thus pointed to the need for the Irish production and broadcast industry to gear up to compete.

However, the report argued that historically RTÉ had made only limited use of independent production to augment its in-house production, despite the requirement under European Union (EU) law that it source at least 10 percent of its material from independent producers. The report also suggested that in the absence of commissions from RTÉ, independent producers in Ireland had been forced to look overseas for work and, as a result, had developed a strong export orientation. This, together with their Anglophone status, made them potentially attractive coproduction partners for other European producers.

In short, external conditions had created an opportunity for a huge expansion in the scale of the Irish independent production sector, which could be facilitated by an integrated government response. Specifically the report recommended passing legislation to ensure RTÉ's adherence to EU law on independent commissioning, appointing an independent commissioning editor with RTÉ, coordinating state policy on encouraging audiovisual production, and amending **Section 35** to allow individuals to use it and to increase the amount of money that could be invested under the scheme.

The report was published in August 1992, within a month of the *Coopers and Lybrand Report*, some of the conclusions of which it closely echoed (hardly surprising given that both were informed by interviews with either the same individuals or individuals with similar production backgrounds). In particular, the recommendations on Section 35 were virtually identical. As such it would become a key influence on the conclusions of subsequent Special Working Group on the Film Production Industry *Report to the Taoiseach* in December 1992.

***THE INFORMER* (1929).** Liam O'Flaherty's novel (1925) lends itself easily to adaptations, and to date there have been a number of them, including **John Ford**'s classic in 1935, Jules Dassin's 1968 version, and Michael Byrne's 1992 version. Flaherty was heavily influenced by the silent German expressionist film of this period in writing the novel, and the central antagonism between a hard man (Gypo Nolan) and a gunman (Commandant Dan Gallagher) has produced an effective means of staging political conflict. The silent version of 1929 is even considered by some to compare favorably with Ford's classic version.

The original script breaks into four parts. In the first there is an announcement that there will be a cessation of hostilities, but this is followed by a shoot-out, and Francis McPhillip kills the chief of police and escapes. In the second there is a price on his head, but before going to America he cannot resist seeing Katie and his mother. Katie's boyfriend Gypo betrays McPhillip to the police, McPhillip is shot while trying to escape. In the third part Katie stands by her man in the face of revenge-thirsty rebels, but in the final act the rebels get their way as Gypo, in a heightened melodramatic moment, shouts out, "Francie, Francie, your mother has forgiven me" and dies with the shadow of the crucifix across his prone body.

Flaherty used an extensive array of visual metaphors that have been applied in the various adaptations—including the fog as representing moral confusion, the continuing images of the wanted poster to illustrate betrayal, and the ship as a symbol of freedom—a grammar that was also prevalent in classic film noir narratives like Carol Reed's *Odd Man Out*.

INGRAM, REX (1893–1950). Born Reginald Ingram Hitchcock in Dublin, a son of a Church of Ireland clergyman, at 18 he left Ireland for America, never to return. He never showed a particular predisposition to reflect his native culture, but then in Hollywood this was never a high priority. Following the popular and critical success of *The Four Horsemen of the Apocalypse* (1921), which he directed and which made Rudolph Valentino a star, he went on to make *The Conquering Power* (1921), *The Prisoner of Zenda* (1922), *Scaramouche* (1924), *The Arab* (1926), *The Magician* (1926), *Mare Nostrum* (1927), *The Three Passions* (1929), and *Baroud* (1933), among others, becoming a very prolific and successful Hollywood filmmaker.

INSIDE I'M DANCING (2004). **Damien O'Donnell's** film stars James McEvoy as Rory O'Shea (the title under which it was released in the United States), who suffers from Duchenne muscular dystrophy and can move only a couple of fingers and his head to communicate. He allies with Michael (Steven Robertson), who has cerebral palsy and a bad speech impediment, to fight for independence and a noninstitutionalized life. The use of nonhandicapped actors to take on such roles remains a Hollywood tradition and calls to mind the towering performance of Daniel Day-Lewis in *My Left Foot*, who won an Oscar for his role. However, the narrative is not trying to preach around issues of disability but instead seeks to humanize such stories. The two able-bodied actors worked hard to replicate the symptoms of their disabilities. The characters come together in a long-term residency home for the disabled, and life is transformed when they can communicate and understand each other for the first time. The rebellious nature of the outsider—reminiscent of *One Flew Over the Cuckoo's Nest* (1975)—allows them and the film to rise above indulgent sentimentality. They eventually set up a flat on their own and take on a headstrong and very inexperienced female helper. Of course romantic rivalry for her affections ensues in this effective and affecting movie.

INTER-DEPARTMENTAL COMMITTEE ON THE FILM IN-DUSTRY. In 1938, **Sean Lemass**, as minister for industry and commerce, established a three-man committee with a broad remit to examine and report on every aspect—actual and putative—of the Irish film industry. The report was a response to two sets of pressures. The first was the trickle of private proposals relating to the establishment of Irish film industry (most of which centered on the building of a film studio) that the department had been in receipt of since 1928. Second, Lemass appeared to have treated with growing concern calls made from April 1937 by Jesuit priest Father Richard Devane for a government enquiry into all aspects of cinema. Lemass might conceivably have ignored Devane's calls were it not for the fact that on 22 April 1937 the priest wrote to Prime Minister Eamon de Valera requesting a meeting to pursue the idea of an enquiry. Seeking to head off any possibility that the de facto determination of cinema policy might fall to Devane, Lemass instructed John Leydon to establish a small interdepartmental committee (representing Industry and Commerce together with the Departments of Finance, Education, and Justice) to examine difficulties standing in the way of a national film production enterprise. Lemass further suggested to de Valera that any meeting with Devane should await the conclusions of that committee.

Those conclusions were long in coming. In June 1937, John Leydon wrote to his opposite number at Finance (J. J. McElligott) seeking sanction for Lemass's proposed committee. Finance refused, fearing that the report would be used to justify state subsidies for a putative film industry. However, it acceded to the committee's creation when Leydon argued that in fact the primary function would be to collate information that would allow the Department of Industry and Commerce to deal with (and implicitly reject) private appeals for subsidy.

The three-man committee, made up as it was of three middle-ranking civil servants from Industry and Commerce, Finance, and Education (Justice declined a role), was far from expert in the field of the cinema. None of its members had ever been inside a film studio, for example. This ignorance would delay the completion of the report by years: The committee had planned to travel to London to witness the work of British studios but had to first postpone, then cancel the trip when war broke out in September 1939. Consequently, the committee's deliberations were informed by evidence or representations received from bodies or individuals mainly associated with either the film industry in Ireland or the Catholic Church. The committee finally submitted a completed draft in March 1942.

The report was divided into chapters dealing with **exhibition, distribution**, production, and **censorship** of films in Ireland. The penultimate chapter discussed how the establishment of a national film institute could address some of the problems discussed in the earlier chapters. As a result it represented a comprehensive oversight of (and offered a profound insight into) official thinking on the role of cinema in Irish cultural affairs. Furthermore, the fact that it was written on the understanding that it would not be made public led the committee to express its views in relatively unguarded terms.

The opening chapter on exhibition noted a growing concentration of cinema ownership and recommended placing a ceiling on the total number of seats cumulatively held by an exhibitor or group of exhibitors. It also described as "undesirable" (apparently) increasing Jewish ownership and control of Irish cinemas given the part played by cinema in the social and cultural life of the community.

Similar concerns were voiced with regard to distribution and the fact that "alien" film distributors could determine the extent and nature of films available to the Irish public. This was particularly significant for the committee's core interest—production. Noting that even low-budget films could not recoup their costs within Ireland, the report concluded that access to international distribution was a prerequisite for a commercially successful indigenous industry. However, the committee was tentative in discussing how this might be achieved. Although suggesting that the Irish state could "encourage" American distributors to acquire one or two Irish features a year by threatening import restrictions on Hollywood films, it cautioned that such a move might provoke a punitive response from Hollywood, such as entirely withholding film supplies from Ireland. Thus the committee recommended that the state adopt at most a *"reasonably firm attitude"* with regard to distribution.

Moving to production, the report cited far more prosaic difficulties, chief among which was the absence of any substantial studio facilities or of any company regularly producing films on any scale. Since neither gap looked likely to be filled by private capital, the committee proposed building a modest (£25,000) studio. The committee concluded that further state assistance in the form of partial reimbursement of actual production costs would be essential. The committee further recommended that initial domestic production be concentrated on newsreels, where it felt there was a gap in market provision.

In sum, however, with regard to production the conclusions of the report were somewhat gloomy:

> A native film industry could never hope to replace to any large extent imported films by native films. . . . Its prospects of ever becoming self-supporting would depend on the extent to which a foreign market could be secured. . . . Obstacles in the way are so great that it would be wise in considering the question of the establishment of a small-scale film industry to proceed on the assumption that its products would seldom procure exhibition outside the country. The greater portion of the cost of films produced in this country would in these circumstances have to be met from public funds. (*Report of the Inter-Departmental Committee on the Film Industry*, 1942)

The question of precisely how those public funds might be dispensed was addressed via discussion of a national film and cinema board. It was envisaged that the board would regulate the exhibition sector and act as a focus for production activity, offering encouragement, advice, and—on occasion—funding for prospective producers. Finally, the board would advise on the question of a state-funded film studio and on encouraging overseas producers to film in Ireland. In short, the board would take day-to-day responsibility for defining film policy in Ireland.

What is striking about the report, viewed from a distance, is the persuasive power the committee explicitly and tacitly ascribed to cinema. The committee argued that the promotion of film for purposes of education, culture, and general propaganda would be the most important function of the Film Board, suggesting that there was no subject that could not be dealt with via cinema. The Irish language in particular was singled out as a subject that could be mainstreamed by cinema.

Yet if cinema's power for good was stressed, so too was its darker side. The report's final chapter—reflecting representations from the Catholic hierarchy and other Catholic organizations—addressed the practice of film censorship. The report referred to films informed by a materialist philosophy that threatened Ireland's values as a small Christian nation. Particular attention was drawn to the cumulative negative impact on young people of watching such films. Despite these views, the committee advised against making any substantive changes to the existing censorship code. Ironically it did so on the grounds that such changes might have the opposite outcome to that sought by the hierarchy, that is, that forcing the censor to operate within a more strictly defined code might restrict the freedom permitted under the existing code to cut or ban films.

Lemass's immediate response on receiving the report is not recorded. However, he can hardly have been encouraged. The conclusions on production effectively confirmed what the Department of Finance had long asserted—that a commercially viable Irish film industry was impossible. Thus Lemass strategically "parked" the report lest its gloomy conclusions be seized upon by others (in particular Finance) as definitively closing the question.

Nonetheless, some of the report's recommendations relating to the educational potential of cinema were passed on. In December 1943, a further interdepartmental committee (this time representing Education, Finance, Industry and Commerce, Agriculture and Local Government, and Public Health) considered the original report's recommendations relating to educational films and films in the Irish language. This committee would ultimately recommend the advancing of funds to the **National Film Institute of Ireland** (NFII), which was established under (ironically) Father Richard Devane in July 1943. Thus from 1945/46, the NFII was voted £2,000 via the annual science and art vote of the Department of Education for the purposes of acquiring a library of educational films and producing films on behalf of government departments.

However, the report would ultimately have a much more substantial impact on the shaping of the state's longer-term policy on film production. By impressing on Lemass the difficulties entailed in creating an Irish film industry, it led him instead to consider how to encourage the development of a *film industry in Ireland*, that is, one based on foreign direct investment from American and British production companies.

***INTERMISSION* (2003).** An extremely ambitious project for first-time director John Crowley, the film has over 11 interlinked story lines and 54 characters, seeking to emulate the type of narrative popularized by Robert Altman's *Nashville* (1975). The Dublin-based film has been very successful at home, with its stellar cast, including **Colin Farrell**, **Colm Meaney**, and **Cillian Murphy** working alongside several other fine Irish actors.

The narrative opens dramatically with Lehiff (played by the now cult A-list Hollywood star Colin Farrell) apparently wooing a shop assistant while speaking of the possibility of love at first sight. She is swooning at his verbal dexterity, and one must assume the audience is also seduced by the star's power to attract women. Without warning, he savagely punches her in the face, drawing blood. Audience response to such a violent and taboo action has been varied, with some shocked at such violence and others bemused by its apparent dark humor and subversive postmodern irony. The multiple story lines weave together a large number of contemporary Irish characters. Most notable among these is the aggressive policeman, played with great panache by Colm Meaney, reprising the "Dirty Harry" cop trope, while at the same time the character affirms his love of soft romantic Irish music. The film actively seeks to present itself as capturing the authenticity of contemporary life through strong Irish accents, colloquial and colorful language, rich characterizations, and interwoven contemporary story lines that appeal to native audiences.

At the time of its release the film became the most successful independently produced Irish film released by the second Irish Film Board. By the end of 2003 it had taken over €2.3 million at the Irish box office and was still running in suburban cinemas 10 weeks after its initial release, a feat unequalled by any other independently produced Irish film. Initial press reports suggested that the film, produced by **Neil Jordan** and Stephen Woolley's company with **Parallel Films,** would be distributed internationally by Dreamworks, then Miramax, before it was finally released in March 2004 by the Independent Film Company. It received only a limited release, playing in only 10 theaters across America and earning just $39,540 in its opening weekend. Showings were expanded to 26 theaters the following week, and the film increased its box office to $128,802, but peaked in its fourth week, playing at 69 theaters, when its take dropped 25 percent, having achieved a box office total of $579,085. The film appears unlikely to break the $1 million mark, and the fact that it was awarded an R rating in America, no doubt primarily due to its coarse language and initial violence, has unfortunately seriously curtailed such a possibility.

INTO THE WEST **(1992).** Produced by **Little Bird** with **Parallel Films,** from a **Jim Sheridan** screenplay and directed by Mike Newell, the film opens with **Traveller** Grandpa Ward (**David Kelly**), being followed from the beach to his Ballymun encampment by an enormous white horse. There he encounters his son-in-law, Papa Riley (**Gabriel Byrne**), a former Traveller "king" who has lived among the settled community with his two sons, Ossie (Ciaran FitzGerald) and Tito (**Rúaidhrí Conroy**), since the death of their mother. The horse forms an instant attachment to Ossie and moves into their Ballymun flat. When the neighbors complain, the police remove the horse and then illegally sell it to a racehorse owner.

Ossie and Tito steal the horse back, however, setting off across the country to avoid recapture, pursued both by the police and by their father, who enlists the help of the Travelling community to track down the boys. They race through the midlands before the boys and the horse are cornered by the police on the edge of the Atlantic Ocean. Papa arrives just in time to see Ossie and the horse dive into the sea to evade capture. Both disappear under the waves, apparently drowned, but while the horse disappears, Ossie reemerges, having magically encountered his mother under the sea. The film concludes with Papa vowing to return to the Travelling life, his sense of self-worth reinvigorated by his rediscovery of his old life.

Into the West faces several obstacles from the outset: Not only is the screenplay carried largely on the backs of two children and a horse, but the film also attempts to convincingly portray a part of the Irish population that is generally ignored by the mainstream media. The film successfully hurdles the first of these obstacles with a combination of a well-chosen cast and skillful direction. As Ossie and Tito, Fitzgerald and Conroy successfully convey the essential innocence of their characters despite their necessarily outwardly tough appearance and demeanor. As for the horse itself, clever shot framing and editing combine to give the horse a dramatic physical presence and even the illusion of acting.

At overcoming the second hurdle, however, the film is less successful. When portraying the relationship between settled and Traveller society, the film is relatively comfortable because there is a perspective that both the filmmaker and a settled audience can understand. As in reality, the Travellers of *Into the West* are a mystery to the settled community and thus reviled by them: Papa Riley's brutal treatment at the hands of the police is both comprehensible and credible.

The film's portrayal of Traveller culture itself, however, is less credible. By presenting the Travellers as familiar (notably by casting cuddly **Colm Meaney**, friendly Johnny Murphy, and most awkwardly, sultry Ellen Barkin, in key Traveller roles), the film suggests that Travellers are pretty much the same as everyone else and that blind ignorance alone prejudices the settled community against Travellers. However, the film does this by ascribing the same virtues of domestic stability that characterizes settled life to the Traveller community. The film is unwilling or unable to deal with the possibility that traveller society *is* different. Thus instead of offering any genuine insight into the Traveller community or its culture, the film resorts to an unconvincing public relations job on their behalf. Indeed, the format of a mainstream film aimed at a mainstream audience was never likely to lend itself to an exploration of what is a fundamentally different culture.

Consequently, *Into the West* is only tangentially concerned with portraying Traveller culture. Instead it pursues a more universally comprehensible story, a tack signaled by Papa Riley's comment that "there's a bit of a Traveller in everybody. . . . Only a few of us know where we're going." Hence the film unashamedly weaves generic elements into its pattern: The movie's plundering of the Western genre is evident not just from the title but also by explicit references within the text to *Butch Cassidy and the Sundance Kid* (1969) and the implicit identification of Ossie and Tito during their flight across the country as desperadoes. More surprisingly, the film also borrows elements from magic realism, and it is when the film is in this last mode, however, that it is most successful. The scenes of the horse in a Ballymun flat and Ossie's aquatic encounter with his mother are easily the most entertaining and affecting.

IRISH DESTINY (1926). Directed by George Dewhurst, *Irish Destiny* is essentially a love story set against the backdrop of the War of Independence. The film opens with the arrival of a Black and Tans troop in the village of Clonmore, home of Irish Republican Army (IRA) man Denis O'Hara and his fiancé, Moira. When O'Hara learns of a plan to raid a secret IRA meeting, he travels to Dublin to warn his colleagues. On arriving he is shot and captured by British soldiers. People in Clonmore believe that O'Hara has died: The shock of this news leads his mother to lose her sight, while local poitín maker Beecher (who is in league with the British) takes the opportunity to kidnap Moira. O'Hara is in fact quite alive but imprisoned at the Curragh Camp in Kildare. Despite his injury he escapes, arriving in Clonmore just in time to rescue Moira. The film concludes with the dramatic burning of the Customs House in Dublin and the signing of a truce with the British.

Irish Destiny was written and produced by Dr. Isaac Jack Eppel (1892–1942), a Jewish doctor who ran a general practice and a pharmacy in Mary Street, Dublin. Although he harbored ambitions for a theatrical career, his middle-class background dictated that he pursue the more respectable path of medicine. However, he maintained a presence in the entertainment world as owner of the Palace Cinema (later the Academy) in Pearse Street.

Determined to make a movie about the War of Independence, Eppel used his own and borrowed funds to hire an English director, George Dewhurst, and a cameraman, Joe Rosenthal, to shoot the film. Dewhurst had established a modest reputation since his debut short in 1917 and his 1922 version of the stage play *A Sister to Assist 'Er*. (Remarkably he would direct four further film versions of the same play between 1927 and 1948.)

The film was shot on location in Wicklow, and Shepherd's Bush Film Studios in London were used for interior scenes. The all-Irish cast was mostly amateur: Several had never acted before. Paddy Dunne Cullinan, who played O'Hara, for example, was employed largely because of his equestrian skills. Eppel's son Derek and his brother Simon also appeared as extras, while Kit O Malley, formerly of IRA's Dublin Brigade, played the local IRA commandant.

Released on Easter Saturday 1926, to coincide with the anniversary of the Easter Rising, the film was reviewed in glowing terms in the domestic press and, unusually, was retained for a second week in the Corinthian cinema, where it set a new box office record. Overall, however, it was not a financial success. Because of its subject matter it was banned in the United Kingdom, then cut to remove the IRA and the Black and Tans confrontations and rereleased as *An Irish Mother*. Eppel also released the film in the United States, where, although Irish Americans warmly embraced it, reviewers compared it unfavorably with the more polished Hollywood product.

As a result *Irish Destiny* was Eppel's only film production. He incurred enormous debts in making it that took him, his wife, and his brother years to clear. He later emigrated to England, divorced, and remarried, and when he died in 1942, he was largely forgotten in Ireland.

The same was true of *Irish Destiny* until 1988, when an original poster for the film turned up under the linoleum of a Dublin house. This prompted a search for the film itself, which ultimately led to the Library of Congress in Washington, D.C., where, for copyright reasons, all films distributed in the United States must be deposited. The library had retained an original nitrate print, from which a modern print was struck, which was given to the **Irish Film Archive**. Thus in 1993 the National Concert Hall in Dublin saw the first Irish screening of *Irish Destiny* in nearly half a century.

IRISH DREAMTIME. Both the initial financing and the rationale for Irish Dreamtime's existence owe much to **Pierce Brosnan**'s stint as James Bond. The Los Angeles–based company was formed by Brosnan (with producing partner Beau St. Clair) in 1996 on the back of a first-look deal struck in 1996 with Metro Goldwyn Mayer (MGM) after his successful debut as Bond in *Goldeneye*. Brosnan was motivated by a concern that the Bond role threatened to typecast him, and Irish Dreamtime has allowed him to secure roles beyond 007. This has indirectly benefited the Irish film industry: Although Irish Dreamtime's highest-profile production to date has been *The Thomas Crown Affair* remake, as of 2005 the company had also shot three Brosnan vehicles in Ireland. Brosnan's role in the first of these, *The Nephew* in 1998, was relatively low profile, since that story focused on a young black American man returning to Ireland to scatter his mother's ashes and find her roots. However, in *Evelyn* (2002) he took on the main role, playing against type as a down-at-the-heels, drunk, and despairing single father taking on the courts and the Irish Catholic Church to get his three kids out of children's homes. Finally, in 2004, Brosnan again starred (opposite Julianne Moore) as a shabby but effective lawyer in Dreamtime's *Laws of Attraction*.

Although the Irish films have received generally positive reviews, their financial performance has been more mixed in their primary English-language markets. *The Nephew* was never released in the United States and earned less than half a million dollars in Britain and Ireland. The generally well-received *Evelyn* took just over $1.4 million at the United States box office, compared to the $2.2 million it took in the much smaller British and Irish market. However, the also favorably reviewed *Laws of Attraction*, boosted by a setting and cast more familiar to American audiences, earned $17 million in the United States. Thus although the company's higher-profile pictures are likely to remain confined to the Western Hemisphere, the improved performances of the "Irish" pictures, coupled with Brosnan's obvious desire to shoot in Ireland (evinced by the fairly successful decision to use Dublin as a double for New York in *Laws of Attraction*), suggest that the company will remain a significant originator of projects destined to be set and shot in Ireland.

IRISH FILM & TELEVISION ACADEMY. The Irish Film & Television Academy (IFTA) was established in August 1998 to promote Irish film and television, nationally and internationally. Although the academy nominally existed to facilitate dialogue between film and television practitioners and to provide an independent forum for debate and discussions of those issues affecting the industry, in practice its main activity was limited to the organization of an annual awards ceremony, which first ran in 1999.

Eligibility for the awards reflected the composition of the governing body, which included representatives of the Irish film and television industry, from both Northern and Southern Ireland. **RTÉ, TV3,** TG4, UTV, and BBC Northern Ireland were all represented on the academy's council, which also included professional bodies such as the **Irish Film Board**, the **Irish Film Institute**, the **Northern Ireland Film and Television Commission, Screen Producers Ireland,** and the Royal Television Society.

Unfortunately the academy ran out of steam within three years of its establishment. However, the acronym IFTA has been sustained by the intervention of the Irish Film and Television Network, which maintains a website dedicated to the Irish audiovisual sector, and which now runs the annual Irish Film & Television Awards (IFTAs).

IRISH FILM ARCHIVE. Although an "official" national film archive in the sense of a dedicated space came into being only with the opening of the **Irish Film Centre** in 1992, the idea of an archive has a much longer history. Prior to the 1980s, what little archiving occurred was done by interested individuals. Notable examples of this were the cataloguing undertaken by **George Morrison** when he assembled material for **Mise Eire** and *Saoirse?* and **Liam O'Leary**'s single-handed crusade to preserve as much Irish material as possible (although the bulk of O'Leary's material was in the form of documents rather than actual film stock).

Speaking at the Dublin Arts Festival in 1976, O'Leary complained that the absence of a national film archive had created a situation whereby a new generation had little or no knowledge of cinema's contribution to shaping the life of the nation. Some moves to address the situation were made in 1984 when the **Irish Film Institute** (IFI) received some funding from the **Irish Film Board** to carry out work on the possibility of creating an archive. This subsequently led to the employment by the IFI of an individual to promote the need for an archive, and to produce a profile of an archive and a report on the technical aspects of doing so.

The first moves to coherently preserve material commenced in 1986, when the IFI officially established an archive section and began to isolate Irish material from the film lending library it had built up since the 1940s. By the mid-1980s, the library was infrequently called upon, as educational institutions increasingly switched to using videotape for in-class screenings. The Irish material culled from this source would constitute the core collection of the embryonic national film archive. The work was initially carried out by two IFI staff members. Although third-level qualifications in archiving did not exist at the time, they were both sent to the National Film and Television Archive in Britain, where they received training.

The Irish Film Archive proper came into being in 1992, when the Irish Film Institute moved to its current premises in Eustace Street, and four vaults were commissioned specifically to house the archive's collections. As of 1986, the archive held perhaps 800 films. An active film search commencing in 1986 unearthed chunks of additional material from sources such as Bord Fáilte, the Department of Foreign Affairs, the National Safety Council, indigenous production companies, and individual filmmakers like Vincent Corcoran. As of 2006, the archive held over 20,000 items—a comprehensive collection of extant indigenous production in and about Ireland. Holdings range from full prints of professionally made films that were released commercially (the Irish Film Board requires that any film that receives board support deposit a copy in the archive) to advertising footage and home movies.

The film collections are held in vaults, which are temperature- and humidity-controlled at optimal levels for long-term preservation. These vaults are in turn protected by a sophisticated system of fire and flood alarms. Two vaults store master material, which is acquired solely for preservation. However, there is also a viewing vault that houses all "access material," film and tape available to researchers. The archive also has a climate-controlled paper vault, housing documents, posters, stills, scripts, press packs, production-related correspondence, and other paper material.

IRISH FILM BOARD. Although an Irish Film Board was inaugurated in 1981, proposals for such a body date back to the 1942 *Report of the Inter-Departmental Committee on the Film Industry*. In 1954, after his attempts to establish a National Film Studio had been frustrated by the refusal of the Department of Finance to countenance such a facility, **Sean Lemass** instead proposed the establishment of what he termed a film board. Although nominally influenced by the example of the National Film Board of Canada, the body he proposed was to do the following:

- produce films, including films in Irish
- encourage and coordinate filmmaking by other Irish producers
- encourage the making of feature films in Ireland by outside organizations
- foster the general development of a film industry in Ireland

In effect, Lemass proposed a single institution that would perform not only the functions of a film board but also a production company and a screen commission. In any event, the proposal lapsed after Fianna Fáil lost the May 1954 general election.

The idea was revived, however, by the 1968 *Report of the Film Industry Committee*, which, in the course of proposing the creation of a fund to finance low-budget feature and short film production, suggested that the fund be administered by a putative film board. The idea was incorporated into a 1970 bill, simply entitled the Film Bill. Unfortunately, because of a totally unrelated matter of domestic politics, the bill was sidelined, and it was not until the late 1970s that the idea of a film board was revisited.

In 1977 then minister for industry and commerce Desmond O'Malley commissioned an independent report on the operations of the **National Films Studios of Ireland** (NFSI). The report concluded that the NFSI was not contributing to the development of a domestic film industry and suggested instead creating a £4.1 million production fund to be administered by a film board. At the same time, members of the Association of Independent Producers (AIP), including **Tiernan MacBride**, had been lobbying O'Malley for a board. The combined effect of the report and lobbying was the passage of the 1980 Film Board Bill. During the Dáil debate on the bill, several deputies requested that a passage be inserted stipulating that the board should exclusively fund the work of Irish filmmakers. The minister (again Des O'Malley) refused to do so on the grounds that this would needlessly restrict the board's scope (although it was also suggested that it would contravene European law).

The board commenced its work in 1981 despite the fact that only three of the seven board members had actually been appointed. Controversy immediately surrounded it when the partial board awarded half of its first year's funding (£200,000) to a single picture—**Neil Jordan**'s debut, *Angel*—then returned the rest of the year's allocation to the state. The AIP interpreted this as effectively suggesting that there were no other Irish projects worthy of support. The controversy was fuelled by the fact that a board member, **John Boorman**, was also the executive producer on the film. Eventually board chairman Louis Heelan resigned in frustration at the response to *Angel*'s funding, and five new board members were appointed.

Over the next six years the board would go on to put money into 10 feature projects as well as a number of short and experimental works. The full list of features was *Angel*, *The Outcasts*, *The Country Girls*, *Anne Devlin*, *Pigs*, *The End of the World Man*, *Eat the Peach*, *Budawanny*, *Reefer and the Model*, and *The Courier*.

On the whole, however, even the many features supported by the board would have been regarded as avant-garde: The films made by **Joe Comerford, Cathal Black**, and **Pat Murphy** with Film Board support were textbook examples of national cinema. In part because of their avant-garde nature, the films—with the exception of *Eat the Peach*—did not perform well either at the Irish box office or overseas, and the original idea that the board would eventually become self-funding, using profits from earlier films to fund investment in later ones, never came to fruition. Thus, although technically the board gave soft loans rather than grants, in practice the loans were rarely repaid. As late as 1992, of the IR £1.247 million advanced to the 10 feature films, only IR £106,000 had been reimbursed to the board. Consequently, in 1987, a new Fianna Fáil government, facing a national economic crisis, suspended the operation of the board, arguing that it constituted an unsustainable drain on the economy. Filmmakers retorted that the direct return to the board failed to fully reflect its economic impact. Former chair of the board Muiris Mac Conghaile argued that the IR £1.2 million in loans had jump-started work with a total budget of IR £6.1 million, 20 percent of which (IR £1.2 million) had been returned to the state by way of direct and indirect taxes. The government was unmoved, however, pointing to the introduction weeks earlier of the **Section 35** tax break and the promise of the European Union's **MEDIA** program as more than compensating for the loss of the board.

Nonetheless, the board remained in stasis, not actually closed down but not operating either for a six-year period. During this time the number of indigenous projects declined significantly (just one Irish film was made in 1991), demonstrating how important the development function of the board had been.

In 1992, however, several factors led to a revival of the board: The lobbying of industry groups such as **Film Makers Ireland** was supplemented by a series of reports (most notably that prepared by **Coopers and Lybrand**) pointing to the economic potential of the audiovisual sector in Ireland. Most significant, in January 1993, **Michael D. Higgins** became minister at the new Department of Arts, Culture and the Gaeltacht. Two months later Higgins declared that he had secured cabinet approval for the immediate reactivation of the board, which, in keeping with a (usually only rhetorical) commitment to administrative decentralization, was given new head offices in Galway. Veteran producer **Lelia Doolan** was appointed chair, and former **Channel 4** commissioning editor **Rod Stoneman** became the chief executive and thus assumed day-to-day responsibility for running the board.

As of 2004, the Film Board received in the region of € 12 million per annum in capital and administration funding from the state. This has been used to fund loans and equity investment for independent Irish filmmakers to assist in the development and production of Irish films. In this way the board was a critical driver of the explosion in production activity that took place in the 1990s. Nearly 100 Irish features and television series and 300 short films received funding in the decade up to 2004, and a further 500 projects received development funding. The board has also funded **animation** and **documentary** projects. In addition the board has promoted a series of initiatives with **Radio Telifís Éireann (RTÉ)**, TG4, and **Film Base** intended to allow neophyte filmmakers to develop their craft (mainly via the production of shorts). These schemes include Short Cuts, Short Shorts, Frameworks, Oscailt, and Irish Flash.

The second board in particular has adopted a broad interpretation of Section 4 of the Film Board Act, which outlines the general functions of the board. The section notes that the board may "assist and encourage by any means it considers appropriate the making of films in the State." In practice this has seen the board cooperate with a range of other Irish semistate agencies (notably the **Arts Council**, FAS, and the **Northern Ireland Film and Television Commission**) with a view to improving the marketing, sales, and distribution of Irish films and to promoting training and development in all areas of filmmaking. (It should be noted that the employment of Irish film workers and the use of ancillary Irish services is usually regarded as a crucial consideration in the board's assessment of applications.)

Furthermore, the 1980 act empowered the board to establish subsidiaries (technically "committees") to carry out functions that the board considered might be "better or more conveniently performed by a committee." Consequently, the board established the **Irish Screen Commission** in 1997 to promote Ireland as a film location. Initially the commission was established as a separate entity with its own offices in Dublin. However, in 2001, the commission was replaced by a Location Services unit, which was folded back into the main board and which now provides comprehensive information about all aspects of filming in Ireland, from tax incentives to locations, casting, crews, equipment, and facilities.

In terms of the films supported by the Stoneman board, it has been argued that, notwithstanding the chief executive's expressed policy of "radical pluralism" (i.e., supporting the widest range of films possible), it was somewhat more commercially minded than its predecessor. Some critics noted an increasing trend toward more formally conservative filmmaking, especially in comparison with the culturally engaged, critical cinema of the 1980s. However, while it is undeniable that most of the board-funded films since the 1990s have adopted more universally comprehensible narratives (*see Circle of Friends*, *About Adam*, or *Dead Bodies*), the board has continued to support a more critical cinema, including *Adam and Paul*, *Disco Pigs*, *All Souls' Day*, and *Nora*. Moreover, it is largely due to the board that there has been constant activity since 1993, in contrast to the previously stop-start nature of production.

In 2003 Stoneman resigned as head of the board to take up a professorial position with the Huston School of Digital Media in Galway. His successor, **Mark Woods**, came to the position having been head of acquisitions and investment for the Showtime and Encore film channels in Australia. He, in turn, left in April 2005, and a seven-month interregnum followed in which the board effectively had no chief executive. In November 2005, however, **Simon Perry**, former head of British Screen Finance, was appointed to take over the position.

IRISH FILM CENTRE (IFC). The concept of an Irish Film Centre dates from an **Irish Film Institute** (IFI) proposal in the early 1980s to create a physical nexus for the often disparate activities of film-related bodies in Ireland. In 1985 the IFI drew up plans for a center on the corner of Trinity Street and Andrew Street in Dublin, but these were abandoned the following year when the IFI acquired most of what was then the Friends Meeting House at 6 Eustace Street in Dublin's Temple Bar. Architect Sheila O'Donnell drew up an award-winning plan to rework the interior in line with the IFI's requirements for a space containing two cinemas, a film archive, and a library (to which a bar and restaurant and a bookshop were later added). The project was given a political fillip in January 1987 when the government's first white paper on cultural policy, "Access and Opportunity," singled out the Film Centre project as deserving support, and later that year the **Arts Council** provided a £95,000 capital grant to the IFI (over and above a direct grant of £20,000) to allow it to complete the purchase of the building. The building was then occupied on an interim basis by the institute along with **Film Base**, the **MEDIA program**'s EVE initiative, and the Traditional Irish Music Archive. In 1989 the Arts Council established the Irish Film Centre Building Ltd. (IFCB) to oversee the development of the project. Having raised £350,000 of National Lottery funds via the Arts Council in December 1989, with a further £600,000 of European Union structural funds in November 1990, the IFCB Ltd. commenced a major redevelopment of the building in June 1991.

The newly refurbished building, redevelopment of which ultimately cost £2.25 million, eventually opened in September 1992, following the merger of IFI and the IFCB. Though logical administratively, the merger was not an entirely happy one, as it led to "rationalization" of staff numbers and initial tensions between staff from the formerly separate organizations. Nonetheless, the main public focus of the center, the two cinemas, enjoyed early success. Around 15,000 people became members in the first 12 months—three times the targeted figure. This was financially significant given that Arts Council support to the IFI was limited to supporting education and archival and informational work, that is, not the cinemas. Furthermore the remit that the cinemas limit runs to two to three weeks and reserve a percentage of screenings for repertory and archival material imposed programming constraints that a purely commercial cinema would have eschewed.

The financial limitations imposed by the remit would become a pressing issue for a period in the mid-1990s as membership—and therefore the cinemas' income—dropped off. When in March 1995 the IFC announced plans to screen Oliver Stone's *Natural Born Killers*, which the film censor had banned on an open-ended basis, it was suggested that the decision was driven less by ideological objections to **censorship** and more by the need to keep the cinemas afloat. In any event the screenings were prohibited by the Department of Justice, which threatened garda intervention. The financial position of the cinemas improved after 1996, when the **Light House** cinemas closed.

In addition to the cinemas, by the mid-1990s the IFC was home to **Media Desk**, EVE, **Film Base**, the Federation of **Irish Film Societies**, the Junior Dublin Film Festival, **Film Makers Ireland**, and Hubbard Casting. By the first decade of the 21st century, the center was widely recognized as being at the heart of film culture in Ireland, and it has become a model for proposed similar initiatives in other Irish cities.

IRISH FILM FINANCE CORPORATION (IFFC). The Irish Film Finance Corporation was established in 1960 as a response to changes in the operation of the British Cinematograph Films Act of 1957. Prior to 1959 films made by Irish citizens or companies were considered British under that legislation and could thus avail of Eady levy funding, a tax on all cinema going in Great Britain. Thus, for example, it appeared that the promoters of **Ardmore Studios**—the building of which started in 1957—assumed that such funding would be available for productions shot at the studios. However, in 1959 the British Board of Trade amended the operation of the levy so that only films made by British residents or by companies registered, managed, and controlled in the United Kingdom qualified for funding.

The absence in Ireland of any alternative organization offering to provide risk capital for producers wishing to make films at Ardmore Studios posed a serious threat to that operation's viability. Within six weeks after the changes to the Eady levy came into effect, however, the state-owned Industrial Credit Company responded by establishing a subsidiary, the Irish Film Finance Corporation Ltd.

Between 1960 and 1967, the IFFC would invest £506,317 of public funds in 15 films. Of these, however, only 2 dealt with Irish subjects. More significantly Irish employment on all of these films was limited to carpenters, plasterers, and canteen and office workers at Ardmore. This was because—surprisingly—the IFFC was not explicitly established to support Irish film production but rather to consider applications from *film producers in Ireland* for financial assistance by way of loans.

Indeed neophyte Irish film companies were virtually unable to access IFFC funding for two reasons: first because the IFFC required that any project they considered had previously secured distribution guarantees—that is, a commitment from a distributor to pick up the film once completed. Second, the IFFC preferred to provide "end money," the remaining capital required by a producer to finance a film after the producer received credit from commercial institutions. Both of these conditions meant that IFFC funding was of use only to those producers with a track record impressive enough to convince distributors, banks, or building societies to invest in their films. Since there was no history of consistent feature production in Ireland, there were no such producers based in Ireland. Not surprisingly, a 1967 civil service assessment of the IFFC concluded that "the IFFC is serving no useful purpose as a credit institution for regular film production in Ireland" (National Archive, 1967).

IRISH FILM INSTITUTE. The origins of the Irish Film Institute date back to the mid-1930s when Jesuit priest Father Richard Devane's interest in cinema was piqued by an *Irish Press* campaign castigating elements of the **exhibition** industry for its effect on public morality. Although supporting the campaign, Devane's critique of cinema was more nuanced: He called for a government enquiry into all aspects of cinema to enable a fuller understanding of its cultural, educational, and "national" potential. He would repeat this call in April 1937, notwithstanding the publication in the interim of Pope Pius XI's encyclical on cinema, which advocated a censorious approach to the medium. For Devane, by contrast, the establishment of an enquiry would enable Ireland to use cinema as a powerful instrument of cultural development. Ultimately he expected the enquiry to recommend that this be achieved through the establishment of a national film institute.

Devane's call for an enquiry was indirectly answered by the decision of **Sean Lemass** to establish the **Inter-Departmental Committee on the Film Industry** in 1937. In its eventual 1942 report, the committee considered the pros and cons of a national film institute, which it envisaged (among other functions) as acting as a focus for production activity, funding prospective producers, and advising the state on running a putative state-funded film studio. In short the committee envisaged a body that would effectively bear de facto responsibility for defining film policy in Ireland.

However, the committee described as "perhaps the most important function" of the institute the promotion of film for purposes of education, culture, and general propaganda (Inter-Departmental Committee on the Film Industry, 1942). Demonstrating almost limitless faith in the power of the medium, the report asserted that there was no subject of the school curriculum that did not lend itself in a greater or lesser degree to film treatment. Similarly, with regard to cinema's cultural potential the report suggested that

an important contribution could be made towards the development of national culture by the exhibition of films dealing with the history and institutions, traditions and customs, literature, music, games and pastimes of the people. (Inter-Departmental Committee on the Film Industry, 1942)

Although many of the committee recommendations were not acted upon, the one exception to this related to a national film institute, in part because other actors took a hand in the matter. In July 1943

Devane (with the imprimatur of Archbishop John Charles McQuaid) announced the intention to establish the National Film Institute of Ireland (NFII). The following December saw a further Inter-Departmental Committee representing Education, Finance, Industry and Commerce, Agriculture and Local Government, and Public Health reconsider the original committee's comments on educational films and films in the Irish language. This new committee recommended state funding of the Film Institute to facilitate the acquisition of a library of education films and the production of films on behalf of government departments. Thus from 1945/6 onward the NFII was in receipt of funding via the annual science and art vote of the Department of Education.

In effect the state co-opted the Film Institute, imposing upon it the dual responsibilities of a national film unit and a film education board, without giving it sufficient funds to fulfill either remit. However, from the perspective of the Catholic hierarchy, it seems likely that state funding was interpreted as a tacit endorsement of the institute as the state's "official" film body, thus obviating the possibility that a more secular body such as the **Irish Film Society** might occupy that role.

In general terms, the institute identified its function as being to direct and encourage the use of the motion picture in the national cultural interests of the Irish people. However, the approach adopted by the institute to realizing this broad objective changed dramatically in the late 1970s, so that the NFII's history can be divided into two periods — its "Catholic" phase from 1945 to 1979 and its secular one since 1979.

The Catholic phase was inaugurated by the initial grant of state funds, which permitted the institute to begin a concerted program to acquire a substantial library of educational films. By 1950 it had already amassed 800 films, although at the time relatively few schools were equipped with projectors. These were augmented by a range of films commissioned by the state in the 1940s and 1950s. Key among these were *A Nation Once Again* (1945), a documentary commemorating the centenary of Thomas Davis's death, and *W. B. Yeats—A Tribute* (1950), although most of the films commissioned were more mundane public information shorts, relating to subjects like road safety and hygiene.

In 1948, the institute launched a journal that would remain in existence in one form or another until the late 1960s. *Irish Cinema Quarterly* (1948–1949) became *National Film Quarterly* (1950–1956), then *Irish Film Quarterly* (1957–1959), before eventually being retitled *Vision* (1965–1968).

Beyond film library, production, and journal functions, the institute operated some sporadic education outreach programs, initiating a course on educational films for teachers in 1946, and in theory it acted as an advisory committee on state film policy. In practice the institute's influence in this regard was limited by its resources. In 1955 minister for industry and commerce William Norton requested that the NFII look into "the whole question of a film industry." Although the institute did hold some meetings to attempt to devise some kind of film strategy, the resulting document, only a few pages long, obviously fell well short of what Norton had been expecting. Despite the institute's ability to carry out in-depth research, such a request continued to be hampered by the limited financial resources made available by the state. In 1967, for example, the Department of Education grant to the institute was £5,250, only slightly greater than the 1945 grant in real spending terms.

However, even if such resources had been adequate, it was unlikely that the institute would have undertaken a more ambitious program of action. At the institute's annual meeting in 1965, during a speech intended to complement its members on their Catholic character, Archbishop McQuaid made comments that indirectly acknowledged how he perceived the relevance of the organization in the wider society:

> I invite you to be glad at being treated with a sardonic contempt. If you had not standards of Christian Reverence, you would not be regarded as uneducated, illiberal, and inexperienced. ("Irish 'Accept and Want' Censorship," 1965)

Hence, by 1978, **Kevin Rockett**, although noting that the institute had a library of 6,000 films and two traveling projectors touring the country, described the institute as ineffectual and largely dormant, operating outside contemporary developments in film screening and writing.

Nevertheless, Rockett would be one of the key individuals in the cultural revolution that transformed the institute at the close of the

1970s. In 1978, Rockett had noted that the institute's connections with what remained a largely Church-run education system placed it in a unique position to drive forward a film education policy through the appointment of a film education officer. This coincided with **Arts Council** thinking on encouraging the institute to modernize and professionalize through financial incentives.

A first step in this direction was taken when the board of the institute (some of whose members had been in situ for two decades) invited Kevin Rockett to join the board. He was later followed by figures like Ciaran Benson (later chair of the Arts Council) and renowned cultural theorist Luke Gibbons. In 1979, the Arts Council responded by increasing the institute's grant from £200 to £7,400, an increase conditional on the appointment of a dedicated film education officer, Martin McLoone (who has written extensively on Irish film). By 1983 the grant went to £21,000, permitting the appointment of a full-time director. Thus, when David Kavanagh became director of the Irish Film Institute in 1983, he inherited a staff of six and an annual turnover of £130,000.

This purging of the board of its old guard continued through the early 1980s. By the time Kevin Rockett became chair in 1984, it had become possible to secularize the institute's Articles of Association, a shift reflected in the redesignation of the body as the Irish Film Institute.

In practical terms, these changes led to a dramatic transformation in the way the institute went about its business. Film education changed from merely screening approved material in schools to a more progressive, pedagogically informed approach typified by publications like *Every Picture Tells a Story* (1985) and *Roll It There, Colette* (1986), visual culture and media studies texts for secondary schools. This followed logically from a broader call for changes in the curriculum to reflect the growing influence of the mass media articulated in institute publications like Martin McLoone's *Media Studies in Irish Education*. Third-level education was also addressed in the 1984 copublication (with RTÉ) of *Television and Irish Society*.

From 1984, the institute began to receive seed funding from the Irish Film Board to develop an **Irish Film Archive**. However, arguably the most ambitious activity of the institute in the 1980s was the quest to find a new home, one that would allow the institute to operate a permanent cinema. The institute had had a taste of the exhibition business in 1983, when it was called in by the Arts Council in an attempt to revive the flagging fortunes of the **Irish Film Theatre** (IFT). Although the IFT closed in May 1984, the IFI pursued an exhibition strategy, curating the well-received Green on the Screen season of Irish and Irish-related material as part of the 1984 Contempor-Eire festival. In 1985 the institute announced plans for an **Irish Film Centre** (IFC), but acknowledging that it would take some time to raise the necessary funds, engaged in a partnership with Neil Connolly to establish the **Light House** Cinema as an interim measure to maintain some kind of continuity in art-house exhibition. This relationship came to an amicable conclusion with the opening of the Irish Film Centre in September 1992.

Kevin Rockett stood down as chair of the IFI in 1991, to be followed by Niamh O'Sullivan (who was in turn followed by Martha O'Neill and later **Alan Gilsenan**). Yet despite the opening of the IFC and a spectacular increase in Arts Council funding (reaching £330,000 by 1995), the early 1990s were a politically difficult period for the board. In early 1993 the IFI and Irish Film Centre Building Ltd., the ad hoc body charged by the Arts Council with the establishment of the IFC, merged, bringing two sets of staff together, and creating a new entity, the Film Institute of Ireland (FII). This led to a period of "rationalization" and redundancies and an internal dispute over the appointment of a chief executive, which ultimately led former IFI director David Kavanagh (who by 1994 oversaw 45 staff and a turnover of £1.5 million) to resign from the organization. Matters were compounded by the fact that the center as a whole lost money in 1994, in part as a result of the initial failure of the IFC's bar and restaurant to earn the profits that had been earmarked to cross-subsidize more overtly cultural activities.

In September 1994, however, a new chief executive, Sheila Pratschke, was appointed, and with the aid of substantial ongoing funding the environment at the FII became more settled. In 1999, in part driven by the Arts Council publication of a three-year arts plan, the FII published its own five-year plan, identifying the organization's core functions. These included the operation of the IFC cinemas, the promotion of the education department, supporting the Irish Film Archive, and performing a research and information function for all aspects of film and filmmaking in Ireland. Most of these mapped neatly onto the film policy emphases laid out in the Arts Council document, and they have subsequently remained the main foci of institute activity.

In 2003, driven by a concern that there was a lack of public appreciation of the institute's activities (many people were unaware that the Irish Film Centre housed much more than its cinemas), the FII board voted to revert to the IFI name. As part of this shift, the Irish Film Centre building became the Irish Film Institute.

As of 2004, the IFI employed 70 people and had an annual turnover of approximately €2.6 million (including a €600,000 Arts Council revenue grant and €14,000 for education from the Department of Education). The main objective of the current chair, **Alan Gilsenan**, is to acquire national cultural institute status for the IFI, a move that would put it on a par with other national cultural bodies like the National Library, the National Gallery, and the Abbey Theatre.

IRISH FILM SOCIETY (IFS). The society was founded in 1936 by **Liam O'Leary**, Edward Toner, Sean O'Meadhra, and Patrick Fitzsimons. Membership grew quickly, and branches were set up around the country. Although the main objective of the society was to exhibit classical and foreign films, by 1943 the work of the society had expanded to include running the School of Film Technique, the Children's Film Committee, which trained teachers to use film as a pedagogical tool, and working with the element of the Irish cinema trade to sponsor children's matinee screenings. In addition the society was responsible for publishing *Scannán*, the only regular indigenous film journal. The school collapsed in 1948 as the society—not surprisingly, given the absence of a film industry—found it difficult to hire adequately trained instructors. Before this, its members produced a series of short films including the well-received *Foolsmate*, a 20-minute fiction piece directed by Brendan Stafford (who later pursued a directorial career in the British film industry), and *Aiséirghe*, directed by **Liam O'Leary**, which in critiquing the nation's practical commitment to the ideals of 1916 arguably prefigured O'Leary's 1948 film *Our Country*.

However, the society's most important cultural contribution was to bring to Ireland foreign language films, which had largely disappeared from mainstream cinemas since the introduction of sound and the ensuing Anglo-American dominance of the Irish **distribution** sector. And while side projects such as the film school and *Scannán* gradually came to a conclusion, the society's core function of exhibition has persisted into the modern era. Although with the advent of the **Irish Film Theatre** in 1976 (and subsequently the Light House and the Irish Film Centre), the society was no longer the sole avenue for art-house material in Ireland, it remained crucial for audiences based outside Dublin or Cork who lacked access to a dedicated art-house venue.

In 1977 the IFS was superseded by the Federation of Irish Film Societies (FIFS), which acted as an umbrella body for all of the country's local film societies. The FIFS provided a centralized film-booking agency for its members from its head office in Dublin. Typically the FIFS organized biannual screenings of new material on offer (especially in the 16 mm format that was the preferred option for societies), to allow local societies to draw up seasonal screening programs. By the early 1990s the federation was bringing in approximately 250 titles annually for 25 societies with aggregate membership in the region of 4,500 people. It was also arguably developing an audience for more permanent art-house venues. As of 1990 the society at the Triskel Arts Centre in Cork City was operating four days a week for 25–30 weeks of the year, a consideration that indirectly influenced the decision to open a permanent venue (the Kino) in the city in November 1996.

By the end of the 1990s, the widespread availability of material for home consumption in VHS and DVD formats and doubts over the long-term availability of 16 mm material along with the emerging possibilities of digital cinema began to raise serious questions over the future role of the federation. In addition an increasing number of regional arts centers were using their theater spaces to screen art-house material alongside the operation of local film societies. In response in 1998 the federation commissioned a development plan to outline new directions for the organization.

This in turn led to the rebranding of the organization in 2001 as ACCESS Cinemas. ACCESS continued to advise local societies on film selection, technical issues, and presentation standards, and to block-book and ship films on behalf of local film societies. However, these activities were now presented as taking place within a broader remit to promote regional cultural cinema programming in general, for example in partnership with arts centers and other local cultural organizations.

IRISH FILM THEATRE. In many ways a forerunner of the **Irish Film Centre** cinemas, the Irish Film Theatre (IFT) was established in March 1976 after the success of the European Film Fortnight held in January of that year in Dublin's International Cinema. The aim was to satisfy the demand for films that would not otherwise receive commercial release. In effect the IFT represented the nearest thing Ireland had at the time to a national film theater. Despite this and the fact that the Film Fortnight had been run by the **Arts Council**'s Film and Literature officer **David Collins**, and that the IFT was legally a subsidiary of the Arts Council, it received no Arts Council funding. Encouraged by the success of the European Film Fortnight the council felt that the IFT could be financially self-sufficient, particularly in light of the fact that it would be constituted as a club and thus would not have to pay **censorship** fees. Despite this view, David Collins summed up the section on film in the 1976 Arts Council report by stating that the council's overall level of finance for film was still inadequate.

The initial success of the IFT, however, seemed to confirm the Arts Council view. By 1980 membership had reached 12,000 people, and annual admissions topped 100,000: an extraordinary figure considering that there were only two screenings a day, all taking place in the single-screen, 240-seat Earlsfort Terrace cinema. The initial success owed much to the availability of product, as there was a huge backlog of art-house material that had never been screened in Ireland.

Such was the euphoria that, in 1980, a second cinema was leased from the **Ward Anderson** group in Limerick. It was intended to be the first stage in an ambitious plan to establish a national circuit of IFTs. The 1982 Arts Council annual report, however, made it clear that all was not rosy: Plans to establish a third IFT in Cork were abandoned when a disturbing trend of diminishing audiences in the Dublin IFT during the last quarter of 1982 prompted the IFT board to introduce a change in programming policies and discard the membership requirement for admission. The ongoing lack of subsidy was exacerbated by several other factors. The Limerick IFT was a disaster from the start: Poorly located, it had never broken even financially. Furthermore, by 1980 the Dublin IFT had exhausted the backlog of blue-chip art-house material and was increasingly forced to rely on newer material, which proved less reliable in drawing audiences.

As a result, in 1983 the IFT administrative offices were closed, and the Arts Council was forced to pay out £105,953 to cover the debts of its subsidiary. Despite handing over programming policy to the **Irish Film Institute**, attendances continued to drop, from their 2,000 a week peak in 1979 to 500 a week in 1984. In May of the same year £50,000 was provided to wind up the IFT's affairs. The 1984 annual report concluded with the hope that "a new way of providing for the public who wish to see and support a programme of art-house films will emerge" (Arts Council, 1984).

The significance of the IFT as a model (particularly for the Irish Film Centre cinemas) cannot be overstated: Its spectacular rise and fall made explicit the possibility of screening art-house material but also drew attention to the commercial pitfalls of doing so.

IRISH SCREEN COMMISSION. When, in January 1996, the minister for finance introduced changes to **Section 481**, they were—to the consternation of both the state and the Irish film industry—reported in international film industry journals as signaling a shift away from encouraging international productions to shoot in Ireland. Although in the longer term Hollywood companies continued to arrive in Ireland, the changes drew attention to the absence of any state mechanism for countering the effect of such stories. The response in March 1997 was the creation of an Irish Screen Commission, as a subcommittee of the **Irish Film Board**. The new body was charged with promoting Ireland internationally as a filmmaking location. In addition the commission was to facilitate both incoming *and* indigenous productions by acting as a one-stop information source for filmmakers, offering advice on liaising with local authorities and on potential locations for filming.

The commission did not commence actual operations until Roger Greene was appointed chief executive in August 1998. Greene had previously worked as a public relations consultant to **Strongbow** film and television productions, **Ardmore Studios**, and the **Irish Film Institute** in the 1980s and had founded his own production company — Charlemont Films — in 1987. Immediately before taking on the commission position he had worked in England, lecturing in media at the University of Lincolnshire and Humberside and directing television coverage of horse racing.

Although officially constituted as a subcommittee of, and funded by, the Irish Film Board, the Screen Commission had its own offices in Dublin (120 miles from the Film Board's headquarters) and from February 1999 maintained an office in Los Angeles. However, the commission proved relatively short-lived as a stand-alone body. In November 2000, as part of a package of measures growing out of the *Kilkenny Report*, it was decided to fold the commission's activities back into the Irish Film Board, a decision that took effect in September 2001. Much of the responsibility for the commission's activities fell to the location services unit, within the Film Board's new marketing department. Since 2001, however, the location services manager has been renamed screen commissioner to reflect the broad range of activities that comes under the rubric of the position. These included maintaining a database of potential locations, offering information on financial incentives for shooting in Ireland, maintaining a database on local production personnel, and acting as a hub for the developing network of regional film commissions and Film Dublin, which works to facilitate film production in the capital city.

In May 2005, government minister **John O'Donoghue** announced that the Irish Film Board would appoint a deputy film commissioner, based in Los Angeles, to liaise with the major studios there and to effectively link these studios with the services and supports available in Ireland.

– J –

JORDAN, NEIL (1950–). Born in County Sligo but raised in Dublin, he studied English literature and history at University College Dublin. He made his initial impact as a writer of literary fiction, establishing the Irish Writers' Cooperative in 1974 and winning the Guardian Fiction Prize in 1976 for *Nights in Tunisia*, a collection of short stories.

(He has subsequently had four other novels published, the most recent being *Shade* in 2004.) He began his filmmaking career with a documentary on **John Boorman's** *Excalibur* (1981). However, having originally scripted **Joe Comerford**'s *Traveller* (1981), he was very unhappy with the finished film, which he claimed lacked narrative and cohesion. His first feature, *Angel* (1982), began his preoccupation with representations of violence and the Northern "**troubles**." It was a well-produced, driven revenge narrative, and a calling card for Jordan, which was well received critically.

Throughout his career, Jordan has been one of the most important native writers and directors. His preoccupation with representing the political "troubles" in Northern Ireland and the Provisional Republican movement (PIRA) in particular helped to carve out a revisionist identity for Ireland. From *Angel* up to the more recent *The Crying Game* (2002) and the Irish success of **Michael Collins** (1996), Jordan's films have dealt closely with Irish nationalist issues, while his directorial talents have been used to great success internationally within a wide variety of genres.

Joining up with British producer Stephen Woolley, Jordan directed a number of successful small-scale films in the mid-1980s, beginning with the very stylish horror rites-of-passage narrative *The Company of Wolves* (1984), which was coscripted from the original story by Angela Carter. The film is a surreal allegory with men morphing into wolves as in the Little Red Riding story. Beware of men whose "eyebrows meet in the middle," warns this gothic and magical exploration of desire and budding sexuality. Critics reviewed the film very favorably, and even with its relatively small budget the film includes some very effective special effects that captured the dark magic realism of the original source. Coproduced by George Harrison's Handmade Films, Jordan's next feature, *Mona Lisa* (1986), was also both critically and commercially successful. Bob Hoskins plays a retired petty criminal who is hired by his former boss, Michael Caine, to chauffeur chic prostitute Cathy Tyson between jobs in London.

High Spirits (1988), from Jordan's own script, was probably his most ill-conceived comedy attempt and a commercial failure, costing over $12 million. It focused on a haunted house farce set in an Irish castle and starred A-list Hollywood cast including Daryl Hannah, Steve Guttenberg, **Peter O'Toole**, and Beverly D'Angelo. Irish actors on the film included **Donal McCann**, **Liam Neeson**, **Ray McAnally**, and Tom Hickey. The cringing and stilted comedy lacks overall pace and narrative drive, a fact defended by Jordan, who argued that he had little postproduction input or control. *We're No Angels* (1989) followed, again with an A-list cast of Robert De Niro, Sean Penn, and Demi Moore. This story of two escaped convicts is a conventional and poorly received reworking of Michael Curtiz's 1955 movie of the same name.

Having being somewhat burned by the Hollywood experience, Jordan returned home to a more intimate and less expensive form of filmmaking and made *The Miracle* (1991), which is set in a seaside town of Bray, County Wicklow, near his home. Two teenagers spend their time inventing imaginary stories about the local townfolk who pass them in the street, but when glamorous actress Beverly D'Angelo comes to town, the boy, Jimmy, soon becomes obsessed with her. Only as the film progresses is the truth about her relationship to him revealed.

This romantic rites-of-passage narrative was followed by the surprise hit *The Crying Game* (1992), which also became an academic staple for analysis in a slew of gender and queer theory essays and studies. The runaway success of the film had seemed unlikely. How could one sell a film mixing a controversial gender-bending twist with ethnic debates and a narrative steeped in the Northern "troubles" to a mass audience? But Miramax marketed the film as a straightforward thriller and traded on the film's gender twist and teaser, "The movie that everyone's talking about, but no one is giving away its secrets." Between its release in November 1992 and the **Academy Awards** in the following March, over a thousand release prints were issued, and the film was nominated for six Academy Awards including Best Film and Best Director. It won the award for Best Screenplay and grossed over $60 million at the U.S. box office alone, which to this day remains one of the greatest Irish success stories.

Jordan then went on to make *Interview with a Vampire* (1994), an adaptation of Anne Rice's cult gay novel starring Brad Pitt and Christian Slater along with Tom Cruise and Antonio Banderas; it did well at the American box office. As with *The Miracle*, Jordan again turned to homegrown Irish themes for his next two films with the support of Warner Brothers and Geffen Pictures, following the success of his vampire film. In *Michael Collins* (1996) he addressed the very controversial Irish historical debate around the 1916 rebellion and the cult status of Collins, played by **Liam Neeson**, against the foregrounding of the struggle for Irish independence. Within the Irish media, debates raged over the historical authenticity of the story as framed against a revisionist peace process, which was going through various crises in the North. The British press was generally very hostile to the film's portrayal of the old Irish Republican Army (IRA) and its sympathetic representation of Irish nationalism generally. The film was shot over a 14-week schedule in over 80 locations throughout Dublin and County Wicklow.

With *The Butcher Boy* (1997) Jordan adapted an acclaimed novel by Pat McCabe. Irish critics in particular regard the resultant film as Jordan's crowning achievement, citing its successful retention of the novel's unique authorial voice, its toying with the clash between tradition and modernity in early 1960s Ireland, and the extraordinary visual tropes used to depict that clash. But unfortunately the difficult terrain of violent childhood imaginings made it hard for the film to attract a wide mass audience, especially since the film's release coincided with widely reported real-life stories of violence meted out by dysfunctional children.

His next picture, *In Dreams* (1998), was a supernatural psychological thriller that remained overly generic and formulaic (but was better than some of Jordan's own pronouncements on the film suggested). This preoccupation with generic material continued with his stylish remake of Jean-Pierre Melville's *Bob le Flambeur*, *The Good Thief* (2002), starring Nick Nolte. He completed his second adaptation of a McCabe novel, *Breakfast on Pluto* (2005).

JOYCE, JAMES (1882–1941). Joyce is the most recognized Irish literary artist. He wrote most of his greatest literature while an emigrant in Europe, including *Ulysses*, which focused on the minutiae of his beloved Dublin at the turn of the 20th century. The seminal Russian filmmaker Sergi Eisenstein, admiring its revolutionary stream of consciousness and modernist cinematic aesthetic, wanted to film the difficult text. While this prospect was very appealing to the writer, unfortunately the project never got off the ground. Nevertheless, there have been at least two versions made of the book—**Joseph Strick**'s version and ***Bloom***—alongside a very superior version of his short story "**The Dead**," which was director **John Huston**'s swan song. Joyce himself became very interested in the medium of film and even went so far as to set up one of the first cinemas in Dublin, called the Volta, in December 1909, which showed a wide range of European art-house films. But unfortunately the project failed and he quickly left his homeland again.

JOYRIDERS (**1988**). Directed by Aisling Walsh and set in contemporary Dublin, the film tells the story of a woman, Mary (Patricia Kerrigan), who is forced to abandon her home with her two kids and faces the prospect of being homeless on the streets. She decides in the opening sequences to have them taken into care, abandoning them at a main train station and calling the police to pick them up. She is alone and distressed, and her troubles worsen when two sailors looking for a good time in an all-night café harass her. The occasional joyrider—slang for car thief—Perky Rice (Andrew Connolly) saves her, bringing her to a public house, where despite or because of her seething anger at her situation, he becomes attracted to her. His situation becomes more complicated, however, when gangsters track him down and demand a payoff for some earlier misdemeanor. He decides to escape the city and asks her to accompany him. So begins a road movie romance—he steals a car that she chooses, and they head off to the coastal town of Killeel, where she had her honeymoon, a source of fond memories. As in many such journeys, all has changed when they reach their destination, and she finds a town peopled by bachelors and a seedy hotel proprietor (**John Kavanagh**). Nonetheless the pair form a friendship with washed-out dance hostess Tammy (Billie Whitelaw).

The joyride gravitates to the West and a farm on which Daniel, an aging widower (**David Kelly** in another stand-out performance), lives, more asleep than awake. In this rural refuge, the city dwellers find redemption in hard work on the farm while Daniel realizes his need for a family. The film's closure follows the protagonists as they return to the city en famille. The film's attempt to merge the gangster movie conventions that characterize the opening section of the story with the romantic road movie of the latter section does not fully come off, but the feel-good love story has wide appeal.

JUST IN TIME **(1998).** As in all their well-regarded art films, directors John Carney and Tom Hall focus on relationships and their difficulties in this story. A middle-aged academic, Frank (Gerard McSorley), spends a weekend in the country with his painter wife (Frances Barber), leaving his lover behind in London. Their mood of recollection is broken when an old friend turns up with his young mistress.

– K –

KALEM COMPANY. The Kalem Company was formed in the United States in 1907 by George Kleine, Samuel Long, and Frank Marion and shot the first feature made in Ireland, entitled *The Lad from Old Ireland* (1910). This melodrama is described as the first feature film produced by an American company outside America. **Sidney Olcott** was the main driving force behind the Irish operation, and he favored producing rebel Irish nationalist stories. Initially the local parish priest denounced the production company from the pulpit, but eventually he was removed to another parish and the filmmaking continued. Later, with the British taking exception to the screen treatment and romantic representation of rebels, and their American masters concerned about their investments, Olcott turned to the safer themes of Dion Boucicault's romantic melodramas during the remainder of his stay.

Notable examples of films made by Kalem include *The Colleen Bawn*, *Arrah-na-Pogue*, and *The Shaughran*. Less-distinguished shorts, which made excellent use of the beautiful scenery and other facets of Irish Life, include *The Kerry Dancers*, *The Kerry Gow* [Blacksmith], *The Fisherman of Ballydavid*, *The Girl of Glenbeigh*, *A Puck Fair Romance*, and *Ireland 50 Years Ago*.

KAVANAGH, JOHN (1946–). Born into a Dublin family, Kavanagh grew up in the suburb of Milltown, where he attended the local national school. As a teenager he was determined to work in cinema, albeit as a technician rather than an actor. (Ironically, he regarded acting as a means of getting into technical work.) After leaving school at 16 he worked as a caddy at a local golf club, later returning to a technical school to complete his Leaving Certificate. He then trained as an actor at the Brendan Smyth Academy, which he joined when he was 19, and in 1967 he joined the **Abbey Theatre**, where he would remain for a decade before becoming a freelance actor.

He made his film debut with a small part in *Paddy* (1970), based on a play by local writer Lee Dunne, but it was his performance more than a decade later as the Bowser Egan in **Pat O'Connor's** *Ballroom of Romance* that established him as a screen actor. Kavanagh was perfectly cast in the adaptation of the William Trevor short story, his occasionally peevish visage embodying the cautious rural culture the heroine of the story finds herself trapped within. He has continued to work with O'Connor on features ever since, including *Cal*, *Fools of Fortune* (another William Trevor adaptation), *Circle of Friends*, and *Dancing at Lughnasa*. Kavanagh has also become a familiar face to British audiences, although mostly for major roles in single dramas or miniseries set in Ireland or with an Irish theme. He is perhaps less well recognized outside the United Kingdom and Ireland, although American audiences would know him from roles in **Neil Jordan's** *Michael Collins* and *The Butcher Boy* and more recently from Oliver Stone's *Alexander* (2004).

Like most Irish actors he has combined his screen appearances with stage work, winning acclaim for playing Magwitch in *Great Expectations* and Astrov in Anton Chekhov's *Uncle Vanya*, and becoming inextricably associated in the minds of Dublin theater audiences with the role of Joxer in Sean O'Casey's *Juno and the Paycock*—especially in a 1980s production opposite **Donal McCann**. He has also worked on stage in London's West End and on Broadway in New York.

KELLEGHER, TINA (1967–). Born in Dublin, she became a household name with her powerful role as working-class Sharon Curley in *The Snapper*, which dealt with teenage pregnancy. Since then she had roles in *Widows' Peak* and *The Disappearance of Finbar*, and several well-remembered roles in effective television miniseries like *The Hanging Gale* (1995), *Ballykissangel* (1996), *Sinners* (2002), and *Showbands* (2004).

KELLY, DAVID (1929–). Born in Dublin and educated at the famous Synge Street School, he started acting at the tender age of eight with the

Gaiety Theatre. Of late he has become the grand old man of Irish theater and film with a long and distinguished career. Most famously home audiences remember his groundbreaking leading performance as Rashers Tierney, a down-and-out character in the most successful historical production of all time, *Strumpet City* (1980), made and broadcast by the Irish national broadcaster **Radio Telefís Éireann (RTÉ)** and successfully sold throughout the world. His extensive Irish film credits include an adaptation of Brendan Behan's *The Quare Fellow* (1962), Edna O'Brien's *The Girl with the Green Eyes* (1964), **James Joyce**'s *Ulysses* (1967), *Joyriders*, *Into the West*, *Waking Ned* (aka *Waking Ned Devine*), *Ordinary Decent Criminal*, *Puckcoon*, *Mystics*, and more recently *Charlie and the Chocolate Factory* (2005). Kelly received a Lifetime Achievement award from the Irish Film Industry in 2005.

KENNEDY, MARIA DOYLE. She initially came to public attention in Ireland through music as a backup singer for the Hothouse Flowers and subsequently as lead singer for the Black Velvet Band. Her musical background eased her transition to acting when she came to prominence with her strong role as Maria in **Alan Parker**'s quasi musical *The Commitments*. Although she continues to work as a recording artist, she has interspersed albums with roles in *A Further Gesture*, *The General*, *I Could Read the Sky*, and *Spin the Bottle*. She has also had strong roles in the well-regarded television series *Queer as Folk* and miniseries like *No Tears*.

KEOGH, GARRET. Garret refined his acting skills while doing the fringe and theater circuit in Dublin in the 1970s, performing in a wide range of genres and acting styles. This variety has served him well as he continues to work between television, theater, and film over the years. On television he has had a major part in *Ballykissangel* playing Mossy Phelan, alongside an Irish football series, *On Home Ground*, the very popular *Fair City* soap, and most recently in the doctor series *The Clinic*. In film he had important parts in *The Bargain Shop* and more recently *Veronica Guerin*, playing the overly clean-cut Tony Gregory—who is a well-known Dublin inner-city independent member of parliament. Other roles include *Excalibur*, on which many Irish actors got a start in film, alongside *Widows' Peak*, *Angela's Ashes*, *Saltwater*, and *Evelyn*.

THE KILKENNY REPORT. See STRATEGIC DEVELOPMENT OF THE IRISH FILM AND TELEVISION INDUSTRY 2000–2010.

KILLANIN, LORD (1914–1999). Born Michael Morris, he inherited the title Killanin when the previous lord—his uncle—died in 1927. Having been educated at Eton, the Sorbonne, and Cambridge, he went to work as a reporter first for the *Daily Express* and then for the *Daily Mail* in the 1930s. During this period he came into contact with Irish director **Brian Desmond Hurst**, for whom he began writing scripts. While on assignment in Hollywood he encountered director (and apparently his distant cousin) **John Ford** for the first time. Anticipating the coming conflict with Germany, he joined the British Army in 1938. During the war he was decorated on several occasions, took part in the D-day landings in Normandy, and by 1945 had been promoted to brigade major. With the fighting over he returned to his ancestral home in Spiddal, County Galway, which he rebuilt in 1945. In 1951 his relationship with Ford moved onto a professional plane when he played a substantial role in location scouting and production work on *The Quiet Man*. In the same year he established **Four Provinces** films, through which he produced a number of films. The first of these was *The Rising of the Moon* in 1957, followed a year later by another Ford-directed picture, *Gideon's Day* (1958). This was in turn followed by Hurst's adaptation of *The Playboy of the Western World* in 1962. In 1965 he acted as associate producer on Ford's *Young Cassidy*, based loosely on Sean O'Casey's early life. His final film credit came in 1969 when he again acted as associate producer, this time on Clive Doner's *Alfred the Great*.

In addition to his film work he engaged in an extraordinary range of other activities. Most notable among these was his work with sporting organzations. Having been president of the Olympic Council of Ireland since 1950, he became a member of the International Olympic Committee in 1952. In 1972 he effectively became the most powerful man in international sport when he was appointed IOC president, a position he retained until 1980, when Juan Antonio Samaranch replaced him. Meanwhile, in Ireland, in addition to a number of commercial directorships, he also sat on a range of state bodies, several of which had a cultural dimension, including the **Cul-**

tural Relations Committee from 1949 till 1972, the Film Industry (Huston) Committee in 1968, and the Dublin Theatre Festival, which he chaired from 1958 to 1970. Indeed he was an active campaigner for state support of the film industry, especially in the 1950s, when he made a series of suggestions in that regard to the Department of Industry and Commerce. He had four children, one of whom, Redmond Morris, himself became a producer working on most of **Neil Jordan**'s films since the 1990s. *See also REPORT OF THE FILM INDUSTRY COMMITTEE.*

KNOCKNAGOW **(1918).** Based on Charles J. Kickham's famous novel, the film was directed by Fred O'Donovan, scripted by Mrs. N. F. Patton, and starred Brian Magowan, Fred O'Donovan, and Arthur Shields. The story uses the backdrop of the Great Famine as it focuses on poverty, stereotypically wicked land agents, and absentee landlords in County Tipperary. In particular Pender, a vicious agent, grossly mistreats the tenants. After falling in love with Mary, Arthur gives up his chance of becoming a priest, while she remains oblivious to his affections. As is reminiscent of the form of fatalism in a Thomas Hardy novel, she does not receive a letter he sends her on the eve of his ship's departure for America. Meanwhile, Pender plots to have Arthur arrested as the ship docks at Liverpool, but Arthur is vindicated, and of course the story ends happily. Unfortunately many sections of this archival film are difficult to piece together as the only surviving print is somewhat incomplete.

KOREA **(1995).** The capacity of the past to send shockwaves through time lies at the core of *Korea*, director **Cathal Black**'s densely layered and richly visual adaptation of John McGahern's short story. Set in a small Cavan village in 1952, the film opens with the death in the Korean War of local emigrant Luke Moran, leaving the community in mourning. The Moran family receives scant sympathy from John Doyle, a widower who fishes the freshwater lake with his son, Eamonn. Doyle still nurses a feud with Luke's father, Ben, that began when they chose opposite sides in the Civil War. Luke's death coincides with change in the community: The rural electrification scheme is reaching the village, promising to "sweep away inferiority complexes," tourism is developing as a local industry, and two of the "first generation born in freedom," Eamonn and Ben's daughter Una, are entering upon their first romance.

The historical setting of *Korea* is critical, for if the years from 1959 to 1963 are widely recognized as the era in which modern Ireland was born, it was the economic and demographic crises of the preceding decade that forced change. In *Korea*, John Doyle becomes the vehicle through which the dawning of this transformation is shown. The opening shot follows John Doyle rowing on the lake while Eamonn pays out a fishing line. As the camera angle disguises any progress across the water, Doyle is represented as a man literally going nowhere. Thus director Black eloquently establishes his role: John Doyle remains the defeated antitreatyite, for whom change is not synonmous with progress. He is already suspicious of the advent of electricity, which will bring both literal and figurative light to the village. The imminent tourist invasion threatens the withdrawal of Doyle's license to fish so that fish stocks might be built up for tourists. Faced with an uncertain future, he clings to the dark ages of his own past despite the pain engendered by his memories—atrocities witnessed in the Civil War and the death of his wife.

Ironically, by focusing on the experience of one individual, Black makes comprehensible the persistence of Civil War politics in Ireland, which can be obscured by explanations that refer to the nation as a whole. *Korea* offers a complex study of the nature of memory and, both in content and in form (re-creating the Ireland of 40 years ago), examines the re-creation of the past. In *Korea*, Civil War iconography pervades the Doyles' home. A photo of John Doyle as a young man in his Civil War uniform brings him back, recalling images of reprisal executions. But the process works two ways: The photo has the power to stare back, his past self challenging his present. Doyle, however, is unable to answer that challenge: His loyalty to the cause has won him little. Indeed if anything the cause has betrayed Doyle: It is after all a de Valera–led, Fianna Fáil government that threatens to withdraw his fishing licence. The Ireland that emerged from the ashes of war bears scant resemblance to his romantic and patriotic visions of it. Betrayed by his own nation he looks to send Eamonn to America, away from "this fool of a country." Yet Eamonn, educated, in love with Una, and part of the generation that will lead Ireland into the 1960s, is unwilling to leave. The resulting confrontation between the old and the new forces Doyle to face his own past and so come to terms with the present.

– L –

LALLY, MICK (1945–). After graduating from Galway University, he became a teacher, but when he was almost 30, he, Garry Hynes, and Marie Mullen decided to set up the Druid Theatre Company in Galway, which has become highly successful over the years. Lally solidified his theater acting while becoming a household name for his role as a bumbling farmer in the long-running television soap *Glenroe*. While continuing to command theater audiences for his roles in John B. Keane's *The Chastitute* and J. M. Synge's plays, he has had numerous character roles in films as diverse as *The Fantasist* (1986), *The Outcasts* (1982), *Fools of Fortune* (1990), *A Man of No Importance* (1994), *The Secret of Roan Inish* (1993), *Circle of Friends* (1995), and *Alexander* (2004).

LAMB **(1986).** Made for **Channel 4** and based on a Bernard MacLaverty novel, *Lamb* is a remarkably moving account of the relationship between two contrasting figures who nonetheless have much in common. Owen Kane (**Hugh O'Conor**), an eight-year-old offender with epilepsy, is brought by his mother to Saint Killian's, a school for difficult children, run by Christian Brothers. There he is taken under the wing of Michael Lamb (**Liam Neeson**), a brother facing a crisis of faith. As he learns about Owen's life—the absence of any father figure and the consistent abuse at the hands of his drunken mother—Michael despairs at the world at large and questions his own faith. Owen is trapped in a miserable life not of his own choosing, while Michael is unable to legitimately escape the control of his order. In short, neither has much to look forward to. The impact of their age difference is somehow mitigated, since life has forced Owen to become streetwise, growing up faster than most, while Michael, by contrast, has never really been without a father figure—be it actual or spiritual.

Michael's father dies, leaving him money and a way out. His order, however, seeks to claim his father's estate by invoking Michael's vow of poverty. Michael flees to England with Owen only to find that the order has reported his act as a kidnapping. With £2,000 from his father's estate, Michael and Owen are able to live comfortably for a while. Thus, for both characters, the escape from the boy's home represents an escape from fates that would otherwise be set in concrete. The brief idyll comes to a sharp end, however, when Owen suffers an epileptic fit at a football match. Soon after the pair are conned out of their money, forcing them to return to Ireland. Pursued by the police, Michael ultimately takes both their fates in his own hands with terrible consequences.

The film is almost entirely carried by its two leads, Neeson and O'Conor, both of whom used the film as a launchpad for their subsequent careers. The performances are matched by careful direction from Colin Gregg, who opts for an unobtrusive style that allows the story to unfold at it own pace. Indeed it is a tribute to the skill with which actors and filmmakers work to convey the characters' inner emotional lives that the terrible final act in the film is rendered almost merciful. "Almost," because the film also allows the possibility that Michael's act is not the correct choice, but that the pressure of the situation has caused an essentially good man to carry out an evil act.

LAMENT FOR ART O'LEARY [*CAOINEADH AIRT UI LAOIRE*] **(1975).** The film was financed by the Workers' Party (an unusual occurrence) and lauded by many film critics of the time, being the first independently produced Irish-language film and indeed the first major indigenous production of the 1970s. The lament was written by O'Leary's wife after the death of her husband, an 18th-century descendent of Gaelic aristocrats dispossessed by the English. **Bob Quinn**'s film concerns the last few years of O'Leary's life, from 1767 to 1773, after his return to Ireland. Reminiscent of the radical historical style of Peter Watkins's celebrated *Culloden* (1964) and its re-creation of a famous battle, this film is, as **Kevin Rockett** affirms, structured around an amateur drama group in an Irish-speaking area of Connemara, County Galway, rehearsing a stage production of the story of O'Leary under the direction of an Englishman (John Arden) (Rockett, Gibbons, and Hill, 1988). In a complex multimedia mixing of past and present, fronted by (later Irish-language television personality) Seán Breathnach in the title role, the film poses various questions around the cult of personality and the usual techniques of historical referencing.

***THE LAST BUS HOME* (1997).** Considered by many as a critique of Celtic Tiger Ireland and its obsessive focus on fiscal success, the film follows the rise and fall of a punk band from 1979—somewhat reminiscent of the story of ***The Commitments*.** As in ***The Bargain Shop*,** director **Johnny Gogan**'s concerns are with the compromises that come with success and the realizations that come with failure. It is tempting to read the apparent suicide of Petie (John Cronin), the gay punk band member, as motivated by his parents' narrow-minded, "old Ireland" fear of queer sexuality. Great use is made of the deserted streets of Dublin, when most of the population attended the papal mass of the late Pope John II's only visit to Ireland in Phoenix Park, which contrasts with later scenes in dark venues as frustrated teenagers connect with the music.

***THE LAST OF THE HIGH KINGS* (1997).** Based on a novel by Ferdia MacAnna and adapted for the screen by writer-director David Keating on a budget of IR £2.25 million, *Last of the High Kings* is a lighthearted coming-of-age picture that follows Frankie (Jared Leto) as he awaits his Leaving Certificate results through the summer of 1977. With his actor father (**Gabriel Byrne**) working overseas and his mother (Catherine O'Hara) involved in ultranationalist activities, Frankie is left to pursue local girls (loss of virginity is identified as synonymous with coming of age) and plan an end-of-summer beach party. The film was reasonably well received at the Irish box office, but despite careful cameo casting (Christina Ricci, **Colm Meaney**, and **Stephen Rea**) it failed to travel successfully.

***THE LAST SEPTEMBER* (1999).** Based on the novel by Elisabeth Bowen, the film was directed by Deborah Warner and stars Maggie Smith, **Michael Gambon**, **Fiona Shaw**, and Keeley Hawes and is set in Danielstown, somewhere in the South of Ireland. This is the country town of Sir Richard Naylor (Gambon) and his wife, Lady Myra (Smith). The story takes place around the time of the Irish War of Independence in the early 1920s. Behind the façade of dinners, tennis parties, and dances, all know that their way of life is coming to an end. Lady Myra's niece, Lois (Keeley Hawes), who is being courted by a captain in the British Army, is lured by the menacingly playful and violent young man who has taken up residence at the bottom of the garden. What unfolds is a portrait of the demise of a way of life and a young woman's coming of age in a brutal time.

This story outline hints at the period-costume nature of the film. National conflicts serve as a conventional backdrop for a story that includes a police officer who is indecently stripped before being shot in the head, and the head of the household, who attempts to protect his beloved. But, of course, all the women escape back to "civilization" and Britain before the natives' "animalistic" passion breaks loose.

LEAVING CERTIFICATE FILMS. A small group of films that reflect teenagers' rites of passage after they complete the Irish state exam known as the Leaving Certificate. The exams are usually taken in June, leaving students in a state of limbo over the course of the summer as they await the results that are often depicted as determining the range of options open to them for their rest of their lives. Examples of films set during this limbo and its aftermath include Fergus Tighe's well-regarded *Clash of the Ash* (1987), in which the main protagonist is effectively driven from his southern home toward **emigration** and escape to London by the parochial drudgery of life in the community. Other fine examples include David Keating's *Last of the High Kings* (1996), Owen McPolin's *Drinking Crude* (1997), Graham Jones's *How to Cheat in the Leaving Certificate* (1997), and **Johnny Gogan**'s *The Last Bus Home* (1997).

LEMASS, SEAN (1899–1971). Lemass, who became taoiseach (prime minister) in 1959, was minister for Industry and Commerce for 21 of the 27 years from 1932 to 1959. For much of that period he pursued the goal of developing if not an Irish film industry then at least a film industry in Ireland.

The Department of Industry and Commerce was receiving private proposals to establish a film studio at least as early as 1928, but these had generally been rebuffed on the grounds that the Irish market was too small to support such an industry. However, in 1938, apparently prompted by a concern that other (specifically, Catholic Church–

driven) agendas might seek to drive film policy, Lemass began to push for some official consideration of film in Ireland. In the face of stiff opposition from officials in the Department of Finance he succeeded in establishing the **Inter-Departmental Committee on the Film Industry** with a remit to examine all the difficulties standing in the way of a national film-production enterprise. Lemass was unhappy with the pessimistic appraisal the committee offered of the possibility of jump-starting a domestic film industry when it finally reported in 1942, and he effectively mothballed their report.

Once the war was over Lemass returned to the subject of film policy. Now, however, rather than focusing on the creation of an indigenous industry his attention shifted to the possibility of attracting overseas producers to use Ireland as a location for their films. Key to this strategy was the building of a national film studio. Over a period of 17 months in 1946 and 1947 the Department of Industry and Commerce prepared a series of memos to the cabinet seeking more than £250,000 (later revised to £500,000) to build two sound stages, an administrative building, and a laboratory. A further £70,000 was sought for the annual administrative costs of the studio. Draft legislation was even prepared to put this into effect. Lemass's film policy at this point worked around the gloomy conclusions of the Inter-Departmental Committee's 1942 report. If American and British companies dominated the English-language film **distribution** market, then the most pragmatic means of generating filmmaking activity in Ireland was to attract film production companies from those countries. Such companies would require studios that could accommodate larger-scale productions.

Lemass's confidence in the spin-off benefits of such a studio was not widely shared by the rest of the cabinet. Even his own department expressed doubts about the viability of the scheme. But the most substantive critique of the proposals came from the Department of Finance, where Minister Frank Aitken, in addition to expressing doubt over the economic viability of the putative studios, argued that it would be most undesirable, nationally and culturally, that the shape and character of an Irish film industry should be determined on the basis of the needs of wealthy foreign industrialists. Thus, although Lemass twice submitted his national film studio proposals to cabinet, they were dismissed on both occasions.

In the mid-1950s, Lemass returned to the subject of film in a more sporadic fashion (at least in part because he was out of power between 1948 and 1951 and 1954 and 1957). In 1951 he briefly raised the possibility of creating a film production fund along the lines of the Eady levy in the United Kingdom (a levy on cinema tickets that was used to fund domestic film production), and in 1954 he directed that a memo be drawn up outlining a proposal to establish a national film unit. This was to be a much more modest enterprise than his earlier studio plans and returned to the idea of setting up a native film industry starting with the production of **documentaries** and shorts on a limited scale. The proposal was set aside, however, when Fianna Fáil lost the May 1954 election.

By the time Lemass returned to the Department of Industry and Commerce in 1957, however, there was a newer prospect in the offing. **Louis Elliman** and **Emmet Dalton** had established Dublin Film and Television Productions Ltd. to film **Abbey Theatre** plays for the American television market. In August 1957, apparently convinced that there was a substantial market for this material, Elliman and Dalton acquired a site for a film studio at **Ardmore** Place, Herbert Road in Bray, County Dublin.

The studios were completed by March 1958. A month later Lemass officially presided over the opening of the studios, where he praised the enterprise as generating exports and employment and training Irish citizens in the complex processes of the industry. He acknowledged that when Elliman and Dalton had initially approached him, he had promised the greatest possible aid the Department of Industry and Commerce could give.

The nature of this aid was largely financial. Ardmore's construction was initially budgeted at £161,000, of which £45,000 was raised from an Industrial Development Authority (IDA) grant. Furthermore, the Industrial Credit Corporation (ICC) advanced a further £217,750 to Ardmore by way of a debenture loan. ICC assistance to the studios did not cease there. In 1960, in an effort to encourage production at Ardmore, the ICC established the **Irish Film Finance Corporation** (IFFC) to consider applications from film producers in Ireland for financial assistance by way of loans. Between 1960 and 1962, the IFFC would invest £385,000 of public funds in 15 films.

Although Lemass had no overt hand in these funding decisions, it would seem unlikely that he was entirely out of the loop given that both the ICC and IDA were very much creatures of the Department of Industry and Commerce. Thus in many respects it is arguable that Ardmore Studios were an explicit realization of Lemass's national studio plans from the 1940s. Indeed, the extent of state funding to Ardmore meant the studios were de facto state owned (via the ICC), even if Elliman and Dalton were nominal owners. When, in 1964, the studios ran into financial difficulties, it was the ICC that appointed a receiver. Yet if Ardmore represented a secret victory for Lemass, it was not an entirely straightforward one. It would be 20 years after his death before the studios were consistently used for indigenous production, and longer still before overseas productions shot in Ireland began to use local talent in creative production roles.

THE LIGHT HOUSE. Neil Connolly established the Light House in 1988 to fill the programming gap left open by the collapse of the **Irish Film Theatre** (IFT) in 1984. Connolly, a former accountant at **Ardmore Studios**, had acted as IFT programmer in its last year of operation, when the **Arts Council** drafted in the **Irish Film Institute** (IFI) in an unsuccessful attempt to save the IFT. However, the IFI saw in the Light House the possibility of an interim solution to the lack of a national film theater that could exhibit nonmainstream material. Accordingly, it took a 50 percent interest in the cinema, which was situated in the shell formerly occupied by a mainstream cinema (the Curzon) on Dublin's Abbey Street. It had two auditoriums, the main cinema having a capacity of 280 seats, the other 80 seats.

The films screened on the opening night of the cinema—Eric Rohmer's *4 Adventures of Reinette and Mirabelle* (1987) and Pedro Almodovar's *Law of Desire* (1987)—set the tone for subsequent programming policy: "blue chip" art-house titles mixed with more adventurous material where possible. In autumn 1991, with the construction of the **Irish Film Centre** (IFC) finally underway, the IFI amicably severed its links with the Light House, leaving it as an independent commercial cinema. Thus, in a single move, the cinema lost a sponsor and acquired a competitor. Remarkably, however, despite the added presence of the IFC in the Dublin market, the finances of the Light House remained in the black.

Indeed, in part, the significance of the Light House lay in the simple fact that it remained in existence, exhibiting exclusively art-house material in a period when most independent cinemas faced dwindling audiences and when even the **Ward Anderson** group was facing the possibility of retrenching its operations in the face of competition from globe-spanning competitors such as United Cinemas International (UCI). More importantly, however, the Light House introduced Dublin audiences to work that was simply inaccessible elsewhere — one-off screenings at **festivals** aside — and thus made a unique contribution to the artistic life of the city.

However, in September 1996, the curtains at the Light House closed for the last time. The closure reflected not a downturn in business but rather the opposite: The Light House building was leased from Arnotts, a major Dublin department store that, amid the mid-1990s economic boom, decided to expand its premises, taking in the site of the Light House (and another former cinema, the Adelphi).

At the time of the cinema's closure it was publicly mooted that the two directors of the cinema — Connolly and Maretta Dillon — might establish a new cinema in a new shopping development on Dublin's O'Connell Street, but when that venture failed to come to fruition, the cinema plans were also abandoned. However, in May 2005, nearly a decade after the cinema closed, the cultural cinema consortium, a joint initiative of the Arts Council and the **Irish Film Board**, charged with the task of expanding the range of cinema in Ireland, announced that it was offering €750,000 in capital funding to two groups, one of which — Lighthouse@smithfield — was headed by the directors of the Light House cinema.

LINEHAN, ROSALEEN (1937–). Born in Dublin to a middle-class family (her father was a Fine Gael TD for Donegal from 1932 till 1961), she attended school at Loreto College on Stephen's Green before going on to study economics and politics at University College Dublin, which was unusual for an Irish woman in the 1950s. At university she joined the famed college theater society Dramsoc and within two years of graduating had commenced a professional acting career. She quickly became a household name through her stage and radio work, albeit one associated more with comedic roles than "serious" theater. She made a couple of appearances in filmed roles in the late 1960s in **Joseph Strick**'s adaptation of James Joyce's *Ulysses* and *A Portrait of the Artist as a Young Man*. Her subsequent inability to find big-screen work—13 years would elapse before she appeared in a film again after *Portrait*—may have been due to the clash between her clownish persona and the preference of indigenous filmmakers for a realist, quasi-avant-garde approach to telling filmed stories.

However, in the mid-1980s, Linehan successfully reinvented herself as a serious actress, taking on a series of heavyweight roles in works such as Anton Chekhov's *The Seagull*, Federico Garcia Lorca's *House of Bernarda Alba*, and Peter Sheridan's *Mother of All the Behans*. Key among these was her role as Winnie in Beckett's *Happy Days*, for which she received critical plaudits and which she would reprise onscreen in Patricia Rozema's contribution to the project of filming all of **Samuel Beckett**'s works. Since 1990 she has sustained a series of character roles in film such as ***Snakes and Ladders***, ***About Adam***, and ***The Butcher Boy***, in which she often plays conventional gossipy mother figures.

LITTLE BIRD. Among the production companies in Ireland that have been in existence the longest, Little Bird has quietly become one of the most prolific screen production entities in Ireland. Indeed, since the company has established offices in Dublin and London and built partnerships with British, German, and South African companies, it can legitimately claim to be in the second tier of leading European film and television production companies.

The company was established in 1982 by James Mitchell, who was originally an entertainment lawyer based in Great Britain, and his business partner, Jonathan Cavendish, to produce the light comedy *The Irish R. M.* for **Channel 4** in the United Kindgom. The show, which eventually ran to three seasons, was sold to over 50 territories worldwide. Since then the company has continued to produce a regular output of television drama. Even more remarkable, however, is the fact that Little Bird managed to sustain a semiregular output of feature film titles through the difficult years of the late 1980s, commencing with ***Joyriders***. Since then the company has produced and shot a sequence of films in Ireland including Mike Newell's ***Into the West***, Suri Krishnamma's ***A Man of No Importance***, and three

Thaddeus O'Sullivan pictures, *December Bride*, *Nothing Personal*, and *Ordinary Decent Criminal*.

Regularly cited by industry journals as among the powerful figures in the Irish film industry, Mitchell and Cavendish have also gained substantial overseas clout. For example, its London branch produced Mike Hodges's *Croupier* (1997) and Paul McGuigan's *Gangster No. 1* (2001) in partnership with FilmFour, and it coproduced the two film adaptations of Helen Fielding's *Bridget Jones* novels with Working Title films. In 2001 the company established a distribution entity (Zephir Films) in Germany with local coproduction partner TatFilm. Finally, in 2002 Little Bird established a financial services company to raise funds for international film projects shot in South Africa with South African financial services company Coronation Capital.

The company owes much of its success to its (unusual by Irish standards) careful nurturing of distribution that goes well beyond the establishment of Zephir, referred to above. In 1993, James Mitchell and Little Bird producer Jane Doolan established Clarence Pictures not only to distribute Little Bird material in Ireland but also a wider range of nonstudio pictures and indigenous films. Clarence, which later spun off from Little Bird and rebranded as Eclipse Pictures in 2002, developed distribution relationships with FilmFour and Mel Gibson's Icon Production and Distribution Company, the latter leading to the reciprocal distribution by Icon of *Ordinary Decent Criminal* in Britain.

A LOVE DIVIDED **(1998).** Directed by Sydney McCartney and set in Fethard-on-Sea in County Wexford, the film is based on a true story of religious sectarianism that divided the area in 1957. Catholic Sean (**Liam Cunningham**) marries Sheila (**Orla Brady**), who is a Protestant, but when their eldest child reaches school age, Sheila decides to send her to the local Protestant school. The Catholic parish priest forbids such a move, claiming it violates a pledge Sheila signed on her wedding day stating she would bring up her children in the **Catholic** faith. Outraged at the priest's interference and her husband's inability to change matters, she flees to Belfast and then Scotland, where she takes refuge on a farm. Meanwhile, back at home, her family and the other Protestant villagers become the victims of a boycott initiated by the Church. Eventually Sheila returns (after Sean travels to

Scotland), and the boycott is ended by the intercession of the more politic local bishop, but the bitterness continues as Sean and Sheila educate their children at home.

LYNCH, JOHN (1961–). Lynch grew up in Corrinshego outside Newry as the eldest of five children (including his sister, actress **Susan Lynch**). His parents met in London, where Lynch spent his earliest years, but returned to Northern Ireland in 1968, just as the "**troubles**" were breaking out, and as a consequence he grew up in what he has described as an oppressive atmosphere. On leaving school, he was offered a place at the Central School of Speech and Drama in London. He secured his first major role—the lead in *Cal* opposite Helen Mirren—while still attending the school. He was cast as a young IRA recruit who falls in love with the widow of a member of the Royal Ulster Constabulary. *Cal* was an instant breakthrough for Lynch after the film received critical plaudits and achieved modest box office success. Despite this it was another six years before he would appear in a second feature film: Tthe roles offered in the wake of *Cal* were mainly Northern Irish, and fearing typecasting, Lynch retreated to concentrate on theater work for the rest of the 1980s, including an 18-month spell with the Royal Shakespeare Company in London.

When he did return to film, however, it was precisely in Northern Irish parts that he drew critical praise. He played Paul Hill opposite Daniel Day-Lewis's Gerry Conlon in *In the Name of the Father*, a Catholic father caught up in sectarian violence in *Nothing Personal*, and Bobby Sands in *Some Mother's Son*. Indeed, for a period, Lynch's haunted visage with its piercing eyes became synonymous with representations of the Northern Irish.

In 1994, he appeared in **Mary McGuckian**'s *Words upon the Window Pane* and collaborated on three further films: *This Is the Sea* (on which he also acted as second unit director), *Best* (which he cowrote), and McGuckian's Hollywood debut *The Bridge of San Luis Rey* (2004). Their close working relationship is in part explained by the fact that they have been romantic partners for more than a decade and married in 2002.

Although he has appeared in other Irish films (including *Evelyn*, *Puckoon*, and—with his sister Susan—*The Secret of Roan Inish*), he has also established something of an international reputation. Derek Jarman cast him in *Edward II* (1991), and he played the male lead in the Australian art-house hit *Angel Baby* in 1995. However, outside Ireland, he is possibly best known for his performance opposite Gwyneth Paltrow in the comic *Sliding Doors* (1998). Most recently, in addition to lead roles in the Charles Sturridge–directed version of *Lassie* (2005), which was shot in Ireland, he has turned his hand to writing with the publication of *Torn Water*, a semiautobiographical coming-of-age story set in Newry.

LYNCH, SUSAN (1971–). Born in Newry in Northern Ireland, she is most recognized for her commanding role in Pat Murphy's period costume drama *Nora*, where she takes on the role of the wife of **James Joyce**. Although she came to public attention in the early 1990s for her stage work (including a version of *Hamlet* in Galway, which also starred her brother **John Lynch**), she quickly moved to screen roles and has become a fixture on British and Irish television. She has won three Irish Film & Television Academy awards for acting, with memorable roles in *The Secret of Roan Inish*, *Waking Ned*, *The Mapmaker*, and most recently *Mickybo and Me*. After her performance in *Nora* drew critical plaudits, she also secured several leading roles in British films, including *Beautiful Creatures* (2000), *From Hell* (2001), and *Enduring Love* (2004).

– M –

MACAVIN, JOSIE (1920–2005). Born in 1919, set designer Josie MacAvin learned her trade with touring theater productions. These included pantomimes with Irish stage actress Maureen Potter, a European tour with *Joan of Arc*, and a production of Michael Mac Líammoir's *Playboy of the Western World* in Edinburgh. She began her film work in 1959 on Michael Anderson's *Shake Hands with the Devil*, one of the first films shot at **Ardmore Studios**.

MacAvin's employment on that film was unusual for the era: Typically films shot in Ireland by overseas production companies (as was the case for *Shake Hands with the Devil*) did not employ local talent in senior creative positions. Her employment reflected an appreciation of her abilities. This was confirmed in 1964 when she was nominated for an Oscar for her work on the Albert Finney version of *Tom Jones* (1963). Two years later she was nominated again for her work on Martin Ritt's adaptation of John Le Carré's *The Spy Who Came In from the Cold* (1965), which used Dublin as a double for East Berlin.

From that point on MacAvin was employed on virtually every major film shot in Ireland: David Lean's **Ryan's Daughter**, **John Huston**'s **The Dead**, Ron Howard's **Far and Away**, and **Neil Jordan**'s **Michael Collins** (she was also set designer on Jordan's later **Butcher Boy**). Nor was she averse to working on smaller films; during the period of the first **Irish Film Board** she worked on **Eat the Peach**, and in the early 1990s she was the set designer on two low-budget films by director **Ron O'Leary**: *Diary of a Madman* and *Hello Stranger*. Her work was not confined to films shot in Ireland, however; her non-Irish shoots included Michael Cimino's *Heaven's Gate* (1980), and she won an Oscar for her contribution to Sydney Pollack's *Out of Africa* (1985), which entailed her living in Africa for nine months.

Remarkably MacAvin continued working into her 80s. At the age of 75, she won an Emmy for Outstanding Individual Achievement in Art Direction for her work on the *Gone with the Wind* sequel *Scarlett* and was 82 when she completed work on her last major production, *Evelyn*, produced by **Pierce Brosnan**. She died in January 2005 at the age of 85.

MAEVE **(1982).** *Maeve*, directed by Pat Murphy (with **John T. Davis**), remains one of the most sophisticated films ever made about the "**troubles**" in Ireland, developing a coherent analysis and critique of the stifling stasis imposed by the past (real or imagined) on the present.

The film opens when Maeve Sweeney returns from London to visit her Catholic family in Belfast, a trip that brings up memories of her childhood in Northern Ireland. The story cuts back and forth between three temporal planes: Maeve as a young girl, as a teenager, and in the present. She recalls her family leaving their home in a Protestant area of Belfast in the face of threats from the locals. However, the family's move to a Catholic area means living amid people on the other side of the political spectrum: nationalist republicans. She remembers, too, traveling around the North with her determinedly neutral father, selling cakes from their van, all the time encountering hostility from republicans, unionists, and the British Army. As Maeve enters her later teenage years, even her sympathetic boyfriend pressures her to take a stance on the "Northern Question." Unwilling to take sides in a conflict that she sees as based on a mythologized version of the past, Maeve is finally unable to find a place for herself in Northern Irish society.

The protagonist Maeve has moved beyond national politics, which she perceives as rooted in conflicts of the past, memories of which have been reimagined and reshaped, and selectively edited, to suit the current mind-set. The film argues that it is memory that provides the framework that allows the older generation (particularly of IRA leaders) to retain their sanity in the face of decades of violence. However, memory frequently depends on reference to events that have been mythologized out of all recognition. These past events then trap those living in the present in imposed categories: For those unwilling to accept the label unionist or nationalist, the past offers them no identity. By being neither, one has no option but to leave. For those seeking to go beyond this, as Maeve does by embracing feminism, there is simply no place to exist: The dominant (indeed the only permissible) discourse is unionist against nationalist, Protestant against Catholic. Other struggles—women against patriarchy—are subsumed into this. So Maeve escapes to England, a country so turned in on itself that "people can grow up here without being imprisoned by the history. . . . They've disconnected themselves from their own neuroses."

THE MAGDALENE SISTERS (2002). Based on the horrific true story of the incarceration of over 30,000 women over the course of the 20th century in Ireland who had been disowned by their families because they were pregnant or in some way regarded as "fallen women." They were dispatched into the hands of **Catholic** nuns, who used their labor to run a number of laundries throughout the country until their closure in the 1970s. The ethos of the institutions was that hard work would help make up for the alleged sins the girls committed. It took the passion of Scottish filmmaker and actor Peter Mullan, filming in an unused Benedictine convent in Dumfries, Scotland, to bring the story to the big screen following a similarly themed television dramatization, *The Sinners.*

The composite story of three girls, generically framed as a "prison movie" in the tradition of *One Flew Over the Cuckoo's Nest* (1975) and *The Shawshank Redemption* (1994), ensured its wide appeal to audiences. It opens with a close-up of a priest, building to a crescendo as he plays traditional Irish music on a bodhrán at a wedding celebration. The party initially appears to replicate a stereotypical *craic*, or the Irish at play. But this is thrown into sharp relief by intercuts to the scene in an upstairs bedroom of the attack on and rape of one of the protagonists, Margaret, which proceeds as the music grows more raucous. The impressively choreographed opening scene concludes with the priest being told in hushed tones of what has happened. However, it becomes obvious through the display of looks that it is the female victim who will suffer most as a consequence in this regressive paternal and religious community. The following morning scene confirms this, as a lone car with a priest inside takes Margaret away with the quiet consent of her family.

Next we are introduced to Bernadette at Saint Attracta's Orphanage, who has a healthy eye for the boys and is quite able to banter with them. When the nuns running the orphanage note this, they decide to move her to the laundry in a bid to temper her curiosity. Finally we are introduced to Rose, who has just had a baby. A priest working for an adoption agency informs her that a child born out of wedlock is a bastard and convinces her to sign away her child, a decision she immediately regrets. After this preamble of three backstories, the camera tracks through a long list of names of such unfortunate girls, reminiscent of a memorial plaque for war victims. As our three new recruits enter, the deliciously evil head nun, played by Geraldine McEwan, informs them that eternal salvation will come only by doing penance in this life.

Throughout their incarceration the girls endure numerous indignities, especially if they refuse to accept their situation or try to escape. Serious misdemeanors receive the strongest punishment, including having all their hair ceremoniously cut off. Their pariah status in the outside world is exemplified by the laundry man warning his young apprentice not to look at or talk to them.

All of the performances by the young actresses—Anne-Marie Duff, Dorothy Duffy, Nora-Jane Noone, and Eileen Walsh—are of a very high standard. Although the film ends on an upbeat note as the other two main protagonists hatch and carry out an escape plan, the postscript telling of their subsequent lives outside the institution is silently countered by the knowledge that most inmates were not so lucky. The film has been very successful at the box office, passing the €1 million mark at home and almost £2 million in the British market.

MAN ABOUT DOG (2005). Directed by **Paddy Breathnach,** the film stars Allen Leech, Tom Jordan Murphy, and Ciaran Nolan as Mo Chara, Scud Murphy, and Cerebral Palsy, three luckless losers from Northern Ireland whose main aim in life is simply to survive while having the best time possible. However, whether running a mobile shop, selling dope, or gambling, the trio—initially at least—are no match for the crooked bookie (**Sean McGinley**), who thwarts their ambitions.

The comic road movie caper charts their revenge as they travel down south with a thoroughbred greyhound that they hope will bring them luck. When the dog initially fails to perform, they sell it to a group of Travellers (led by the comic Pat Shortt), at which point the dog suddenly demonstrates a remarkable turn of speed. Stealing their dog back, they head for the "holy grail" of dog racing in Clonmel, County Tipperary, where the story culminates and all their newfound enemies congregate. The dialogue throughout is scattered with risible colloquialisms and scatological references. The obligatory sex scenes display no evidence of any hang-ups, and the characters' political observations are equally casual. Of course they know Irish republican activists are dangerous to upset, but they nevertheless enjoy fantasizing about how well-known political figures like Gerry Adams or Ian Paisley would look if they were drugged sufficiently.

The film was not received well by Irish critics, but despite this it became the most successful indigenous film in Ireland in 2004. Given its generic appeal, its success is perhaps not that surprising and confirms the preference of local audiences for local stories, even if told using a universally accessible narrative structure.

MAN OF ARAN (1934). Robert Flaherty's famous poetic **documentary** filmed on the Aran Islands off the west coast of Ireland remains a defining image of primitive cultural endurance and the romantic representation of rural Irish identity. When the film was first seen by the political elite, it was said that Eamon de Valera—the leader of the Fianna Fáil political party who above all others helped define a post–Civil War identity that continued well into the 1950s—wept at its heroic portrayal of Irish people. The film reflected a preoccupation with the West as defining a pure strand of Irish identity and was marketed internationally as a realist document of life in that period.

As in all his films—*Nanook of the North* (1922), *Louisiana Story* (1948), and others—Flaherty remained preoccupied with showing primitive societies embodying the universal human trait of endurance and the ability to survive against all odds. The fact that the family in the film was constructed and that the central activity of the film, the hunting of the whale for oil, had not actually being carried out in recent times, remains problematic for many critics, as the film is often labeled a truthful documentary. While filmmakers like Flaherty's erstwhile friend John Grierson wanted to capture the specific truth of poverty and corruption, Flaherty was more focused on valorizing man's struggle with nature and was willing to "shape" the truth to this end. The result in *Man of Aran* is a form of hard primitivism, a portrayal of the enormous hardship the natives have to endure on the island to eke out a living.

Flaherty's filming method involved living for up to a year in the environment with his subjects, producing extensive footage in an attempt to capture the essential tenor of their lives. Even if one took issue with the film's evocation of the reality of the period, it is impossible to dismiss the cinematic style of his oeuvre and his experiments with lenses of different focal lengths in the film, which contributed enormously to expanding film grammar. Finally, however, it is little wonder that the story of the islanders' attempts to fight the wild but beautiful sea and the poetic hardship of breaking up rocks and carrying seaweed up the cliff face to make precious fertile soil remains an enduring testament to an idealized Irish rural mythos, which was also emulated in the nationalist revivalist writings of the playwright J. M. Synge and his stoic testament to female endurance in *Riders to the Sea*, for example.

Nonetheless, it is also noteworthy that when anthropologist John Messenger interviewed islanders in the late 1950s and mid 1960s about literary and filmic representations of the Aran Islands and the way of life there, *Man of Aran* was consistently identified by islanders as the most distorted. Somewhat puritanically, Messenger cited over 50 "abuses of reality" (Messenger, 1988) in the film and also noted that many of the islanders bitterly resented the indelible image of their home the film created.

***A MAN OF NO IMPORTANCE* (1994).** Directed by Suri Krishnamma, the film is a modest attempt at retelling the life of Oscar Wilde through the parallel experience of a Dublin bus driver, Alfie Byrne (Albert

Finney), in the 1960s who feels forced by a very conservative Ireland to conceal his **homosexuality**. He finds pleasure by dressing up in flamboyant attire and wearing makeup in the privacy of his own home. Later he attempts to stage Wilde's *Salome* in his local community, allowing his secret to be revealed, with some tragic consequences.

THE MAPMAKER **(2001).** Evoking a theme that has become well known in Irish theater and embodied by the debate around place names in Brian Friel's *Translations*, for example, director **Johnny Gogan**'s film deals with politics and the impact of mapping and renaming space. When cartographer Richie Markey (Brian F. O'Byrne) travels to a border area of County Fermanagh to make a hill-walking map, his arrival arouses the suspicion of locals. The landscape holds secrets, particularly in relation to the disappearance of a local farmer 10 years earlier who was suspected of being a police informer: It emerges that completing the map will require that Markey first discover the fate of the missing farmer. This psychological thriller, which Gogan also scripted, is effective and engaging but unfortunately was not very successful at the box office.

MARCUS, LOUIS (1936–). Born in Cork, the son of a picture framer, he completed an English and French degree at University College Cork before George Morrison took him on as assistant editor on *Mise Éire*. He also worked on that fim's sequel, *Saoirse?*, before the Irish-language cultural organization **Gael Linn** hired him to make documentaries. As a result Marcus was one of the very few individuals working outside **Radio Teilfís Éireann (RTÉ)** who was able to make a full-time career of filmmaking in the Ireland of the 1960s. Noted films from this period include *Peil* (1962), on Gaelic football; *Rhapsody of a River* (1965), commissioned by the **Cultural Relations Committee**; and arguably, his best work of that decade, *Fleá* (1967), a cinema verité record of the Kilrush, County Clare, music festival. This last film was widely screened internationally, won Marcus the Silver Bear award at the Berlin Film Festival in 1967, and was nominated for an **Academy Award** the following year.

By the late 1960s, however, Marcus was becoming as well known for his lobbying on behalf of an as yet nonexistent film industry as he was for his creative work. As early as 1959, he had written articles for the *Irish Times* critiquing government film policy and arguing that organizations like **Ardmore Studios** were contributing little to the development of an indigenous production sector. In 1967, he wrote a further series of articles for the same newspapers, which the **Irish Film Society** subsequently published as a single pamphlet, decrying the failure of Ardmore and, more generally, of successive governments to treat cinema seriously. The articles drew Marcus to the attention of then Irish resident **John Huston** and indirectly led to the establishment of the Film Industry Committee and the publication of *The Huston Report* in 1968.

Marcus was also a member of that committee, and it is apparent that he had a substantial influence on its conclusions and recommendations. Unfortunately the Dáil never passed the legislation that was to have put those recommendations into action in 1970, and the emergence of an Irish film industry was delayed by at least a decade as a consequence. This was particularly damaging for Marcus himself, as Gael Linn, the major sponsor of his output in the 1960s, withdrew from filmmaking activity in 1973 (though not before Marcus completed his 1971 documentary, *Dubliners: Sean agus Nua*).

From the 1970s on, Marcus produced a mix of promotional documentaries such as *The Heritage of Ireland* (1978) and *Discovering Ireland* (1983) and more aesthetically engaged work. His 1973 film *Paistí ag Obair*, made for RTÉ, looked at a Montessori School in Dublin and was nominated for an Academy Award. This was followed in 1975 by the stunning cinematography of *Conquest of Light*, a documentary about Waterford Crystal. Later in the decade he made the first of his (very) occasional forays into drama, with his production of *Revival*, a drama-documentary about the life and thinking of one of the 1916 martyrs, Padraig Pearse. Now in his 70s, he has produced over 80 documentaries and short films and continues to do so. He was appointed chair of the **Irish Film Board** when **Lelia Doolan** retired in 1996, and in 2005, he was the subject of a lifetime tribute at the film **festival** in his native city of Cork.

MARY BREEN FARRELLY PRODUCTIONS (MBF). Mary Breen Farrelly Productions (MBF) is included in this volume not because of an impressive track record as a production company but rather because of its central role in the production of the science-fiction movie *Space Truckers* (1996), the near-collapse of which led to a substantial tightening up of the administration of the **Section 481** tax incentive. MBF Pro-

ductions was launched in May 1992, with the promise that it would re-
vitalize the Irish film industry by way of an IR £70 million film production package. The company was launched by the eponymous Mary
Breen Farrelly and her partner, John Avery. Farrelly's
experience in the industry derived from her work in the accounts departments of a range of British film companies in the two decades preceding the establishment of MBF Productions. The IR £70 million never
materialized, but with the expansion of the Section 481 tax incentive the
company acquired funding for an animation series based on Bible stories (*Sign of the Fish*) and for the **Ronan O'Leary** feature *Driftwood*.

In 1994 MBF came into contact with U.S. producer Peter Newman,
who was seeking a location to shoot *Space Truckers*. Promised by
MBF that £7 million could be raised via Section 481, the production
duly came to shoot in **Ardmore Studios** in July 1995. In fact, however,
only £4.1 million had been raised by the time the film commenced production, and the project soon ran into financial difficulty. The minister
for arts, culture and the Gaeltacht, **Michael D. Higgins**, whose department had originally certified the project for Section 481 funding, called
in producer **Morgan O'Sullivan**, film lawyer James Hickey, and AC-
CBank to attempt to retrieve the film. Mary Breen Farrelly resigned as
producer of the film and was replaced by Morgan O'Sullivan, who succeeded in securing further Section 481 funding to complete it.

However, while salvaging the finances of *Space Truckers*, AC-
CBank found that of the £4.1 million raised under Section 481 for the
film, only £1.5 million had actually gone into its production budget.
Of the remaining £2.6 million, £850,000 had been diverted to *Driftwood* and another £250,000 to *Sign of the Fish*. The remaining money
was simply unaccounted for. This was bad news for the original Section 481 investors who'd put money into *Space Truckers*: Since not all
of their money had gone into that film, they were no longer entitled to
avail of a tax break on their investment and found themselves faced
with an unexpected tax bill.

The film effectively marked the end of MBF Productions in Ireland,
although the company was granted a further Section 481 certificate for
a film called *Feeney's Rainbow*. That project never came to fruition,
and the collapse of the *Sign of the Fish* project meant that *Driftwood*
was only the film begun and finished by MBF. However, the impact
of MBF Productions lingered in the way in which investors and Irish

tax officials subsequently viewed Section 481. For investors, Section 481 no longer appeared to promise a guaranteed return. For the revenue commissioners, the project offered evidence that unscrupulous producers were using the tax break in an illegal fashion. More concretely, in the January 1996 budget, the minister for finance announced that, henceforth, Section 481 certification would be granted only to films made by production companies established solely for the purpose of the production of one and only one film. Furthermore tax relief for investors would commence only from the date of principal filming of the project (i.e., when production actually commenced).

MASCULINITY AND COLONIZATION. Irish cultural theorists have long argued that Ireland's colonial past has been influenced by the ineffective family or remote father figure, a failing exacerbated by new inheritance structures that emerged after the famine, whereby farms that had once been subdivided among the male offspring of a farmer were now consolidated and passed on in their entirety to only one son. Because this was not necessarily the eldest male, the sons competed for the father's approval, and his relationship with the children took on a more economic dimension. In turn, the mother became the focus of most of the affection and emotion, acting as the mediator or communication link between father and children, a relationship powerfully exemplified in **Jim Sheridan**'s *The Field* and his earlier film *My Left Foot.*

It has also been argued by several critics that, in the case of formerly colonized nations, there is a specifically gendered relationship between the colonizer and the colonized. Historically, the Irish were identified as "feminine" in an attempt to justify the relationship between colonizers and colonized: If the country was configured as female, the implication was that she therefore must be governed.

It is unsurprising, therefore, that much contemporary indigenous cinema strives to challenge these rigid definitions of masculinity within a postcolonial environment. This has also coincided with a historical moment when European social thinking began to filter into Irish consciousness, as reflected in films like **Cathal Black**'s *Our Boys*, which exposed the institutionalization of violence in the education of Irish males, or in **Kieran Hickey**'s *Exposure*, which provides a complex exploration of patriarchal bonding that lurks beneath the respectable veneer of middle-class Irish masculinity. Most recently, the novels and films adapted from the Dublin working-class novelist **Roddy Doyle** (*The Commitments*, *The Snapper*, and *The Van*) have effectively foregrounded issues of masculinity in Irish film and signaled a close connection between debates around masculinity and particularly working-class culture in Ireland. *The Most Fertile Man in Ireland,* for example, presents a humorous correlation between politics in the North and the potency of Irish masculinity. However, more ambiguous middle-class representations are articulated in *About Adam* and *When Brendan Met Trudy*, where the war of the sexes is less polarized or clearly defined.

MCANALLY, RAY (1926–1989). McAnally was born in Buncrana in County Donegal and became a well-known international actor, a consummate professional who could effectively take on a wide range of parts. Significant roles in Irish films include Paddy Nolan in the classic *Shake Hands with the Devil*, a Northern detective in *Angel*, the authoritarian, working-class father in *My Left Foot*, as well as roles in *Cal*, *The Outsider*, *High Spirits*, and **Neil Jordan**'s Hollywood remake *We're No Angels*. He worked extensively in television in a wide number of series and films, including *The Death of Adolf Hitler* (1973), *A Very British Coup* (1988), *Great Expectations* (1989), and many more. He also worked on a wide range of international film projects and had major roles in *The Mission* (1986), *White Mischief* (1987), and *The Fourth Protocol* (1987). He was nominated four times for a British Film and Television Academy (BAFTA) award and won three times— for *The Mission*, *A Very British Coup*, and *My Left Foot*. He was helping to script *The Field* with **Jim Sheridan**, with the intention of starring as the Bull McCabe, when he died suddenly, a great loss for Irish film acting.

MCARDLE, TOMMY. A very eclectic scriptwriter, director, and theater director who has produced three small-scale but nonetheless highly innovative films over the years, namely *The Kinkisha* (1977), *It's Handy When People Don't Die* (1980), and *Angela Mooney Dies Again* (1996). All of his stories draw on various mythological stories, superstitions, and Irish history that deserve to be told before they are lost along with much of Ireland's oral history and culture.

McArdles's first film drew on a unusual and obscure Irish superstition, namely that a child born on Whit Sunday will either kill or be killed unless he or she in turn kills a robin. At just 60 minutes in duration *The Kinkinsha* is somewhere between a short and a full feature but nonetheless evocatively portrays this story for a contemporary audience. In his next film, Tommy deals with history and the revolutionary fervor in the year 1798 as the United Irishmen stage their uprising. The story deals with a reluctant conscript, Art, who witnesses the carnage from afar. This film's puncturing of historical myths of glorious revolution indirectly questioned the manner in which history has been used to legitimate political violence during the "troubles." *Angela Mooney Dies Again*, his most recent film, remains the most technically accomplished and deals quite effectively with mental illness and a concurrent major social malaise on the island, namely suicide. To use comic excess to deal with such an issue at first appears to be in very poor taste. Nonetheless, the film is able to make some interesting dramatic points around the topic and established McArdle as an effective film maker, capable of directing major stars like Mia Farrow.

MACBRIDE, TIERNAN (1933–1995). When Tiernan MacBride died in 1995, Michael Dwyer wrote that no other individual had campaigned quite so vigorously and so ceaselessly for the Irish film industry ("Tiernan MacBride Dies, Aged 63," 1995). At his funeral **Lelia Doolan** called him the father and mother of Irish film. A decade later it is difficult to quibble with these assessments.

MacBride was a son of Sean MacBride and grandson of Maud Gonne MacBride. In addition to his work for an Irish film industry he was an activist on various political issues, including campaigns to release the Birmingham Six and Guildford Four. He went to University College Dublin to study architecture in 1951 and subsequently worked in an agricultural company before moving to the Arks Advertising Agency. Starting as a projector operator he progressed through the film department before moving to the United States for half a decade to work as a commercials director in Detroit and New York.

On his return to Ireland MacBride joined the television department at McConnells Advertising and then established his own company,

Advertising on Film, which built up a substantial national and international client list. During this period (1978) he also directed his only fiction film, a short entitled *Christmas Morning*. In 1985 Advertising on Film closed, and MacBride shifted his considerable energies to feature films by establishing Roebuck Moving Pictures (the company was named for the house MacBride grew up in). He would subsequently act as executive producer on Bill Miskelly's *The End of the World Man* and on Vinny Murphy's *H for Hamlet* and received a posthumous production credit for his partner **Pat Murphy**'s *Nora*.

However, it was in the field of lobbying and campaigning for support for Irish film that MacBride's impact was felt the most. He was on the board or a member of virtually every film-related organization included in this volume. In the 1970s he was a pivotal figure in the establishment of a Film Section in the Irish Transport and General Workers Union and was chairman of the **Irish Film Theatre.** He was a member of both the Association of Irish Producers (AIP) and the Assocation of Irish Film Makers and as such was one of several key figures in lobbying then minister for industry Desmond O'Malley to revive the idea of an **Irish Film Board.** Ironically he subsequently led the AIP's boycott of **Neil Jordan**'s *Angel* at the 1982 Celtic Film Festival (in protest at the manner in which the Irish Film Board and **John Boorman** had funded the film). In a further twist, he himself was subsequently appointed to the Film Board.

MacBride was also one of the prime movers behind the 1986 establishment of **Film Base**, going so far as to personally finance the purchase of video equipment for the organization. When the Film Board closed in 1987, MacBride was at the forefront of the campaign to reestablish it and as a member of **Film Makers Ireland** was vociferous in his criticism of **Channel 4** when in 1989 the channel abruptly canceled its *Irish Reel* documentary series.

When the European Union's **MEDIA program** commenced, MacBride was appointed to the board of MEDIA Desk Ireland and was Irish representative on the Madrid-based MEDIA Business School. Finally, by the time of his death, he was one of the longest-serving members of the board of the **Film Institute of Ireland**.

Happily MacBride lived to see his campaigning bear fruit: When **Michael D. Higgins** became minister for arts, culture and the Gaeltacht in January 1993, MacBride led a group of placard-wielding filmmakers not to protest but—uniquely—to welcome his appointment. He was famously combative in pursuing his lobbying objectives but was equally renowned for his generosity of spirit and his willingness to assist younger filmmakers as they attempted to break into the industry. Given this, it was fitting that, after his death, the Film Institute of Ireland renamed their annual script funding award in his name.

MCCABE, RUTH. The daughter of novelist and playwright Eugene McCabe and in whose *King of the Castle* she appeared at the **Abbey Theatre** in 1989. (She would later appear in his television adaptation of several of his famine-era short stories, *Tales from the Poorhouse*.)

McCabe began her acting career in the mid-1970s onstage. Her first screen roles came a decade later when she became a cast regular on the indigenous soap *Fair City*. She has played recurring roles in subsequent British and Irish television shows including *Silent Witness* and *The Clinic*. Her first film role was in *My Left Foot*, in which she played the woman who would eventually become Christy Brown's wife. She has since secured a steady flow of work in indigenous films such as *Circle of Friends*, *Intermission*, and *The Snapper* (playing Kay Curley) and in overseas productions shot in Ireland, including *Scarlett* (1994) and *An Awfully Big Adventure* (1995).

McCabe has also continued to work onstage, securing a Best Supporting Actress nomination for her part in the Abbey's 2004 production of Federico Garcia Lorca's *House of Bernarda Alba* and directing a play, penned by **Brendon Gleeson**, for the Passion Machine Company in 1994. More recently her big-screen work includes roles as Annie in *Inside I'm Dancing* and Ma Braden in **Neil Jordan**'s *Breakfast on Pluto*.

MCCANN, DONAL (1943–1999). When McCann died, the *Irish Times* devoted an editorial to his passing, describing him as the best Irish actor of the 20th century (and possibly the best ever). Although it is widely acknowledged that his best performances were reserved for the stage, and that filmmakers had largely failed to make use of his talents, he remains a mesmerizing figure on the small or large screen.

He acquired his zest for acting from his father, a former TD (Irish member of Parliament) and lord mayor of Dublin who wrote plays for the **Abbey Theatre** in the 1950s. McCann debuted onstage in 1962, appearing in a Terenure College past pupils' production of one of his father's own plays: *Give Me a Bed of Roses*. In college he studied architecture but left to work as a copy boy at the *Evening Press*, a job that allowed him to moonlight as an actor. He received formal acting training at the Abbey School of Acting and made his first professional stage appearance with the Abbey company in Padraic Colum's *Thomas Muskerry*. He continued to receive second billing, however, until he was cast in the Abbey's enormously successful 1968 production of Dion Boucicault's *The Shaughraun*, which both revived the playwright's reputation and ensured that McCann was subsequently offered only lead stage roles.

By this time he had already broken into cinema, appearing in a 1966 Disney take on early modern Irish history, *The Fighting Prince of Donegal*, and in 1969 in **John Huston**'s *Sinful Davey*. However, his first successful screen role was in the British Broadcasting Corporation's (BBC) serial adaptation of Anthony Trollope's novel *The Pallisers*, in which he played the dashing Phineas Finn. He followed this the following year with another successful screen role, this time as Gar Public in an adaptation of Brian Friel's ***Philadelphia, Here I Come!*** (1975).

However, for a period in the late 1970s and early 1980s, his work rate dropped, due in part to something of a disenchantment with the world of acting but due also to chronic alcoholism. Nonetheless, he turned in another striking performance as the menacing Sleamhnan in **Bob Quinn**'s *Poitín* opposite **Cyril Cusack** and **Niall Toibin**, and he achieved local fame with his role in the successful **Radio Telefis Éireann** (RTÉ) series *Strumpet City*. Onstage, he produced what is still regarded as one of the most astounding Irish theatrical performances of the decade as Captain Boyle (opposite **John Kavanagh**'s Joxer) in Sean O'Casey's *Joxer and the Paycock*. He would later be equally mesmeric in Brian Friel's *Faith Healer*.

However, one of his screen roles from the mid-1980s is arguably the equal of either of these frequently cited performances. John Huston cast him opposite his daughter, Angelica Huston, in his 1986 feature adaptation of **James Joyce**'s short story "**The Dead**." McCann's performance as Gabriel, Joyce's most enigmatic outsider, is the core of the film. Everything that occurs is observed through his impeccably mannered but impassive gaze, and his soliloquy at the close, following on the story's climatic revelation, is heartbreaking in its evocation of a heart that cannot break.

He did make other impressive screen appearances in that decade, most notably in **Pat O'Connor**'s *Cal*, **Neil Jordan**'s *Angel* and *The Miracle* (he also appears in *High Spirits*, but, like the film, this is best forgotten), and as the tortured but defiant priest in Bob Quinn's *Budawanny* (later refilmed as *The Bishop's Story*). The nature of that last film—at least in its original silent version—offered something of an insight into McCann himself: self-effacing and almost entirely without ego yet carrying with him the constant threat of anger when he found fault with others. Something of the same character is also evident in the screen performance that capped off the 1980s for McCann—the brooding Hamilton in **Thaddeus O'Sullivan**'s *December Bride*.

By the 1990s, he had won his battle with alcohol, and it was reflected in the quality of his work—especially onstage. In 1995 he was awarded the London Critics Circle Theatre award for his tormented portrayal of Thomas Dunne in Sebastian Barry's *The Steward of Christendom*, a play that toured both sides of the Atlantic and won McCann extensive praise everywhere. Arguably his cinema work in that period was a little less interesting, although he was increasingly called on by internationally renowned directors such as Bernardo Bertolucci and Phillippe Rousselot, for *Stealing Beauty* (1996) and *The Serpent's Kiss* (1997), respectively. One can only speculate as to where his career might have gone had not pancreatic cancer brought him to an early grave at 56.

MCCOURT, EMER. Northern Irish actress McCourt came to prominence with her endearing and empathetic performance as Goretti in *Hush-a-Bye Baby* alongside a young unknown cast including the singer Sinead O'Connor. After roles in **Johnny Gogan**'s *The Bargain Shop* and Ken Loach's *Riff-Raff* (1990), she had roles in *Boston Kickout* (1995) and *Sunset Heights* (1997). In 1999 she turned producer for the film *Human Traffic* (1999), which featured **Lorraine Pilkington**, and, in 2003, switched roles again when Virago published her warmly received first novel *Elvis, Jesus and Me*.

MCDONALD, PETER (1972–). Originally from Mount Merrion in Dublin's south side, McDonald considered attending acting college after secondary school but opted to study English at University College Dublin instead. He was very active in Dramsoc, the college drama society, and it was there that he first met **Conor McPherson**, with whom he has subsequently worked on several occasions. In 1992, McDonald and McPherson were key figures in the establishment of the Fly By Night theater company, which concentrated on the production of original plays.

McDonald concentrated on stage work for the first five years of his career, but his film debut, when it came, made a major impact. The film, *I Went Down*, was directed by **Paddy Breathnach**, but Conor McPherson scripted it. Cast opposite **Brendan Gleeson**, McDonald made an instant impression as Git, conveying a winning mixture of steadfastness, intelligence, and vulnerability. After the film became a hit in Ireland, McDonald (like Gleeson) was offered a series of screen roles, and for several years his stage work took a backseat. *I Went Down* was followed by smaller roles in Atom Egoyan's *Felicia's Journey* (1999) and **Pat Murphy**'s *Nora*, playing James Joyce's brother Stanislaus in the latter film. He would work with Breathnach again in the poorly received *Blow Dry* (2001) but received better reviews for his next McPherson collaboration, *Saltwater*. In this film, adapted from McPherson's own play *This Lime Tree Bower* (in which McDonald had already performed in a British radio adaptation), McDonald played the key role of Frank, the oldest son in an Irish-Italian family, who resorts to desperate measures in an attempt to save his father's chip shop from financial ruin. The same year he took the key role in *When Brendan Met Trudy,* playing an ineffectual secondary school teacher whose life is turned upside down when he meets a cocky petty criminal. The self-referential comedy was a major success at home and, along with *I Went Down*'s Git, is the role McDonald is best known for.

After appearing in a lead role opposite Christopher Walken in the poorly received independent U.S. picture *The Opportunists* (2000), he concentrated on television work for a period. In 2000, for the first time, he worked with another ongoing collaborator, Michael McIllhatton, who wrote *Paths to Freedom*, a hit **Radio Telefís Éireann (RTÉ)** sitcom. In the show, McDonald played Tomo, the long-haired guitarist in a no-hope Dublin band fronted by recidivist criminal Rats (McIllhatton). The series spawned a feature film spin-off in 2003, *Spin The Bottle*, and McDonald appeared in another McIllhatton-scripted sitcom, *Fergus's Wedding*, in 2002.

Since *Spin the Bottle* he has worked mainly in British television, including a recurring role in the British Broadcasting Corporation series *Sea of Souls* from 2004. However, he remains one of the most recognizable Irish screen actors, especially for younger audiences.

MCGARVEY, SEAMUS (1967–). While working with still photography at school, McGarvey was encouraged by his art teacher to experiment with Super 8 film. In 1985 he left his native Armagh to do a three-year film course at a London polytechnic, as part of which he produced a short road movie. This attracted the attention of **Thaddeus O'Sullivan**, who offered him a camera trainee job on *December Bride*. From this he began shooting a series of low-budget shorts funded by the British Film Institute (BFI) and **Channel 4**, before graduating to working with some of the emerging talents of early 1990s British cinema. These included Michael Winterbottom, on whose directorial debut, *Butterfly Kiss* (1995), McGarvey acted as cameraman, and actor-directors like Alan Rickman (*The Winter Guest* [1997]) and Tim Roth (*The War Zone* [1999]). In the late 1990s he moved to larger-budget pictures with Stephen Frears's *High Fidelity* (2000) and *Enigma* (2001) before in 2003 working on both *The Hours* (for which he won the Evening Standard British Film Award for Best Technical/Artistic Achievement) and **Conor McPherson**'s *The Actors*.

MCGINLEY, SEAN (1956–). Born and raised in Ballyshannon, County Donegal (where his mother taught him at the local primary school), McGinley trained to be a teacher at University College Galway. While working on a university theater production, he was talent-spotted by Garry Hynes and Marie Mullen (whom McGinley later married), who were looking for actors to work with their new company, the Druid Theatre. McGinley duly became a key element of what was the first professional Irish theater company set up outside Dublin. He stayed with the company for nearly a decade, helping build its premises and—in stark contrast to his subsequent screen career—was frequently cast in the role of the quiet simpleton.

In 1986 Garry Hynes, who had become director at the **Abbey The-atre,** cast him against type in a production of Tom Murphy's *Whistle in the Dark*. The role proved revelatory—McGinley was suddenly violent and domineering in a production that won him awards and toured in the United Kingdom. The role dramatically altered the trajectory of his career, and he quickly secured roles in production of Eugene O'Neill's *The Iceman Cometh* and Anton Chekhov's *Three Sisters* at the Gate Theatre. This was followed by a nine-month stint at the National Theatre in London.

He made his first screen appearance as a priest in **Jim Sheridan**'s film *The Field*. Though rarely receiving first billing in features, McGinley secured a steady line of small and big screen work. Much of this has been in the United Kingdom, where he has made guest appearances in a wide range of dramas including *Minder*, *Cold Feet*, and *Waking the Dead*. However, his best television work has been on Irish television, where he has played leading roles in three key dramas of the past decade: *Family, Making the Cut,* and *On Home Ground*. *Family*—directed in 1994 by English director Michael Winterbottom from a **Roddy Doyle** script—seared McGinley's screen persona into the consciousness of Irish audiences. He played Charlo, a seductive but spectacularly violent patriarch of a working-class Dublin family. The character was capable of switching from apparent calm to untrammelled fury in an instant, and McGinley imbued him with a sense of constant menace. The role has arguably influenced much of McGinley's subsequent casting.

It also made him a star in Ireland, and when **Radio Telefís Éireann** came to produce the detective series *Making the Cut* in 1997, then the biggest drama undertaking in the station's history, McGinley was cast in the lead role of a Waterford-based detective. He was again the obvious choice in 2001 for the station's prime-time Gaelic football drama, *On Home Ground*.

Family also led to an apparently endless series of offers for feature film work: Indeed, such was the demand for his services that he did not work again in theater until 2000. McGinley has appeared in nearly 15 Irish features since 1994 and also secured roles in Irish-themed films such as *The Informant* (1997) and *The Closer You Get* (*American Woman,* 2000). Many of these play on the air of danger if not psychosis established with Charlo: His detectives in *Michael*

Collins and *Dead Bodies* are by turns savage and sinister, while his sidekick roles in *Trojan Eddie* and *Resurrection Man* carry more than a whiff of menace. He is more than capable of playing outside these confines, however: He plays a gentle garda sergeant in *The Butcher Boy* and exhibited fine comic timing as Gary opposite Brendan Gleeson in *The General*.

In 2002, he was cast (along with **Brendan Gleeson** and **Liam Neeson**) in Martin Scorsese's *Gangs of New York*, playing one of the gang leaders. For the most part, however, he continues to do most of his screen work in the United Kingdom and Ireland, where he remains remarkably busy. He appeared in seven productions between 2003 and 2005, including *Freeze Frame*, *Man About Dog*, and *The Mighty Celt*.

MCGUCKIAN, MARY (1964–). The daughter of a well-known agricultural entrepreneur, McGuckian graduated from Trinity College with an engineering degree. Despite this she moved into theater, becoming an actress, and then a producer, beginning with *Macbeth*, which she devised with **Alan Gilsenan.** Since 1994 she has produced and directed more films than most Irish directors and has worked with some of the biggest stars in Hollywood. Unfortunately many of the resultant films have had mixed reviews, and her work has not yet been subject to extensive critical analysis.

McGuckian's film debut, *Words upon the Window Pane* (1994), featuring Geraldine Chapman and Ian Richardson, is somewhat reminiscent of classic European art cinema, and she was apparently encouraged to direct the film by **Pat O'Connor** as well as **Jim Sheridan**, taking over three years to raise the €3 million budget. Based on a W. B. Yeats one-act play, it focuses on Jonathan Swift's (Jim Sheridan) relationship with his two lovers, Stella (**Brid Brennan**) and Vanessa (**Orla Brady**). The stories of these historical figures are told by a medium, Mrs. Henderson (Geraldine James), using flashbacks.

McGuckian's next feature, *This Is the Sea* (1997), is a conventional "love-across-the barricades" story dealing with the "**troubles**" and set in contemporary Belfast—a romance between Protestant Hazel (Samantha Morton) and Catholic Malachy (Ross McDade). More recently *Best* (2000) recounts the life and career of the famous football player George Best, portrayed by McGuckian's partner,

John Lynch, who is, according to critics, badly miscast in the role. In 2004, she adapted Thornton Wilder's *The Bridge of San Luis Ray*, a classic novel much loved in America, with the phenomenal cast of Harvey Keitel, Kathy Bates, F. Murray Abraham, and Robert De Niro. Her great skill at co-opting and working with some of the most recognized actors in Hollywood is certainly to be commended. Unfortunately the film got a roasting from American critics, and did not receive a theatrical release in Ireland.

McGuckian's latest release, *Rag Tale* (2005), focuses on the activities of a down market tabloid newspaper and its preference for celebrity gossip over more conventional news. The film uses striking camera angles and staccato editing to emulate the brash style of the tabloid world and has been described by one unnamed critic as *"Natural Born Killers* on speed." The exposure of the print trade is part of a trilogy she hopes to complete. The second part, *Funny Farm*, will deal with therapy culture, while the third will focus on the film industry. As a director-producer, she is certainly prolific, but it remains to be seen whether her future work will earn her the commercial and critical success that has thus far eluded her.

MCKENNA, SIOBHAN (1922–1986). Born in Belfast, she grew up in County Monaghan speaking fluent Gaelic and got involved with the theater in her early teens. Over the years she became a well-known and respected actress in Ireland and Great Britain as well as in off-Broadway classics like *Saint Joan*. She even appeared on the cover of *Life* magazine. Although primarily a stage actress, she appeared in a number of films including *King of Kings* (1961), *Of Human Bondage* (1964), and *Doctor Zhivago* (1965). Her most significant Irish role was in **Brian Desmond Hurst**'s 1960s version of *The Playboy of the Western World*, although at 42 she was arguably too old to play the ingénue role of Pegeen Mike.

MCKENNA, THOMAS PATRICK (T. P.) (1929–). Born in Mullagh, County Clare, the son of the local auctioneer, McKenna was educated in Saint Patrick's College, near Cavan Town, where he developed keen interests in Gaelic football (he would play at county minor level) and politics. His family was staunchly Fine Gael, but although McKenna's own politics proved more flexible, he generally voted for the left-wing Labour Party. (He remains a member of the British Labour Party to this day.) He also developed something of a reputation as a boy soprano, and in his first stage performance played the female lead in a production of Gilbert and Sullivan's *The Yeoman of the Guards*.

After leaving school he worked in a bank but spent his evenings as a semiprofessional actor. In 1954 he spent an entire season at the Gaiety Theatre, working under Irish theater legend Anew McMaster, before becoming a full-time actor the following year when he joined the **Abbey Theatre** company, with which he remained until 1963.

His first film roles were bit parts in films shot at **Ardmore Studios**, including *A Terrible Beauty* (1960) and *The Quare Fellow* (1962). Then he secured more prominent roles in the thinly disguised Sean O'Casey biopic *Young Cassidy* (1964) and in **Joseph Strick**'s *Ulysses*, in which he played Buck Mulligan. However, by the mid-1960s he was increasingly in demand for theater productions in London, and in 1967 he spent a year in the United Kingdom playing in David Storey's *The Contractor*. This lead to a wide range of television work, and over the course of the 1960s and 1970s, McKenna's became a well-known face on British screens. (Indeed, since 1972, McKenna and his family have lived in London, having previously resided in Sandymount, in South Dublin.) This included playing three different roles in episodes of the hit show *The Avengers* between 1964 and 1968. Interestingly, he was also usually and unproblematically cast in British roles. Only in the last decade has he been cast as Irish on a more regular basis; he has appeared in a growing number of Irish-made series, including *Ballykissangel* for BBC Northern Ireland and *Fair City* for **Radio Telefís Éireann (RTÉ)**.

By the 1970s he was an established character actor and appeared in a number of notable films, including Sam Peckinpah's *Straw Dogs* (1971) and Lindsay Anderson's *Britannia Hospital* (1982). However, although he has rarely worked in Irish cinema—an eye-catching role in **Kieran Hickey**'s short *A Child's Voice* (1978) apart—he has frequently been cast in Irish roles in films produced by other countries. He worked with Joseph Strick again in 1977, playing Simon Daedalus in *Portrait of the Artist as a Young Man*. He appeared in *The Outsider* (1979), opposite Sterling Hayden, in which a Vietnam veteran joins the Irish Republican Army (IRA), and he worked with

Pierce Brosnan in *The Mannions of America* in 1981. Since 1990 he has appeared in relatively few feature films, although his television work continues unabated and he still makes occasional appearances on the London stage.

MCPHERSON, CONOR (1970–). McPherson grew up on the northside of Dublin city, living in Coolock and going to school in Raheny (an experience he apparently hated). As a teenager he dabbled with music, playing in a number of bands between the ages of 14 and 20 before studying English and philosophy at University College Dublin (where he encountered **Peter McDonald** on the stage of the institutions famed Dramsoc). He gradually came to concentrate more on writing plays than on acting in them and in 1992 established the Fly-By-Night theater company (with McDonald), which served largely as a vehicle to produce his early plays. By his mid-20s he had already established himself as one of the country's foremost dramatists with internationally successful plays like *The Weir, Port Authority*, and *Shining City*. His script for *I Went Down* (which, though this is unacknowledged by McPherson, clearly draws on his 1994 monologue play *The Good Thief*) represented his first entry into filmmaking. In an interview, the film's director, **Paddy Breathnach**, stressed how involved McPherson was throughout the production (Power, 1997). Despite some alcohol-related health issues in the late 1990s (he ended up on a life support system), a time when his professional career seemed to be going well, it was seemingly inevitable that he would turn to directing himself. This he did in 2000, adapting his own play *This Lime Tree Bower* into the film *Saltwater*, which (inevitably) starred Peter McDonald opposite Brian Cox. The film was generally well received although some critics complained that it seemed more suited for television than the large screen. Since then he has continued to work mainly in theater, although he has made the occasional cameo acting appearance on the small screen. He undertook one of the more substantial elements of the project to film all of **Beckett's** works in 2000 when he shot *Endgame* with **Michael Gambon** and David Thewlis. His most recent directorial foray into film, however, was not overly well received. Based on a story from **Neil Jordan**, *The Actors* (2003) starred Michael Caine and Irish comic Dylan Moran in a crime caper that was widely dismissed as lightweight if not actually trite. Perhaps as a result, though he has been linked with several possible projects, McPherson has not directed a film since.

MCSORLEY, GERARD (1950–). McSorley attended school at Saint Columba's in Derry, and it was there that he first considered acting as a career. After school he went to Queen's University Belfast to study English and history but then returned to acting, making his first major impact in *The True Story of the Horrid Popish Plot*, a play directed by Hilton Edwards at the Gate Theatre in Dublin. More work with the Gate followed, but he was also involved in the Project Theatre during the mid-1970s during the tenure of **Jim Sheridan** and his brother Peter. Having worked as a freelance actor for several years he joined the **Abbey Theatre** in 1981 but left before his contract ended, citing discomfort with having to fit into the Abbey's schedule.

He had in any case already begun to branch out into screen work; he appeared in **Joe Comerford**'s *Withdrawal* (1982) and had a small role in **Neil Jordan**'s *Angel*. He also made appearances in the British television programs *The Irish R.M.* and *Bergerac*. Given the sporadic nature of screen production in Ireland in the 1980s, the bulk of his work in that decade remained stagebound. However, when Irish audiovisual production began to take off in the early 1990s, McSorley was well poised to benefit: In 1995 alone, he appeared in eight major productions, including *Moondance*, *Braveheart*, and *Nothing Personal*. Arguably his success in this period owed much to a well-honed cameo in Jim Sheridan's *In the Name of the Father* as a Belfast detective. Although his screen time in that film was limited to a couple of minutes, his portrayal of the psychologically subtle policeman was among the most memorable in a film heavily populated with impressive performances.

Subsequently (and appropriately for a Northern Irish actor) McSorley seems to have appeared in virtually every film made relating to the "troubles," including *Michael Collins* (as Cathal Brugha), *Bloody Sunday*, and *The Boxer*. Key among these was the lead role in *Omagh*, which took its title from the town where the main character grew up. In the film he played the real-life figure of Michael Gallagher, who lost his son in a terrorist bombing that killed 28 people in 1998. In what is a remarkable, sympathetic performance,

McSorley's character becomes a proxy for the other grieving relatives, and thus much of the picture is carried on his shoulders.

Michael Gallagher could hardly have been more different from the character McSorley portrayed in his previous performance in Joel Schumacher's *Veronica Guerin*. McSorley had already appeared in two productions about Dublin gangster Martin Cahill—a British Broadcasting Corporation (BBC) production called *Vicious Circle* (1999) and **Thaddeus O'Sullivan**'s ***Ordinary Decent Criminal***—but in *Veronica Guerin* he took on the role of John Gilligan, the Dublin criminal who was ultimately imprisoned for his role in Guerin's murder. His portrayal of a career criminal is horribly fascinating, repulsive yet compelling, especially in a scene where he threatens harm to Guerin's young son.

In addition to all his big-screen work (McSorley has appeared in 30 features since 1993), he continues to do stage work from time to time. He has been particularly successful in the works of dramatist Brian Friel, especially in the role of Michael in the Abbey Theatre production of ***Dancing at Lughnasa***, which played in Dublin, London, and New York in the early 1990s. Finally, Irish audiences have also been exposed to his more comedic side, in the local sitcom *Fergus's Wedding* and his scene-stealing one-off role as Father Todd Unctious in the absurdist **Channel 4** sitcom *Father Ted*.

MEANEY, COLM (1953–). Sometimes referred to as the "first Irishman in space," Meaney will be forever associated with *Star Trek*, holding the unique distinction of having appeared in 14 seasons of the *Next Generation* and *Deep Space Nine* series between 1987 and 1999. However he is also one of the busiest screen actors to have come out of Ireland, and although he began his career in the theater, his stage appearances have been rare since the mid-1980s.

He grew up in Finglas on the north side of Dublin and attended both the Dublin Drama Centre and the **Abbey Theatre** Training School in the late 1960s and early 1970s. He was based in London for most of the 1970s, where he developed an impressive stage curriculum vitae and—toward the end of the decade—made a number of smaller television appearances, beginning with a role in the classic British police series *Z-Cars*. In 1982 he moved to New York and worked on Broadway before moving into television roles. He made appearances in both *Moonlighting* and *Remington Steele* (opposite **Pierce Brosnan**) before securing the recurring role of Miles O'Brien on *Star Trek*. When *Deep Space Nine* began in 1993, he negotiated the right to do feature film work while working on the television series. As a result he was able to appear in two or three features a year through the mid-1990s while still appearing on *DS9*.

Although he had appeared in an American Public Broadcasting System (PSB) production of J. M. Synge's *The Playboy of the Western World* in 1983 (opposite then wife Bairbre Dowling), his first significant Irish feature role came in 1987, when he was cast in **John Huston**'s *The Dead*. Smaller Hollywood roles quickly followed in *Dick Tracy* (1990), *Die Hard 2* (1990), and Alan Parker's *Come See the Paradise* (1990) before he took on the role of Jimmy Rabbitte Sr. in Parker's adaptation of **Roddy Doyle**'s novel *The Commitments*. The boisterous working-class father with the heart of gold remains the role with which he is most readily associated in Ireland, and although he played a relatively minor part in *The Commitments*, he was the unquestioned star of the show when he reprised the character in *The Snapper* and *The Van*.

Although based in New York, he has always maintained a home in Glasnevin on the north side of Dublin, and this dual residence is reflected in his screen work. He has made 10 feature films in Ireland since 1993, including appearances in *Into the West* and *Last of the High Kings*. However, his most substantial Irish roles in recent years came in *How Harry Became a Tree*, playing the eponymous Harry, a man obsessed with besting his rival, and the New Age Irish music-loving detective in the ensemble piece *Intermission*.

However, although in his Irish work he generally plays comic (if not absurd) characters, he has secured a broader range of work in the United States and is frequently cast as an American. Thus he has played an FBI agent in *Con Air* (1997), a small-town mayor in *Mystery, Alaska* (1999), and a pimp in *Claire Dolan* (1998). He has also maintained a presence on American television screens, playing an occasional role in *Stargate: Atlantis* and appearing in *Law and Order: Criminal Intent*.

MEDIA DESK. Run since its inception in February 1992 by Siobhan O'Donoghue (who wrote the influential *Independent Television*

Production Sector Report for **Film Makers Ireland**), Media Desk Ireland was set up to provide information for Irish filmmakers on various aspects of the **MEDIA program**. Media Desk's function is to provide current, accurate, and comprehensive information and consultancy services regarding access by Irish filmmakers to money for many aspects of filmmaking. Media Desk holds ongoing briefing meetings, seminars, and workshops with Irish film professionals. There is also a regional antenna of Media Desk in Galway, which has a particular responsibility for the development of Irish-language projects.

MEDIA PROGRAM. First begun on a pilot basis in 1987, before becoming a full-fledged program in 1990, the MEDIA program of the European Union (EU) represents a concerted attempt to slow the steady decline of the European film industry. In fact there have been four MEDIA programs, running in succession since 1987: MEDIA '95, MEDIA II, MEDIA Plus, and the current MEDIA 2007, which is due to run until 2013. All of the programs have been informed by the same cultural and economic considerations. Culturally, the dominance of American audiovisual product has been seen (particularly in France) as undermining the very fabric of European society through cultural imperialism. At the same time, American domination of European cinema and television screens has had a damaging economic influence on the U.S.–European balance of trade: In 1993 there was a £3.7 *billion* deficit in terms of European audiovisual trade with America.

Rather than directly funding European production—this was felt to be the province of national film boards, and in any case **Eurimages** was already funding pan-European production—the programs sought to address the structural factors underpinning the perceived weakness of the European audiovisual sector. Although the MEDIA '95 program split its €200 million budget across 19 separate projects in areas as diverse as encouraging multilingualism in television programs and support of the **animation** sector, subsequent programs concentrated their efforts in three areas: supporting development, **distribution**, and training.

Given the condition of the Irish audiovisual industry in 1989/90 when MEDIA '95 was established, most notably the "retirement" of the **Irish Film Board** in 1987, the program was embraced by both Irish producers and by successive Irish governments as—**Channel 4** aside—the most promising source of finance for Irish producers (albeit upstream and downstream of actual production funding). The Irish government reacted enthusiastically to the MEDIA program initially because it displaced responsibility for the domestic audiovisual industry onto the shoulders of the then European Community.

From the outset Irish films and companies punched above their weight in terms of receipts from the program (Ireland accounted for 1 percent of the EU population in 1990 but typically secured 2–3 percent of the MEDIA budget). Early Irish beneficiaries included *Reefer and the Model*, *The Miracle*, and *Hush-a-Bye Baby*, which cumulatively received 600,000 ECU (European Currency Units—a pre-Euro currency) from the theatrical distribution support agency EFDO. However, for Irish producers the MEDIA program was beneficial in ways difficult to capture in monetary terms. For example, the EAVE program (aimed at enhancing the skills of European producers) allowed Irish producers to meet and work with producers from other European countries, thus giving them access to a network of pan-European contacts and facilitating subsequent coproductions. Thus while direct funding to Irish production from the MEDIA program amounted to £0.6 million in 1993, much of the £0.8 million that went into Irish production from other EU sources results from the network of contacts established by MEDIA for Irish producers.

The MEDIA '95 program officially came to a close on 31 December 1995 but was immediately followed by MEDIA II, a program with more money (€310 million) that concentrated on training, development, and distribution. The changes were a response to the complaint from many European producers that MEDIA '95 funding had been spread too thinly over too many projects. Similarly the decision to concentrate some 60 percent of the total MEDIA II budget on distribution acknowledged the limitations of EFDO and EVE (the two MEDIA '95 bodies responsible for distribution) given the size of their budgets.

In addition, although MEDIA II followed the same basic remit as its predecessor, there was markedly greater emphasis on the influence of market forces and more concentration of activity with money targeted on significantly fewer projects. Administrative and budgetary power was also concentrated: Whereas in MEDIA '95 each EU member state (apart from Greece) had at least one MEDIA project situated in its territory with the power to decide its own spending priorities, the new projects were to be financially administered from Brussels.

This tripartite division introduced by MEDIA II was largely retained by the MEDIA Plus program, which commenced in 2001 with an operational budget of €400 million. MEDIA Distribution continued to swallow up the bulk of this finance to fund its support for distribution of European works across theatrical, broadcast, and domestic (i.e., video and DVD) markets. To support cinema distribution, the project operates a combination of what are termed automatic and selective schemes. Automatic schemes are post hoc in that they "automatically" reward distributors and sales agents who successfully distribute European works across European borders by offering them funds—the precise amount is based on the box office performance of previous European films—to support further distribution of European works. In selective schemes, by contrast, funds are awarded in advance of release to facilitate the subsequent pan-European distribution of European works. Both automatic and selective schemes are designed to encourage the emergence of pan-European distribution networks capable of competing with the operations of the U.S. majors in Europe. MEDIA Development supports the development not only of individual projects but also, through the provision of slate funding (i.e., supporting a range of projects associated with one company), encourages the development of production companies with a long-term strategic outlook. Finally, the MEDIA Training Program encourages the establishment of pan-European training initiatives to allow filmmakers to develop their competence and their competitiveness on the international market—in 2003, a fourth strand, European Film Promotion, was added to support access of European productions to international markets and festivals.

The overall impact of the MEDIA project is difficult to assess objectively. Judged by European audience figures for European films over the last 15 years, the project would not be regarded as a success, considering that since the beginning of the MEDIA programs European attendance at European films has declined. Against this, it might be argued that only the existence of the MEDIA program has prevented the situation from being much worse. Certainly the European

Commission is confident of the importance of retaining the scheme. Although MEDIA Plus would wind up in 2006, in 2004 the commission published proposals for MEDIA 2007, which was due to commence on 1 January 2007 with a budget of over €1 billion, almost doubling the budget for the current program. In practice the final sum voted for MEDIA 2007 in November 2006 was capped at €755 million, which would fund the program until 2013.

From an Irish perspective the €20 million awarded to various elements of the domestic audiovisual sector since the inception of the MEDIA program has certainly contributed to the emergence of a series of relatively healthy production companies, working across a range of media. Much of this has been facilitated by the operation of **MEDIA Desk** Ireland.

MERLIN FILMS. John Boorman and well-known accountant Kieran Corrigan founded Merlin Films in 1989 as a production company and vehicle for raising **Section 481** funds for other production companies. Corrigan, who was born in 1954 and grew up in Tyrone and Belfast, studied economics and law at Trinity College, later qualifying as a barrister. From Trinity, however, he joined Arthur Andersen, trained as an accountant, and specialized in tax law, a field in which he subsequently established his own consultancy.

By the 1990s, he had an established profile in Irish business circles and was appointed to the board of the Industrial Development Authority, sat on the Custom House Docks Development Board, and chaired the National Building Agency. However, although he has retained an interest in nonfilm activities since 1989 (unsuccessfully bidding as part of a consortium for a national mobile phone license in 1995), his public profile is now that of a film accountant and producer.

Corrigan became involved with film and John Boorman when he advised the director on the funding of *Excalibur* in 1981. In 1987 Corrigan and two partners, Philip King and Nuala O'Connor, set up Hummingbird Productions to produce a major documentary on the impact of Irish music overseas, *Bringing It All Back Home*. Two years later he and Boorman created Merlin, the vehicle through which Boorman has produced the bulk of his films since, including *I Dreamt I Woke* (1991), *Two Nudes Bathing* (1995), and the John Le Carré adaptation *The Tailor of Panama* (2001) with **Pierce Brosnan.**

From an Irish perspective, however, Merlin's most notable Boorman production is *The General*. Unusually for an Irish production company, Merlin financed the film largely independently (as opposed to funding it through presales), borrowing much of the budget from a bank on the basis of estimates of box office sales and Corrigan's own reputation. As a consequence the company owned the rights to the film when it was completed and was able to sell it across a number of territories. Indeed, Corrigan is on record as declaring it to be a Merlin group ambition to "build up a library of rights," and the group has successfully raised production funds on international markets.

In addition to producing non-Boorman pictures such as *Angela Mooney Dies Again* and *This Is My Father*, from the early 1990s Merlin actively sought to expand its interests into a range of media-related areas. In 1992, in a joint venture with finance firm Media Assets, Merlin became co-owner of the Dublin-based Don Bluth Animation Studio, which, although in financial difficulty at the time, was the largest non-Disney feature **animation** production company in the world. (In 1994, Merlin unsuccessfully attempted to purchase the studios outright.) The group also includes a music division—Hummingbird Records—and in 2001 the group acquired the long-established Dublin publisher Wolfhound Press, which became part of Merlin Publishing.

The company now maintains offices in Dublin, London, Los Angeles, and Shannon. The last of these is explained by Corrigan's involvement with Alliance International Releasing, a Shannon-based film distribution company owned by Canadian film production company Atlantic Alliance. Shannon was also a base for Corrigan's dealings with Cinar, one of the biggest animation producers in the world.

Finally, Corrigan is also a director of Concorde Film Studios, **Roger Corman**'s European production base located in Connemara. Corrigan largely engineered Corman's decision to establish in Ireland, and Merlin has subsequently been the vehicle through which Corman productions have accessed Section 481 funds (although Merlin have also provided such services to Hummingbird Productions, Don Bluth Studios, and Irish television production companies like Tyrone Productions and Time Horizon Productions).

METROPOLITAN FILMS. One of the busiest Irish production companies, Metropolitan Films is run by James Flynn and Juanita Wilson and describes itself as producing films for the international market, stressing an ability to offer executive production services for European coproductions. Despite this international focus (which accounts for the vast bulk of the 25 or so projects the company has been associated with thus far), the company has also been behind a range of domestically originated Irish films. These have included *Inside I'm Dancing*, *Cowboys and Angels*, *H3*, and *Nora*. For the most part Metropolitan Films uses a strategic alliance with **World 2000** embodied in a third company—Octogon Films—to service incoming productions, many of which have been large-budget films. In recent years these have included *Reign of Fire* (2002), *The Count of Monte Cristo* (2002), *King Arthur* (2004), and *Tristan and Isolde* (2006).

James Flynn was formerly head of business affairs at the **Irish Film Board** before leaving to become an independent producer in the late 1990s. He has subsequently been a prominent spokesperson for the industry, sitting on the board of **Screen Producers Ireland** and the Irish Business and Employers Confederation's (IBEC) Audiovisual Federation.

Several of the company's Irish narratives have themselves been coproductions—*Nora* involved production partners in Italy and Germany, and *Inside I'm Dancing* is technically an Irish-French-British coproduction.

***MICHAEL COLLINS* (1997).** This film consolidated **Neil Jordan**'s status as Ireland's premier national filmmaker. It traces Collins's involvement in the establishment of the state from the 1916 Rising, through the War of Independence (1919–1921), to the Civil War (1922–1923) and the establishment of the border between Northern Ireland and the Irish Free State. Any discussion of history in Ireland almost inevitably has a resonance for modern-day politics, but these moments in particular are regarded as central in modern Irish history and have particular significance for the subsequent conflict in Northern Ireland.

Given this, the film's release during the nascent Northern peace process unsurprisingly prompted much debate about its historical accuracy and its meaning for contemporary national politics. According to some critics, not since *The Dawn* (1936) and its historical representation of rebellion has Irish nationalist history been visualized so effectively, while for others the film represents a revisionist history designed to validate the contemporary political situation and obfuscate difficult historical issues.

Certainly Jordan takes some liberties with historical accuracy to make the story fit the classic narrative structure. Some of these are relatively minor—amalgamation of several real-life individuals to create **Stephen Rea**'s character, Ned Broy, for example. Others are more open to question: The Croke Park killings of 1920, although terrible, did not involve armored cars, as depicted in the film, but rather were carried out as the army and police searched for IRA assassins.

In any case, Jordan's masterly use of the narrative techniques of Hollywood cinema and the gangster genre lends a dynamic energy and emotional depth to complex historical events. In particular the relationship between Collins (**Liam Neeson**) and his friend Harry Boland (**Aidan Quinn**) is the film's principal affective drive, functioning to personify the two opposing sides that fought over the partition of the island in the Civil War.

Indeed at a glance the real Collins is arguably the most cinematic figure of modern Irish history: a young warrior and lover who took on a massive empire and forced it to the negotiating table before being tragically killed in his prime. Thus the Collins of Neeson and Jordan is a likeable, rabble-rousing man more comfortable with the gun than the pen. The Collins of history, however, was also the first Dail's minister for finance, whom historians widely regard as the most effective member of that first Irish cabinet. In part the film's portrayal of him seems prompted by the need to contrast him with his eventual nemesis, de Valera, who is portrayed by Alan Rickman as an ascetic, aloof, and intellectual figure. It is only when the plot seeks to address modern politicians, by stressing Collins's attempt to take the gun out of Irish politics after the treaty, that a more bucolic figure emerges.

Similarly, although the casting of American star Julia Roberts as Kitty Kiernan, Collin's fiancé, was clearly done with an eye to the international market, it indirectly resulted in an underwriting of her character. In the final scene, while Kitty is shopping for her wedding dress, her fiancé is being ambushed. This can be read as symbolizing, albeit through a highly conventional Hollywood cliché, selfless sacrifice by all who loved this enigmatic rebel hero. Collins was sent to negotiate a peace settlement against his wishes. He believed that the treaty, which included the partition of Ireland and having to swear an oath of allegiance to the British monarchy, was the best deal Ireland could get from Britain at that time. While accepted by a majority of the people in a vote, this set in train a violent civil war. De Valera and his followers were unable to accept such a compromise or stepping-stone, while Collins pleaded for the resolution in Anglo-Irish conflicts. The working out of this schism has taken a number of violent decades. Many critics assert that the film remains an important representational and historical marker of the national political struggle.

However, taking the story as just that—a story—and judging *Michael Collins* simply as a piece of filmmaking, one cannot but be impressed by Jordan's ability. *Michael Collins* is arguably the first epic of Irish cinema, dwarfing even **Jim Sheridan**'s *In the Name of the Father* by dint of its scope of ambition, which recalls the myth-making ability of a David Lean. *See also* THE "TROUBLES."

MICKYBO AND ME (2005). Starring **Adrian Dunbar** and **Ciarán Hinds**, the Terry Loane–directed film tells the story of two young boys in 1970s Belfast at a critical time during the "**troubles**." The two escape the confines of their urban world by becoming their heroes—Butch Cassidy and the Sundance Kid. Micky Boyle, otherwise known as "Mickybo" (John Joe McNeill) plays a kid who is always up to some mischief and striving for attention in a large Catholic family, particularly from his mother (Julie Walters) and father (Dunbar). Johnjo (Neill Wright), on the other hand, is an only son who receives lots of attention from his guilt-ridden father (Hinds), who is having an affair. Through their imagination they flee the imploding city for the freedom of the Australian outback with dramatic results. While the ending might seem out of place in such a lighthearted children's adventure, nevertheless it serves to underscore the pervasive influence of the "troubles" on all the characters' lives as it disrupts the possibility of community solidarity.

THE MIRACLE (1991). Starring Beverly D'Angelo and **Donal McCann**, this small-budget story—compared to **Neil Jordan**'s large Hollywood narratives—evokes the tone and mood of a small seaside town near Dublin, where a young man, Jimmy Coleman (Niall Byrne), is growing up and trying to resolve some family issues. Based on one of Jordan's short stories—"Night in Tunisia" (1976)—the resultant narrative is arguably let down by a heavy-handed plot; the thinly veiled Oedipal drama is predictable and gets in the way of the story. (One could probably suggest that Jordan learned this scripting lesson for *The Crying Game*, in which a related psychodrama is more carefully suggested but not labored in its execution.) D'Angelo arrives in the town, and Jimmy becomes enamoured with her, not knowing her true identity and reason for coming back to Ireland. His family situation is difficult, with his musical father feeling unfulfilled in life and unable to activate his son's imagination. In spite of such difficulties, the gentle story remains memorable and engaging and helped to develop Jordan's skill at effective characterization and storytelling.

MISE ÉIRE [*I AM IRELAND*] (1959). Directed by George Morrison, *Mise Éire* was the first of a projected trilogy of films on Irish history (and in particular the struggle for independence) covering 1896 to 1939. (A second film, *Saoirse? [Freedom?]*, was released in 1961, but the third film was shelved.) Made by **Gael Linn**, an independent but state-aided Irish-language and cultural organization, *Mise Éire* was the first feature-length (90 minutes or longer) Irish-language film.

The film traces the development of the revolutionary movement in Ireland between 1896 and 1918, exclusively using film footage from the period (most of which had to be found outside Ireland). The film divides its treatment of the era into three sections: Awakening (1896–1915), The Rising (1916), and The Dawning of the Day (1917–1918). The history of this period is well known, but in brief, it follows the rise of Sinn Féin in the first decade of this century against the waning power of the Irish Parliamentary Party, noting too the rise of (unsuccessful) revolutionary wars against the British Empire in the same period (most notably the Boer War).

As the narrative enters the 1910s the unionist reaction to the passing of the Third Home Rule (setting up the Ulster Volunteers) is mirrored by the establishment of the Irish Volunteers. Although with the outbreak of World War I in 1914, the Home Rule Bill is shelved and the majority of the Irish Volunteers join the British Army, two years later in 1916, the Easter Rising breaks out with fewer than 3,000 men and women on the Volunteer side. The Rising is swiftly crushed, but as the leaders are executed afterward, Irish public opinion, initially hostile to the Rising, turns to support the rebels. In the closing segment of the film, Sinn Féin's political success at the 1918 general election is interpreted by the film as offering strong evidence that the tide of history is turning the way of Irish nationalism.

A knowledge of history is crucial for understanding *Mise Éire*. The release coincided with a key moment in modern Irish history, in particular for national economic development. The growth in national self-confidence that resulted from the film made it possible to celebrate the foundation of the state in a way that would have been harder to justify previously. Consequently as a piece of **documentary**, *Mise Éire* is far from the ideal held up by some practitioners of the art: objective recording of actuality. Although **Louis Marcus**, who acted as one of the assistant editors on the film, agued that the raw footage had not been slanted politically, this is hard to square, however, with the film's actual mode of representation, which fairly nails its political colors to the mast. While the Sinn Féin movement is venerated as holding the torch of "true nationalism," it is implied that the Irish Parliamentary Party (IPP) was a dupe of the British Empire, especially in the wake of IPP leader John Redmond's call to the Irish Volunteers to join the British Army. Meanwhile the Ulster unionist case is simply not put forward: They remain characterized as "the invaders."

Nonetheless, judged as a piece of propaganda, *Mise Éire* is pretty effective. The painstakingly assembled footage is cleverly used to tell a linear narrative: In the absence of Irish material from the 1890s, the film uses instead contemporaneous Boer War footage to suggest a parallel struggle against the empire. Furthermore, director Morrison was clearly a member of the Robert Flaherty school of Irish symbolism: While the British Empire in Ireland is represented by stone statues of snarling lions, the image of Ireland as timeless and indomitable and indeed the persistence of "the Irish revolutionary spirit" are symbolized by footage of waves crashing and breaking against rocks on the Irish shore. Finally, the producers were lucky to find composer **Seán O'Riada** in top form: His lush score has subsequently become one of the classic pieces of 20th-century Irish music, classical in form yet undeniably Celtic in tone.

MISKELLY, WILLIAM (BILL) (1940–1991). Born in Belfast, Miskelly joined the BBC in 1967 initially as a film editor. He later moved to directing and before parting company with the broadcaster in the early 1980s directed over 40 documentaries and dramas. In 1983, he and Marie Jackson established Aisling Films as an independent production company.

The first Aisling production was *The Schooner* (1983), a one-hour drama for television based on a short story by Michael McLaverty. The story followed an eldery woman's final coming-to-terms with the loss of her husband at sea many years before, a process brought about by her encounter with her young nephew.

In 1985, the company produced *The End of the World Man*, a ecologically themed children's film partially financed by the **Irish Film Board.** Well made from an intelligent script, with its heart in the right place, the film is most impressive for the absence of any sense that the filmmakers are talking down to children. Perhaps the most remarkable fact about the film, however, is the almost total absence of any comment or explicit reference to the political environment of Northern Ireland. Perhaps inevitably the "troubles" do have an impact on the narrative, but they do so in an almost incidental manner. *The End of the World Man* reminded viewers that life in the six counties had another side, that shooting and bombings did not represent normality.

As was the case for so many Irish filmmakers, the closure of the Irish Film Board made it difficult for Miskelly to continue in feature production. Sadly, by the time the board was reestablished in 1993, he had prematurely passed away. The **Northern Ireland Film and Television Commission**, together with Miskelly's family, has commemorated his work by establishing an annual film script award in his name.

MONTGOMERY, FLORA (1974–). Born in Northern Ireland and certainly a rising star, she is most recognized for her commanding role as Trudy in *When Brendan Met Trudy*. Her feisty performance and ability to creatively speak to a new generation has made her marketable. She also had a major role in *Goldfish Memory* and made numerous appearances in television films and series such as *The Bill*. Most recently she appeared in *Basic Instinct 2: Risk Addiction* (2006), which hinted at the possibility of a Hollywood breakthrough.

MOONDANCE (1994). This rite-of-passage story, based on *The White Hare* by Francis Stuart and directed by Dagmar Hirtz, stars Ian Shaw, **Rúaidhrí Conroy**, and Jasmine Russell. Two brothers, 21-year-old Patrick and 14-year-old Dominic, lead an idyllic existence, living alone in a rambling country house, together with their greyhound. They spend endless days swimming, fishing, and hunting while their mother is in Africa. Eventually they make the acquaintance of a young German girl, Anya, who becomes their tutor and eventually comes to Dublin with them. Critics suggest that this German-Irish production is somewhat uneven and overly focused on presenting local (admittedly magnificent) scenery; the overall story is certainly fascinating, but ultimately the film reads as an unfinished script requiring more detailed characterization.

MOORE, JOHN (1970–). Born in Dundalk, he developed a fascination with film while pursuing a production course in Rathmines in Dublin, after which he set up Clingfilm Production Company along with his friend **Damian O'Donnell**—who later made his feature debut with *East Is East* (1999)—and where they learned their trade producing shorts and advertisements. Moore got his big break when Hollywood executives saw his Sega games advertisement, and he was invited to make *Behind Enemy Lines* (2001), a taut war story based on the recent Bosnian struggle, starring Gene Hackman and Owen Wilson. More recently he directed the $60 million remake of *Flight of the Phoenix* (2005), starring Dennis Quaid, which unfortunately has not done so well at the American box office.

MORRISSEY, EAMON (1943–). Morrissey made a household name for himself as a comic actor working on series like *Hall's Pictorial Weekly* on **Radio Telefís Éireann (RTÉ)** and, more recently, *Father Ted*, *Ballykissangel*, and *The Irish R.M.* Major roles in film include his well-honed comic persona in *Eat the Peach*, *Philadelphia, Here*

I Come, **How to Cheat in the Leaving Certificate**, *This Is My Father*, and most recently *The Trouble with Sex*.

MORRISON, GEORGE. Born in County Waterford, George Morrison first became interested in still photography in the mid-1930s. He shot his first moving film in 1942 with a 16 mm at Bram Stoker's *Dracula* (although the shortage of film stock during the war meant the film was never completed). When the war ended, he became involved in documentary production, subsequently working with the production company run by Michael MacLiammoir and Hilton Edwards of the Gate Theatre. As early as 1949 he submitted a proposal to the BBC to support the cataloguing of archival footage from key history, but it was after a 1952 meeting of the International Federation of Film Archives in Amsterdam that the real work of cataloguing Irish-related archival material began. This would constitute the basis of his most famous work, *Mise Eire*, produced for **Gael Linn** and completed in 1959.

Although Morrison himself would describe the technique of relying exclusively on "found footage" to recount the history of the Irish struggle for independence that constitutes the main body of *Mise Eire* (and its 1961 sequel *Saoirse?*) as entirely novel, there were several antecedents for this, most notably Esther Shub's seminal 1927 documentary *The Fall of the Romanov Dynasty*. (Indeed there is evidence that the Fianna Fail administration of the 1930s contemplated a project similar to *Mise Eire* but rejected it on cost grounds.)

Morrison has continued to work as a filmmaker since the 1960s: Subsequent productions include *Rebellion* (1963), *These Stones Remain* (1971), and *Two Thousand Miles of Peril* (1972). He is currently one of a handful of filmmaker members of Aosdana, a council created by the **Arts Council** in 1981 to honor those whose work has made an outstanding contribution to the arts in Ireland.

***THE MOST FERTILE MAN IN IRELAND* (2001).** Eamonn Manley, a **Catholic**, lives in post-ceasefire Belfast working in a dating agency and is in love—initially unrequited—with a local Protestant girl, Rosie, who works in a funeral parlor. Meanwhile, however, Eamonn finds that his loins are unusually productive: Each of his romantic encounters leads to conception. This lighthearted comedy, directed by

Dudi Appleton, challenges conventional representations and perceptions of Northern Ireland by placing Eamonn's fertility against the
backdrop of a conflict in which the Catholic nationalists are "out-
breeding" their Protestant unionist enemy. This film is particularly interesting for its sympathetic representation of loyalist culture: The
"Glorious Twelfth," for example, generally understood by nationalists as an exclusivist demonstration of triumphalism, is depicted here
as more akin to the St. Patrick's Day celebration.

MOTHER IRELAND. Discourses on nationalism have pervaded Irish
cultural and political life for centuries, within which images of the female have been appropriated by their male protagonists either for in-
spirational purposes, as in the case of the nationalism explored by
the plays of W. B. Yeats's in the **Abbey Theatre**, or for the practical
purpose of ensuring its own hegemonic role, as in the case of the
Catholic Church. These images have served to mythologize and
therefore conceal, to some extent, the actual roles played by Irish
women in the shaping of history. These representations have been explored in documentary works such as Anne Crilly's *Mother Ireland*
and affirmed by other feminist filmmakers like **Pat Murphy** in
Maeve, *Anne Devlin*, and most recently *Nora*. Margo Harkin's
Hush-a-Bye Baby also explores the problems inherent in the lack of
fit between these images and the reality they purport to represent.

MOXLEY, GINA. Originally from Cork, she began her film acting career with Fergus Tighe's 1987 production *The Clash of the Ash* and
has gone on to various roles in *Joyriders*; *Hear My Song*; *The Sun,
the Moon and the Stars*; *The Butcher Boy*; *This Is My Father*; and
most notably *Snakes and Ladders*, which was written around two
characters created by Moxley and her costar Pom Boyd a decade earlier. However, although she still appears on small and big screens, the
focus of her career since 1996 seems to be the stage. In that year her
debut as a playwright, *DantiDan*, a tale of sexual awakening in 1970s
Cork, produced by the Rough Magic company, became a massive
critical hit, winning a Stewart Parker award and transferring to
London after a successful Irish run. A film version of the play—
apparently to be directed by Moxley herself—has long been in ges-
tation, having received a substantial commitment from the **Irish Film**

Board. Meanwhile she has continued to write plays, including *Tea Set* for Fishamble Productions and *A Heart of Cork* as part of that city's 2005 Festival of Culture, and, in 2002, her work was included in the *Field Day Anthology of Irish Writing*.

MURPHY, CILLIAN (1976–). The first child of four born into a family of pedagogues (his father is a school inspector, his mother a French teacher), Cillian Murphy grew up in Cork. He became interested in theater and acting while studying at the Presentation Brothers College. He studied law at University College Cork but left midway through his degree to pursue acting as a career. He was quickly cast in a starring role in the original stage production of Enda Walsh's **Disco Pigs**, which received universally enthusiastic notices when it toured internationally. Murphy's performance as the near-psychotic Pig was singled out for attention, and when Kirsten Sheridan came to film the play in 2000, he was the obvious choice to reprise the role. His screen performance was equally impressive, by turns seductive and terrifyingly unpredictable.

His progress since then appears to have been meteoric, but in fact he had already appeared in seven films, including *Sweety Barrett*, *On the Edge* (as a suicidal psychiatric patient), and most effectively as the unresponsive son in *How Harry Became a Tree*. Despite this, until the filming of *Disco Pigs* he was best known to Irish audiences for his stage roles, most notably in Druid Theatre adaptations of *Juno and the Paycock* and *The Country Boy* and in a 2002 production of Neil LaBute's *The Shape of Things* at the Gate Theatre.

In 2002 Danny Boyle cast him in a lead role in the contemporary horror *28 Days Later* (2002), which became a surprise hit in America and brought Murphy to the attention of a much wider audience. This has led to a series of roles in "respectable" **Academy Award** fodder such as *Girl with a Pearl Earring* (2003) and *Cold Mountain* (2004) and starring roles as Dr. Johnathan Crane/The Scarecrow in *Batman Begins* (2005) and in Wes Craven's thriller about aircraft-bound passengers, *Red Eye* (2005).

He has also continued to work in Irish cinema, as part of the ensemble cast for the local hit *Intermission* and most recently in the main role as a transvestite prostitute in **Neil Jordan**'s *Breakfast on Pluto* (2005). In some respects he is perhaps best understood as a more "actorly" counterpart to **Colin Farrel**. While Farrel has been largely trapped in pretty boy lead roles since his turn in Joel Schumacher's *Tigerland* (2000), Murphy retains the potential of securing less lucrative but more intrinsically interesting roles, especially if he can avoid the trap of being typecast in on-the-edge psycho roles.

MURPHY, PAT (1951–). Murphy has been a very influential feminist film director and teacher and has been an important artistic force for explicating many radical ideas within Irish film. She began her film career with the formally experimental and highly innovative *Maeve* (1982), which was jointly directed with **John T. Davis** and explores the themes of republicanism and feminism within the political vicissitudes of Belfast. Similar themes are dealt with from a historical context in Murphy's next film, *Anne Devlin*.

After *Anne Devlin,* Murphy experienced a 16-year hiatus in filmmaking, which was indicative of a change on the part of the industry. Although production activity increased dramatically in the 1990s, the globalization of the film industry made the maintenance of a discrete national cinema increasingly difficult. It is argued that Hollywood's increasing role in Irish cinema placed limits on the freedom of Irish filmmakers to tell their own stories, and the feminist work of Pat Murphy did not seem to fit into the new commercially oriented orthodoxy of Irish cinema.

Consequently, when Murphy did return with *Nora* (2000), the story based on Brenda Maddox's biography of **James Joyce**, she had a difficult time getting it financed. The film has had mixed reviews — it is so different from her earlier films. Nevertheless, she has remained a compelling feminist voice in the Irish film landscape.

MY FRIEND JOE **(1995).** Based on a successful book by German novelist Peter Pohl-Jann and directed by Chris Bould, the film is unusual among recent Irish features in that it is unashamedly made with an audience of children in mind. Set in modern Ireland, the narrative centers on Chris, who comes from a "normal" middle-class family, and his friendship with Joe, who lives in a trailer with his violent uncle. Joe has spent his life traveling with a circus, and as a consequence he craves some stability, in contrast to Chris, who wants to escape what is perceived as a boring existence. The film concludes with a gender twist that forces the young protagonists to entirely reevaluate their relationship.

MY LEFT FOOT (1989). This film is often cited as single-handedly reviving the Irish film industry. Its success certainly played a major part in developing the pressure on the government to take an active role in developing the Irish film industry. In some respects the film came as a bolt out of the blue: Director **Jim Sheridan** and producer **Noel Pearson**, fresh from their partnership at the Abbey Theatre, came together to produce a feature film on a relatively small budget about a disabled Irish writer who had published only two books and who had in any case died nearly 15 years earlier. On paper this can't have looked like box office gold, and indeed although initial reviews were universally positive, public reaction was more muted. Even in Ireland the film failed to set the box office alight on its first release. Then came the **Oscars**—nominated in four categories, the film surprised by winning two: Daniel Day Lewis and **Brenda Fricker** for Best Actor and Best Supporting Actress, respectively. Re-released on the strength of that performance the film did enormous trade in both Ireland and the United States and in doing so raised the possibility of making films in Ireland that both in financial and creative terms could be internationally successful.

Examined on its own merits, the film remains far superior to many of the Irish pictures that followed in its wake. It opens in 1963 when Christy Brown (Day-Lewis) is a guest at a fund-raising gala held in his honor. As he waits to be presented to the crowd, he recounts his life to the nurse assigned to him. Born with cerebral palsy into an impoverished and large working-class family in 1932, his parents are informed by the doctors that he will remain a vegetable for the rest of his life. This defines his father's (**Ray McAnally**) initial relationship with him, although his mother (**Brenda Fricker**) is not convinced by the diagnosis. Ten years pass, however, before Christy is able to communicate his fierce intelligence: In a pivotal scene he picks up a piece of chalk with his left foot to write the single word "M-O-T-H-E-R" on the ground.

Thereafter Christy begins to explore his artistic side: Although almost his entire body is affected by the palsy (including his mouth, which slurs his speech), he retains control over his left foot, which he uses to paint with. At the age of 19 he enters a new clinic for cerebral palsy patients. There he meets Eileen, a specialist in treating palsy, who works with Christy to overcome his speech impediment. When she announces her engagement to Peter, the gallery owner who exhibits Christy's first public exhibition of art, Christy is heartbroken, and he abandons painting as a means of expression in favor of writing.

As the story returns to the present, Christy asks Mary, his nurse, if she'll go out with him. Initially reluctant, she eventually agrees. The film closes with the pair on Killiney Hill, drinking a toast with champagne to "Dublin, where Christy Brown was born." As the credits close, a postscript tells us that Christy and Mary married in 1972.

The performances in the film are immaculate. Given that the real Christy Brown was confined to a wheelchair, Day-Lewis's role was always likely to be the scene-stealer, but the actor still imbues his character with an extraordinary physicality: Unable to easily and rapidly express his frustrations with life through speech, his Christy communicates with his entire body, most notably in a confrontational restaurant scene where Eileen announces her engagement. Nor is his Christy an always sympathetic character: Given to fits of depression he also allows himself to wallow in self-pity. And it is this warts-and-all portrayal that lies at the center of the picture. Equally impressive, however, in less dramatic roles are Fricker and McAnally as Christy's parents. As noted above, Fricker's performance was recognized with an Oscar, but McAnally, given the difficult job of embodying a character unable to communicate with his own flesh and blood and frequently taking refuge in the bottle, nonetheless skilfully gives the audiences an insight into his character's frustrations with his own failings.

However, the film also reveals director Sheridan as a consummate storyteller. He altered the original biographies of Christy Brown (*Down All the Days* and *My Left Foot*) upon which the film was based so that, for example, Christy's father, although still gruff in the film, was rendered a far less brutal figure than in Brown's own depiction. But it is Sheridan's unerring ability to make such judgments, in the pursuit of a universally comprehensible narrative, that has often been cited as a critical factor in the international success of his pictures.

However, although *My Left Foot* helped create the circumstances in which an indigenous industry could emerge, it also raised the stakes for those Irish films that followed. No longer is it sufficient to make an artistically accomplished film in Ireland: To match *My Left Foot*, it must also be a financial success. It is notable then that much of the criticism leveled at the post–*My Left Foot* crop of Irish films often focuses less on the actual quality of the films themselves and more their financial performance. In the longer term, however, these two criteria tend to blur into one another so that commercial failures are automatically dismissed as critical failures. This leaves the question of the difficulty of accessing distribution channels in a global market dominated by Hollywood and creates an environment where good work is simply dismissed as failing to reach an audience.

My Left Foot also created an environment where Irish filmmakers have been subjected to the mantra that only "universal" narratives can succeed commercially overseas, a piece of cant that has arguably contributed to a noticeable tendency in 1990s Irish cinema to eschew cultural specificity and to embrace genre production, a strategy that has had only mixed results.

MYSTICS (2003). This caper comedy was directed by David Blair and features veteran actors **Milo O'Shea** and **David Kelly** as Dave and Locky, who are unable to secure thespian employment and run fake séances above a Dublin public house to earn cash. The story is complicated when a recently deceased Dublin gangster (played by Ronnie Drew) begins using Locky to communicate with his family. What is considered by some critics as a sitcom pilot could be compared with *Waking Ned*, which was more successful in its attempts to milk not dissimilar comic situations.

– N –

NATIONAL FILM INSTITUTE OF IRELAND. *See* IRISH FILM INSTITUTE.

NATIONAL FILM STUDIOS OF IRELAND. *See* ARDMORE STUDIOS.

NEESON, LIAM (1952–). The only boy in a family of four children, Neeson was born to a working-class **Catholic** family in staunchly loyalist Ballymena in Northern Ireland. As a child he nurtured ambitions to be a priest, although he also joined the local All Saints Boxing Club at an early age. He attended Ballymena Technical College, then spent an abortive year at Queen's University in Belfast studying physics and mathematics before taking up a place in an actor's training course in Newcastle-upon-Tyne in England. He returned to Northern Ireland, approached the Lyric Theatre, and was immediately cast in their next play. While touring a play in Dublin, Neeson was spotted by Peter Sheridan, who offered him a part in a play called *Says I, Says I*. This led him to move to Dublin, where he worked onstage with—among others—**Brid Brennan** and **Gabriel Byrne,** appearing in several plays at the **Abbey Theatre** and the Peacock. From there he moved to his first major film role as Gawain in **John Boorman**'s *Excalibur*.

In 1982 he moved to London, where he worked on a succession of American miniseries shot there and on the occasional British film, including *The Bounty* (1984) and *The Mission* (1986). It was the production of *Lamb* in 1986, however, that brought his name to the attention of a popular audience in Ireland. His casting as gentle giant Michael Lamb played on his large frame (Neeson is 6 feet 4 inches): His powerful physique stood in marked contrast to the sense of impotence the character experiences in the face of the corruption and unfairness of life. In 1987, Neeson moved to Los Angeles, where he made an immediate impact in Peter Yates's *Suspect* (1987), playing a deaf-mute homeless man opposite Cher and Dennis Quaid.

In 1988 while still in Los Angeles he was cast in Neil Jordan's *High Spirits*, the first collaboration between the two. Leading roles in Sam Raimi's *Darkman* (1990) and Woody Allen's *Husbands and Wives* (1992) followed, but it was his role as the charismatic wartime profiteer turned Holocaust hero Oskar Schindler in Steven Spielberg's film based on Thomas Keneally's novel *Schindler's List* (1993) that definitively placed him in the firmament of A-list Hollywood stars.

Indeed, such was his star status that his casting as **Michael Collins** instantly signaled that the film was going to be a biopic—albeit an unusually sophisticated one—rather than a critical examination of the politics underlying the foundation of the Irish state. His portrait of Collins is that of a physical, vigorous man of action, a general in charge of an army. The fact that the real 1920s republican rebel Collins had among his responsibilities the more sedate role of minister for finance was not one easily accommodated by this casting.

Since then Neeson has increasingly been cast in mentor roles, playing Qui-Gon Jinn opposite Ewan McGregor's Obi-Wan Kenobi in *Star Wars: The Phantom Menace* (1999), Henri Ducard in *Batman Begins*, and even the voice of Aslan in *The Chronicles of Narnia: The Lion, the Witch and the Wardrobe* (2005). Even in his most recent collaboration with Jordan, **Breakfast on Pluto**, Neeson plays a priest guiding the young "Kitten" (**Cillian Murphy**) through his formative years.

Over the years, he has occasionally returned to his stage roots and appeared opposite future wife Natasha Richardson (with whom he has two children) in a 1993 Broadway production of *Anna Christie*, for which he received a Tony nomination. A decade later in 2002, he received a second nomination for his part in a Broadway revival of Arthur Miller's *The Crucible*.

THE NEPHEW (1998). Produced by **Irish Dreamtime**, and thus financed almost totally outside of Ireland, the film, directed by Eugene Brady, mobilizes a mythic rural narrative style aimed at the American market, playing on a stereotype of the Irish as quirky yet welcoming. When a young black man comes to the rural town of Inishdaragh, his clothes and music fascinate the locals, although younger locals are already familiar with his culture from their exposure to MTV. However, although the film seeks to posit the Irish as open to outside cultures, some critics have noted that Chad is fully accepted by the locals only on their own terms: after he has sung a song in Irish at a wake. The film has a strong cast, including **Donal McCann, Pierce Brosnan**, and Sinead Cusack.

NIGHT TRAIN (1998). Directed by John Lynch (not the actor of the same name but a former RTÉ director), from an Aodhan Madden script, the film stars Brenda Blethyn as Alice, an older single woman who feels trapped by life and eventually takes in a lodger, Poole, played by John Hurt. It transpires that Poole is on the run from a Dublin criminal gang and spends most of his time operating his beloved model train in his room. The somewhat unrealistic plot developments that lead the pair to flee from the capital do not hamper a solid study of character and romance. Furthermore, the film is unusual—and welcome—in its willingness to give some narrative expression to the lives and loves of older people.

NORA **(2000).** This recent historical film by director Pat Murphy is a re-creation of the life of **James Joyce**'s wife, who has been famed in much of his writing. Most surprisingly, the Scottish actor Ewan McGregor plays Joyce, but of course his name helped the project to be finally green-lighted after a long struggle to bring the script to the screen. He plays opposite **Susan Lynch**, who performs with panache as Joyce's apparently stereotypical naive and innocent partner, Nora. The marital struggles are affectively played out and serve to affirm Nora's independent identity. Some critics regarded the film as a moving away from the formal affirmation of a feminist discourse toward endorsing the Hollywood conventions of romantic period drama. Others, more generously, suggest that the film represents a commercially necessary and pragmatic realignment of strategies to represent the new postfeminist worldview.

NORTHERN IRELAND FILM AND TELEVISION COMMISSION (NIFTC). The NIFTC grew out of the Northern Ireland Film Council (NIFC), which was established in 1989 as a voluntary body following recommendations in the **Derry Film and Video Co-Operative**'s 1988 *Fast Forward* report. Two years late the NIFC published its own *Strategy Proposals* outlining its ambition to create a vibrant film and video culture and industry in Northern Ireland. From the mid-1990s, the NIFC was in receipt of British National Lottery funds, which it used for film project development. In July 1997 the NIFC became the NIFTC with a much broader remit and more substantial funding from the Department of Culture, Arts and Leisure, Invest Northern Ireland, and the British Film Council. In addition, the commission also administers lottery funding for films in Northern Ireland on behalf of the Arts Council of Northern Ireland.

In many respects the responsibilities of the NIFTC mirror those of its counterpart in the Republic of Ireland, the **Irish Film Board**. However, while both institutions bear responsibility for funding film development and production, and both operate screen commissions in their respective jurisdictions, the NIFTC's remit is much broader. The commission focuses on seven objectives: production and development, business development (focused on developing production companies rather than simply individual productions), skills development and training, education (embedding audiovisual study into the primary and secondary school curricula), heritage (archiving), exhibition, and marketing and information.

In addition to funding short film and television production, the NIFC and NIFTC have been involved in financing virtually every feature shot in Northern Ireland since 1997, from *Sunset Heights* and **Titanic Town** to **Mickybo and Me** and *The Mighty Celt*. Both the council and the commission have had close working relations with the Irish Film Board, with which they have cofunded several productions (especially—and appropriately—those with cross-border or community themes such as **The Most Fertile Man in Ireland**, *A Love Divided*, and **Puckoon**). Northern and southern institutions have also collaborated on exhibition issues, jointly funding research into a putative pan-Ireland art-house cinema network and cofunding the purchase and running of a mobile cinema, the Cinemobile.

NOT AFRAID, NOT AFRAID (2001). Left by her husband of 25 years and convinced she is dying of cancer, Paula (Dianne Wiest) summons her son (Jack Davenport) and his wife to inform them of her impending demise and of her decision to embark on a nostalgic journey to visit her ex-lovers. Her journey is complicated when she brings her grandson, who has Down's syndrome, along for the ride. Produced by an independent American production company in conjunction with **World 2000**, and directed by Annette Garducci, the film has never received a theatrical release in America or Europe, suggesting a degree of unhappiness with the finished product on the part of potential distributors.

NOVEMBER AFTERNOON (1997). This is a small-scale theatrical film directed by **John Carney** and **Tom Hall**, shot in black and white, about an illicit relationship between a brother and sister. The tone and aesthetic of the film recall European art movies from the 1960s and 1970s; the film was made using lots of roaming cameras and apparent improvisations. In spite of some forced dialogue, the narrative is strangely hypnotic and engaging, even if the diegesis of the story (nominally set in Dublin, the interiors are more reminiscent of New York) seems somewhat unconvincing.

The story is structured in three acts, which play out over a long weekend, as Karen (Jayne Snow) and her husband, John (Mark Doherty), arrive home from London and proceed to her brother Robert's (Michael McElhatton) flat in inner-city Dublin. Reversing conventional Irish stereotypes, the English husband is very fond of his drink, while Robert follows jazz—a music not often associated with Ireland. An apparently conventional narrative technique of emigrants returning home with and to "skeletons in the cupboard" coupled with varyious unhappy relationships does not detract from what is a well-conceived and highly visualized story line that concludes with a spectacular revelation. Great confidence is shown in dealing with a taboo story in an engaging and nonsensational way.

– O –

O'BYRNE, JOE. After completing a degree in German and English literature at University College Dublin, he became closely involved in theater as artistic director of the Dublin Co-Motion Theatre Company from 1985 to 1998. He directed many critically acclaimed plays as well as developing innovative audiovisual theatrical experimentations. Directing the award-winning *Frank Pig Says Halo*, an adaptation by Pat McCabe from his novel *The Butcher Boy*, has lead to several other collaborations. While he become a very skillful and imaginative translator of literary drama, Byrne has always wanted to direct film also and began as a script editor on **Johnny Gogan**'s low-budget *The Bargain Shop* (1992). He wrote the screenplay for Cathal Black's *Korea*, adapted from a short story by John McGahern and set in 1950s Ireland. In 1998 O'Byrne wrote and directed his first children's feature, *Pete's Meteor*, starring **Brenda Fricker**, Alfred Molina, Dervla Kirwan, and Mike Myers. Pete (Myers) is an ex-junkie in the process of turning his life around when his two best friends die unexpectedly, so he steps in to help raise the deceased's children. Along with their grandmother (Fricker), they all witness a miraculous event—a meteor lands near their back yard. Unfortunately, critics regarded the story line as mawkish, which ruined the possibility of the film's getting a cinematic release. O'Byrne continues to write and direct a wide range of theatrical production at home and abroad.

O'CONNOR, PAT (1943–). Though born in Ireland, he enrolled in a liberal arts program at the University of California and then continued his education in Canada, returning in 1970 to work in **Radio Telefís Éireann (RTÉ)**, where he learned the craft of directing. He served his apprenticeship in television production and was particularly acclaimed for *The Ballroom of Romance* (1982), which dealt with frustrated gender relations in a rural society where the only respite was the local dance hall. It went on to win a British Academy Film and Television Award (BAFTA) for Best Television Drama in Britain and acted as a springboard for a feature film career.

His first feature, *Cal*, was produced by highly regarded British producer David Puttnam. He followed this in 1987 with *A Month in the Country*, based on the novel by J. R. Carr. The film, which helped to establish the film careers of Colin Firth and Kenneth Branagh, is set in Britain after World War I. Firth and Branagh play two traumatized and shell-shocked war veterans who get summer jobs in a beautiful English country village—one to uncover a mural in a local church, the other to uncover the grave of a famous luminary. They become friends as they unearth secret Muslim influences in the area and discover the religious tensions between churches. They also become attracted to the Natasha Richardson character, who appears unhappily married to the pastor. The novel's complexity is well expressed and executed if overly pointed at times. However, O'Connor's star became somewhat dimmed by his subsequent features, namely *Stars and Bars* (1988) and *The January Man* (1989). O'Connor returned to successful form, however, with his brand of heritage cinema in *Fools of Fortune* (1990), adapted from another William Trevor novel, which follows the fortunes of a wealthy middle-class Irish family during a violent political time in the early 1920s. The film has a large British cast, including Julie Christie and Iain Glenn.

Drawing on the large audiences already secured by the author, Maeve Binchy, the adaptation of *Circle of Friends*, with its all-star cast, was a great commercial success. O'Connor moved into more classic literature with ***Dancing at Lughnasa***. Frank McGuinness was commissioned to write the screenplay based on the classic play by Brian Friel. The story is set in the small village of Ballybeg in rural County Donegal in the summer of 1936. The play, which culminated in an exuberant Irish dancing sequence, had been highly successful touring abroad as well as in Ireland. The film, with its all-star cast, is a successful transcription.

Although the size of his output compares with that of Sheridan and Jordan, critics have afforded O'Connor less critical analysis and credence, judging unfairly that his extensive output lacks authorial distinctiveness and dismissing in an elitist fashion what they call his generic filmmaking. O'Connor has directed many other "non-Irish" films, including *Fools of Fortune* (1990) and *Sweet November* (2001), and continues to be an active filmmaker.

O'CONNOR, SINEAD (1966–). O'Connor is a controversial singer and performer who has built up a major international musical career. Her distinctive voice has been heard on numerous Irish film soundtracks including ***Angela's Ashes*** and ***In the Name of the Father***, which features the devastating "Thief of Your Heart" over the end credits. Indeed, directors have a peculiar preference for deploying her music at the denouement of the narrative: In ***Michael Collins*** she performs "She Moved through the Fair" over the final montage and contributes a haunting ballad to the close of ***Veronica Guerin***.

O'Connor's very strong beliefs and internationally publicized criticism of the Catholic Church in particular—she later toyed with being a priest herself—frames her changing Madonna-like persona and her evolving sexual politics. This has been reflected in her two film roles to date. In ***Hush-a-Bye Baby*** (for which she again produced the theme music), she plays a young girl growing up during the Northern "**troubles**." Though her character makes a relatively brief appearance, a scene where she dresses up as a nun has resonances with her larger public persona. Clearly playing upon this, **Neil Jordan** cast her as a blasphemous Virgin Mary in ***The Butcher Boy***. The star performance effectively and intertextually reflects her real-life persona, and the film explores the range of contentious debates over sacred divinity within the country and its contemporary traumatized sexual politics. *See also* WOMEN AND FILM.

O'CONOR, HUGH (1975–). In *Red Hot* (1993), Hugh O'Conor plays a teenager living in 1950s Russia who attempts to set up a rock and roll band. He was well equipped for such a musical role: The actor is the son of John O'Conor, the internationally acclaimed pianist and director of the Royal Irish Academy of Music. Hugh O'Conor himself plays guitar, piano, and clarinet. He made an arresting debut at the age of nine opposite **Liam Neeson** in *Lamb*. A role in *Da* (1988), an adaptation of a Hugh Leonard play, followed before he took on the role of the young Christy Brown in *My Left Foot*. His performance as the palsied writer was again remarkable, and several critics cited it above even Daniel Day-Lewis's Oscar-winning performance as the older Christy.

From 1993 to 1995, he studied drama at Trinity College, Dublin, but continued to make films such as the acclaimed *The Young Poisoner's Handbook* (1995). This last, a British-French-German coproduction, suggested a willingness to work in European cinema: He has subsequently made films in Turkey, Italy, and France. By contrast, his appearances in Hollywood productions have been few and far between: He played King Louis in the 1993 version of the *The Three Musketeers* and appeared in *Chocolat* (2000), but the majority of his other screen appearances have been in Irish or British productions. These include a winning turn as the older brother in *The Boy from Mercury* and, in a definitively adult role, as Stephen Dedalus in *Bloom*.

O'DEA, JIMMY (1899–1965). Before taking up a performance career, O'Dea studied to become an optician. His long association with stage and film is best remembered for the creation of the renowned character Biddy Mulligan, "the Pride of the Coombe," and his numerous one-person shows and storytelling on **Radio Telefís Éireann (RTÉ)**. He had roles in films including **John Ford**'s *The Rising of the Moon* and *Darby O'Gill and the Little People*.

O'DONNELL, DAMIEN (1967–). His childhood heroes were Buster Keaton, Charlie Chaplin, and Harold Lloyd, and it is little wonder that O'Donnell remains an unpretentious director who produces gentle comedies. His first forays into film were with the award-winning short *Thirty Five a Side* (1995) and the setting up of a production company, Clingfilm, with other film school graduates, most notably **John Moore**—who went on to make *Behind Enemy Lines* (2000). O'Donnell directed *East Is East* (1999) in Great Britain, which became the most popular cross-over success in Asia and helped develop his reputation. Incidentally, there is some debate within Irish national film culture about the legitimacy of working abroad, and such success demonstrates that filmmakers do not have to be insiders to appreciate and capture the comic aspects of cultural diversity. More recently, back in Ireland, O'Donnell directed *Inside I'm Dancing* (aka *Rory O'Shea Was Here*), which has been a minor success, following in the path of *My Left Foot*, with its focus on a character's disability. O'Donnell's range and adaptability are beginning to flower as he stretches his creative abilities.

O'DONOGHUE, JOHN (1956–). O'Donoghue succeeded Sile de Valera as the minister with responsibility for film policy in June 2002. Born and raised in Caherciveen, County Kerry, O'Donoghue was a solicitor by trade and was elected TD (Irish MP) for the Fianna Fáil Party in 1987 (and at each subsequent election). In 1997 O'Donoghue was appointed minister for justice, having campaigned on a hard-line "zero tolerance" policy in that year's election. He remained at that department until 2002 when, in a move widely regarded as a demotion in the cabinet, he was appointed to Arts, Sport and Tourism, a new department that took on elements of the previous Departments of Arts and Culture and of Tourism.

O'Donoghue's bullish public persona prior to this appointment made him a surprising choice to many. Few commentators would have ascribed to him the sympathetic and sensitive qualities generally regarded as sine qua non for such a position. Despite this, he is generally regarded as having been a quite effective defender of state support for the film industry during a period when there was substantial pressure from the Department of Finance to withdraw all film support. In autumn 2002 an independent estimates review committee, brought in to advise then minister for finance Charles McCreevy on the budget for the next year, recommended the abolition of the **Irish Film Board**. It is apparent that O'Donoghue intervened to ensure that the board was retained, and he was able to make an announcement to that effect in December 2002. Similarly when

McCreevy then announced his intention to end the **Section 481** tax incentive at the end of 2003, O'Donoghue employed **PriceWaterhouseCoopers** to write a report recommending the retention of the incentive (as subsequently occurred).

Since then, despite his varied portfolio, O'Donoghue has continued to play a key role in the industry. In 2005 in particular, when production levels fell to their lowest in five years, he intervened to augment the level of funding available to the Film Board, and in summer 2005 he announced the appointment of a Los Angeles–based screen commissioner to promote Ireland as a filmmaking location.

O'HARA, MAUREEN (1920–). She remains the best-known face of Irish film, solely from her feisty starring role as Mary Kate Danaher in the seminal *The Quiet Man* (1952). Her career commenced after she did a screen test for Charles Laughton in London. Legend has it that while the test was very poor, he became hypnotized by her eyes, which had a powerful quality, and she was signed up on a seven-year contract. Her first major film was in Alfred Hitchcock's *Jamaica Inn* (1939), and she also starred alongside Laughton in *The Hunchback of Notre Dame* (1939). Other major films include *Dance Girl Dance* (1940), *How Green Was My Valley* (1941), *This Land Is Mine* (1943), *Buffalo Bill* (1944), *Rio Grande* (1950), *The Rare Breed* (1965), and more recently *Only the Lonely* (1991). She remains one of the most beloved of Hollywood's golden age icons for all the classic films she has appeared in. Recently she wrote an autobiography, *'Tis Herself: A Memoir*.

O'HERLIHY, DAN (1919–2005). He studied architecture at the National University of Ireland and worked as a theater set designer before turning to acting with the Abbey Players and Radio Éireann—the forerunner of RTÉ. His first film role was in Carol Reed's 1947 classic *Odd Man Out*. Later moving to America, he joined Orson Welles's Mercury Theater and was cast as McDuff in his 1948 film version of *Macbeth*. Other notable film roles included those in *Imitation of Life* (1958) and *McArthur* (1977) before he came home to act in **John Huston**'s adaptation of **James Joyce**'s classic story "**The Dead**" (1987). In all he starred in over 60 cinema and television films and was nominated for an Oscar in 1955 for his intense portrayal of the title role in *The Adventures of Robinson Crusoe*, directed by the great Spanish director Luis Buñuel.

O'LEARY, LIAM (1910–1992). Liam O'Leary was arguably the single most active and influential figure in the establishment of a film culture in Ireland. Over the course of his life he was an author, an actor, a filmmaker, the cofounder of the **Irish Film Society**, and—in his later years—he almost single-handedly gathered and preserved the nucleus of what would become the National Film Archive.

Born in Youghal, his formative cinema experiences were in Wexford, where his family moved when he was a child and where he became an avid cinema goer. While studying at UCD, he expanded his interests to include theater, and in 1934 he cofounded the Dublin Little Theatre Guild. While still a student he partook in an extraordinary protest at the screening of *Irish Eyes Are Smiling* in the Savoy Cinema in Dublin. The protestors (who included **Cyril Cusack** and later president of Ireland Cearbhall O'Dalaigh) demanded the removal of the film, which, they argued, represented the Irish as stupid and backward. In O'Leary's account (L. O'Leary, 1945) the cinema manager then called for the aid of armed detectives before agreeing to discuss the film with protestors. The protestors achieved their end, however, and the film was removed.

He was formally employed as a civil servant, but his interest in and commitment to film were evident in his extracurricular activities, which included working as film critic for *Ireland Today* and cofounding the Irish Film Society in 1936. After a decade in the civil service, he was seconded to the **Abbey Theatre** as a producer, but left to freelance in radio and journalism and as an occasional actor for director Brendan Stafford. He played a priest in the latter's *Men against the Sun* and a gangster in *Stranger at My Door*.

This period also saw the publication of O'Leary's *Invitation to the Film*, the first book written on Irish cinema. Published in 1945, the book argued passionately for the establishment of an indigenous industry, pointing to the need for a well-equipped national studio (thus coinciding with **Sean Lemass**'s contemporaneous ambitions) and a native newsreel service. Contending that film had a unique role to play in "national renaissance," he argued that "not to use it would be almost an acknowledgement of terrible failure" (L. O'Leary, 1945).

In that same book he argued that "cinema must be used to open the eyes as well as the hearts of our people." That philosophy clearly informed his own work in the 1940s when he became a director of short films in his own right. The most notable of these was his production of *Our Country,* commissioned by Sean MacBride as part of Clann na Poblachta's 1948 election campaign. The eight-minute film dwelled on national poverty, unemployment, and emigration and implicitly cited the incumbent Fianna Fáil administration as the cause of these ills. Certainly Fianna Fáil regarded the 100-print release of the film as a factor in their loss of the election.

Sean MacBride became minister for external (foreign) affairs in the government that followed the election, and he appointed O'Leary to sit on the newly established **Cultural Relations Committee**, which immediately began to commission a series of films on Ireland. O'Leary and Brendan Stafford collaborated on *Portrait of Dublin,* the third of these. However, by the time the film was completed in 1952, Fianna Fáil had returned to power, and *Portrait of Dublin* was effectively suppressed.

Effectively deprived of the only realistic means of making a film in Ireland, O'Leary moved to London in 1953, where he was appointed acquisitions officer of the British National Film Archive. This indirectly benefited Irish cinema culture, since O'Leary negotiated an arrangement with the British Archive that allowed him to use their facilities to preserve any historic Irish films. In consequence several crucial productions from the **Kalem Company** and **Film Company of Ireland** were held for a period by the British National Film Archive.

O'Leary returned to Dublin in the 1960s, finding employment with **Radio Telifís Éireann** as a film viewer, a job he held until his retirement in 1986. However, it was his leisure activities during this period that had a much more lasting impact. In 1976 he organized an elaborate exhibition on the history of film in Ireland at the invitation of the Dublin Arts Festival. He also researched and wrote a major biography of the Dublin-born silent era director **Rex Ingram**, which was published in 1980. Most importantly he continued collecting a vast range of rare and valuable material relating to Irish cinema, which he stored in his Dublin flat until 1986 when the National Library gave him an office and a room for his archive.

Fittingly, his efforts led him to become the subject of a documentary celebrating his life and times, **Donald Taylor Black**'s *At the Cinema Palace—Liam O'Leary*. Further tacit acknowledgment of his key place in Irish cinema history came when—only months before passing away—he was invited to preside over the opening ceremony of the **Irish Film Centre** in 1992. This was especially apt given that the center was home to the then **Irish Film Institute**'s archive.

O'LEARY, RONAN. The most notable thing about Ronan O'Leary's career is perhaps not so much the quality of the films he has made but the fact that he has made them at all. Between 1987 and 1992, widely acknowledged as the most barren period for Irish production in three decades, O'Leary managed the not inconsiderable feat of completing four drama productions: *Riders to the Sea*, *Fragments of Isabella*, *Diary of a Madman*, and *Hello Stranger*. Ironically, however, since 1993, the period during which the Irish production sector took off, his output has dwindled to virtually nothing: just one feature (*Driftwood*). However, viewed in its totality, his work arguably lends itself more to an auteurist analysis than that of many Irish directors, with his films invariably set in a single location (in part for budget reasons) and, as a result, characterized by an occasionally overwhelming sense of claustrophobia.

Ronan O'Leary began his career as a drama producer-director for the Public Broadcasting Service (PBS) in Los Angeles in 1983, making a number of drama-documentaries and some profiles on filmmakers like Oliver Stone and David Puttnam. His "Irish" debut with an adaptation of J. M. Synge's play *Riders to the Sea* in 1987 was heavily criticized at home, but its small budget meant that even the modest TV and video sales it achieved in the United States were enough to allow O'Leary to move to his next production, *Fragments of Isabella*, in 1989. Both this and his third film in 1990 (a film version of Gogol's *Diary of a Madman*) received more positive reviews, which focused mainly on the manner in which O'Leary had managed to transcend the limitations imposed by what were obviously low budgets.

His fourth film—*Hello Stranger*—was nominated for four awards at the 1993 Monte Carlo Television Festival. After *Hello Stranger*, O'Leary took on screen-writing duties, working with Michael

Lindsay-Hogg and Chet Raymo to adapt the latter's novel *The Dork of Cork* into the screenplay for **Frankie Starlight**. However, when **Mary Breen Farrelly Productions** (MBF) set up shop in **Ardmore Studios** in 1992, O'Leary became a part of that operation, working as an editor on *The Sheltering Desert* (1992), a film that the company picked up and completed when the original production company—Kusier Films—went bust.

It was thus with MBF Productions that O'Leary made *Driftwood* (1997). Although he was operating with his largest budget to date, the resulting film was poorly received internationally, and virtually all reviews cited Rob Reiner's *Misery* as an obvious—and superior—influence.

His work since 1997 has been much more sporadic; most recently he directed a documentary—*Hold the Passion*—in 2003. It is worth noting that over the course of his films O'Leary has managed to assemble quite remarkable casts and crews. He has worked with four Oscar winners—actress Geraldine Page, cinematographers Walter Lassally and Billy Williams, and set designer **Josie MacAvin** (who worked on three of his films). Similarly, James Spader, who appeared in *Driftwood*, had previously won a Best Actor award at the Cannes Film Festival for *Sex, Lies and Videotape* (1989). If nothing else this demonstrates a remarkable capacity to sell his projects, one perhaps not entirely reflected in the finished products.

Ó'RIADA, SEÁN (1931–1971). Widely regarded as the most significant Irish composer of the 20th century, Ó Riada first came to wide public attention through his score for the **Gael Linn** film *Mise Éire*. Born in Cork, Ó Riada grew up and was schooled in Limerick before going to University College Cork to study arts. He graduated with first class honors in music in 1952 and in 1953 was appointed assistant director of music at Radio Éireann (later to become RTÉ). Although he enjoyed aspects of the job—namely, concert arranging and the occasional opportunity to have his own music recorded—he was less interested in the administrative side and in 1955 resigned his post. This led Ó Riada to approach the recently formed **Gael Linn** for work, initially writing a few articles on music for *Comhar*, the organization's magazine. In 1959, he visited the Kerry Gaeltacht on the Dingle Peninsula and for the first time experienced what he termed

An Saol Gaelach (literally "The Irish Life"). On his return to Dublin he encouraged Gael Linn to record two of the singers he had encountered in Kerry, and subsequently when the organization decided to make its first long-playing record of Irish music, Ó Riada was invited to produce it.

When Gael Linn turned its focus to the production of a major Irish film based on archival material (***Mise Éire***), the organization naturally turned to Ó Riada to compose the music for it. The film's director **George Morrison** agreed, despite his misgivings about Ó Riada's youth. The resulting score remains a high point in the history of not merely 20th-century Irish film music composition but arguably of all Irish music. The score drew heavily on arrangements of traditional Irish songs but arranged them in the kind of lush romantic style that characterized mainstream European composition. At a stroke, then, Ó Riada conjured up an Irish classical tradition informed by a nationalist vision. He also, it is worth stressing, created a fantastically emotive score—the "Roisín Dubh" sequence, where the music swells to a crescendo as independence is achieved, is as stirring as any moment in film music history.

Ó Riada continued to work with Gael Linn on *Saoirse?*, the 1961 sequel to *Mise Éire*, and on **Louis Marcus**'s 1966 film (also for Gael Linn) *An Tine Bheo*. He was also commissioned to score the **Four Provinces** production of *Playboy of the Western World* (1962), **John Ford**'s thinly disguised Sean O'Casey biopic *Young Cassidy* (1965), which permitted Ó Riada a brief sojourn in Hollywood, and *Kennedy's Ireland*, a documentary made in the wake of President John F. Kennedy's 1963 visit to Ireland.

He went on to work with the **Abbey Theatre** through the 1960s and made a major contribution to the revival of Irish traditional music through the establishment of the Ceoltóirí Cualann musical group; a recording of their performance at the Gaiety Theatre in the late 1960s became the best-selling Gael Linn record *Ó Riada sa Gaiety* [*Ó Riada in the Gaiety*].

Less well known is the fact that Ó Riada set up his own production company—Draíon Films—in the mid-1960s to make short films for some of the **Radio Telefís Éireann (RTÉ)** television shows with which he was involved. He had planned to make an Irish-themed feature-length film for the American market but was forced to abandon the scheme when he realized that color television had become the norm in the United States: His own equipment was exclusively for black-and-white production.

Sadly Ó Riada's life and work were cut short in his 40th year. Decades of drinking had contributed to cirrhosis of the liver, and in 1971 he was admitted to a Cork hospital, and from there he went to King's College Hospital in London, where he died after a series of heart attacks.

O'SHEA, MILO (1926–). O'Shea has become a successful character actor and is quite recognizable with his big bushy eyebrows, resonating voice, and impish smile. He married an Irish actress, Kitty Sullivan, and both have taken out American citizenship and reside in the United States. Irish films he has had important roles in include *Ulysses* and *The Playboys*. He has also had numerous roles in international films as diverse as *Barbarella* (1967) and *Purple Rose of Cairo* (1985).

O'SULLIVAN, MAUREEN (1911–1998). She was born in Boyle, County Roscommon, and attended a convent school in Dublin before attending the famous high-class finishing school in Roehampton in England, where the actress Vivien Leigh was one of her classmates. After a successful screen test, she got a role in *Song o' My Heart*, which also starred the Irish tenor Count John McCormack. After completing this film in America, she went on to appear in six more movies and in 1932 signed with Metro Goldwin Mayer (MGM) studios. She later appeared as Jane Parker in *Tarzan the Ape Man* opposite Johnny Weissmuller and in five sequels. Her marriage to John Farrow produced seven children, one of whom—Mia—became a movie star in her own right. She also starred with William Powell and Myrna Loy in *The Thin Man* (1934), *Anna Karenina* (1935), and *Pride and Prejudice* (1940). Later, when her daughter Mia became involved with Woody Allen, she had a cameo role in some of his films.

O'SULLIVAN, MORGAN. *See* WORLD 2000 ENTERTAINMENT.

O'SULLIVAN, THADDEUS (1948–). Born in Dublin, O'Sullivan first came to public attention as a cinematographer. His earliest work, however, was as director on a number of semiexperimental shorts, including *A Pint of Plain* (1975), which deals with the often-displaced Irish in London, and *On a Paving Stone Mounted* (1978), which also explores the results of **emigration.** Throughout the 1980s, however, he worked in Ireland and the United Kingdom on a combination of features and large-scale television series. On the features in particular he worked with just about every significant Irish director making films that decade: He shot **Joe Comerford**'s *Travellers*, Bob Quinn's TV series *Atlantean*, **Cathal Black**'s *Pigs*, and **Pat Murphy**'s *Anne Devlin*.

His work was singled out for its composition and color and for the manner in which the characters in the films he shot seemed trapped within landscapes both rural and urban. He brought this approach to his first "straight" narrative, *The Woman Who Married Clark Gable* (1985)—an adaptation of a Sean O'Faolain short story—in which **Brenda Fricker** played a character seeking to escape the straitjacket of 1950s Ireland through immersion in Hollywood romances.

Later he returned to making features with *December Bride* (1990), which is a beautiful evocation of a historical rural Irish Protestant community. The film explores sexual politics between a Catholic woman and two Presbyterian brothers (**Donal McCann** and **Ciarán Hinds**). The look of the film, and its careful placement of the leading characters in a timeless landscape, lent the film a European art-house appearance, reminiscent of the languid work of Theo Angelopolous, and secured it a substantial audience and critical acclaim.

He followed *December Bride* with a number of well-received dramas for British television, including *In the Border Country* (1991), set in Northern Ireland, territory to which he would return for his second feature, *Nothing Personal* (1995). Also set in Northern Ireland during a short-lived truce in the war between republican and loyalist paramilitaries in the 1970s, it was unusual in that it focused on the loyalist side. The film suggests that violence was tolerated within an embattled community controlled by paramilitary godfathers and filled with crime, unemployment, and political powerlessness. The film's more brash style (at least when compared with *December Bride*'s), invoking gangster movie tropes and using a 1970s pop soundtrack, led to an offer to direct the Robert de Niro–produced *Witness to the Mob* series in the United States.

When O'Sullivan returned to working in Ireland, he remained focused on gangsters, this time with the overly Hollywood-influenced *Ordinary Decent Criminal* (2000), which starred Kevin Spacey and Linda Fiorentino. Like **John Boorman**'s *The General*, the film was based on the life of real-life gangster Martin Cahill. Unlike Boorman's film, which won an award at the 1998 Cannes Film Festival, *Ordinary Decent Criminal* was universally panned, and in an interview, O'Sullivan, though stressing that he enjoyed making the film, tacitly conceded that it was somewhat underwritten ("Thaddeus O'Sullivan Interview," 2000).

His next film as director, *The Heart of Me* (2002), a British picture following the adulterous three-way relationship between a husband, wife, and her sister in 1930s middle-class England, reprised the central theme of *December Bride* and received much better reviews. Of late O'Sullivan's work has been somewhat erratic with numerous projects falling through. He spent a long time, for example, trying to bring John Banville's novel *The Book of Evidence* to the screen. More recently he was contracted to direct the second series of the **Radio Telefís Éireann (RTÉ)** television gangster thriller *Proof* in 2005.

O'TOOLE, PETER (1932–). He received a scholarship to the Royal Academy of Dramatic Arts in London from 1952 to 1954, where he learned his craft. Afterward he performed in many plays in Brighton and London, including classics like *Waiting for Godot* and *Look Back in Anger*. In 1962 he was catapulted to international stardom when David Lean cast him as the male lead in *Lawrence of Arabia*. He married Sian Philips in 1959; the marriage produced two daughters and a son and lasted till 1979, after which he married model Karen Brown (Summerville); that marriage lasted from 1982 to 1988. He received an honorary Academy Award in 2003 for a long career in films, which included *Goodbye Mr. Chips* (1968), *My Favourite Year* (1982), **Neil Jordan**'s comic Irish fairy tale *High Spirits* (1988), *The Last Emperor* (1987), and *Troy* (2004), among many more. On being notified by the Academy that he was to be a recipient of an Honorary Oscar at the 75th annual awards, he initially appeared to reject the offer but graciously accepted the accolade in the end.

***ODD MAN OUT* (1947).** This film noir classic is part of a trilogy from the British director Carol Reed that deals with various forms of fatalism, including later adaptations from stories by Graham Greene, *Fallen Idol* (1948) and the better-known *The Third Man* (1949). *Odd Man Out* explores the character of Johnny (James Mason), a disaffected leader of the "Organisation"—an old Irish Republican Army (IRA) unit—who emerges from prison full of doubts about the continued use of violence to further republicanism. Still loyal to his ideals, however, and unwilling or unable to accept the pleadings of his girlfriend, Kathleen (Kathleen Sullivan), he goes ahead with one last robbery to replenish resources for the movement. Inevitably things go awry: A man is killed, and Johnny is seriously injured while attempting to steal a textile mill payroll in Belfast.

Johnny finds himself wandering the mean streets of Belfast, which are filmed using expressive low-key, chiaroscuro lighting that effectively captures the postwar blitzed-out buildings in the docks area of the city. Most people ignore the wounded man as he tries to find his destiny, but Kathleen, following her heart, in spite of all entreaties not to do so, hatches an escape plan for them both. Trying to capture the escaped convict in this divided city is the Royal Ulster Constabulary inspector (Denis O'Dea), who embodies the forces of reasoned law and order, as he seeks to discover where Johnny is hiding. At one stage, in a scene reminiscent of the famous child and ball sequence in Fritz Lang's *M* (1931), the children playing in the street notice the outlaw, which ensures that he will be discovered. Kathleen unwittingly leads the police to her beloved, accompanied by her priest, Father Tom, who wants to save his immortal soul. Following some engaging meanders into public houses and scenes of artists trying to capture the soul of such a terrorist, the spiral of the story eventually moves to its inevitable fatalistic conclusion.

As snow begins to fall—reminiscent of the ending of *The Dead*—Kathleen eventually locates Johnny. While ostensibly trying to escape on an emigrant ship at the docks, their fate together is sealed as the police surround them and Kathleen decides to draw their fire. After both are shot dead in a hail of bullets, the camera majestically swoops around their bodies in the snow as the priest blesses them and the camera tilts to a close-up of a (Big Ben) clock—time has finally run out for them—and the sound of the horn of the ship that could have taken them away is heard on the soundtrack. The critic John Hill speaks of the fatalistic evocation of atavistic violence in such narratives that corresponds to an attitude toward the political problems in the North. Generic or stylistic conventions implicit in film noir can also promote a attitude and approach toward ethical questions about human agency that are universal, beyond local or political explications. Either way *Odd Man Out* has remained a canonical text for Irish studies.

OLCOTT, SIDNEY (1873–1949). Born in Canada to parents who had emigrated there from Cork, Olcott became a child actor before moving to New York as a young man. In 1904, he became a film actor with Biograph Studios before graduating to direct films for and ultimately manage the company. He began to work with the **Kalem** (Film) **Company**, established in 1907 by Frank Marion, Samuel Long, and George Klein, which went on to become one of the largest U.S. producers of the 1910s. Olcott became a director noted for his careful preparation and a—more than unusual—tendency to write his scripts in advance of shooting. Cinema legend has it that as a reward for the success of his films—especially a version of *Ben Hur* (1907) —in the U.S. market, the Kalem Company offered him the chance to do a location shoot anywhere in the world.

His ancestry inevitably dictated that he would choose Ireland, to which he returned every summer from 1910 to 1914, shooting at **Beaufort** near Killarney. The location determined the themes of the 29 films shot by Olcott in Ireland, from the first, *The Lad from Old Ireland* (1910) to *Bold Emmet, Ireland's Martyr* (1915). Not all of these were shot for Kalem, however. In 1912, Olcott took the company to Palestine to film *From the Manger to the Cross*. Budgeted at $35,000, the film took in an incredible $1 million in U.S. theaters. However, despite being president of the company, Olcott's share in the earnings amounted to no more than $350. By now feted as America's greatest director, he no longer felt he needed the support of Kalem and, in 1912, Olcott and Gene Gautier, his leading lady at Kalem, left the company to form Gene Gautier Feature Players. It was this company that returned to Beaufort in 1913 and was followed in 1914 by Olcott's own Sid Films.

The outbreak of World War I brought his Irish sojourns to a conclusion and put paid to his stated plans to build a permanent studio in

Ireland. The body of work left behind, however, ranged from romantic melodrama such as his adaptation of Dion Boucicault's *The Colleen Bawn* (1911) to more overtly politicized material such as *Rory O'More* (1911), which drew the ire of the British authorities in Ireland when it was asserted that the film's popularity in Ireland was undermining the British Army's recruiting drive there. The films were made largely for the diasporic audience in America—several of the films identified America as a potential haven for those forced by economic or political circumstances to flee Ireland—thus the eponymous hero of *Rory O'More*, having escaped execution by the British at the scaffold, escapes to America, and the end titles of *For Ireland's Sake* posit the West (in this case, America), as "the land of the free."

However, it was not merely the themes of these films that drew U.S. audiences in droves to watch them. Olcott's use of authentic locations and landscapes particularly appealed to Irish exiles in the United States and ensured the success of his films there. Olcott retired from filmmaking in 1927, although he continued to return to Ireland for holidays until his death in 1949.

OMAGH **(2004).** Directed by Pete Travis, *Omagh* re-creates a recent horrific chapter in the **"troubles"** when a bomb killed 29 people in the small northern town of Omagh on 15 August 1998. Based on a screenplay by Paul Greengrass, who also directed *Bloody Sunday*, the film stars **Gerard McSorley** as Michael Gallagher, whose 21-year-old son died in the blast. Gallagher becomes a spokesman for the victims' families and thus the focal point for the narrative. The semi-documentary style of the film has become a very common format for addressing such traumatic events of late. The film is an earnest endeavor to capture the authenticity of events from the terrible bomb scene (as shot in Navan, County Meath) to the families' immediate reactions, and later their coming to terms with the grief following their—still unresolved—pursuit of justice.

ON THE EDGE **(2000).** Directed by John Carney, this very sensitive and rare drama on teenage suicide—which has become a major social issue in Ireland—is made most effective by outstanding performances from **Cillian Murphy** and Tricia Vessy, with excellent support from a number of other young actors. Jonathan Breech (Murphy) is unable to accept life and, sparked by the death of his father, drives a stolen car over a cliff. But he survives and ends up in a mental hospital alongside other damaged young people, who also cannot accept themselves for what they are. The psychiatric environment is controlled by the undemonstrative **Stephen Rea**, who tries to get his patients to understand their problems. However, Jonathan and a few others, in a manner somewhat reminiscent of the characters in the classic *One Flew Over the Cuckoo's Nest* (1975), try to subvert this form of behavior analysis and rebel in various ways, while having to wear their pajamas at all times. A process of bonding between the inmates eventually helps the main protagonists to discover and face up to themselves. While at times the narrative is somewhat clunky and uneven, the drama remains very powerful.

ON THE NOSE **(2000).** This comedy, produced by **Subotica** for Sky Pictures and directed by David Caffrey, appeared to have made more with a television than a cinema audience in mind. *On the Nose* stars Robbie Coltrane as Brendan, a university janitor with a betting addiction. Having gambled away his daughter's college fund, he is forced to earn it back when she accepts a university place in Trinity College. Happily, at work Brendan discovers the preserved head of an aboriginal tribesman, which has the power to pick racehorse winners. The lead cast also includes Dan Ackroyd and Brenda Blethyn.

ORDINARY DECENT CRIMINAL **(2000).** Following a spate of gangster movies based on the notorious Dublin gangster "The General," this all-star cast, directed by **Thaddeus O'Sullivan**, milks the story for generic laughs. Kevin Spacey plays a loveable rogue who dreams up robberies with panache that rarely fail to endear him to the public. The last is a prestigious art-gallery theft that dumbfounds the police, Interpol, and the rest of the criminal fraternity generally. As the blurb for this underdeveloped narrative asserts, the main character is driven by two fundamental beliefs—loyalty to his own and to hell with everyone else.

OSCARS. *See* ACADEMY AWARDS.

OURSELVES ALONE **(1936).** The film recounts how, during the War of Independence in the 1920s, a Royal Irish Constabulary (RIC) inspector takes responsibility for the killing of a republican leader to allow the real killer—an English officer—to develop a relationship with the victim's sister. The cast of the **Brian Desmond Hurst** film includes Maire O'Neill (Nanny), Clifford Evans (Commandant Connolly), Antoinette Cellier (Maureen Elliott), and Paul Farrel (Hogan). At times the film strives too hard to set a tone of balance while appearing to legitimate both sides in the conflict.

THE OUTCASTS **(1982).** This difficult to categorize film was directed by Robert Wynne-Simmons and was financed by a combination of the **Arts Council** Film Script Award for 1981 and funding received from **Channel 4**. Set in mid-19th-century Ireland, the film follows Maura's (Mary Ryan) relationship with Scarf Michael (**Mick Lally**), a man cast out from the local community because of his dealings with the world of the supernatural. Maura seeks to leave the community to be with Michael, but he refuses her company, and a series of catastrophes subsequently befalls the locality. Believing this to be Maura's fault, the locals move to drown her, but Michael intercedes and takes her away. The film is uneven in tone and direction but fascinating nonetheless. Its originality lies in the straightforward manner in which it fuses the natural and the supernatural, constructing a quasi-pagan Ireland that draws little distinction between religion and superstition.

– P –

PARALLEL FILM PRODUCTIONS LTD. Set up in 1993 by Tim Palmer and Alan Moloney, Parallel is unusual among larger-scale indigenous production companies in that it has focused almost exclusively on indigenous narratives. The company debuted with *Into the West*, which they coproduced with **Little Bird**. This was followed by *The Last of the High Kings* and *A Love Divided*, the latter produced with financial support from **RTÉ**, BBC Scotland, the **Irish Film Board**, and the Arts Council of Northern Ireland.

The company also specializes in large-budget, high-quality drama series. In 1998 it produced for the BBC and RTÉ two television miniseries, *Amongst Women* and *Falling for a Dancer*, based on books by John McGahern and Deirdre Purcell, respectively. These were followed in 1999 by *DDU* (District Detective Unit) for RTÉ; starring **Sean McGinley**, the series arguably constituted the first — and to date only — Irish TV "cop show."

In 2000, Alan Moloney, in partnership with Michael Colgan of the Gate Theatre, established the Blue Angels production company to undertake the ambitious Beckett on Film project, the filming of **Samuel Beckett**'s 19 theater works. The project attracted an extraordinary group of international behind- and in-front-of-camera talent including Anthony Minghella, David Mamet, Atom Egoyan, Julianne Moore, Kristen Scott Thomas, and Jeremy Irons.

Since then Parallel has continued to produce for television and feature release. Since 2002, they have produced four seasons of *The Clinic*, RTÉ's flagship drama series, and two seasons of *Showbands*, a drama set in 1960s Ireland. They have also developed a working relationship with **Neil Jordan**, coproducing *Intermission* with Jordan's Company of Wolves and producing his most recent film as a director, ***Breakfast on Pluto***.

***PARK* (1999).** A quasi-experimental and self-consciously small-scale film, directed by **John Carney** and **Tom Hall**, that opens with a woman seeking a psychiatrist's aid in interpreting a recurring dream in which she stabs a man in the street for no apparent reason. Later under hypnosis she eventually regresses back to when she was a teenager to reveal the truth. The re-creation of the park of her dreams is very rich and evocative. The film captures a sense of innocence and escape from the rigors of school as she walks around in her school uniform, only to be met by Adam, the park keeper. Eventually he entices her to have a meal with him after he teases her about whether she had a boyfriend. The borderline between friendly banter and seedy talk is very carefully maintained. Apparently she likes to lead him on and be nice to him, while he appears to look after her and pay her attention. The first part of her remembering process ends with her going through the black door of his hutch, and she seems to be heading toward a space where more traumatic memories are deeply buried.

Evidence of what eventually happened and its tragic consequences are withheld as the story moves forward to an old people's home, where the keeper is still enjoying the pleasures of female attention. This realization leaves a very bad taste for the audience when the full revelation of what happened is finally dramatized. Overall, in spite of some odd narrative lapses, the piece, with its art-house format, remains memorable.

PARKER, ALAN (1944–). Born in London and characterized by journalists as a working-class boy who made good, he began working in advertising. He claims to have made over 500 ads, which certainly gave him the confidence, like his contemporary Ridley Scott, to make effective Hollywood fiction films. His big break came with *Bugsy Malone* (1976), followed by *Midnight Express* (1978) and *Fame* (1980). The latter echoes the musical story of his Irish film *The Commitments* (1991), which had a very successful release and brought **Roddy Doyle**'s comic vernacular to a world audience.

Following numerous other Hollywood films, including his other foray into Irish culture—the historical re-creation of a poverty-ridden Limerick environment, *Angela's Ashes* (1999)—and after harshly criticizing the British Film Board for its lack of commercial realism, he took over as chairman of the newly formed Film Council and has been very active in film politics and production on both sides of the Atlantic.

PEACHES (2000). This Irish-produced film, directed by Nick Grosso, is set in London but was shot in Dublin. It follows student Frank (Matthew Rhys) as he prepares to leave college and face up to living in the real world, and in particular to dealing with real women rather than the fictional ones he has hitherto boasted of to his friends. Production Company Stone Ridge Entertainment, which made the film, is associated with **Ward Anderson**, a fact that helped ensure that the film received an unusually wide domestic release.

PEARSON, NOEL (1943–). Ferndale MD and producer Noel Pearson has asserted that the instinct for film production is not something one can learn by taking a course. Producers, he argues, are *made*. If so, Pearson the film producer was two decades in the making. Born in

1943, he initially considered the priesthood, but after graduating from a junior seminary he rejected the idea and went to work in the Dublin fruit markets. He began his entertainment career as manager of the Chessmen, a Dublin pop group, before taking on responsibility for the internationally renowned folk group The Dubliners. In 1972, while still their manager, he produced an adaptation of Brendan Behan's *Richard's Cork Leg* at the **Abbey Theatre** as part of that year's Dublin Theatre Festival production, which subsequently transferred to London's Royal Court. However, it was Pearson's subsequent success with lavish theatrical productions of *Joseph and the Amazing Technicolour Dreamcoat* and *Jesus Christ Superstar* that established him as Ireland's leading theatrical impresario.

From the late 1970s he began to bring stage productions to the United States, including a 1979 New York run for a ballet version of J. M. Synge's *Playboy of the Western World*. Arguably this orientation toward the U.S. market has been reflected in his later film work. His first direct contact with the world of film came in 1982 when, despite having never made a film, he was appointed to the **Irish Film Board**, a position he maintained until the board's activities were suspended in 1987. Ironically, the closure of the board meant Pearson was unable to secure state funding for what would become Ferndale's first film, **My Left Foot**. Pearson had nursed the idea of a film adaptation of Christy Brown's two-volume autobiography since the 1960s and had finally approached **Jim Sheridan** and Shane Connaughton to adapt it as a screenplay. As the project underwent development, Sheridan also emerged as the director.

Although the film was shot on a shoestring, Pearson's experience as a producer seems to have been very positive. Amazingly, he brought the UK £1.5 million project (which had been substantially funded by Granada Television) in on time and under budget. The phenomenal success of the film secured Pearson and Sheridan a first-look deal with Universal, under which they were due to produce at least two films over a three-year period. The first of these was another Ferndale production, an adaptation of John B. Keane's play *The Field*. However, this also proved to be the last (to date) Pearson-Sheridan collaboration. Later Sheridan established **Hell's Kitchen** with Arthur Lappin, and for a period Pearson focused on theatrical production again.

Pearson had in any case been chair of the Abbey since 1987 and was appointed artistic director of the Abbey, replacing Vincent Dowling, in 1989. He stepped down from the latter position in 1991 (to be replaced by Garry Hynes) but remained as chair until 1993. This led indirectly to his triumphant multi-award-winning Broadway production of Brian Friel's *Dancing at Lughnasa*, and he has subsequently brought two further Friel plays—*Wonderful Tennessee* and *Translations*—to Broadway. (Ferndale also made a documentary on Friel.)

Pearson returned to filmmaking in 1994 with **Frankie Starlight**, an adaptation of the Chet Raymo novel *The Dork of Cork*, but without the support of Universal, which—by Pearson's own account—had passed on every project he put their way after **The Field**. This was quickly followed by another novel adaptation, **Gold in the Streets**; indeed, to date Pearson has never produced a film from an original screenplay. In 1998, he returned to Friel, choosing **Pat O'Connor** to direct a screen adaptation of *Lughnasa*, with Meryl Streep as one of the leads. The lukewarm response to the film version, however, led to another screen production hiatus. It was 2005 before Pearson's next film, an adaptation of Maeve Binchy's *Tara Road*. Like *Lughnasa*, it was clearly designed for the export market, in particular the United States, where the source novel had sold five million copies.

Despite Pearson's on-off relationship with film, Ferndale Films remains a leading Irish production entity, not least because it regularly operates at medium (i.e., €10 million plus) budgets. It has also made the occasional documentary—one about the aforementioned Brian Friel, and another, *Luke*, about former Dubliners balladeer Luke Kelly.

PERRY, SIMON (1944–). The **Irish Film Board** appointed Perry as the new chief executive in November 2005, replacing **Mark Woods**, who resigned in April 2005 after just 18 months in the job. Perry was born in England and brings a broad range of experience to this very challenging post. Having produced two microbudget films in the mid-1970s, he worked for three years in the London bureau of the leading international entertainment industry paper, *Variety*. In the early 1980s he served for three years as the head of the British National Film Development Fund and set up his own production company, Umbrella Films, while producing and coproducing 10 feature films, including *1984* (1984) and *White Mischief* (1987). In 1992 he produced *The Playboys*, and for a nine-year period till 2000 he worked as chief executive of British Screen. Since 2000 he has been cofounder and president of Ateliers du Cinema Europeén, a Paris-based training initiative for European film producers, as well as a film financing consultant for the Swedish regional film center and a course supervisor and lecturer at the International Film School in Cologne.

***PHILADELPHIA, HERE I COME!* (1975).** Adapted by Brian Friel from his seminal play, and directed by John Quested, the film develops an authentic version of his story about a young man—Gar O'Donnell—who emigrates to America. The adaptation constructs an authentic—if now somewhat dated due to the Celtic Tiger economy—exploration of Irish-American relations, as his aunt comes home to snare her only nephew to bring him to Philadelphia. The play uses a very effective theatrical device of presenting "public" and "private" versions of the main protagonist to outline the surface and interior life of this troubled man. Gar must leave his taciturn father and cannot himself express any emotion, even with his few male friends, who lack the courage to escape their tedious rural backwater. **Donal McCann** delivers a strong performance in the title role as he apparently sniggers at the lack of sophistication of his American cousins, who revel in not having a past and in a culture that endorses material wealth. At the same time Gar celebrates a vibrant popular culture that enables him to find solace. Without such escape, one suspects, he would become like his drunken old teacher, who speaks of dreams of escape. But we know this will never happen as the teacher presents his former pupil with a self-published copy of his "cries from the heart" poetry. While there remains a strong critique of the crassness of Americana and the inevitable lure of the metropolis, there are echoes of **Jim Sheridan**'s much later assertions about the script of *In America* and the escape from Ireland and its "death culture."

The theatrical device of two actors playing the same role is less effective within the mimetically realist format of film. The extrovert alterego Gar (Des Cave), in a very loud red jumper, unseen by all but Gar, does not get across the complexity of the characterization but remains effective enough. Meanwhile, **Siobhan McKenna** is very convincing as the surrogate mother figure who helps out in the home and tries to bring father and son together, though it becomes clear this is an impossible task as this laconic yet very humorous story reaches its inevitable dénouement.

PIGS (1984). Directed by **Cathal Black**, *Pigs* is a pessimistic but also cautionary and social realist story of an underclass living in squats in Dublin—long before it became hip to represent a nihilistic drug culture in cult films like *Trainspotting* (1995). Jimmy (Jimmy Brennan, who also cowrote the script) takes up residence in a decrepit but once elegant building in the city and is soon joined by other squatters— George, an erstwhile businessman trying to retain some dignity, along with Tom and Ronny, a drug dealer. These are joined by Orwell, a Jamaican pimp, and his prostitute, Mary. All critics speak of the film's complex representation of various marginal groups, which was ahead of its time, and its evocative **Thaddeus O'Sullivan** cinematography, which captures this underclass with great skill and effect.

PILKINGTON, LORRAINE (1975–). Raised in the middle-class Dublin suburb of Malahide, Pilkington has maintained a consistent presence on the large screen. She made a striking debut as a spiky 16-year-old in **Neil Jordan**'s modestly budgeted but warmly received *The Miracle*. That role established a template for her early career:At 21 she was still playing a rebellious 17-year-old in *The Last of the High Kings*. After a series of undemanding roles in *Gold in the Streets*, *The Disappearance of Finbar*, *The Boxer*, and *The Nephew*, she left Dublin to live in the United Kingdom. Her role as the brash Irish clubber Lulu in the Welsh independent hit *Human Traffic* (1999) hardly depicted a person one would have found at home, although she arguably remained a grown-up version of Rose from *The Miracle*. However, as she reached her late 20s the good roles as the bad-girl were increasingly replaced by roles as more subdued characters. A turn in the BBC hit *Monarch of the Glen* (2000) and her role opposite Richard Harris in the *King Lear*–esque *My Kingdom* (2001) preceded a maternity-inspired hiatus, although she made a confident comeback in **Radio Telefís Éireann**'s (RTÉ) drama *The Clinic* (2003–). Onscreen she has yet to match the impact of her debut, but her stage work suggests that her most interesting film work may yet lie ahead.

THE PLAYBOY OF THE WESTERN WORLD (1962). Produced by Lord Killanin's **Four Provinces** company, the film of J. M. Synge's renowned comic play concerns Christy Mahon, who escapes from his family and finds shelter in another part of the rural West of Ireland, where he meets Pegeen Mike and recounts his story. **Siobhan McKenna** plays the daughter, who becomes romantically attracted by his gallant deeds but has to defend her growing love from the voracious Widow Quinn, who is also interested in this "violent" outsider. Of course all is not as it seems as Mahon's father, who was supposed to have been killed, comes back for his son, only to have the comedy of violence and the retelling of such deeds echo throughout the story. While remaining overly theatrical, the adaptation, directed by **Brian Desmond Hurst**, nonetheless captures the essence of this classic play for another medium.

THE PLAYBOYS (1992). Based on the writings of Shane Connaughton and filmed in County Cavan, like *The Run of the Country*, the film is directed by Gillies MacKinnon. Albert Finney plays a strong-willed local sergeant who has had trouble with alcoholism but is now trying to control his life and his excess. Unfortunately this does not last when his secret love Tara gives birth to their son. We find out later that she swore him to secrecy regarding their affair. But the truth burns inside him, as he dearly wants a family. His competitor for Tara is a local farmer (**Adrian Dunbar**), who, affected by incessant rain and his cows dying, along with rejection in a marriage proposal, soon commits suicide. This brings matters to a head, and the local priest calls on Tara from the pulpit to name the father, affirming how "one sinner can infect us all." The priest pleads with her to realize that "scandal is a contagion." But our (far too modern) Tara will not be forced to marry and is well able to withstand the bile of the community, affirming how "if everyone around here owned up to their sins—there would be a queue at confessionals a mile long!"

As in all classic Hollywood narrative structures, an outside force arrives in the shape of a traveling theater company ("playboys"), led by **Milo O'Shea** and including **Aidan Quinn**. The outsiders bring excitement but also raise doubts about the moral center of the enclosed community. At one stage the outsiders describe themselves as a "bunch of cut price Tinkers" (Travellers). Now faced with a much more potent competitor for Tara's favors in the form of the outsider playboy, the sergeant loses his grip on reality, leading finally (after some engaging theatrical spectacle) to a rather too neat narrative closure.

***THE PLOUGH AND THE STARS* (1936).** Scripted by Dudley Nichols from Sean O'Casey's nationalistic play, the film, directed by **John Ford**, stars Barbara Stanwick as Nora Clitheroe and Preston Foster as Jack alongside the commanding comic performance of **Barry Fitzgerald** as Fluther Good. Ford was strongly drawn to this play, which echoed his own nationalist republican sympathies. Focusing on the desire to fight for the struggle to make Ireland free and independent, Casey's masterpiece counterpoints the great poverty of the period and local Dublin characters (including Nora) who found it very difficult to accept their men going out to possibly die for a somewhat intangible cause. Ford's film version effectively fleshes out the theatrical classic and serves its polemical agenda.

***POITÍN* (1978).** In this film directed by **Bob Quinn,** Michil (**Cyril Cusack**) hands over his latest batch of illegally distilled poitín to his "agents," Labhcas (**Niall Toibin**) and Sleamhnan (**Donal McCann**), to sell on his behalf. Local guards confiscate the poitín, but the two agents retrieve most of the consignment after the guards are rendered unconscious by sampling the drink themselves. Labhcas decides to hide the retrieval of the poitín from Michil, however, and after selling the lot, he and Sleamhnan keep the money for themselves. Having squandered the proceeds on more drink, they return to Michil demanding more poitín. Michil proceeds to calmly extract a revenge for their betrayal.

Poitín, Bob Quinn's second long film after *Caoineadh Airt Uí Laoire*, was financed largely by the first **Arts Council** Script Award in 1977. Quinn, who at the time was based in Connemara in County Galway, had been approached by local writer Colm Bairéad with a story that reminded Quinn of Guy de Maupassant. Certainly the film's direction is informed by a Maupassantian simplicity and economy of expression. In an interview Quinn has spoken of his desire to portray something of the "terrible bleakness" of existence on the economically depressed western seaboard during the 1970s (Quinn,

2004), and the film certainly succeeds in that respect. The world of *Poitín* is one of casual cruelty where alcohol offers what is apparently the only escape—however brief—from the harshness of existence. It also makes compelling viewing, despite the fact that it was shot in a language—Irish—of which most natives have a poor working understanding. That much of narrative requires no understanding of any spoken language is a tribute to Quinn's quiet mastery of visual grammar. In this respect he was clearly aided by the work of a crew that reads like a who's who of Irish cinema: **Cathal Black, Joe Comerford**, and **Seamus Deasy**, among others, were all involved in the production of the film.

PRICEWATERHOUSECOOPERS REPORT. In the wake of the *Kilkenny Report*, minister for finance Charlie McCreevy had extended the operation of **Section 481** until the end of 2004. In December 2002, however, he indicated that it was not his intention to renew the tax incentive after the December 2003 budget. This prompted a major campaign on the part of the film industry, spearheaded by **Film Makers Ireland**, to convince him to change his mind. The minister for arts, culture and the Gaeltacht **John O'Donoghue** also commissioned the international accountancy firm PricewaterhouseCoopers (which in a previous incarnation had produced the *Coopers and Lybrand Report*) to address the question of whether there was an economic or competitive justification for maintaining fiscal support for the Irish film industry after 2004. Less overtly, the report was also intended to address the sotto voce assertion that unscrupulous producers had been abusing the Section 481 mechanism.

The report's conclusions were interesting in that they clearly identified the key role played by overseas productions in the post-1993 boom, the importance of Section 481 in attracting those productions, and the extent to which Ireland now faced international competition for such productions.

The report noted that hitherto, large-scale offshore productions had been attracted by a combination of Section 481, production infrastructures, and personnel. Reflecting their larger scale, the report concluded that such offshore productions were more likely to result in a net gain to the exchequer than indigenous productions with budgets of less than €5 million. However, many of the overseas productions were "location neutral," that is, they could be shot in any number of countries, and the filmmakers would tend to choose the location that offered the most attractive financial incentives. In this respect Section 481 was key: The report therefore concluded that had Section 481 not been in place between 1999 and 2001, something in the region of €150 million in offshore funds would have been lost to the Irish economy.

However, the report also noted that while Section 481 had constituted a major advantage in attracting offshore productions in 1993, the introduction by other countries of competing incentives in the interim had eroded Ireland's competitiveness. In particular, the report concluded that limiting to €10.48 million the amount in Section 481 funds that could be raised for any single picture did not facilitate its use by large-scale offshore productions.

Given this, the report considered other production incentive models such as tax credits and direct subsidy but concluded that for ease and cost of administration, Section 481 was superior to the alternatives. Thus it recommended not only retaining the tax incentive but also substantially increasing the amount that could be raised for any individual film to €50 million. Because of a perception that Section 481 was subject to occasional abuse, the report recommended that the Department of Arts employ budget experts to review budgets before allowing a producer to raise Section 481 funds and that the commissioners be allowed to audit the level of Section 481 spent on randomly selected productions after they were complete.

The report was delivered to Minister O'Donoghue in September 2003 and clearly formed a key element in his submission to the minister for finance on the future of Section 481. It had the desired impact: In December 2003, McCreevy announced that rather than prematurely winding up Section 481, he would instead extend it until 2008. Furthermore, he announced an increase in the sum of money that could be raised per picture via Section 481. However, rather than the €50 million figure suggested by the report, he limited the increase to €15 million. The other recommendations were also largely implemented: As of 2004, primary responsibility for overseeing the operation of Section 481 shifted from the Department of Arts, Sports and Tourism to the revenue commissioners.

PROJECT CINEMA CLUB. Driven by a **Kevin Rockett** policy document (Rockett also programmed the cinema) stressing the need to look at cinema in a wider critical context, the Project Cinema Club operated from 1976 to 1980 in a 70-seat theater within the Project Arts Centre in Dublin's Temple Bar. The Arts Centre emerged from a three-week festival at the Gate Theatre in November 1966, which included avant-garde theater, experimental music, and visual arts. The success of the festival led to the establishment of the Project Gallery on Lower Abbey Street as a permanent venue for alternative takes on performing and visual arts. In 1969 the gallery became the Project Arts Centre and provided a venue for the early work of writers and directors like Jim and Peter Sheridan and **Neil Jordan**. After a two-year sojourn in South King Street, the project moved to a former print works at East Essex Street (a building that was purchased outright with Arts Council assistance in 1977).

Although regarded as alternative, the early project was only politely radical until July 1976, when a new board committed to an oppositional cultural policy was elected. Arguably the subsequent failure to develop a theoretical underpinning to serve as a basis for settling disagreements about wider cultural policy limited the new project's critical impact. Nonetheless, Rockett's policy document chimed well with the new dispensation created by the new board, and from October 1976 screenings began, starting with seasons of new German cinema, previously unscreened Irish material, and other noncommercial films. From the winter 1977/78 program, the club also ran a series of screenings followed by talks and discussions to overtly situate films in a critical context. The series were organized around themes such as feminism and cinema and avant-garde cinema, and high-powered academic names such as Laura Mulvey traveled to Dublin to give lectures.

In 1978, the club programmed *Film and Ireland*, which screened more than 100 Irish and Irish-themed films organized into loose groupings such as Family, Foreign Images of Ireland, and Irish Literary Traditions on Film. As such it was the largest assembly of Irish films hitherto gathered together and influenced later events in London and the Irish Film Institute's (IFI) even more ambitious 1984 Green on the Screen season.

The project also planned more ambitious ventures such as a film workshop and a 16 mm distribution organization, but these proved difficult to achieve in the absence of sustained funding. In any case with the development of the **Irish Film Theatre** and the (partially Rockett-inspired) revamp of the **Irish Film Institute**, the club's screening and education functions were gradually usurped, and the club's operations ceased in the early 1980s. Nonetheless the club represented a key moment in the emergence of an Irish film culture and created a space in which the early work of pioneers like **Bob Quinn** and **Joe Comerford** could find an audience.

PUCKOON **(2001).** A British-Irish coproduction directed by Terence Ryan, *Puckoon* is based on Spike Milligan's surrealist first novel. Set during the work of the 1925 Boundary Commission (which was to finally agree on how Northern Ireland and the Irish Free State would be geographically divided), *Puckoon* traces the consequences of their efforts for one village that finds itself split down the middle by the new border. Despite a star cast (including Elliott Gould and Richard Attenborough), the film found it difficult to secure a release and sank without a trace domestically and internationally.

PURCELL, NOEL (1900–1985). Purcell has always been characterized as the definitive Dubliner who had a long career in theater and film and along with a small number of other character actors kept Ireland in the public gaze. After he had a distinguished career on the Irish stage, Purcell's performance in *Captain Boycott* (together with his distinctive voice and strong bearded features) sufficiently impressed Pinewood Studios for them to effectively make him a contract player, and he spent much of the 1950s appearing in British films. He was frequently called upon to play stock Irish roles in films such as *Talk of A Million* (1951), *Rooney* (1958), and *The Rising of the Moon*, and his old sea salt appearance led to his being cast in a disproportionate number of nautical roles, including **John Huston**'s *Moby Dick* (1956), *Mutiny on the Bounty* (1962), and *Lord Jim* (1965). By the 1960s he was an internationally recognized character actor, although he increasingly began to appear in television roles as that decade progressed. In his last feature roles in the early 1970s he played a ferry boat captain (inevitably) in *The McKenzie Break*

(1970) and a rabbi in a singing and dancing Dublin in *Flight of the Doves* (1971), among others.

THE PURPLE TAXI (*UN TAXI MAUVE*) (1977). A little-seen oddity, this French-Irish-Italian coproduction directed by Yves Boisset is based on a book by French novelist (and Irish resident) Michel Deon. Philippe (Philippe Noiret) is a French journalist who relocates to Connemara in the wake of his son's death. There he meets Jerry (Edward Albert), a youthful American expatriate and heir to a family fortune, and his sister, Sharon (Charlotte Rampling), with whom he becomes infatuated. The cosmopolitan group is completed by Taubelman (Peter Ustinov), a Russian exile, and his ward, Anne, who is (apparently) mute.

Unusually the film was partially financed by the **National Film Studios of Ireland** (i.e., **Ardmore Studios**), where the film was partially shot. The studios paid £260,000 for a 7 percent stake in the film's profits from English-language territories. This proved a poor investment, but nevertheless the film was a box-office hit in France—for many French tourists the film's representation of Ireland as a primitive paradise untouched by the trappings of modernity (albeit peopled by brawling and savage locals) is a key factor in encouraging them to visit.

– Q –

THE QUIET MAN (1952). John Ford's classic film has remained a dominant representation of a romantic Ireland that has continued to appeal especially to a diasporic audience, who enjoy its timeless, stereotypical characterization of the Irish as quaint, wild, and pleasure seeking. However, its Technicolor vision of a land of rosy-cheeked colleens and public brawling has little in common with the period in Ireland in which it ostensibly takes place. On its release it received seven **Academy Award** nominations, winning in two categories—Best Director and Best Color Cinematography. The film's enduring intertextual significance is demonstrated, for example, by its playing in the background on television during a domestic scene in Steven Spielberg's *E.T.* (1982). While many indigenous Irish have dismissed the film as a send-up of an idealized Irishness, others read the film more positively as a playful fantasy that helps capture the nostalgic and romantic mood of the country. Luke Gibbons, who has written more than most about the film, speaks of its picturesque exoticism as evidenced by a cover for *National Geographic* in 1961, with a **Maureen O'Hara** look-alike and its endorsement of a soft romanticism especially when compared with the hard primitivism characteristic of works such as Robert Flaherty's *Man of Aran* (Gibbons, *The Quiet Man*, 2002).

The story was a pet project of Ford, and for years before he could confirm funding, he had agreement from Maureen O'Hara (Mary Kate Danaher) and John Wayne (Sean Thornton) to star in the film. The story is based on a short story by Maurice Walsh and Frank Nugent, who did some final work on the screenplay for Ford. The narrative focuses on an Irish American's attempt to recapture the imagined innocence and beauty of his Irish childhood, most notably when Mary Kate sings "The Isle of Innisfree," a song that encapsulates Sean's longing and loss. Sean is returning home from America, having killed an opponent in a boxing match. His Ireland dream records a fairy-tale illusion of his childhood innocence as he explains how Innisfree is another word for heaven. **Barry Fitzgerald**'s role as Flynn, the village matchmaker and wise fool, remains one of the most memorable characterizations in all of Ford's work, yet he is sometimes accused of hamming up his stage-Irish performance.

Other memorable set pieces include the fantastically melodramatic portrayal of a first kiss (the heavens open to affirm Sean and Kate's romantic love) and, of course, the fist fight at the conclusion staged to satisfy Kate's insistence that her stubborn and strong-willed brother hand over her dowry. The long-awaited Western spectacle of a fight is encouraged by the eager natives and extends for a long time for the pleasure of all. As in all Ford's films the ties of community and family are firmly established and worth fighting for, as celebrated in this playful masterpiece.

Lord Killanin, a (distant) relative and production partner of Ford and also active in trying to set up an Irish film industry, believed the film was in fact more of a Western made in Ireland than an Irish film and spoke of its importance for Irish **tourism**, a point echoed by **Sean Lemass** as part of his campaign to secure state support for a film industry in Ireland. Although contemporary audiences continue to chuckle at its humorous invocation of communal rites of violence, the film's appeal endures and indeed—in a postmodern era—has arguably increased.

QUINN, AIDAN (1959–). He spent most of the first two decades of his life living on both sides of the Atlantic, with his academic father getting work in America and commuting back and forth from their Irish home in Birr, County Offaly. He attended St. Joseph's College in Blackrock, where he excelled at sports, history, and English. On leaving school, however, he did not pursue an academic career and for a period worked as kitchen porter. His interest in acting was piqued by lunchtime plays he would attend in Dublin City Center, although, concerned that his American-tinged accent would prove a hindrance, he never considered pursuing an acting career in Dublin. He returned to the United States in his early 20s, where he took acting classes. Two years of stage acting followed before he secured his first screen role opposite Darryl Hannah in *Reckless* (1984). The following year, he appeared as the male lead in his breakthrough film, *Desperately Seeking Susan*, opposite Rosanna Arquette and Madonna. He also made an indelible impression in *An Early Frost* (1985), one of the first pieces of popular drama to address the impact of AIDS on American society.

By the start of the 1990s he was an acknowledged star on U.S. screens, typically third or fourth on the cast list, but occasionally, as in *Benny and Joon* (1993), *Blink* (1994), and *Legends of the Fall* (1994) receiving equal lead billing. His first Irish role did not come until 1992, when he played the amorous traveling player in **The Playboys**. Indeed until the late 1990s, he was perceived in Ireland largely as an American actor with a facility for Irish accents. However, his de facto dual citizenship and his star status in the United States became increasingly useful for casting directors working in Ireland as production activity there took off in the mid-1990s. Quinn's Irish work has typically been in films that are designed or expected to make an impact in the U.S. market—hence his lead role in **This Is My Father**, in which James Caan's character attempts to trace his family history back in Ireland, his role as Harry Boland in **Michael Collins**, and his part opposite **Pierce Brosnan** in **Evelyn**. However, greatest critical praise was reserved for his most recent Irish role, that of an idealistic teacher working in a 1950s Irish school, in *Song for a Raggy Boy*.

Quinn is not the only member of his family to be preoccupied with filmmaking. His brother Declan is a noted cinematographer, with films like *Leaving Las Vegas* (1995), **Neil Jordan**'s *Breakfast on Pluto* (2005), and **Jim Sheridan**'s *Get Rich or Die Tryin'* (2005) to his credit. Quinn's younger sister, Marian, is a successful actress and has appeared in a number of Irish films, including *Broken Harvest* and *When the Sky Falls*. Finally, another brother, Paul Quinn, directed *This Is My Father,* which featured both Aidan and Marian, and on which Declan acted as cinematographer.

QUINN, BOB (1939–). He began his career with **Radio Telefís Éireann (RTÉ)** in the 1960s and attempted to make the public service broadcaster friendlier to independent productions. In 1969 he left to take up residence in his beloved Connemara in the West and set up a production company, where he made his first feature, *Caoineadh Airt Uí Laoire* [*Lament for Art O'Leary*] (1975), which emulates the experimentation of Jean-Luc Godard's polemical work. Next, he made a full-length feature entirely in Gaelic, *Poitín* (1979), starring **Cyril Cusack**, **Niall Toibin**, and **Donal McCann**, which was financed by the **Arts Council** with no expectations of commercial success or even getting its money back. The story demonstrates the brutality of this insular community in the West, which has been hampered by centuries of **emigration** and underdevelopment.

In 1986 Quinn made *Atlantean*, a three-part television series that sought to question the founding myth of Celtic mythology and its suggestions of a pure, rural, self-sufficient race that is uncorrupted by foreign influence. Focusing on the various extensive trade links between the sea people of Britain, France, Spain, and North America together with Ireland, and in particular the port of Galway, the director presented a convincing dramatic thesis of at least possible blood relations between these various seafaring trading countries. Nevertheless, there was vitriolic criticism from many quarters for even posing such a hypothesis.

The line between his 1987 film *Budawanny*, adapted from the novel *Súil le Breith* by Connemara priest Padraic Standún, and his 1993 reworking of this same material in *The Bishop's Story* is somewhat unclear. But both deal with a Catholic priest, played by **Donal McCann**, on Clare Island, off the west coast, and his sexual relationship with his housekeeper (Margaret Fegan). The story has strong echoes of several real-life scandals in the **Catholic** Church, most notably the Bishop Eamon Casey story of his illegitimate son, which have come to light in recent times.

More recently Quinn's feature film output has declined, although his son (Robert Quinn) directed the generic thriller *Dead Bodies* for a new generation. Quinn senior has become an outspoken critic of new Irish cinema, arguing that younger Irish filmmakers are being seduced by the outside world while being led to believe through various government film agencies that they can and should become international cinema figures, rather than simply setting their sights on appealing to a native audience.

QUINN, MARIAN. Part of the Irish American Quinn family who have been heavily involved in making films, most notably *This Is My Father*, on which Paul Quinn was director, Declan Quinn was cinematographer, and **Aidan Quinn** received top thespian billing. (Even the story was suggested by the siblings' mother.) Born in Chicago, Marian migrated back and forth from Ireland, living in Birr, Illinois, and Dublin. As an adult she settled in New York, although after *This Is My Father* she returned to Ireland again with her husband and children to live in Dromahair, County Leitrim. She has also starred in several other Irish films—including *When the Sky Falls* and *Evelyn*—and has made the Irish American story something of a specialty: In addition to *This Is My Father*, she appeared in both *Broken Harvest* and *2by4*. More recently she has turned her hand to directing, with one well-received short and a feature titled *32a* in production.

– R –

RADIO TELIFÍS ÉIREANN (RTÉ). RTÉ is the national public service broadcaster, owned by the state and run by a state-appointed governing authority. Although sound broadcasting began in 1926, the move to television was not seriously explored until the mid-1950s. Government policy throughout that decade worked on the assumption that television would be run on a commercial basis, but in 1959, the cabinet decided that the existing public service broadcaster, Radio Éireann [Radio Ireland], should expand its operations to encompass television. This was given legal effect via the 1960 Broadcasting Authority Act.

The act was relatively unspecific with regard to RTÉ's programming obligations, beyond Section 17 of the act, which stated that "in performing its functions, the Authority shall bear constantly in mind the national aims of restoring the Irish language and preserving and developing the national culture and shall endeavor to promote the attainment of those aims" (Government of Ireland, 1960).

Thus RTÉ faced no particular obligations to engage in drama production or more particularly to support filmmaking activity. Nonetheless (indeed inevitably), RTÉ did produce dramas, the bulk of which were single dramas until the 1980s. However, serial production did commence as early as 1964 with the production of the first Irish television soap opera *Tolka Row* (which ran until 1968). A year later, in 1965, it was followed by a second soap, *The Riordans*, which ran until 1979 and which generated two spin-off dramas—*Bracken* (1981–1982) and *Glenroe* (1982–2001). As the 1970s and 1980s progressed the drama series came to dominate RTÉ drama production, although this took place in the context of an overall reduction in output, especially in the decade from 1985 to 1995.

Direct support of Irish film production did not take place until the 1980s, when the station partially funded **Joe Comerford**'s first feature-length drama, *Traveller*. Film finance remained patchy for the remainder of that decade, although the station did put some funds into **Pat Murphy**'s *Anne Devlin* and **Jim Sheridan**'s *My Left Foot*. Typically, RTÉ came late to these projects, committing funds only once it was clear that the rest of the budget was already in place. Ironically then, Irish filmmakers were more likely to receive funding from British broadcaster **Channel 4** than from their local channel.

But this situation changed somewhat after 1993, with the passage of that year's Broadcasting (Amendment) Act, which transposed into Irish law that part of the European Union's 1989 "Television Without Frontiers" directive, which required European broadcasters to reserve 10 percent of their broadcast time for independently produced work. This resulted in the establishment of a new unit within RTÉ—the

Independent Production Unit (IPU)—charged with commissioning work from production companies outside RTÉ. At the same time the station came under increasing criticism for the decline in its commitment to drama production in previous years.

Happily for RTÉ, the establishment of the IPU coincided with the expansion in indigenous feature production that followed on the reformation of the **Irish Film Board**, with the result that it could become involved in a plethora of extant projects in development while simultaneously fulfilling its obligations to independent production and drama output. Thus in 1994, RTÉ partially funded **Cathal Black**'s *Korea* and **Bob Quinn**'s reworking of his earlier *Budawanny* into *The Bishop's Story*. IPU involvement with feature production continued through the 1990s; it partially funded (among other titles) *I Went Down*, *Nora*, *Borstal Boy*, and *A Love Divided*. However, from 2000 on, support for feature production dried up as RTÉ began to actively commission independently produced drama series. As hit shows like *Bachelor's Walk* and *Paths to Freedom* came onstream, RTÉ was able to fulfill its drama commitments without recourse to feature film funding.

This is not to suggest that RTÉ has entirely abandoned independent film production. Since 1994 it has developed a series of schemes in collaboration with the Irish Film Board aimed at supporting short film and animation production. These include Short Cuts (1994–), which funds 6–15 minute dramas, Frameworks (1995–), which supports animation, and Oscailt (1998–), which is supported by RTÉ's Irish-language channel TG4 together with the Film Board.

Finally it is also important to acknowledge that the simple fact of RTÉ's existence has indirectly (and unintentionally) supported Irish filmmaking by offering at least some small space for writers, directors, and actors to practice their craft. Producer **Lelia Doolan** worked as a drama director and current affairs producer in the 1960s, as did **Bob Quinn**, before both left dramatically in May 1969 in protest at what they characterized as the station's stifling of creativity. Both, however, acknowledged their professional debts to the organization. Further down the line, in 1979 RTÉ director **Pat O'Connor** directed single dramas penned by both Jim Sheridan (*Mobile Homes*) and **Neil Jordan** (*Miracles and Miss Langan*). Indeed, RTÉ cofinanced (with Channel 4) Pat O'Connor's BAFTA award–winning drama *The*

Ballroom of Romance, which led to O'Connor's first feature work on *Cal*. Even *Eat the Peach* director Peter Ormrod worked as a director for RTÉ, most notably on the 1983 series *Caught in a Free State*.

RAT (2000). This is a quirky comedy, somewhat reminiscent of Kafka's story "Metamorphosis," concerning a lazy working-class man (Peter Postlethwaite) who one day wakes up to find himself transformed into a rat. Remarkably his family, including his wife (Imelda Staunton) and Uncle Matt (**Frank Kelly**), quickly accept these unusual circumstances and proceed to bring him around to his usual haunts. This absurd comic-fantasy directed by Steve Barron and scripted by Wesley Burrows, who is remembered for the long-running rural television soap *The Riordans*, has the unforgettable tag line "He might eat maggots and live in a cage but he's still our Dad." The resultant film remains engaging.

REA, STEPHEN (1946–). Born in Belfast, Rea was the only boy in a family with four children. At university he joined the politically driven Young Irish Theatre Company before moving to Dublin to work with the **Abbey Theatre**. From there he moved to the London Stage, where he worked in virtually every major theater, including the Old Vic, the Royal Court, and the English National Theater. In the course of this he worked through the canon of modern theater from Henrik Ibsen through Anton Chekhov to Bertolt Brecht. In 1980, Rea returned to Northern Ireland, where, with playwright Brian Friel (and later internationally renowned poet Seamus Heaney and academic and writer Seamus Deane), he founded the Field Day theater company, which sought to create a cultural space to interrogate a more constructive historical identity from within the specter of the "troubles."

Rea first became known as a screen actor with *Angel* (1982) and has maintained a close relationship with **Neil Jordan** ever since, making seven appearances in the director's subsequent films. These include most recently *Breakfast on Pluto* (2005), an adaptation of the Graham Greene novel *The End of the Affair* (1999), in which he plays the cuckolded Henry Miles, as well as *The Company of Wolves*, *The Butcher Boy*, *Michael Collins*, *In Dreams*, and *Interview with the Vampire*. Critics often call attention to his understated acting style, as evidenced by the starring role in *The Crying Game* (1992), for which he was nominated for an Oscar. His screen characters rarely go to emotional extremes regardless of their circumstances. However, Rea's performances nonetheless allow the audience glimpses of the turmoil and thinking that lies beneath the surface.

Although he has occasionally returned to stage—most notably for the much-praised Broadway run of Frank McGuinness's *Someone to Watch Over Me*—the bulk of his work is now on the large screen. Beyond his work with Jordan, he has also appeared in numerous other Irish films—often in cameo roles—including *The Halo Effect*, *Bloom*, *Evelyn*, *On the Edge*, *This Is My Father*, *A Further Gesture*, *The Last of the High Kings*, *Trojan Eddie*, and others. He is also in steady demand for roles in smaller-scale European and U.S. films, especially since the *Crying Game* Oscar nomination. These include *Life Is Sweet* (1990), *Prêt-a-Porter* (1994), and *Fever Pitch* (1997).

REEFER AND THE MODEL (1988). Starring Ian McElhinny, Eve Watkinson, and Carol Scanlon, among many other Irish actors, the **Joe Comerford** film is set off the west coast and begins when what could only be described as an aristocratic ex-republican man gives a lift to Teresa, a woman with a shady past. When he takes her in to live on his boat, which is occasionally used as a ferry between the mainland and the islands, we are introduced to his crew—Spider, who is on the run from the British, and Badger.

The dialogue is often overly stilted and didactic and critical of conventional forms of romanticism as displayed within Hollywood-like narratives. Teresa speaks of how she could not have an abortion and now craves a family, a difficult scenario to imagine within such an environment. Like much of Comerford's work, nothing is as it seems, and audiences have to work hard to unpack the multilayered meanings of his narratives.

One can possibly better understand *Reefer and the Model* by ignoring specific elements of the narrative and focusing instead on the impact of the whole. Here the film is somewhat more successful, particularly if one is mindful of the political context in which the film was made in the mid-1980s, a period characterized by occasional news stories about shoot-outs between the Irish Republican Army (IRA) and the gardaí, and IRA members on the run. Thus Reefer is portrayed as an IRA man attempting to put the past behind him but who is thwarted both by the tendency of his past to catch up with him and by an unwillingness to completely abandon past methods of survival in moments of crisis. In short, as a portrayal of the reality of the glamorous gangster image of the IRA, as it is understood in some quarters, Reefer begins to make more sense, although it remains impossible to definitively say what the filmmaker thinks or feels about his main character.

Indeed, Comerford's overall objective in making the film remains unclear as the credits roll. One possibility is suggested by the content of the film. Since one of the objectives may be to portray an alternative to the "terrorist madmen," television news version of the IRA, the question of the politics of representation is brought to the fore. By adopting his own rules of cinema, Comerford implicitly rejects the very filmic language traditionally used to effect such a portrayal, arguably prompting a reconsideration of the validity of such modes of representation. Yet while such a theory is at least plausible with regard to the film as a whole, the absence of a coherent philosophy of either what the film is about or what the film is trying to say about the act of representation still leaves the viewer somewhat dazed and confused.

**REPORT OF ENQUIRY INTO THE SUPPLY AND DISTRIBU-
TION OF CINEMA FILMS (1977).** In 1970 the Fair Trade Commission (FTC) received a number of complaints from independent cinema owners to the effect that they were experiencing difficulties in getting access to films. The complaints clearly implied that **Ward Anderson** and the **distribution** sector were colluding to give Ward Anderson cinemas preferential access to prints. As a result the commission engineered the establishment of the Cinema Trade Complaints Committee in May 1970 to deal with such complaints. However, in 1976, faced with an ongoing flow of complaints, the examiner of the Restrictive Practices Commission (which superseded the FTC in 1972) met the Irish Cinemas Association, which represented independent cinema owners. The association asserted that Dublin suburban cinemas had to wait 2–14 months for product due to the privileged status of Ward Anderson's Green Cinema, and further

that Ward Anderson–controlled provincial cinemas got all the first runs outside Dublin.

The examiner proceed to examine the exhibition patterns of 17 films and concluded that priority was indeed given to the Adelphi-Carlton group, Rank Odeon, and Ward Anderson's Green Group and that effectively the major distributors had established Ward Anderson in a monopoly position throughout the country outside Dublin.

The examiner's report led the commission to establish a major inquiry into the supply and distribution of cinema films in Ireland. The enquiry received 23 submissions from distributors and exhibitors and heard evidence from 26 witnesses (5 of whom were barristers or senior counsel: Ward Anderson were legally represented by Peter Sutherland, who would later become a European Union commissioner and head of the World Trade Organization).

With regard to the dominant position enjoyed by Adelphi-Carlton and Rank Odeon in Dublin City Centre, the distributors argued that this was driven purely by commercial interests. Faced with a limited number of prints for any given film, they had to employ some form of priority in distributing them, and the system they employed was based on the revenue-generating capacity of individual cinemas (which in turn was based on the comfort, quality of presentation, and likely run length associated with individual cinemas). The distributors further asserted that the performance of a given film outside Dublin was affected by the success of the Dublin release. In short, the distributors argued that the position enjoyed by Adelphi-Carlton and Rank derived from the financial advantages they offered to distributors.

In response to assertions about Ward Anderson's extra-Dublin dominance, Ward Anderson pointed out that in addition to the fact that they owned 13 of the 15 cinemas based in Cork, Limerick, and Galway (which although placing them in a dominant position was not of itself illegal), it was easier for distributors to book films into Ward Anderson's 40-strong circuit than to make 40 individual bookings with independent cinema owners. They also argued that they had invested more money in their cinemas than their independent counterparts, thus enhancing the revenue-generating capacity of their cinemas.

The enquiry largely accepted these assertions and effectively overturned the examiner's report. With regard to the position enjoyed by Adelphi-Carlton and Rank Odeon it did suggest that some procedures might be adopted that would moderate their dominance, suggesting that the distributors establish a Product Allocation Committee. However, the enquiry found no evidence of any collusion between the Ward Anderson group and the major distributors, citing instead the group's investment in cinemas and skillful exploitation of commercial opportunities as explaining its growth. Indeed, while stating that it would be desirable from the perspective of competition to have more than one major cinema circuit in Ireland, the enquiry found that it was nonetheless in the interest of the consumer to have at least one circuit capable of investing in facilities and offering a counterbalance to the power of distributors.

REPORT OF THE FILM INDUSTRY COMMITTEE. In 1967 then Irish resident **John Huston** invited **Louis Marcus** to his suite in the Gresham Hotel Dublin to discuss the possibility of state support for filmmaking in Ireland. Marcus had recently written a series of articles lamenting the absence of just such support. Following this discussion Huston invited Taoiseach Jack Lynch to Glencree, County Wicklow, where the former was shooting *Sinful Davey* (1969). In a public address to Lynch, Huston suggested that the time was ripe for the establishment of an Irish film industry. Lynch accepted the suggestion, and in November 1967, George Colley, as minister for industry and commerce, established a committee to examine the problems involved in the establishment of an Irish film industry. The 24-person committee was chaired by Huston and included representatives from all sectors of film production (including Marcus and **Lord Killanin**), **distribution**, and **exhibition** in Ireland. The committee also included five civil servants representing the Departments of Finance, Industry and Commerce, Education, and External Affairs.

In conducting its examination the committee acknowledged that state support for industry was usually justified by an expectation of contribution to employment and the economy in return for that support. While not ignoring these considerations, the committee's thinking was also informed by the more culturally significant "lack of a potent means of presenting Ireland, its heritage and its people to the world and of keeping the people in touch with their distinctive environment" (Film Industry Committee, 1968). The committee's thinking was made more explicit when it noted a working assumption that—outside the United States—all countries with a film industry were financially aided either by the state or by a fund formed from proceeds of a levy on box office receipts.

According to Louis Marcus's account (2003) two somewhat competing perspectives drove the committee's work. Huston argued that the state should concentrate any support it might be willing to offer on funding the preproduction of films (i.e., development funding) to be shot in Ireland, a move that would have facilitated the scale of film Huston was used to making. Again according to Marcus, Huston also rejected the idea that the state should fund the actual production of films and threatened to resign as chairman if the final committee report made any reference to short films.

However, when Marcus wrote an internal report for the committee, he pointed out that the cost of developing an international-scale feature could be anything from £100,000 to £250,000, money that would be lost if the film did not succeed in attracting production finance. Thus, in an indirect response to Huston's position, C. J. Byrnes from the Department of Finance argued that the state was unwilling to support preproduction finance for international producers beyond the sum of £10,000 per film. However, the state was interesting in aiding the development of Irish filmmakers, through 100 percent funding of fiction shorts and modestly budgeted (less than £50,000) features. Byrnes's points appear to have formed the basis for the key financial recommendations emerging from the final committee report.

The committee noted that the value of short films lay in the international prestige they conferred upon the country of origin and in their skills training potential. The committee also pointed out that these films received small rental fees and even with worldwide distribution were highly unlikely to recover their production costs. Thus it recommended making between £55,000 and £75,000 available to fund the production of up to seven fiction and nonfiction shorts per annum.

The final report recommended the creation of an agency (effectively a film board) to disburse these funds. However, rather than simply re-creating the **Irish Film Finance Corporation**, the agency would have a broader responsibility to take positive action to secure the production of Irish feature films, not merely through the provision of financial assistance but by becoming involved in distribution, marketing, the negotiation of coproduction agreements, and offering training facilities. The agency would also act as a **screen commission**, offering international producers advice on locations, the availability of technicians, extras, and other elements of filmmaking in Ireland. Finally the agency would be charged with establishing a national **film archive**. In its conclusion the committee report noted the following:

> The agency will have failed if its efforts lead merely to the establishment here of branches of international film companies, producing films that have no significant Irish creative, artistic and technical content. It will have achieved success when Irish creative endeavour, technical ability and artistic talent are combined in making, on a continuing basis, films of a quality and a standard acceptable to audiences in Ireland and throughout the world. (Film Industry Committee, 1968)

The committee submitted its report in autumn 1968 with Huston's name attached (despite his personal misgivings about the conclusions). By November 1969 Colley announced that legislation to implement the main recommendations of the film industry committee was in the course of being drafted. It is apparent that the newly founded **Society of Film Makers in Ireland** was extensively consulted in the drafting of the bill. In July 1970 Colley's successor at the Department of Industry and Commerce, Patrick Lalor, duly introduced the first stage of the Film Industry Bill, which he declared would establish a film board charged with developing a film industry in the state. Although the bill was due to go to a second reading a week later, the fallout from an unrelated political scandal (the arms crisis) saw the legislation effectively shelved. It would reemerge only a decade later in the guise of the 1980 **Irish Film Board** Act.

REPORT ON INDIGENOUS AUDIOVISUAL PRODUCTION INDUSTRY. See COOPERS AND LYBRAND REPORT.

REPORT TO THE TAOISEACH, MR. ALBERT REYNOLDS, T. D., 24 NOLLAIG, 1992. Taoiseach [Prime Minister] Albert Reynolds announced the establishment of the Special Working Group on 23 September 1992 at the official opening of the Irish Film Centre, adding that he expected a completed report within two and a half months. This short time reflected the fact that the group was not expected to conduct new research but rather to consider the conclusions of the two major reports published in the summer of 1992, the **Coopers and Lybrand Report** and the **Independent Television Production Sector Report**, and to make specific policy recommendations based on those considerations. The group was constituted in such as way as to include persons from virtually every state agency in any way connected with film as well as a smattering of actual filmmakers. The 32-member group thus included civil servants from the Departments of the Taoiseach, Industry and Commerce, Finance, and Tourism, as well as (among others) representatives of the Industrial Development Authority (IDA), **Radio Telefís Éireann (RTÉ)**, the **Arts Council**, the **Irish Film Institute (IFI)**, **Film Makers Ireland**, and the **Irish Film Centre**.

The group submitted the report on 24 December 1992, although it would be the new year before its conclusions were made public. The group rehearsed the conclusions of the Coopers and FMI reports for building an argument for state support for the development of employment and economic potential in the audiovisual sector. However, the report also recorded some concerns from the Departments of Industry and Commerce and Finance. Industry and Commerce pointed to the high risk associated with film production and the need, at a time when the state's finances were being tightly squeezed, to ensure that resources were concentrated on those projects with the best chance of yielding *sustainable* employment. The use of "sustainable" clearly expressed Industry and Commerce's doubts about the freelance nature of the industry and may have been influenced in part by the contemporaneous difficulties being experienced in the **animation** sector.

For its part, the Department of Finance's contribution was at pains to stress that the film industry should not receive preferential treatment from the state "because of ill-defined cultural or artistic characteristics."

Despite these caveats the report argued that the international success enjoyed by Irish and Irish-themed films shot between 1986 and 1991 (i.e., non–Irish Film Board projects) had created a "window of opportunity" for Irish producers and directors. However, since a clear decline in the momentum of activity within the industry had occurred in 1992, there was a risk that the opportunity to exploit the goodwill enjoyed by Irish filmmaking in previous years was fast disappearing and that there was a need for state intervention to ensure that this did not happen.

Specifically, then, the report made five groups of recommendations, relating to the role of the IDA, **Bord Fáilte**, the Irish Trade Board, RTÉ, and the State Training Agency; the need to amend the 1990 Broadcasting Act and to establish an Irish-language television channel; the need to amend **Section 35**; the provision of state subventions for developing and producing audiovisual productions; and a set of miscellaneous recommendations relating to European funding and coproduction agreements. Of these, the discussions of tax breaks and state subvention were most significant. On tax, the group restated the need to extend Section 35 to individuals and to increase the amount of film investment allowed for tax relief. The report stated that a majority of the group favored some kind of annual state subvention to be administered by a specialized agency funded by the Oireachtas. As for which agency, the group considered the Arts Council, the Irish Film Board, or a third agency. Although it could see merit in both the Arts Council and Film Board options, the group recommended establishing a new agency. A new agency could be customized to the conditions relating to film and television production in the 1990s rather than relying on an institution created by legislation drawn up largely in the 1970s. The report also acknowledged that perceptions about the board's past failures might make it politically difficult to revive it.

The report went on to make specific recommendations about the level of finance to be made available to the new agency and to suggest that it be subject to periodic review such that, if after five years it was not considered to have been a success from a creative and economic perspective, the agency should be discontinued.

The report's arrival at the Department of the Taoiseach preceded by mere weeks the appointment of **Michael D. Higgins** as the state's first minister for arts and culture. Such was the speed with which Higgins moved to introduce change, however, that by the time the report was ready for general publication, a number of its recommendations were either already in place or had been superseded. Thus Higgins's introduction to the published version of the report noted the inclusion in the 1993 Finance Bill of changes to Section 35, the introduction of a Broadcasting Authority (Amendment) Bill requiring RTÉ to commission more independent work, and—most significantly—the reestablishment of the Film Board. The last decision, in particular, clearly clashed with the report's recommendation on establishing a new body, suggesting that for Higgins at least, there were no "perception" difficulties relating to the old Film Board. Nonetheless, the report's stress on reviewing the new board's activities within five years must have created an interesting working environment within that institution.

***RESURRECTION MAN* (1998).** Tapping into serial killer and new gangster conventions, the film, directed by Marc Evans, focuses on the sectarianism of a well-known sadist who led a maverick Ulster Volunteer Force (UVF) gang known in real life as the Shankill Butchers, who were responsible for several brutal, ritualistic murders of Catholics (and even Protestants deemed disloyal to the cause). While the film made no claim to historical accuracy, Pierre Aim effectively photographed 1970s gritty Belfast urbanism, while the ambient sound track also succeeds in capturing the mood of the time. **Stuart Townsend** plays the eponymous "resurrection man," Victor Kelly, who is brought up by an overzealous and protective mother (**Brenda Fricker**) and a weak father (George Shane). As a child the boy is seen to identify with the seminal image of Jimmy Cagney in *Public Enemy* (1931), and prompted by his dysfunctional sexual nature, seeks the recognition of the media for his evil deeds. The critic Lance Pettitt suggests that the film probes how individual psychosis is intimately connected with the normality of a dysfunctional society, heavily militarized and suffocating under surveillance (Pettitt, 2000). Others suggest that such a film contributes to the popular perception of loyalist paramilitaries as essentially monstrous.

Some British critics walked out of previews of the film, and it was very critically reviewed in the South of Ireland. This film and **Thaddeus O'Sullivan**'s *Nothing Personal* both appropriate loyalist agency and the "**troubles**" to explore violent **masculinity**.

REYNOLDS, EMER. Now arguably the busiest film editor in the country, Reynolds first made an impact with her work on Orla Walsh's politically charged short *The Visit* (1992). She confirmed her talent when she cut **Paddy Breathnach**'s feature debut, *Ailsa* in 1994. Since then she has rarely been out of work, and directors who work with her usually retain her on their next project. Thus, in addition to working again with Walsh (on *Bent Out of Shape* [1995]) and Breathnach (*I Went Down*), she has also worked with **Cathal Black, Conor McPherson**, and Dearbhla Walsh. Her collaborations with **Alan Gilsenan** stand out in this regard—between 2001 and 2004, she edited four of his productions including a short, a feature (*Timbuktu* —for which she won an IFTA in 2004), and two documentaries.

In more recent years she has turned her own hand to directing, with three shorts since 2001. She has also begun to secure more television drama work, including—in 2004—**Radio Telefís Éireann**'s (RTÉ) *The Big Bow Wow* and Channel 4's *Shameless*.

RHYS MEYERS, JONATHAN (1977–). He survived a difficult childhood, having been born with a heart condition, and his father is said to have abandoned his mother and three younger brothers when he was only two and half, following which the family moved to Cork. He was allegedly kicked out of school at 16 and gained a strong interest in acting with his first leading role as an unhappy man in *The Disappearance of Finbar*. Since then, aided by his striking good looks, which have made him popular with audiences and filmmakers alike, he has worked with major directors including **Neil Jordan** in *Michael Collins*, Ang Lee in *Ride with the Devil* (1999), and Mike Figgis in *The Loss of Sexual Innocence* (1998). He also appeared in Gurinder Chadra's big hit *Bend It like Beckham* (2002) and Todd Haynes's *Velvet Goldmine* (1998). In 2006 he received a Golden Globe for his performance in a U.S. television miniseries on the life of Elvis Presley.

***RIDERS TO THE SEA* (1987).** This is the second (after **Brian Desmond Hurst**'s 1935 version) adaptation of Synge's classic play about a woman who loses her husband and her six sons to the sea and was **Ronan O'Leary**'s directorial debut. Made on a shoestring budget (even considering the play's short 45-minute duration) of £95,000, with support from the Public Broadcasting Service (PBS) in the United States, O'Leary pulled off a remarkable casting coup in securing the services not just of Barry McGovern and Amanda

Plummer but also Oscar winner Geraldine Page in what would prove to be her penultimate screen performance. Although widely criticized after its premiere at the Cork Film Festival, it nonetheless succeeded in achieving modest TV and video sales in the United States, sufficient to allow O'Leary to move to his next production.

THE RISING OF THE MOON (*THREE LEAVES OF A SHAMROCK*) (1957). The film was the first production of **Lord Killanin's Four Provinces** company and was designed to showcase the possibilities of shooting in Ireland. It also emanated from **John Ford's** deep sense of romanticism, which his biographer Joseph McBride described as so extravagant that it could come only from a first-generation American (J. McBride, 2001). In the opening sequence of the film we hear an Irish tenor singing with laconic passion, "The Garden of Eden has vanished, they say, but I know the lie of it still. . . ."

The film is made up of three vignettes of Irish country life that are based on a series of short episodes, with the Hollywood star Tyrone Power, in his last movie, introducing all three stories. In the first voice-over, he describes the story as being "about nothing, yet, perhaps it's about everything." Frank O'Connor's "The Majesty of the Law" tells of the reluctant visit of a Galway police inspector (**Cyril Cusack**) to serve a search warrant on an old man (**Noel Purcell**) who makes his home next to the ancient ruins of his family castle. Another story, "A Minute's Wait," can be appreciated, according to some critics, as Ford's paean to the irrepressible anarchy of the Irish spirit, while also reinforcing the idea of Ireland as a backward island with loveable incompetents, indulging the director's dreamlike romantic vision of his childhood. Naturally the resultant stereotypical Irish blarney caused offense in some quarters when the film was released, but the overall wit and good-natured camaraderie of the production displays the talents of many fine **Abbey Theatre** actors.

ROCKETT, KEVIN (1949–). With the possible exception of **Liam O'Leary**, Rockett has done more to develop the idea of an Irish film culture than any other individual. While studying architecture in London in 1973 he came across what was—at the time—the first university video studio. Gradually his interest shifted from his nominal subject (although architecture and film might both be considered elements of visual culture) toward film culture, and he became involved in community video in London.

After he returned to Dublin in 1976, Rockett was invited to join the board of the Project Arts Centre by its administrator, John Stephenson, at a point when the center was undergoing something of an artistic revolution under the direction of **Jim Sheridan** and his brother, Peter. Rockett immediately outlined a film policy for the project, which was realized through the establishment of the **Project Cinema Club**. His work at the project was informed by his annual attendances at the British Film Institute's residential summer schools at Stirling and the Edinburgh Film Festival, where he encountered such luminaries of early British film theory as Laura Mulvey, Peter Wollen, and John Hill (with whom he would later collaborate in writing). This clearly shaped the fact that the project films were not merely one-off screenings but opportunities to explore the idea of film culture.

In 1978 he became a lecturer on the fine arts course at the National College of Art and Design (NCAD). Although he was initially employed to teach video production, his duties soon expanded to include the first third-level modules on film history and theory taught in Ireland. Within a year, this work, combined with his project activities (and an influential 1978 *Screen* article on constructing a film culture in Ireland), led the then moribund **National Film Institute of Ireland** to invite him to join the board. This occurred despite the fact that institute board members had publicly criticized the explicit content of some of the films he had screened at the project. His appointment was the first of a series that would revolutionize the role of the institute, changing it from an extension of the Catholic hierarchy to an advocate for film culture in Ireland. By 1984 he had become the chair of the institute board, in which capacity he oversaw the efforts to establish an **Irish Film Centre**, including the decision to sell the institute's old building on Harcourt Street and acquire new premises on Eustace Street in Temple Bar.

Rockett left NCAD in 1983 to begin work on his doctoral dissertation (under John Hill), *Cinema in Ireland*. Large elements of this would find their way into the seminal *Cinema and Ireland*, which he cowrote with Hill and Luke Gibbons and which was published in 1987. Although Rockett has published extensively since, it is unlikely that any work will surpass the impact of this tome, which at a stroke established a template for subsequent academic study of Irish film culture and policy. When dedicated film studies courses began to emerge in the early 1990s, *Cinema and Ireland* was usually the key text on reading lists, and Rockett's contribution on political economy in particular remains essential reading for understanding the industrial and policy dimensions of Irish film culture.

After completing his thesis in 1989, Rockett remained at the institute for a further two years before moving to University College Dublin to lecture in 1992. During this period he assembled and published the massive *Irish Filmography*, an index of 2,000-plus films that not only included virtually every feature and short ever made in Ireland but also referenced all overseas films that even referred to Ireland or the Irish. In 2000 he was offered a post at Trinity College, Dublin, where his publishing activities continued. He collaborated with his wife, Emer, on a critical study of the films of **Neil Jordan** and their production contexts in 2003, and in 2004 he published *Irish Film Censorship*, another massive undertaking, which entailed examining censors' reports on 18,000 films. Appointed associate professor of film studies in 2005, his latest projects include a definitive history of Irish cinema exhibition and a second Irish filmography, this time dealing with nonfiction material, and the updating of the first volume—all of which were made available on the Internet at the end of 2006.

Judged in terms of the breadth and scope of Rockett's work on Irish cinema, it is difficult to overstate his influence: An examination of virtually any substantive academic work on Irish cinema will show his name in the bibliography, and it is likely to remain there for decades to come.

***THE ROCKY ROAD TO DUBLIN* (1968).** Irish-born journalist Peter Lennon had produced a series of pieces for *The Guardian* newspaper while working in Paris that caused enormous controversy in Ireland for their severe criticism of the Irish establishment. The response inspired him to make a film along the same lines. He secured financing from an American businessman and persuaded legendary French Nouvelle Vague photographer Raoul Coutard to film the documentary. The premise of Lennon's thesis was what do you do with your revolution once you've got it? Recounting the revolutionary period of 1916 and the struggle for independence, the director's polemical voice-over argues that the nation had been locked into a backward, Church-controlled republic that did not follow through on the heroic struggle of the revolutionary's vision of the past.

To dramatize his thesis, the director interviews a Gaelic Athletic Association (GAA) official, who justifies the outright ban on their members playing English games, while focusing on **Catholic** priests and their pernicious influence on society. Lennon got permission to film one well-known "singing (or swinging) Priest" (Duane, 2004), Father Michael Cleary—who later caused a scandle for fathering a child of his own. With the benefit of this hindsight, Cleary's insights appear hypocritical, especially when he talks about how the Church is not against "sex" per se but extols the virtues of celibacy for the priesthood. Older school children spout their religious indoctrination for the camera. Yet the documentary concludes with one of the most engaging scenes in Irish film history, as many of these kids in their school coats are filmed running toward the motorcycle-mounted camera, symbolically escaping the clutches of their repressive society.

Furthermore, the changing pleasures of the adult society are beautifully dramatized through the cinema verité–style observation of various dance-hall sequences alongside the diegetic use of traditional and popular Irish music. Only in disembodied voice-over are we presented with a hidden counterdiscourse. A young married woman explains how she had several children and did not want more, but the Church's advice on contraception was limited to abstinance and accepting her lot in life. Well-spoken middle-class male university students discuss the inequality in Irish society and their inability to express their political view, while a leading dissident writer of the time, Sean O'Faolain, refers to the control exerted by the Church with great passion and conviction.

The reception of the film probably ensured its cult status. Even though despised by people in the censor's office, they could not cut the documentary since there was no sex in it. Neverthess, while seen only for a few weeks in one Dublin cinema, it was buried in Ireland after this and was never shown on television. However, its spectacular life grew from its showing at the 1968 film festival—the last film shown before the infamous closing down of the festival that year, spurred by Godard and others, as a result of the students' revolution begun in Paris. The documentary was subsequently taken to heart by the revolutionary movement in Europe and shown widely. It remains a provocative exposé of an important period in Irish cultural history.

THE RUN OF THE COUNTRY (1995). Based on Shane Connaughton's semiautobiographical novel of Cavan in the 1950s, the film, directed by Peter Yates, stars Albert Finney, Mat Keeslar, Victoria Smurfit, and **David Kelly**. Danny argues with his father, the local garda sergeant, and moves in with his friend Prunty (Anthony Brophy), who "has the run of the country" and was mixed up with the old Irish Republican Army (IRA) as well as embodying the spirit of rural enterprise. As Danny learns about such a life from his friend, he finally finds the courage to talk to Annagh Lee, a girl he has long been attracted to who lives across the border. When she becomes pregnant, however, Prunty offers to give them money from selling turf from his mother's farm to pay for an abortion (a switch from the source novel, in which she has a miscarriage). Danny initially wants to follow her to America and decides to emigrate with the support of his father, but he eventually goes to college in Ireland instead. This story of impossible love across the border is particularly notable for the evocation of place and the unique drumlin landscape of County Cavan.

RYAN'S DAUGHTER (1970). After the enormous success of *Lawrence of Arabia* (1962) and *Doctor Zhivago* (1965), David Lean considered several subjects for his next film. However, when Robert Bolt produced a script version of Gustave Flaubert's novel *Madam Bovary*, this was eventually turned into a script for this film. Set in County Kerry in 1916, the film cost over $6 million and used more than 115 hours of film stock. Initially the film was a great success with Irish audiences but was ridiculed in Great Britain and elsewhere, much to the shock of the director, who did not make a film for a long time afterward.

The story deals with conventional historical romantic issues of love, passion, revolution, betrayal, heroism, and cowardice. All of these are evocatively framed by the magnificent landscape, as is conventional in romantic melodrama, and extremes of weather correspond to changing emotional states in the chief protagonist, Rosie (Sarah Miles). Rosie is the daughter of an ambivalent patriot and local publican and marries well-mannered schoolteacher Charles Shaughnessy (Robert Mitchum), who is an older widower and far from spontaneous and romantic. Sexually unsatisfied, she has a passionate affair with a troubled and shell-shocked young British officer, Major Doryan (Christopher Jones), who has been temporarily transferred from the trenches to the relatively minor disturbances in Ireland. Rosie's personal betrayal of her husband is mirrored by her father's betrayal of the old Irish Republican Army (IRA), whose men are captured as they land guns on the shore, with the active support of the community, for a future rebellion. In the dénouement of the long, episodic film Major Doryan shoots the IRA leader, and the villagers take their revenge on Rosie by tarring and feathering her, assaulting her, and cropping her hair.

Many critics focus on the representation of the "village idiot," Michael, played by John Mills, who serves as an important narrative driver for the film. His exaggerated grotesque features deliberately represent, according to some critics, the simian caricature of Victorian cartoons, which seek to affirm a colonial discourse. In spite of much criticism the film has helped promote a **touristic** image of Ireland and remains a classic archetypical representation of Irish identity at a specific period in time.

– S –

SALTWATER (2000). Based on his 1995 play *This Lime Tree Bower*, three overlapping monologues, **Conor McPherson**'s directorial debut *Saltwater* follows the experiences of three members of the Beneventi family (played by Brian Cox, **Peter McDonald**, and Laurence Kinlan) who run a chip shop in a small east coast Irish town. Frank (MacDonald) is determined to free his father from the fiscal clutches of the local gangster/gombeen man (played by **Brendan Gleeson**), while Joe (Kinlan) must defend himself from the (as it emerges unfair) charge of date rape. These stories are juxtaposed with that of Ray (Conor Mullen), a UCD lecturer, experiencing an early midlife crisis.

Critical reaction to the film was mixed: The film's humor deriving from McPherson's knack for the pithy one-liner and his eye for the absurd were welcomed, but the busy nature of the script, which saw often only tangentially related plotlines vying for screen time, suggested a reluctance to reconfigure the original stage script for the big screen. McPherson's own absence from the big screen since (apart from his adaptation of **Beckett**'s *Endgame* he has only made one other film—the poorly received *The Actors* in 2003), suggests that his heart remains with the theater.

SAMSON FILMS. Although certainly one of the busiest Irish-based production companies (the company was involved in producing 12 films in the decade starting in 1995), Samson is perhaps less oriented toward originating projects than it is toward acting as a coproduction partner or an executive producer on projects originally developed by other companies. Managing director David Collins has been involved in feature film production since the mid-1980s, making him an éminence grise by the standards of Irish film production.

As part-time film officer with the **Arts Council** of Ireland, Collins was responsible in 1976 for setting up the film festival that would ultimately lead to the establishment of the **Irish Film Theatre**. Moving into production in the 1980s, he established Samson Films to produce **Cathal Black**'s 1984 feature *Pigs*. A year later in 1985 he cofounded **Strongbow Film and Television Productions** with John Kelleher—which produced two major TV series and the (local) feature hit *Eat the Peach* in 1986. (Collins also cofounded Radius Television, now one of Ireland's largest independent TV companies.)

Samson has remained a substantial player in the post-1993 revitalization of the Irish audiovisual sector, developing links with film and television funding agencies in Ireland, Great Britain, and Europe, producing and coproducing projects with funding from Universal Pictures, British Sky Broadcasting, **Channel 4**, the **Irish Film Board**, the **Northern Irish Film and Television Commission**, the British Broadcasting Corporation (BBC), British Screen, Eurimages, and **Radio Telefís Éireann (RTÉ)**. It has also accessed significant sums via the **Section 481** tax investment scheme. Among the projects in which Samson has been involved are *Blind Flight*, *The Most Fer-*

tile Man in Ireland, I Went Down, A Further Gesture, and *The Disappearance of Finbar.*

SCREEN PRODUCERS IRELAND. SPI is the latest incarnation of a filmmakers' representative body, which first emerged in 1978. Such bodies had existed before this date—for example it was in large part due to lobbying from the Society of Film-Makers in Ireland that the state acted on the recommendations of the *Huston Report* and brought the Film Industry Bill to the Dáil in 1970. Although the activity of such bodies had little continuity, in 1977 the Association of Independent Producers (AIP) was established in the United Kingdom. The following year an AIP representative came to Ireland to address a group of Irish producers, which led directly to the establishment of an Irish AIP. The major achievement of the AIP was to successfully lobby for the introduction of a state board to support the film industry, culminating in the publication by Minister for Industry and Commerce Desmond O'Malley of the Film Board Bill in 1979. In 1980 the AIP together with the Irish Film and Television Guild and the Irish Transport and General Worker's Union (ITGWU) lobbied for changes to the proposed legislation—specifically demanding that the bill prohibit any **Irish film board** from funding overseas projects. Though unsuccessful in this regard, the AIP did succeed in broadening the board's responsibilities to include responsibility for an Irish film archive for training.

However, the AIP clashed almost immediately with the board following its decision to award half of its initial funds to **Neil Jordan**'s *Angel*. The tension between the two institutions came to a head during the Third International Festival of Celtic Film and Television held in Wexford in 1982, during which *Angel* was premiered. The AIP effectively boycotted the film, calling a committee meeting that coincided with the premiere.

In point of fact the *Angel* protest was simply the culmination of tensions between those individuals, such as **John Boorman**, who were associated with the **National Film Studios of Ireland** (NFSI) and members of the AIP, such as **Tiernan MacBride**. The AIP, echoing **Louis Marcus**'s 1967 *Irish Times* articles on **Ardmore**, had long argued that the NFSI were a drain on state funds that might otherwise have been available for investment in independent production and consequently regarded Boorman's chairmanship of the studios as a missed opportunity. Boorman, for his part, argued that he had consistently acted in a manner designed to serve Irish film best, citing his formation of the Motion Picture Company of Ireland as a case in point.

Given the AIP's position, however, Boorman's appointment (along with that of Louis Heelan and Robin O'Sullivan) to the Irish Film Board in 1982 was likely to provoke a confrontation. When the three-man board (technically the full board had seven members, but these were yet to be appointed) decided to fund *Angel* to the exclusion of any other applications (including several from AIP members), a clash became inevitable. Thus the Celtic festival witnessed AIP member **Bob Quinn** delivering a scathing attack on Boorman, followed by a formal AIP statement to the effect that the decision to fund *Angel* was "at best improper" (Dwyer, 1997). The statement acknowledged that a full board might well have made the same decision, but in the absence of such a board, there was at least the appearance of impropriety.

The long-term effect of the Celtic festival incident was to create a rift between Boorman and Jordan on the one hand and the AIP on the other, one that was only partially healed when AIP chair Tiernan MacBride and Irish Film and Television Guild chair Michael Algar were appointed to the board in 1982.

In the mid-1980s, the AIP became the AIFM, the Association of Independent Film-Makers, in an attempt to reflect the fact that the membership was made up of not merely producers but also directors. With the closure of the Film Board in 1987, the AIFM was effectively replaced in November of that year with Film Makers Ireland (FMI), a more structured body than the Film Board. It was funded by membership subscriptions and in its initial years driven by a clear objective to lobby for the restoration of the Film Board or a similar institution. Initially chaired by film lawyer James Hickey, the FMI committee also included **David Collins**, Tiernan MacBride, **Alan Gilsenan**, and Jane Gogan.

FMI's establishment was significant in that it expressly aimed to educate political representatives as to the nature of the film industry with a view to initiating a public debate about film policy that could occur outside the confines of the Department of the Taoiseach, which had taken responsibility for arts policy in 1986. In particular FMI began to advance the argument that, especially given the high level of unemployment that characterized the Irish economy in the late 1980s, film should be supported as a manufacturing industry capable of creating employment, but that state agencies like the Industrial Development Authority should acknowledge that, as of 1990, the industry was still in a developmental phase and would require some nurturing. Thus, for example, FMI argued that the state venture capital company NADCorp should fund, if not production, then at least film development in Ireland. This kind of thinking found its most advanced expression in a major report commissioned by FMI in 1991. The resulting *Independent Television Production Sector Report*, published in 1992, would become influential in shaping the variety of film policy decisions that occurred in 1992, including the decision to join **Eurimages**, the reestablishment of the Film Board, and the alteration of **Section 481**. Another 1993 decision placed FMI on an entirely new financial footing. Although FMI had employed a full-time administrator for some years, the body's income relied entirely on production companies taking out membership. The vagaries of the production climate in the late 1980s and early 1990s, however, meant that income fluctuated from year to year. This was in large part addressed as a byproduct of the establishment of the Independent Production Unit (IPU) at RTÉ in 1993. As part of the IPU's establishment, it was agreed that a sum equivalent to 1 percent of the value of independent commissions would be apportioned to FMI. This was subsequently augmented by funding from TG4 and a levy on Section 481–funded projects.

Consequently, FMI was able to broaden and professionalize its activities, and, as of 2005, the body has a staff of three. In 2003, the organization adopted a new moniker, Screen Producers Ireland, to reflect the fact that the activities of many of its members, and therefore the focus of SPI's negotiations, related to the television sector. Although SPI continues to act as a lobbying group on behalf of Irish production companies, campaigning for the retention of Section 481 and an increase in funding to the Irish Film Board, it has also become a de facto trade body, negotiating terms of trade with both RTÉ and TG4 on behalf of producers and drawing up collective agreements with trade unions relating to the crewing of feature film and television drama production. SPI also acts as an information resource for producers on upcoming commissioning opportunities and organizes seminars allowing producers to meet and exchange views with domestic and European commissioning bodies.

***THE SECRET OF ROAN INISH* (1994).** Director John Sayles, best known for issue-oriented films like *City of Hope* (1991) and *Matewan* (1987), wrote and directed the film in Ireland essentially because of favorable tax breaks. Based on an Irish folktale and set around 1946, the films opens with a distraught father who has lost his wife and child sending his remaining daughter to her grandparents' house in a rural region of Ireland to seek solace and a new beginning. The 10-year-old girl, Fiona (Jeni Courtney), becomes enchanted by the local folktale of the selkie, a magical creature that is a seal by day and a human by night, and persuades her grandfather to explore the myth by going to Roan Inish [the island of seals].

From the opening sequences a very clear opposition is established between the beauty of the island and the West and the impurity of the East and the city. This is witnessed through the innocent eyes of a young girl with the camera framed at her eye level as she searches for her father in the pub, with the voice of the barmaid affirming that this is nowhere to raise a child who needs fresh air and suggesting that he send her back to her grandparents. The child functions as a conduit to a lost past, through the sea and wild landscape.

The journey begins with her arriving at her grandparents' little house, where her grandfather (**Mick Lally**) confirms that the city is nothing but noise and dirt but also asserts that "love of the sea is a sickness." The girl's sojourn in this primitive but beautiful place is framed by a number of stories told by her grandfather and her cousin. The first of these narrates the shocking primal story of the cousin's little brother and how he was washed out to sea in his distinctive baby cradle. A flashback shows the islanders preparing to leave the island: As they do, a malevolent force of nature expresses its displeasure at this abandonment. The islanders are attacked by everyday seagulls, while unbeknownst to them the cradle is being taken by the tide out to sea. As they try to rescue the boy, the elements suddenly take a turn for the worse, with strong rain and winds and a darkening sky. Subsequently the islanders superstitiously believe that the sea had taken the infant because it was angry with them for leaving their homeland.

The trajectory of the fable works through this imbalance in nature as the islanders realize their loss, and the story finally resolves—after the intervention of the little girl—with their return to their island.

SECTION 481/SECTION 35. Section 481 of the Consolidated Finance Acts of 1997 (formerly Section 35 of the 1987 Finance Act) incentivizes investment in audiovisual production in Ireland (though not necessarily in Irish films) through the mechanism of a tax break. It is significant because it is by far the largest single source of indigenous capital for filmmaking in Ireland. Introduced in 1987 as a sop to the filmmaking community at a time when the **Irish Film Board** was being closed, its arrival represented a philosophical shift in state film policy away from direct state support toward providing incentives for the investment of private capital in the industry.

In its first six years of operation the impact of the incentive was relatively modest—only corporate entities could avail of the tax write-off, and the maximum annual investment was initially capped at IR £100,000. Consequently between 1987 and 1993 a relatively modest IR £11.5 million was raised by using the incentive. However, in 1993, as part of a package of measures aimed at developing the audiovisual sector in Ireland (which included the revival of the Irish Film Board), Section 481 was radically overhauled. The scale of the tax write-off was increased, as was the ceiling on individual investments. Perhaps most significantly the tax break was extended to individual investors: From 1993, individuals could write off film investments of up to IR £25,000 against income tax, a strong incentive to invest at a time when the marginal rate of personal income tax was 46 percent. The subsequent impact of the incentive on filmmaking activity in Ireland is almost impossible to overstate. Between 1993 and 2003 some €640 million in private capital was raised through the scheme, and virtually every film shot in Ireland since 1993 has availed of it.

Nonetheless, the figure of €640 million is somewhat misleading since Section 481 investors often expect the majority of their investment to be secured against income from presales (a commitment from a distributor or television company to buy rights to a film once it is completed). Since the producer must effectively hand over the presales income to Section 481 investors as soon as the film is completed, the actual gain to an average film's budget is in the order of 12–13.5 percent of the total production cost. (It should be noted that presales are not a legal prerequisite: Indeed, such risk aversion strategies on the part of investors is theoretically discouraged since the very existence of the Section 481 incentive is predicated on the assumption that any investment in film production involves a high degree of risk.)

Nonetheless, Irish producers insist that Section 481 is a key ingredient in maintaining production activity in Ireland and have actively mobilized to argue for the retention of the scheme whenever the Department of Finance has mooted winding it up. In this they have been supported by a range of studies, such as the *PricewaterhouseCoopers Report*, commissioned by the **Irish Film Board** and the Department of Arts in 2003, which concluded that the removal of Section 481 would lead to a 65 percent drop in the value of audiovisual production in Ireland and a 60 percent drop in related employment.

In more recent years a debate has emerged about the aims and objectives of the tax incentive, particularly with regard to whether Section 481 is intended primarily to support indigenous production or simply to incentivize audiovisual production in Ireland, regardless of a given production's national origins. In 1996, faced with the perception that large-scale foreign projects such as Mel Gibson's *Braveheart* were sucking up the bulk of Section 481 investment, the minister for finance at the time altered the operation of the incentive to target investment on indigenous productions. Working on the assumption that domestically originated projects were typically characterized by low (less than IR £10 million) budgets, the minister capped at IR £7.5 million the amount of Section 481 money that could be raised for any individual film.

By 2003, however, the *PricewaterhouseCoopers Report* concluded that the cap was beginning to seriously undermine Ireland's capacity to attract larger-budget productions from overseas. The report noted that the introduction of competing tax incentives in other countries (e.g., the United Kingdom, the Isle of Man, and Luxembourg) meant that Ireland was no longer "competitive" for projects with budgets in excess of €15 million. In consequence the report recommended that the per project cap on Section 481 finance be dramatically increased to €50 million to allow Ireland to continue drawing in projects on the scale of *Reign of Fire and King Arthur*. The cap was raised in December 2003, but the increase was limited to just €15 million, a figure that suggests that, officially at least, Section 481 is still considered as targeting low- to medium-budget films (i.e., the kind of films more likely to emerge from within Ireland than from without).

***SHAKE HANDS WITH THE DEVIL* (1959).** Starring the Irish American star James Cagney, together with Don Murray and Dana Wynter and filmed in Dublin and County Wicklow, the Michael Anderson film deals with the turbulent time in Irish history in the early 1920s, when Irish republican forces were fighting the British Army. An Irish American medical student, Kerry O'Shea (Murray), hopes to stay above the conflict, but he gets sucked in while trying to save a wounded friend. He is eventually drawn into the rebellion organization supported by his former professor, Sean Lenihan (James Cagney), who has "shaken hands with the Devil" and also actively supports the rebellion.

The historically based story becomes more complicated when Kerry falls in love with a beautiful English hostage (Dana Wynter), but eventually a ceasefire is called. The general (clearly based on Michael Collins but played by a much older Michael Redgrave) is sent over to broker a treaty in London, but many at home, including the professor, cannot stomach a deal that would lead the nation into civil war. This contentious historical story is of course reprised most effectively in later years by **Neil Jordan**'s *Michael Collins*.

SHAW, FIONA (1958–). Although, like many Irish actresses, Shaw is primarily renowned for her stage work, her recurring role as Aunt Petunia in the successful adaptations of the *Harry Potter* series has made her face more familiar to cinema goers. Born in Cork, she studied philosophy at University College Cork in the late 1970s before moving to London (where she has lived ever since) to study at the Royal Academy of Dramatic Art (RADA). From RADA she became a staple at the Royal Shakespeare Company (RSC), her angular visage and crisp delivery admirably adapted to playing a range of classical female protagonists.

In 1989 Deborah Warner, then one of the RSC's youngest directors, cast her in the title role of Sophocles' *Electra*. The production was the making of Shaw, and her astonishing performance won her a first Lawrence Olivier award. (She would win a second in 1994 for *Machinal*.) The Warner connection has subsequently been sustained on stage and screen: Shaw performed in **Richard II** (a much-maligned production) for Warner and had a relatively minor role in Warner's 1999 film version of Elizabeth Bowen's *The Last September*.

Shaw's first Irish role was in **Jim Sheridan**'s *My Left Foot* as Eileen Cole, arguably in part against type in that she was Christy Brown's (unrequited) love interest. She has subsequently worked extensively in television and on the large screen, where her old-world looks have frequently seen her cast in adaptations of classic plays and novels—*Jane Eyre*, *Persuasion*, *Anna Karenina*—although she has also appeared in a number of contemporary Hollywood dramas—*Three Men and a Little Lady* (1990) and *Undercover Blues* (1993).

Her often severe expression found its natural home in **Neil Jordan**'s *The Butcher Boy*, where she plays the straight-laced returned emigrant Mrs. Nugent, the object of the eponymous protagonist's envy and hatred. However, although she is regarded as willing to undertake massive risks in her theater work—in physical, artistic, and financial terms (she cofounded her enthusiastically received performance of T. S. Eliot's "The Wasteland")—it is arguable that she has not yet found the screen role to tax her in a similar fashion.

SHERIDAN, JIM (1949–). As the eldest of seven children born into a working-class area of Dublin, Jim was no stranger to poverty. Key incidents in his lifetime include the death of his brother Frankie in 1967 when he was only 11 years of age. This traumatic incident informed the personal script written by Jim and his daughters, Naomi and Kirsten (who directed *Disco Pigs*), for *In America* (2002). He graduated from university in 1972 and married the same year. Between 1973 and 1974, he toured Ireland with **Neil Jordan** and their Children's T Company. Following several theatrical performances and helping to develop the project theater company with his brother Peter (who later directed *Borstal Boy*), he left Ireland in 1981 to manage the Irish Rebel Arts Centre in New York.

It was not till 1990 that Sheridan made his first film, *My Left Foot*, based on the autobiography of Christy Brown, a physically disabled writer with cerebral palsy who wrote and painted with his foot. The

film celebrates Christy's individual determination to overcome physical limitations and lead a creative life, while at the same time highlighting his belligerent and complex personality. Most especially the
importance of a close-knit community is dramatized through scenes
of football (soccer) in the street and drinking in the local public
house, personified by his drunken and authoritarian father (**Ray
McAnally**). His father eventually becomes proud of his handicapped
son, who first showed his innate intelligence by scrawling "mother"
with chalk using his foot. *My Left Foot* was nominated for five **Academy Awards**, and both Daniel Day-Lewis and **Brenda Fricker** won
for Best Actor and Best Supporting Actress, respectively, with their
deeply moving performances. This enormous first success had a
strong influence on Sheridan's career path and on Irish filmmaking
generally.

Virtually all of Sheridan's subsequent films deal with emotive Irish
issues, often structured allegorically in terms of familial conflict. In
1990 he directed *The Field*—adapted from the play by John B.
Keane—which tells the story of Bull McCabe (**Richard Harris**), a
tenant farmer who has spent his life cultivating a small rented field in
a barren and inhospitable landscape. Then, in 1992, he wrote the
screenplay for Mike Newell's film *Into the West*, a fable of two **Traveller** children escaping from Dublin to the mythic West.

Sheridan and his producer Arthur Lappin set up a production company called **Hell's Kitchen**, which produced *In the Name of the Father*, a film that focuses on the miscarriage of justice with the so-
called Birmingham Six, who were illegally convicted of the awful
bombings in Britain. The film was nominated for seven Oscars but
unfortunately did not win any. In 1996 Sheridan assisted the production of the **Terry George**–directed *Some Mother's Son*, which dealt
with the 1981 hunger strike in Northern Ireland's Long Kesh prison.
In 1997, he directed another Northern Ireland–themed film, *The
Boxer* (again starring Daniel Day-Lewis), a paean to the need for active citizenship to encourage people to avoid succumbing to tit-for-
tat sectarian violence.

Following this Sheridan worked as producer on *Agnes Browne*
(1999), directed by Anjelica Huston, and *On the Edge* (2000), directed by **John Carney**. Audiences had to wait until 2002 for his autobiographical film *In America*, which he wrote and directed. With

his long-standing theater background, Sheridan is frequently associated with strong acting roles—particularly those played by the method-style actor Daniel Day-Lewis—as well as emotionally strong and well-told stories that appeal to mass audiences. He is a very good self-publicist and in several interviews talks about the need to make Irish stories "universal" so that they resonate with mass audiences. He does not accept the notion that "local" and indigenous Irish films cannot also be universal and successful in their appeal. For some this is his major strength as a filmmaker and ensures that his films remain provocative and enticing, while other critics question his extensive use of emotionalism and contrast his more limited output with the wider and eclectic oeuvre of Neil Jordan.

But such a local Irish debate cannot take away from Sheridan's global importance and his very successful filmmaking over the past decade or so, ensuring his position as one of the most important Irish filmmakers ever to come out of the country. His production profile will hopefully expand greatly in the years to come. His latest film project—50 Cent biopic *Get Rich or Die Tryin*—certainly suggests that he is looking to work with subject matter outside Ireland and the Irish.

SHORT FILMS. Inevitably, given the absence of an infrastructure for filmmaking until the 1980s, the vast majority of early indigenous Irish cinema took the form of shorts. This was in any case the global default format for cinema until the 1910s. However, for the most part early (i.e., pre-1970) Irish shorts, as exemplified by the work of filmmakers like **Louis Marcus** and **Patrick Carey**, were almost exclusively **documentary** nonfiction. Thus, even in the short form, filmed fiction appeared only very sporadically prior to the 1980s. Notable examples in that period include the **Irish Film Society** production of *Foolmate* (1940) and Hilton Edwards's Oscar-nominated *Return to Glennascaul* (1951).

At an official level, however, the short was regarded as a crucial stepping-stone on the path to developing an indigenous industry. The 1942 *Report of the Inter-Departmental Committee on the Film Industry* assumed that, initially at least, the main scope for domestic production would be confined to short films, and much of the report's chapter on production was concerned with the practicalities of establishing such production on a firm footing. It conceded that the developing tendency toward double features and cinema verité had had a deleterious impact on the market for short films but noted that the majority of cinemas still required such films to complete single-feature programs. Thus in 1942 short production was considered very much an end in itself.

This was no longer the case a quarter of a century later when the 1968 *Report of the Film Industry Committee* was published. Although the report also emphasized the need to support short production —indeed the report spent more time discussing shorts than any other form—it also betrayed a tendency to regard shorts as a stopgap measure. Thus although Irish fiction shorts could "provide the domestic audience with a reflection of themselves in that special way that only fiction can achieve," this was to be resorted to only "in the absence of a significant volume of Irish *feature* films." In case the point was not clear enough, the report also noted that short films provided filmmakers "*with potential for making feature films* practical, technical and creative training and experience which a small country could not as readily provide in any other way" ((Film Industry Committee, 1968; italics added). As a consequence, the report recommended that a fund of between £55,000 and £75,000 be provided annually to support short production in Ireland.

Although ultimately nothing came of the report, institutional developments in the 1970s—in particular the beginnings of **Arts Council** film funding—saw the start of more consistent short fiction production. Not surprisingly, the same individuals who would later produce the first wave of indigenous features were associated with many of the shorts produced in this era. **Joe Comerford** directed his first short—*Swan Alley*—in 1969 and followed it with *Emtigon* a year later. In 1976, aided by an **Arts Council** grant, **Cathal Black** directed *Wheels* from a John McGahern short story. A year later **Bob Quinn** directed the comic *Self Portrait with Red Car* featuring painter Brian Bourke, and in 1978, **Kieran Hickey** made his fiction debut with the well-received gothic horror *A Child's Voice*.

From 1984 on, the presence of the **Irish Film Board** began to complement the Arts Council's activities. In 1984 they cofunded Joe Comerford's *Waterbag*, an experimental film that acted as a pilot for his later feature *Reefer and the Model*, and a year later partially financed **Thaddeus O'Sullivan**'s *The Woman Who Married Clark Gable*, based on Sean O'Faolain's short story. Other beneficiaries of Film Board support included **Alan Gilsenan** for *Eh Joe* (1986), City Vision's *Sometime City* (1986), and Siobhan Toomey's *Boom Babies* (1987).

As the 1980s progressed, third-level institutions also became key players in increased short production. Trinity College's film society had been involved with shorts to varying degrees since the late 1960s—*Swan Allen* received its premiere at the Film Society—while **Alan Gilsenan**'s first short, *Shelia* (1986), was credited as a coproduction involving the Film Society. However, it was not until the advent of formal education courses in film production at the National College of Art and Design (NCAD), Dun Laoghaire, and at the Dublin Institute of Technology (DIT) in the 1980s that levels of short fiction production really took off. In 1987 alone, DIT students produced seven shorts, a level of output that Dun Laoghaire matched and surpassed in the following years. Between 1987 and 1989 in particular, Dun Laoghaire shorts showcased a number of directors who would go on to become significant figures in film and television production, including Liam O'Neill (*Frankie and Johnny* in 1987), Kieron J. Walsh (*Goodbye Picadilly* in 1988), and Declan Recks (*Big Swinger* in 1989). The last of these, a comedy starring Tom Hickey as a pirate radio station owner and operator, became a minor hit on the festival circuit and—unusually for the time—was broadcast on domestic television. Meanwhile the early 1990s saw **John Moore**'s debut when he worked on graduation films at DIT and then directed the well-received *Jack's Bicycle*.

Indeed, by the early 1990s, the tropes of student films were sufficiently well established to allow one DIT student, Alan Duffy, to make a student film parodying other student films. The appropriately titled *Student Film* took as its subject the production of a student film called *Belly of a Convent Girl*.

The closure of the Film Board in 1987, however, severely curtailed both short and feature activity, and as a result directors who might have expected to be making their first long-form projects found themselves concentrating on shorter but no less ambitious shoots. **Paddy Breathnach** made an immediate impact with *A Stone in the Heart* in 1991, as did Lenny Abrahamson with *3 Joes*, which won the Best Irish and European Short awards at the 1991 Cork Film Festival.

However, in 1995, short production received another boost when the reformed Film Board instituted the Short Cuts scheme, which provided relatively generous funding for short production. In part as a consequence in 1995 approximately 40 short films were produced in Ireland. Ironically then, short production in Ireland has been at its healthiest in an era when there is virtually no commercial market for such films. This raises the question of what the role of the form is for contemporary Irish cinema. The invariable answer is that they are calling cards, a response that exacerbates the tendency—noted in the 1968 report discussed above—to regard them as a stepping-stone to feature production rather than an end in themselves.

However, if this is true of the majority of shorts produced, Irish film-makers have continued to produce work that acknowledges the short as a legitimate form in its own right characterized by a unique aesthetic. Key examples of this in the past decade or so include Kieron Walsh's *Shooting to Stardom* (1992), Robert Quinn's *Detour* (1994), John Moore's *He Shoots, He Scores* (1995), **Damien O'Donnell**'s *35 Aside* (1995), Alan Gilsenan's *Zulu 9* (2001), and Martin McDonagh's *Six Shooter* (2004).

Indeed, there are filmmakers who have concentrated on the short fiction form and who have used it to work through subjects in a manner that the feature form cannot. Orla Walsh and Stephen Burke provide good examples of this approach. Both have worked in other forms—Walsh, for example, has directed television comedy, and Burke has directed long-form drama for **Radio Telefís Éireann (RTÉ)**—but their short-form output is arguably their most interesting. Walsh directed three shorts in the 1990s—*The Visit* (1992), *Bent Out of Shape* (1995), and *Blessed Fruit* (1999)—all of which explored various aspects of sexual politics in contemporary Ireland in a much more nuanced fashion than contemporaneous features generally achieve. *The Visit*—which follows the wife of a republican prisoner as she visits her husband to inform him that she is pregnant with another man's child—stands out in this regard, raising and exploring a range of ideological issues related to nationalist and feminist politics.

Stephen Burke's two shorts *After '68* (1993) and *'81* (1996) are more overtly connected. The first follows events in Northern Ireland from the civil rights marches in 1968 to Bloody Sunday in 1972, while the second follows the 1981 hunger strikes through the eyes of a French camera crew covering the story. Both films (but particularly *After '68*) engage more directly with the complex realities of living through the **"troubles"** than better-known long-form counterparts such as **High Boot Benny** and **In the Name of the Father**.

SILENT GRACE (2001). Like **H3**, partially funded by both the **Irish Film Board** and the **Northern Ireland Film Commission**, Maeve Murphy's *Silent Grace* traces the experiences of republican female prisoners in Armagh Prison during the early 1980s (the period of the hunger strikes). The narrative follows Eileen (**Orla Brady**), the leader of the Irish Republican Army (IRA) women prisoners, as she encounters the apolitical Áine, imprisoned for car theft, and subsequently traces the development of their friendship. In contrast to *H3*, however, *Silent Grace* is a much more even-handed take on the politics of the period. Thus although prison officers are represented as brutal, this is implicitly accounted for by the backdrop of an assassination campaign being waged by republicans against those officers. Meanwhile the prison governor (Conor Mullen) is portrayed as concerned and even mildly sympathetic toward the women.

SNAKES AND LADDERS (1996). A relatively conventional, almost soap-styled story about two young roommates in search of love, framed against a well-conceived social realist urban environment, which includes a strong comic performance by **Rosaleen Linehan** as Nora. Most of the film's energy comes from the relationship between the two women (Pom Boyd and **Gina Moxley**) and their attempts to succeed as street entertainers, alongside a male love interest in the form of the stand-up comic Sean Hughes. An amiable farce, this very light comedy directed by Trish McAdam lacks the dramatic passion necessary to elevate it above a regular episode of a soap story. Nevertheless, the film is appealing to its gendered audience and confidently tells its engaging story.

THE SNAPPER (1993). Adapted from **Roddy Doyle's** trilogy of Barrytown novels (which also includes **The Commitments** and **The Van**), the film stars **Tina Kellegher** as Sharon, the eldest daughter of a big working-class family in Dublin, who stuns family and friends with the news that she is pregnant. Officially, the pregnancy is the result of a one-night stand with a Spanish sailor, but the film reveals that the actual father is a middle-aged neighbor who took advantage of Sharon's inebriated state outside a pub one night. **Colm Meaney**'s turn as Sharon's father is a comic tour de force, especially in his reaction to his daughter's refusal to reveal the true identity of the father. The comic vernacular and humor of the piece as directed by Stephen Frears is extremely effective and contrasts with the serious realism of the representation of teenage pregnancy in *Hush-a-Bye Baby* in the North. The film was unusual in Ireland in that having been commissioned by and screened on British Broadcasting Corporation (BBC) television, public demand led to a subsequent and successful cinema run.

SOCIETY OF FILM-MAKERS IN IRELAND. *See* SCREEN PRODUCERS IRELAND.

SOME MOTHER'S SON **(1996).** A widowed teacher and life-long pacifist, Kathleen Quigley (Helen Mirren), is shaken out of her comfortable existence when her son is captured after a shoot-out with the British Army during the Northern "**troubles.**" Along with the mother of another prisoner, Annie Higgins (**Fionnula Flanagan**), whose husband was killed by the British and hence accepts her son's political stance, Kathleen finds herself suddenly brought into the middle of Northern Ireland's political conflict; the women are forced to the center of an epic struggle when their sons go on a hunger strike demanding political recognition for their armed struggle.

The film, directed by **Terry George**, aided by **Jim Sheridan**, is a very earnest and well-meaning production. It deals with one of the most dramatic times in Northern Ireland politics. The script tries to focus on personal stories, as a mother has to take responsibility for the impending death of her own child. Informed that she has the right to end her son's hunger strike, the broader political arguments between the clergy, leaders of Irish Republican Army (IRA), and others become muted as the mother—asserting her primal apolitical privilege to save her flesh and blood—steps out of the maelstrom and signs the document to take her son out of danger of imminent death.

340 • *SONG FOR A RAGGY BOY*

Inevitably, the film came in for criticism for failing to overtly or even tacitly critique the actions that led the hunger strikers to be in prison in the first place. The response reflected the extent to which, even in a postceasefire era, it was politically not just untenable but almost inconceivable to represent members of groups such as the IRA as anything other than murdering psychopaths. As a counterview, *Some Mother's Son* arguably fulfilled the function of facilitating debate on the issue, making it possible to conceive of the IRA as human beings. Indeed, arguably the film advanced the pacifist argument that dying for an abstract concept of freedom (defined in terms of freedom from one state that is simply replaced by another) is not a worthwhile endeavor.

SONG FOR A RAGGY BOY (2003). Directed by Aisling Walsh and adapted from Patrick Galvin's autobiography, the film feeds into the current anti-**Catholic** fixation in popular culture driven by a series of clerical scandals. The film takes place in an era when corporal punishment was the norm in most Irish schools. It is based on the well-documented extreme violence inflicted upon young boys who were unfortunate enough to have been incarcerated in Borstals, run by religious brothers and priests during the late 1930s and 1940s.

We are introduced to William Franklin (**Aidan Quinn**) as the chief protagonist, who has lost the love of his life while fighting for the International Brigade in the Spanish Civil War. This is revealed through flashbacks of atrocities and is also (over)signalled by his psychological need for solitude and physical resignation. The only job he can get in the rural Ireland of 1939 is teaching English to poor and troubled children in a boys' reformatory school run by the Catholic Church. The audience is introduced to this troubled institution through his innocent eyes. The film is somewhat reminiscent of Peter Weir's *Dead Poet's Society* (1989) and others that foreground the positive role of the teacher; William tries to spark his charges to find their voice through literature, in this case Spanish love poetry. Furthermore, they demonstrate their group skills by making a beautiful crib for the local church for Christmas.

The story line constructs very strong, if overly black-and-white, character conflicts, particularly the evil Brother John (Iain Glen) as dean of discipline, who has been appointed by the bishop and therefore has to be accepted by the otherwise benevolent director of the institution. He stalks the children and expounds on the need to treat them as animals ("since that is what they are!"). A fellow brother, who appears less sadistic, is later shown to be equally if not more malevolent. Both "bad apples" are eventually taken away, following an extremely sadistic murder, and Franklin has to decide what is best for the children who are left behind.

SOUTHPAW (1997). The feature-length documentary, directed by Liam McGrath, follows the experiences of Francis Barrett, a 19-year-old **Traveller** from Galway, who trains as a boxer and dreams of going to the Olympic Games. Against all the odds, especially as an outsider in Irish society, he eventually succeeds in his ambition. The film follows Barrett through the qualification rounds, culminating in the final trip to Atlanta in the United States, where the Olympics are hosted. In particular the story explores his personal relationship with his trainer and close friend, Chick Gillen. In an era when the documentary form has become almost the exclusive province of television, *Southpaw* is—thus far—almost unique in recent Irish cinema history in that it was expressly intended for cinematic release.

SPECIAL WORKING GROUP ON THE FILM PRODUCTION INDUSTRY. *See REPORT TO THE TAOISEACH, MR. ALBERT REYNOLDS, T. D., 24 NOLLAIG, 1992.*

SPIN THE BOTTLE (2002). Directed by Ian Fitzgibbon, *Spin the Bottle* revives for the big screen the character of Rats, first introduced in the hit **Radio Telefís Éireann (RTÉ)** comedy *Paths to Freedom*. Newly released from prison, Rats (Michael McElhatton, who also cowrote the series and film) enlists members of his former band (**Peter McDonald** and Donal O'Kelly) in a farcical attempt to cure his aunt's terminal obesity by raising money for a trip to Lourdes. The reformed band eventually gate-crashes a national television talent show, leading to a further spell in prison. In contrast to other films set in contemporary working-class Dublin, *Spin the Bottle* is played strictly for laughs: Although the character Rats is ultimately portrayed as sympathetic, there is little attempt to place Rat's recidivist behavior in any kind of larger social or political context.

STARFISH (2004). This quirky narrative directed by Stephen Kane tells the story of Ella (Ailigh Symons), whose relationship with her boyfriend begins to collapse after he is laid off from his software engineering job. In the café where she works as a waitress she befriends a lonely science fiction writer (Pat McGrath), who is obsessed with a fish tank (and the starfish in particular) in the restaurant. The narrative subsequently degenerates into a series of comic vignettes involving a hitchhiking nun and shoplifting as the unlikely trio escape the city with their fish to release it into a sea in the south.

STEMBRIDGE, GERRY (1960–). Raised in Limerick, where he remained until the end of secondary school, Stembridge moved to Dublin to study arts at University College Dublin, where he was very active in student theater productions. He graduated in 1981 and three years later joined **Radio Telefís Éireann (RTÉ)** as a producer-director. He remained there for five years, making a name for himself by writing and performing on a political lampoon radio show called *Scrap Saturday* in the late 1980s. Having written and directed a major one-off drama for RTÉ—*The Truth about Claire*—examining the politics of the abortion debate in Ireland, he made his debut as a feature writer and director with *Guiltrip* in 1995.

Stembridge followed *Guiltrip* with *Bad Day at Black Rock*, a single drama for RTÉ exploring racism and multiculturalism in Ireland. During this time he began to write a romantic comedy, *About Adam* (2000), a seldom seen genre in Irish film production—given the preoccupation in much Irish cinema with identifying social and political problems of the past and the concomitant failure to reflect the growing reality of Celtic Tiger Dublin with its universal cosmopolitanism. During this prolific period Stembridge also served as screenwriter on **Thaddeus O'Sullivan**'s *Ordinary Decent Criminal* (2000) and **Pat Murphy**'s *Nora* (2000).

STONEMAN, ROD (1953–). Rod Stoneman has been a key figure in Irish film production since he was appointed chief executive of the reestablished **Irish Film Board** in 1993. Born in London in 1953, Stoneman grew up in Devon in southwest England. He studied English literature at the University of Kent before completing a postgraduate diploma with the film unit at the renowned Slade College of

Art in London. Having spent some years teaching film in art colleges, working for the British Arts Council, and compiling catalogs for film exhibition, he then ran the Arnolfini art-house cinema in Bristol.

In 1982, Stoneman joined the fledgling **Channel 4**, initially on a consultative basis, but rose to become a commissioning editor with the channel's groundbreaking Independent Film and Video section, sometimes referred to internally as the "channel within the channel" because of the wide range of material made there. During his time at Channel 4, his department commissioned a number of documentaries and low-budget fiction projects dealing with Ireland, including Margo Harkin's teenage pregnancy drama *Hush-a-Bye Baby* and **Joe Comerford**'s *High Boot Benny*, which subsequently became one of the first productions to receive Film Board support.

Although the board members themselves officially take funding decisions at the Irish Film Board, the chief executive of the board has a substantial input into how those decisions are made. Stoneman's philosophy in this regard sought to find a middle ground between, on the one hand, offering funding on a purely commercial, economic basis and, on the other, acting as a purely cultural agency funding film "artists." This philosophy found expression in the phrase *radical pluralism*, a concept borrowed from the early days at Channel 4. In practice this meant supporting the widest possible range of films. Thus the first review of the Film Board's activities included a (Stoneman-penned) (mis)quote from Mao Tse Tsung: "Let a thousand flowers bloom and a thousand schools of thought contend" (Irish Film Board, 1995).

Stoneman justified such radical pluralism on more than simply academic grounds. Starting from the pragmatic basis that the Irish film industry was artisanal in nature (in contrast to the industrial approach of Hollywood), Stoneman argued that the only possible means of maintaining the authenticity and integrity of Irish cinema while keeping an eye on the bottom line was to produce the greatest possible variety of smaller films. For Stoneman, the strength of artisanal film-making lay in its unpredictability, which increased the chances of capturing the public imagination (and thus achieving commercial success) in a fashion that did not require the huge production and marketing resources brought to bear by Hollywood. Stoneman noted, for example, that *The Crying Game* was better geared (the ratio of production cost to exhibition return) than *Jurassic Park*. Indeed, he argued that Hollywood itself had briefly recognized this in the wake of the success of Dennis Hopper's *Easy Rider* (1969), which engendered a wave of small-scale films produced on the basis that although the majority would fail commercially, those that succeeded would earn enough to cover the rest.

In practice, Stoneman's philosophy was exemplified by the early simultaneous funding of the low-budget Irish-language feature *An Gabhan Saor* and **Pat O'Connor**'s overtly commercial *Circle of Friends*. Certainly the remarkable recoupment rate enjoyed by the board during its first year of existence (£200,000 from an investment of £945,000 or 25 percent—an unusually high rate of return for an arts funding body) suggested a certain commercial savvy on Stoneman's part, although such a high rate of return inevitably diminished over his decade as chief executive officer.

Over the course of his tenure Stoneman adopted a broad interpretation of the board's legal mandate to assist and encourage filmmaking in Ireland "by any means it considers appropriate" (Irish Film Board, 1995). Recognizing that production was only one of the issues faced by Irish filmmakers, Stoneman commissioned research on the distribution of Irish (and other European) films in the United States, prepared an analysis of rural cinema exhibition (and of the viability of an art-house cinema network), and examined the Irish facilities and postproduction base. By 1998 Stoneman was laying increasing emphasis on the marketing and development of Irish films while defending the cultural and artistic role of cinema against the *Kilkenny Report*'s emphasis on developing the audiovisual sector as a mainly business undertaking.

By the time Stoneman resigned from the board in 2003 (to be succeeded by **Mark Woods**), he could point to its involvement in the production of more than 100 features, 60 documentaries, eight television series, and 150 short films. The board had grown from a three-person £1 million operation in 1993 to one with 16 staff and €12 million in 2003. Perhaps his most significant achievement, however, lay in the simple fact of the board's continued existence, the result of a successful gauging of how to reconcile the pressure to create audiovisual activities that have significant economic and employment outcomes with the need to support cultural effects.

STRATEGIC DEVELOPMENT OF THE IRISH FILM AND TELEVISION INDUSTRY, 2000–2010. The Film Industry Strategic Review Group was appointed by Minister for Arts and Culture Síle de Valera in June 1998, to assess strategies for the ongoing development of the audiovisual sector in Ireland in the context of the anticipated expiration of **Section 481** in April 1999. However, in addition to that short-term question, de Valera tasked the group (which she characterized as a "think-tank") with the development of a decade-long roadmap for the development of the industry. It was originally envisaged that the report would address the Section 481 question by September 1998, well in advance of the April 1999 deadline, but as the work of the group expanded, the minister decided to extend Section 481's existence by one year to allow the group to complete its full report.

The ambition of the final report was reflected in the scale of activity that informed it. Chaired by accountant Ossie Kilkenny (who would subsequently be appointed chair of the **Irish Film Board**), the group had 17 members, representing groups such as **RTÉ, TV3, Film Makers Ireland**, the **Film Institute of Ireland**, and the Departments of Arts and of Finance. Independent producers were particularly well represented, accounting for six of the positions. Furthermore, in the course of drawing up its own report, the group would commission two more of its own: one from consultants **Indecon**, who three years earlier had written a report casting doubts over the efficacy of Section 481, and a second comparing costs of film production in the United Kingdom and Ireland.

Despite these efforts, for the most part the resulting report made unsurprising reading—its recommendations could best be summarized as "more of the same." It proposed an expanded, better-resourced Film Board with a greater emphasis on strategic business development and marketing. These additional activities were to be funded by a levy on cinema tickets and the sale and rental of videos and DVDs. Similarly the report recommend extending Section 481 for seven years, although it also suggested increasing the tax relief on such investments from 80 to 100 percent for investments in projects with a budget of £4 million or less (i.e., for indigenous films).

The most notable innovation was in the stress laid on the development of stronger production companies characterized by greater scale, capitalization, business acumen, and editorial expertise. While acknowledging the role played by smaller companies, the group emphasized the need to create companies capable of competing on the international market. Implicitly pointing to the Hollywood model, the report stressed the importance of supporting companies that developed libraries that could be exploited over a period of time. This support would be funded by the introduction of a special equity fund that would be established along the lines of Section 481. Private investors would be encouraged to make equity investments in production companies by being allowed to write off such investments against tax.

The report was published in August 1999, but despite the status theoretically accorded to its conclusions, it had little practical impact. Given that the group envisaged that most of the developments recommended would be funded from taxation, the Irish filmmaking community awaited the December 1999 budget (the first after the report's publication) with anticipation. To their dismay virtually none of the recommendations were adopted, although the minister for finance Charlie McCreevy did extend Section 481 for a further five years. Filmmakers were particularly incensed at the failure to increase to 100 percent tax relief on Section 481 projects with budgets of less than £4 million. In the longer term the Film Board did receive an increase in exchequer funding that allowed it to broaden its activities in a manner that at least in part reflected the report's recommendations, although the idea that this might be funded by a film and video levy was never instituted. Ultimately, then, the main long-term effect of the report was the intangible impact of its emphasis on developing film production as a business. Although the report did acknowledge the cultural significance of cinema—and interviewed a number of cultural commentators on that subject—it devoted only 3 of its 122 pages to that perspective.

STRICK, JOSEPH (1923–). Although as a director he has made only 11 films in nearly 40 years, those he has made—including two **James Joyce** adaptations—have rarely been less than interesting. Born in Philadelphia to Jewish immigrants from eastern Europe, his earliest filmmaking experience was gained as an aerial photographer with the United States Air Force. In 1948 while working at the *Los Angeles*

Times, he made his first short film, *Muscle Beach*, a satire on the bodybuilder culture.

From 1954 to 1959 he worked on *The Savage Eye*, an award-winning semidocumentary study of the emptiness of Los Angeles culture. In 1963, Strick directed his first adaptation, *The Balcony*, based on Jean Genet's novel set in a brothel.

In 1967, Strick came to Ireland to make **Ulysses**, which he first read when he was 16. The film rights had become available in 1964, and despite competition from 20th Century Fox, Strick secured them for US$75,000. Although he initially planned to make an 18¾-hour film, which would have included every episode from the book, financial constraints saw the running time cut to just over two hours. By Strick's account the shooting of the film was almost prematurely ended when British Lion, who was financing the film, informed Strick that it was withholding funds despite the fact that shooting had begun. Happily for Strick, the threat coincided with a three-week bank strike in Dublin, so he continued to write checks in the knowledge that the recipients could not attempt to cash them. By the time the strike concluded, Strick simply presented British Lion with the fait accompli of the written checks, which the company agreed to honor.

Although the screenplay was nominated for an Oscar in 1967, *Ulysses* was refused a certificate by both the **censor** and the Film Appeals Board in 1967. (Resubmitted in 1974 to new censor Dermot Breen, it was promptly banned again.) Strick would go on to win an Oscar for Best Short Documentary three years later for *Interviews with My Lai Veterans*.

Through the 1970s Strick continued to direct films looking at the underside of the American dream, including an adaptation of Henry Miller's *Tropic of Cancer* (1970) and the critically well-received *Road Movie* (1974), a Cassavettesean tale of two truckers and a prostitute. Ironically his more radical work was subsidized by his work as a producer on more wholesome fair such as *Ring of Bright Water* (1969).

In 1977 he returned to Joyce to film *A Portrait of the Artist as a Young Man* with Bosco Hogan as Stephen Dedalus, **T. P. McKenna**, John Gielgud, **Rosaleen Linehan**, Maureen Potter, and Niall Buggy. His next visit to Ireland in 2000 to direct Aristophanes's *Ladies Day* at the Granary Theatre in Cork happily coincided with the decision of then censor Sheamus Smith to finally pass *Ulysses* without cuts.

STRONGBOW FILMS. Despite having already established **Samson Films** in 1983, David Collins partnered with John Kelleher the following year to establish Strongbow in large part with a view to raising funds for what would prove to be the company's only feature film, ***Eat the Peach***. Strongbow was designed to take advantage of the recently introduced **Business Expansion Scheme** (BES), which allowed private individuals to buy shares in BES-registered companies and to claim tax relief on that investment. Using the BES scheme, Strongbow was ultimately able to raise £1.4 million for *Eat the Peach* from 300 investors, a sum that was subsequently augmented by £600,000 from **Channel 4** and a further £100,000 from the **Irish Film Board**.

Buoyed by the success of *Eat the Peach* in the domestic market, the company went on to produce a number of drama series for television and succeeded in finding an American distributor (Skouras Pictures, which had previously enjoyed some success with Peter Greenaway's *A Zed and Two Noughts*) for *Eat the Peach*. However, although the film's initial single-print release in 1987 was considered a success (in its first week the film's per screen take was well in excess of the top movie in the United States at the time—Paul Verhoeven's *Robocop*), when the release was broadened to 11 screens at the height of the release, it failed to sustain its performance and was pulled from the U.S. market after six weeks, having earned just over $200,000.

Thereafter, although Strongbow was involved in coproducing at least one more feature (*Inisfree*), it mainly focused on television production, especially after partnering with Green Apple productions, which brought a track record in popular, mass appeal to the joint enterprise.

SUBOTICA ENTERTAINMENT. Named after a city in northern Serbia, Subotica Entertainment Ltd. grew out of Subotica Films, which was established in 1994 by Tristan Orpen Lynch, who has worked as a television and commercial producer since 1989. Subotica Films's first major feature production was ***Night Train***, starring John Hurt and Brenda Blethyn, and directed by Lynch's father, John, himself a former **Radio Telefís Éireann (RTÉ)** director. In June 1999 Lynch and British producer Dominic Wright, along with Paul Moore, the managing director of the Ardmore sound postproduction facility, became directors of Subotica Entertainment, a new company set up to produce feature films and large-scale television dramas. Wright had worked in broadcast television since the late 1980s, first on **Channel 4**'s *Week in Politics* program, and then as production manager of the **Strongbow**-produced Spanish-Irish coproduction *Innisfree*. He subsequently worked with London-based financiers Film Trustees before moving to Dublin to coproduce *Spaghetti Slow* in 1995. He has subsequently been based in Ireland and began working with Subotica in 1996 while maintaining an occasional sideline as a film and television actor.

Since the establishment of Subotica Entertainment, the company has produced a series of features and large-scale television dramas. These include David Caffrey's *On The Nose* and the eight-part period drama *Random Passage* directed by John N. Smith. In 2003 Subotica released Aisling Walsh's *Song for a Raggy Boy,* which became a major festival hit. Arguably the highest-profile work within Ireland, however, has been their productions of two political thriller series for Irish Television, *Proof* and *Proof 2*, which aired in 2004 and 2005 and achieved impressive ratings for RTÉ.

THE SUN, THE MOON AND THE STARS (1996). A rarity in recent Irish cinema, in that it was written and directed by a woman, Geraldine Creed, and is also slightly unusual in that it is a coming-of-age film focusing on young women rather than men. Mo (**Gina Moxley**) abandons her job and her home in Dublin, bringing her two daughters, Dee (Aisling Corcoran) and Shelly (**Elaine Cassidy**), to live in a small seaside resort to escape the unreliable men in their lives, namely the children's father and Mo's employer. Moderately well received by local critics, who were bemused by the casting, which included Angie Dickinson and then heartthrob Jason Donovan, the film received a short and limited Irish release.

SWEETY BARRETT (1999). Barrett (**Brendan Gleeson**) is a giant of a man with the mind of a child. Having lost his job with the traveling circus, he arrives in the seedy port of Dockery, looking for work. He befriends a local woman and develops a close bond with her six-year-old son, Conor, who loves his new playmate. An easy target in this corrupt town, Sweety becomes embroiled in a smuggling operation, which unleashes a spiral of dangerous and unexpected events. In a final twist, Sweety triumphs as the unlikely hero against the evil machinations of detective Bone (**Liam Cunningham**). Writer-director Stephen Bradley's feature debut was heavily criticized as being narratively unconvincing, a criticism frequently aimed at much auteurist-based Irish film, which generally lacks the extensive script doctoring and honing of story lines of the more small-scale art-based films.

– T –

TEMPLE FILMS. *See* ELEMENT FILMS.

THIS IS MY FATHER **(1998).** In this well-regarded Irish-American film directed by Paul Quinn, James Caan plays a burned-out American high school teacher whose mother is dying. The depressed son makes the decision to go back to her homeland in Ireland on a pilgrimage of discovery. Accompanying him is his wayward nephew, who will not knuckle down at school. Back in the boglands of Ireland and framed initially by an incongruous symbol of modernity, a powerhouse chimney spewing out steam in the background of their bed and breakfast accommodation, he tries to discover the true story of his mother's past. Almost too quickly he is told the tragic story of her unrequited love, as seen in flashback with Kieran O'Day (**Aidan Quinn**). In this historical period, as the film's tag-line announces, "When actions were ruled by guilt, fear and prejudice, their love could not flourish." This passionate Irish tale rings true and is successful on narrative and dramatic levels.

THIS IS THE SEA **(1997).** Directed by **Mary McGuckian**, the film is set in Northern Ireland, shortly after the 1994 ceasefire, and addresses a very conventional romance "across the barricades" between a Protestant woman, Hazel (Samantha Morton), and Malachy (Ross

McDade), a Catholic man, who of course has a friend in the republican movement and in turn wants him to fight for the cause. The relationship is doomed to failure as they try to affirm their private love within the context of the "**troubles**."

THIS OTHER EDEN (1959). Directed by Muriel Box, the film is critically considered an acerbic response to the "paddywhackery" of *The Quiet Man*. The director presents an interesting take on the national mores and presents an engaging historical evaluation of the period. As affirmed through critical work on this radical film, the narrator subverts everything from the romanticism and hero worship of the national struggle to the absolute power of the Catholic Church and other sacred cows of the period. It was also arguably the most interesting film produced by **Ardmore Studios** cofounder **Emmet Dalton**.

TIMBUKTU (2004). The second feature release from **Alan Gilsenan** shares much of the fatalism that characterized the narrative of his earlier *All Souls' Day*. When Isobel's (**Eva Birthistle**) brother, a Christian monk (played by Irish singer Liam O'Maonlai) is kidnapped by Algerian rebels, she reunites with their childhood friend Deecy (Karl Geary), and together they set off across the Sahara to find her brother. On arrival they are assisted by a local hustler, whose presence ultimately proves to be a double-edged sword. Again like *All Souls' Day*, the film is characterized by avant-garde camera techniques and the use of multiple shooting formats. The result is less a straight narrative film than a collage of textures and colors that effectively captures the otherness of the Algerian setting. The downside of this technique is underdevelopment of some of the characters: The monk whose disappearance nominally drives the narrative is a chimera, mainly represented by his voice reading letters he has written to his sister. Meanwhile the film hints at some childhood trauma as an "explanation" for Deecy's sexuality but never clarifies what this might be. Nonetheless, the sheer strangeness of the context draws the viewer on, and the film is rarely less than absorbing.

TITANIC TOWN (1997). Starring Julie Walters, **Ciarán Hinds**, Nuala O'Neill, and Elizabeth Donoghy, Roger Michell's film foregrounds the violent "**troubles**" in Northern Ireland. Bernie and her family have become inured to the presence of helicopters hovering overhead, armored cars patrolling their street, soldiers lying on their lawn, and gunmen crouching in their doorways. But Bernie draws the line when one of her friends is caught in crossfire and killed in front of her young son's eyes. Despite friendly warnings not to get involved in politics, she speaks out in public. But the manipulative pro-British press twist her heartfelt words into an antirepublican campaign. This blurring of individual and personal family trauma with more overtly political agency has become a growing phenomenon in Northern Ireland of late.

TOIBIN, NIALL (1929–). In his autobiography Toibin refers to his screen roles as "the compulsory series of priests, IRA men and drunkards that were the lot of your middle-grade Irish Thespian before it started showering Oscars from Heaven" (Toibin, 1995) (the last phrase is a reference to the post–*My Left Foot/The Crying Game* expansion of production activity in Ireland). This is, however, an all-too-modest assessment of his career. Born in Cork, he made his first stage appearance in primary school. On leaving secondary school he took the civil service entrance exam and in January 1947 moved to Dublin to join the Department of Supplies. He would later move to the Department of External Affairs, where he was assigned to work at the **Cultural Relations Committee**. On arriving in Dublin he also joined the Gaelic League, where he renewed his interest in drama. Between 1947 and 1953, he also worked with the Compántas Amharclainne na Gaeilge theater group and did some semiprofessional work at the **Abbey Theatre**.

In 1953, he left the Department of External Affairs to take up a position with the **Radio Telefís Éireann (RTÉ)** Repertory Company, where he remained until 1967. In addition to his radio and (from 1962) television work, he was also a constant presence on Dublin stages. In the latter half of the decade he also became involved in film, acting as narrator on three **Louis Marcus** shorts—*Capallology*, *Golf*, and *Fleadh*. In 1964 he appeared in Brendan Behan's *The Hostage* at the Gaiety Theatre, commencing an association with the playwright that would establish Toibin as the definitive interpreter of Behan's works. (Toibin had known Behan since 1952, before any of his plays were staged, and bore a remarkable resemblance to the writer.) Despite this Toibin did not appear in either of the two English-language features based on Behan's works, *The Quare Fellow* (1962) and ***Borstal Boy*** (2000).

Having played every conceivable type of role in his stint with RTÉ, Toibin went freelance in 1967, attracted by the prospect of appearing in Brian Friel's *Lovers* at the Gaiety. It proved a safe move, for he has rarely been out of work since. In 1968, he appeared in a Disney film shot in Ireland, *Guns in the Heather*, then spent several months in 1969 in Dingle for his role as O'Keefe, a political Irish Republican Army (IRA) member, in ***Ryan's Daughter***. From Dingle he went straight to Broadway to appear in a Tony award–winning production of *Borstal Boy*. In the early 1970s he also developed a comedy sideline, devising a one-man show, which he has continued to perform periodically ever since. (Two comedies produced for RTÉ— *If the Cap Fits* (1973) and *Time Now, Mr T.* (1977)—were considered too risqué to receive extended runs.)

His key film role of the 1970s was in **Bob Quinn**'s *Poitín*, where he played Labhcas, opposite **Cyril Cusack** and **Donal McCann**. Gone was the comic persona Irish audiences had become familiar with, replaced by a sly and ruthless "cute hoor," concerned only with his own advancement.

In 1977 he joined the National Theatre in London, and a slew of roles on British television followed. These included his turn as Slipper—another cute hoor—in the **Channel 4** comedy *The Irish R.M.* He has remained a staple of such series ever since, appearing in the British Broadcasting Corporation's *Ballykissangel* in the 1990s and more recently in RTÉ's *The Clinic*. This work was interspersed with the occasional feature film: He played a comic showband promoter in ***Eat the Peach***, appeared down the cast in **Pat O'Connor**'s *Fools of Fortune* (having earlier appeared in that director's *Ballroom of Romance*), and then played Tom Cruise's father in ***Far and Away***. Now in his 70s, he continues to make regular—albeit often brief— screen appearances in films such as ***Veronica Guerin***.

TOMELTY, FRANCES. Born in Belfast, with a father—Joe Tomelty—who was also an actor, she built up an acting career in television that included stints in the cult British soap *Coronation Street*.

In 1976 she married musician Gordon Sumner (better known as Sting), with whom she had two children before they divorced in 1984. She played Mrs. Kane in *Lamb* and went on to play the stoic, cold-hearted young widow in *The Field* who will not sell the land for a fair price. Her last big-screen Irish role was in *High Boot Benny*, but she has continued to work on television in miniseries like **TV3**'s *Lucy Sullivan Is Getting Married*. She is particularly noted for her attractive voice and as a consequence has maintained a consistent output of radio work.

TOURISM. From the first films made in Ireland by the **Kalem Company**, such as *The Lad from Old Ireland* (1910), the extensive use of a touristic landscape has appealed to millions of Irish emigrants who wished to see romantic images of their homeland. The evocative use of beautiful native landscape as a backdrop to a fictional story became a staple for many Irish-American films, most notably of course *The Quiet Man* and David Lean's romantic adventure *Ryan's Daughter*. Such films have certainly placed the Irish landscape on a world stage and encouraged numerous tourists to the island to experience the idyllic screen landscape for themselves. It is no wonder, therefore, that official tourist organizations from the very start have sought to promote Irish images onscreen, and this has continued up to the present day with active participation by the tourist industry (Bord Fáilte) in promoting film production. Bord Fáilte also sought to use film to increase tourist numbers by sponsoring the establishment of the Cork Film **Festival** in the mid 1950s as part of the larger An Toastal Arts Festival, an arrangement that continued into the 1980s.

TOWNSEND, STUART (1972–). Townsend grew up in Howth, County Dublin, son of international golfer Peter Townsend and international model Lorna Townsend. He made his stage debut at school before appearing in two productions of *Borstal Boy* at the Gaiety Theatre. His first major theater role was in *Intermission* director John Crowley's critically acclaimed *True Lines*, after appearing in a number of student films (including Eve Morrison's acclaimed *Summertime*). Townsend made an eye-catching feature film debut in Gilles Mackinnon's film of Billy Roche's *Trojan Eddie* as a young

Traveller who runs off with **Richard Harris**'s new bride. He immediately followed this with low-budget British indie hit *Shooting Fish* (1997), opposite Kate Beckinsale, which brought him to the attention of a much wider audience.

In 1998 he played the title role in the adaptation of Eoin McNamee's novel *Resurrection Man*, playing an almost seductively psychotic loyalist paramilitary with a perverse sexuality. Further roles in British films followed, before what is arguably his best role to date: the eponymous lead in **Gerry Stembridge**'s *About Adam*. The film again played on Townsend's seductive appeal, but this time it was wrapped up in a much more palatable package: a character whose background alters to suit whatever the listener wants to hear. Adam is quickly established as someone for whom constancy is impossible, but Townsend successfully pulls off the task of retaining audience sympathy for his mysterious Lothario.

Since then, he has worked largely in American cinema, first in *Queen of the Damned* opposite pop singer Aaliyah, then in a series of films that despite A-list stars and directors somehow failed to make an impact. These include *Trapped* (2002) opposite Charlize Theron, who subsequently became his partner; *Shade* (2003), which also featured Gabriel Byrne; and *Head in the Clouds* (2004). Even those films that succeeded in achieving global releases, such as *The League of Extraordinary Gentlemen* (2004), in which he played Dorian Gray, were considered to have underperformed. This is all the more disappointing given that he was cast as Aragorn in Peter Jackson's take on *The Lord of the Rings* trilogy. However, after a few weeks of shooting, he was replaced by Viggo Mortensen, after "creative differences" emerged between himself and Jackson.

More recently he again worked with *Shooting Fish* director Stefan Schwartz on 2005's *The Best Man*.

***TRAVELLER* (1981).** This rarely seen story of a group of **Travellers** (Irish Gypsies) focuses on Angela Devine (Jody Donovan) and Michael Connors (Davy Spillane), who are subjected to an arranged marriage. Michael's father demands a dowry for the marriage, so the newlyweds are sent up North to smuggle radios and televisions back to the South. They pick up a hitchhiker, Clicky (Alan Devlin), whose presence complicates their attempts to negotiate unapproved roads around the border and encounters with the British Army. The **Joe Comerford**–directed story is effectively filmed with lots of traditional music and singing, performed by Spillane, a well-known musician. Critics have singled it out for its surfeit of raw realism and the refusal to apply Hollywood sentimentality or romanticization of its minority community in Ireland.

TRAVELLERS. The Travellers are an indigenous minority of about 25,000 living in Ireland, who are often used to represent the "other" in Irish film and could be crudely characterized as Gypsies. The most widely held belief about their origins holds that they were peasant farmers who had been thrown off the land in the wake of the famine of the 1840s, although other accounts suggest much earlier origins. Many still continue to be involved in scrap collection work as well as horse dealing and other short-term occupations. They have strong **Catholic** beliefs with tight communal and family values. Furthermore, many speak their own dialect—Cant—which is rarely included in Irish film, presumably for commercial reasons, although ironically Hollywood star Brad Pitt delivered a version of it in the comic British gangster film *Snatch* (2000). Boxing is a popular sport among young Travellers, and *Southpaw* dramatizes how the Traveller Francis Barrett from Galway went on to represent Ireland in the Olympics in 1996. Described as a nomadic group, many travel throughout the island while living temporarily in designated halting sites, or more controversially, camp illegally on the side of the road. Over the years many have become "settled," living in various designated sites around the country, but continue to encounter prejudicial and even racial resentment from the majority settled community.

Indigenous films have a history of using the representation of Travellers as a recognizable shorthand for otherness and therefore helping to foreground conflict with the settled community. Such conflicts are evident in films like *The Field*, in which the Traveller's horse is disposed of at the start of the film and whose owners later demand compensation; or *Country*, in which Travellers are scapegoated for a crime; and more recently in *Man About Dog*, in which they are portrayed as comic characters who buy a dog and prove the animal's worth in a subsequent race.

In a number of Irish films, however, Travellers are even more central to the story, probably reflecting a romanticization of the wild nature of the Travellers—somewhat reminiscent of the Native American Indian in recent revisionist American films—who as a group are free to roam the country, unfettered by the socially imposed obligations faced by the settled community. This corresponds most especially with a reading of *Into the West*, which nostalgically re-creates a closely knit Traveller community and follows its young Travellers as they ride their beautiful mythic white horse west to discover their mother.

Alternative examples tend to look more critically and adapt a less nostalgic lens as the Travellers strive to survive and change with the times, as they do in films like **Joe Comerford**'s *Traveller* and *Trojan Eddie*. Scripted by **Neil Jordan**, who was apparently unhappy with the filmed outcome, *Traveller* tells the often-violent story of interfamily rivalry and uses an avant-garde style that often draws attention to its study of the otherness of the Travellers. One throwaway example of this style is the very artificial and crude mapping technique used to illustrate the journey taken by the main protagonists that serves to break any illusion of bourgeois mimetic realism. Nevertheless, the strength of the film comes from its ability to get inside the violence and the pleasures of the Traveller community. Similarly, *Trojan Eddie*, although operating on a more conventional and prosaic level, also foregrounds a very strong and self-contained Travelling community and tries to frame the story from the inside out rather than voyeuristically objectifying this alien community.

More recently in *Travellers* (2001), photographer Alen Weeney (together with director **John T. Davis**) effectively applies a tradition of the ethnographic study of the romantic exoticism of the Travellers, revisiting the Traveller subjects of photographs he took in the 1960s. Similarly, Perry Ogden, who spent a lot of time photographing the Travellers and produced an accompanying book about boys and their ponies (as romanticized in *Crushproof*), made a very sensitive and well-regarded art-house film focusing on a young Traveller girl, *Pavee Lackeen* [Traveller Girl] (2005), which has been a domestic art-house success and won awards for its exquisite composition and direction. The film treads the line between **documentary** realism and fiction, with the audience invited into the life of 10-year-old Winnie

(Maughan), as her family confront various authority figures. The actors are all nonprofessionals from the Traveller community, and reviews suggest that the director does not exoticize the Travellers into "designer ethnic" but creates a very authentic evocation of the real-life experience of this minority group in Ireland. One hopes such positive representations will continue in the future.

TREASURE FILMS. Treasure Films was jointly founded by producer Robert Walpole and director **Paddy Breathnach** in 1992, in the wake of their critically successful 1991 **short film**, *A Stone of the Heart*, which won the Special Jury Prize at the 1991 Cork Film **Festival**. Since then Treasure has produced a wide range of material for broadcast and cinema release.

Walpole studied economics and political philosophy at university before embarking on a film career as a location scout on *The Commitments* and then as an assistant director on *The Snapper*. Breathnach and Walpole's first production as Treasure Films came the following year with *The Road to America*, a **documentary** on Ireland's 1994 World Cup campaign. It was a major hit—it became the third-best-selling video in the country and provided a sound financial basis for the company.

The company initially concentrated on television production work, including the Breathnach-directed *W.R.H.*, a documentary series focusing on a regional hospital in Waterford. Although Breathnach's first feature, *Ailsa*, was produced by **Ed Guiney** for **Temple Films**, its success at the San Sebastian Film Festival, where it won the Euskal Media prize, directly benefited Treasure. Treasure used part of the prize fund to finance the company's first feature, *I Went Down*, which Breathnach directed from a **Conor McPherson** script.

The film was a major commercial and critical success in Ireland and was widely distributed across Europe, where it recorded 240,000 admissions. In 1998, Artisan Entertainment picked up the U.S. rights and released the film in 69 cinemas. Although it performed relatively poorly—peaking at 100,000 admissions—it was nonetheless sufficient to secure Treasure a two-year first-look deal with Fine Line Features, the art-house subsidiary of minimajor New Line. The deal was brokered by Justin Moore-Lewy, a Dublin-based agent for the International Creative Management talent agency, who would subsequently become a director of the company that grew out of Treasure Films, Treasure Entertainment.

Treasure's first project under the Fine Line deal was to have been an adaptation by Dublin author Joe O'Connor of his own novel *Cowboys and Indians*. However, the deal did not bear fruit, and although Treasure's next feature release—*Southpaw*, a documentary on boxer Francis Barrett—was released in the United States, it was distributed by an independent company, The Shooting Gallery.

Since 2000, Treasure has produced three further features. *I Went Down* screenwriter McPherson turned director in 2001, adapting his play *This Lime Tree Bower* as the Walpole-produced *Saltwater*, which premiered at the 2001 Berlin Film Festival.

In 2004, founding partner Breathnach made his second feature for the company, *Man About Dog,* which, despite a lukewarm critical response, was one of the most successful indigenous films of recent years at the Irish box office, becoming the 10th most successful release of 2004. And in 2005, Treasure produced *The Mighty Celt*, directed by *Man About Dog*'s screenwriter Pearse Elliott and starring Robert Carlyle and Gillian Anderson.

TROJAN EDDIE (1996). The film won the San Sebastian Festival's Golden Seashell award. It was directed by Gilles Mackinnon from a first screenplay by the well-regarded Wexford playwright Billy Roche. The eponymous Eddie (**Stephen Rea**) prides himself on his gift of communication at his trade stall, where he sells knick-knacks on behalf of John Power (**Richard Harris**), the self-styled "King of the Travellers." Eddie has separated from his wife and is bringing up two children and wants to do the best by them. But the relationship with Power sours when Eddie's assistant, Dermot (**Stuart Townsend**), runs away with Power's new young bride. Told through Eddie's eyes, the film is unusual in that it positions a member of the settled community (Eddie) as the outsider in a world where the norms and customs of the Travelling community are hegemonic; this contrasts most notably with *Into the West*, where the Travellers' lifestyle is shown as somewhat exotic if not sustainable.

THE TROUBLE WITH SEX (2005). After his feature debut with *Flick* (2000), and numerous documentaries on television, Fintan Connolly went on to make this contemporary romantic drama, which draws on a relatively conventional story line but is imbued with strong sexual and contemporary romantic tension. The story concerns Michelle, a hard-working lawyer who—dissatisfied with her relationship (with Ivan, a doctor) and overwrought by her mother's illness—walks into a pub run by Conor (**Aidan Gillen**). Conor, lonely and single, becomes Michelle's new romantic focus, although she initially fails to mention her relationship with Ivan. By the time she does, an intense sexual bond has been established with Conor, and the trio are forced to work through their new relationships with one another. The enticing tag line certainly signals the distance contemporary Irish sexuality has moved beyond conventional historical religious mores—"The trouble with sex is that you can fall in love."

THE "TROUBLES." A small selection of films dealt with the turbulent short period in Irish history between the 1916 Rising and the achieving of independence in 1922. These include *Irish Destiny* (1926), which was banned on release by the British Board of Film Censors (BBFC); *Guests of the Nation* (1935), a silent version of Frank O'Connor's short story, directed by playwright Denis Johnston; and *The Dawn* (1936), which is still highly celebrated beyond its specific evocation of a nationalist agenda. Arthur Robinson's 1929 silent version of Liam O'Flaherty's novel *The Informer* and **John Ford**'s version in 1935, alongside Ford's adaptation of *The Plough and the Stars* (1936)—O'Casey's seminal Easter Rising play—all contributed significantly to representing this turbulent period in Irish history.

More recently Ford's *The Rising of the Moon* (1957) and his quasi biography of playwright Sean O'Casey, *Young Cassidy* (1964) (which was completed by Jack Cardiff when Ford fell ill), encapsulate the major historical films using this particular period. Other representations include the British-produced *Ourselves Alone* (1936), directed by the Irish-born **Brian Desmond Hurst**. The most famous representation that focuses on the "troubles" is *Shake Hands with the Devil* (1959), starring the Irish American James Cagney and directed by Michael Anderson. Adapted from Rearden Connor's novel of the same name, the story concerns secret Irish Republican Army (IRA) leader Sean Lenihan (Cagney), who recruits Irish American student Kerry O'Shea (Don Murray) into the cause after O'Shea witnesses the shooting of a friend (**Ray McAnally**) by the Black and Tans (British Army). They kidnap a British officer in exchange for an IRA sympathizer who is on hunger strike in prison.

While many contemporary Irish films foreground the pernicious or other influence and power of the Catholic Church on Irish identity, across the border in the North, such religious polarization has been even more divisive. Celebrations by the Catholic nationalist community of religious rituals is frequently regarded by many unionist Protestants as legitimizing nationalist political violence and is perceived by Protestants as a threat to an increasingly tenuous hegemony. Of course, critics suggest the same could be said about the South with its historical hegemonic power of the Catholic Church ranged against other minority religions.

Recognizable shorthand stereotypes of the North have provided a clear background for a number of film narratives over the years, from *Odd Man Out* in the 1940s to **Neil Jordan**'s *The Crying Game* and the continued problematic representation of the "**troubles**" in more recent times. Film representation tends to approve action, heroism, and fighting against oppression and injustice. This is not necessarily because film is intrinsically progressive—in fact many contend the opposite—but because of the nonpartisan mass audiences' identification with the underdogs, like the Catholics or nationalists in the North, which tends to elevate victimhood to the stature of heroism. A large percentage of contemporary Irish films use the Northern Ireland conflict to frame if not drive their varying narratives.

Hollywood has also been quick to exploit the potential for global terrorism in Northern Ireland for fictional narratives, for example, in espionage films like Thomas Clancy's *Patriot Games* (1992), starring Harrison Ford, which involves duplicitous IRA terrorists. Such representations tend to lean toward caricatures of republicans as mad bombers—as exemplified by the Tommy Lee Jones character in *Blown Away* (1994)—and offer little insight into the political context for Northern violence. Alan Pakula's *The Devil's Own* (1997) offers a more sympathetic IRA activist in the form of Brad Pitt, but even here the motivation for Pitt's violence is more personal revenge than being part of a larger political context. In any case, "evil" Irish terrorists have found less favor within the genre especially after 11

September 2001, probably reflecting the sensitivities of a well-established Irish diasporic community in America, who are becoming less sympathetic to extreme forms of Irish republicanism. It is hoped that the current peace process will help to ameliorate the polarization represented in the subgenre of "troubles" films and sectarian narratives generally. *See also TITANIC TOWN, MICHAEL COLLINS, RESURRECTION MAN.*
TV3. TV3 is a commercial television broadcaster that was first licensed in 1989 but did not commence operations in Ireland until 1998 due to financial difficulties. These were largely addressed in 1997 when Canadian media conglomerate CanWest took a 45 percent stake in the station, endowing it with the financial and programming muscle to go on air. British independent broadcaster GranadaCarlton subsequently also acquired a 45 percent stake in the station, leaving the remaining 10 percent in Irish hands.

Although TV3 has come in for consistent criticism for its reliance on imported material and its failure to commission local producers, in recent years at least, it has arguably been more supportive of Irish film than **Radio Telefís Éireann (RTÉ)**, having invested in seven television dramas or films, including *The Mapmaker*, *The Honeymooners*, and *The Halo Effect*. In contrast to RTÉ, which in the mid-1990s, for example, partially funded a series of films as a means of fulfilling public service obligations, TV3's strategy has been to invest small amounts (around €50,000) in low-budget films for commercial purposes with a view to developing long-term business relationships with the filmmakers. TV3 also supports the theatrical release of films it invests in with on-air advertising promotion. Responsibility for deciding which films to invest in lies with Jane Gogan, commissioning editor of TV3 since 1998 and previously a founding member of **Film Base** and an independent film producer in her own right.

***2BY4* (1997).** The central character, Johnny (Jimmy Smallhorne—who also directs the film)—has moments of severe trauma due to well-sublimated memories. He works for his uncle, Trump (Chris O'Neill), who embezzles wages to pay for illicit sex with black male prostitutes. Finally Johnny uncovers the root of his trauma, which occurred when he was a child back in Ireland and involved his uncle. Issues of gay and bisexual identity, which some critics regard as somewhat problematic in its apparent linkage of pedophilia and homosexuality, are transferred to the Irish American diaspora.

– U –

ULYSSES **(1967).** Given cinema's historical tendency to borrow from other media, it was inevitable that someone would attempt to adapt what was arguably the 20th century's most famous novel. However, the very characteristics that won the book renown—stream-of-consciousness narrative, constantly shifting style, and so on—arguably rendered it unfilmable. It is also very long, hardly surprising given that Joyce described his intent in writing it as being to create a picture of Dublin so complete that if the city suddenly disappeared from the earth it could be reconstructed from the book.

Although Joyce suggested in correspondence with Sergei Eisenstein that the great Soviet master himself should film it, it was left to American independent director **Joseph Strick** to make the first stab at portraying the fictional events of 16 June 1904, the day in the life of his beloved city, Dublin, that the emigrant writer **James Joyce** recreates. Nothing if not ambitious, Strick attempted to include each of the book's original "episodes" but adapted an accessible, humorous approach in doing so, one that arguably has more in common with the writing of Flann O'Brien than that of Joyce. The most attractive part of the film is its cast: It is a who's who of Irish actors and actresses, including **Milo O'Shea** (as Bloom), **T. P. McKenna**, Anna Manahan, Maureen Potter, Martin Dempsey, Joe Lynch, **Fionnuala Flanagan, David Kelly**, **Rosaleen Linehan**, Brendan Cauldwell, **Tony Doyle**, Des Keogh, Eugene Lambert, O. Z. Whitehead, Biddy White-Lennon, Tomas MacAnna, and a host of others.

Ironically, despite being shot in Ireland, it was banned by the **censor** when presented for certification, because of Molly's famous sexually explicit soliloquy and other explicit content in the novel that was faithfully adapted. In a double irony Strick's script (written with Fred Haines) subsequently received an **Oscar** nomination for Best Screenplay.

– V –

***THE VAN* (1996).** This film is part of **Roddy Doyle**'s Barrytown novel trilogy, alongside **Alan Parker**'s *The Commitments* and *The Snapper*, which Stephen Frears directed. **Colm Meaney** reprises his *Commitments* role of Jimmy Curley, whose best friend, Bimbo (Donal O'Kelly), loses his job in a bakery, reducing him to the status long endured by Jimmy and the rest of his mates. Out on the town to drown Bimbo's sorrows, the pair curse the lack of a chip van in the locality and decide to invest Bimbo's redundancy money in providing one. As in the rest of the trilogy, Dublin argot and the working-class vernacular are used for humorous effect but do not fully succeed in this version, which lacks identifiable originality according to some critics. Nevertheless, the humorous character-driven story is well realized and effective.

***VERONICA GUERIN* (2003).** Both *Veronica Guerin* (2003), directed by Joel Schumacker, and *When the Sky Falls* (1999), directed by John McKenzie, are based on the true story of a *Sunday Independent* journalist who was assassinated by drug dealers in 1996 and whose death indirectly sparked a radical overhaul of the criminal justice system in Ireland. At the outset one could suggest that this heroic story of human sacrifice is reminiscent of the Irish mythos of self-sacrifice, and that it plays into stereotypical clichés that a Hollywood director can draw on, while making it easier for universal audiences to identify with.

Veronica Guerin in particular conforms to a feel-good Hollywood convention of heroes fighting for justice. Only when individuals take a stand for what is transparently good and right does change for the better take place. Such broad Hollywood narrative trajectories usually privilege personal agency while negating the effectiveness of re-organizing the system in the fight against political and other societal problems. This approach has come under extensive academic criticism under the rubric of what has come to be called "screen theory." Nevertheless, one might argue that such a simplistic structural reading belies a more complex engagement with the representation of the heroine's performance as a journalist.

When the Sky Falls was the first cinematic take on the Veronica Guerin story, although the name of the characters were fictionalized.

American actress Joan Allen plays the Guerin character, with **Patrick Bergin** as Detective Mackie and Pete Postlethwaite as a criminal modeled on The General. This more authentic yet strangely dispassionate version fails to connect with audiences as effective fictional narrative. Nevertheless, it provides sharper dialogue that allows an appreciation of the function of the journalist, and a more explicit critique of the role of the *Sunday Globe* (*Sunday Independent*), where Guerin worked when she was killed. But much of the discursive analysis of the circumstances of Veronica's death is frequently delivered in a nondramatic and somewhat uninteresting fashion. Consequently this version got a very poor press and did badly at the box office, while the later, less-discursive big-budget version, *Veronica Guerin*, was much more successful.

Comparing the two versions of the story, the latter Hollywood cinematic treatment wins hands down. While certainly compromised, at least *Veronica Guerin* provides a stronger sense of drama, empathy, and enjoyment. The film passed the €4.1 million box office mark by the end of 2003 in Ireland, thus eclipsing any other "Irish" film. The casting of Cate Blanchett in the title role, with her proficient Irish accent, is regarded by many as a major reason for its success in Ireland, compared with Joan Allen's more staid and less celebrity-driven performance.

Generically, *When the Sky Falls* fits more neatly into the crime genre, with highly conventional and stereotypical evocations of criminals and the police. This doubtless explains the choice of director John McKenzie, who two decades earlier directed the seminal gangster film *The Long Good Friday* (1979). In particular Detective Mackie (Patrick Bergin) is presented as totally frustrated in his attempts to capture the criminals and blames the switching of resources to protect the border in the North. Like many Hollywood crime busters, he becomes as devious and ruthless as the criminals, supporting the proposition that the end justifies the means. Like similar characters in films like *The Untouchables* (1987), but lacking their ethical values, he calls on his fellow officers to follow him in an attempt to capture the enemy, while citing the slogan over the police station that translates "Let justice be done or the sky falls."

The forces of law and order are less compromised in *Veronica Guerin*, and in a more heroic denouement, the emotional effect of her murder is reinforced by an unseen boy singing the classic Irish ballad "The Fields of Athenry" alongside the hypnotic Gaelic voice of **Sinead O'Connor**, while the audience is visually treated to a bird's-eye view of her body as it lies in a painterly repose with her eyes wide open. Her martyred body is symmetrically positioned within her sporty red car, seen through an open sunroof, whereas in *When the Sky Falls*, the re-creation of her death is less dramatic, both aurally and visually; we see her car sans sunroof, and the scene lacks cinematic potency.

– W –

WAKING NED (WAKING NED DEVINE) (1998). This Kirk Jones–directed film stars Ian Bannen and **David Kelly** as Jackie and Michael, two senior citizens living in the fictional coastal village of Tullymore. When the National Lottery announces that a local has won the top prize, the whole village goes to great lengths to find out who it is. However, when it emerges that the winner—Ned Devine—has died of shock upon discovering his win, the village engages in an elaborate plot to pretend he is still alive to allow them all to collect the money. Shot on the Isle of Man to avail of local tax incentives, the film became an international hit (taking $24 million in the United States), apparently confirming the view that only films representing Ireland as prelapsarian, pastoral, and populated by loveable rogues and amiable drunks find favor in the international market.

WAR OF THE BUTTONS (1993). Based on a 1962 French release *La Guerre des Boutons*, the Irish film was produced by British producer David Puttnam, who has a house in West Cork and planned locations accordingly. Directed by John Roberts, the film tells the story of children from two small towns located on two sides of a West Cork estuary who form small armies and battle each other for supremacy. Oscar-winning screenwriter Colin Welland adapted the story from the French setting by not only transposing the setting but also bringing the narrative into more contemporary times. The showdown of the children marching into battle in cardboard armor and dustbin lids is appealing for its comic pastiche but does not have the same level of comic generic sophistication as, for example, **Alan Parker**'s *Bugsy Malone* (which Puttnam also produced). Incidentally, the film's release was held up following a court injunction by parents of an actor extra, who objected to some nudity. Nevertheless, the film was relatively successful in Ireland, taking over £500,000 on its domestic release.

WARD ANDERSON. Surprisingly, given its perceived dominance of the Irish **exhibition** sector, there is in fact no single company called Ward Anderson. Instead there is a group of at least 50 companies, including Provincial Cinemas Ltd., the Dublin Cinema Group, the Green Group, and others, which are jointly owned by Leo Ward (1919–) and Kevin Anderson (1915–). The two men are half brothers—Anderson's father, Thomas, died when he was two, and his mother, Martha, remarried to John Ward. When Anderson left school, he joined the civil service and subsequently worked in a builder's company. Meanwhile, Leo Ward was working with the Irish International Film Agency, which distributed German films in Ireland. However, when Ward, who also played football for Drumcondra, was offered a contract in England with Manchester City, Anderson took over his place at the agency.

When World War II began, Ward returned to Ireland, and he and Anderson started their own distribution company—Abbey Films—acquiring Irish rights for Irish-themed British and American films like *The Hills of Donegal* (1947) and the Lucan and McShane *Mother Riley* series (1937–1952). Anderson was responsible mainly for looking after the day-to-day finances of the company, and Ward spent the 1940s and 1950s touring the country with prints, building contacts with smaller cinema owners in the provinces. As the industry entered a period of decline in the 1950s, Ward gradually became a partner in many of the cinemas he had been supplying, and eventually the exhibition side of the business became more financially significant than distribution. The acquisition of the cinemas was facilitated by Anderson's success on the stock market, which earned some of the capital used to acquire the cinemas.

Anderson also used this money to dabble in film production. In the early 1950s he used Abbey Films as a vehicle to produce a short film on the United Irishmen, *Who Dares to Speak of '98*, with **Peter Hunt**,

George Fleischmann, Liam O'Leary, and **Cyril Cusack**. He also approached the Department of Foreign Affairs in 1955 seeking support for a documentary project on the Irish in London.

By the 1960s Ward Anderson was the dominant player in the provincial market (i.e., outside Dublin). The first move into the capital came in 1968 when the company purchased the Green Cinema on Saint Stephen's Green. By the mid-1970s the company had added three more city-center cinemas—the Ambassador, the Regent, and the Academy. The company's position in the capital was cemented in 1983 when the Rank Organization sold its Dublin cinemas—the Savoy, the Metropole, and the Odeon.

This dominance enjoyed by the company (at least until the 1990s) was not without its negative aspects. In the early 1970s the Irish Cinemas Association (which represented independent provincial cinema owners) leveled a series of accusations at the company that the group's dominance was due to its being favored by the major distributors. Although an initial report from the examiner of the Restrictive Practices Commission found that there was some evidence of such collusion, a subsequent full-scale enquiry dismissed the accusation, arguing that purely commercial considerations had contributed to the group's dominance. Indeed, Ward Anderson emerged from the enquiry in a stronger position than it had before it started. Not only did the enquiry find that it was in the interests of consumers to have a strong chain like Ward Anderson, but it also recommended some modification of practices in the Dublin city-center market, which had arguably disadvantaged Ward Anderson cinemas relative to the dominant Adelphi-Carlton and Rank Odeon circuits.

Throughout this period Abbey Films continued to act as a distributor, although for the most part it acted as agent for U.K.-based companies like EMI, Hemdale, and Gala rather than acquiring Irish rights outright.

Ward Anderson rode out the exhibition recession of the 1980s, in part by simply closing cinemas when they were no longer viable as ongoing operations but retaining the buildings as potentially valuable properties. With the arrival of multiplexes in 1990, however, the company was forced to consider new strategies. Initially, the company toyed with a direct confrontation with internationally backed players like UCI. When the latter opened a 10-screen cinema in

Coolock, Ward Anderson countered with a 10-screen in Santry, another North Dublin suburb. For the most part, however, subsequent developments concentrated on the provincial market, where the company had long enjoyed a dominant position. As a result the 1990s witnessed the closure of a plethora of older Ward Anderson cinemas in provincial towns and the building of new minimultiplexes (anything from 3- to 7-screen theaters) under the Cineplex and Omniplex brands. They also opened 12-screen cinemas in Limerick and—under the IMC Cinemas logo—in Dun Laoire. Consequently the company still accounts for approximately 40 percent of all screens in the republic.

As of 2005, the Ward and Anderson in Ward Anderson have changed. Paul Ward and Paul Anderson, both sons of the founders, now largely direct the running of the group. Kevin Anderson semiretired in the 1980s but continues to be a significant player on the Irish stock market across a range of companies. Leo Ward by contrast, despite being in his 80s, continued playing a management role into the 21st century. Abbey Films also continues to occupy a small but significant role, although the company continues to serve as agent for smaller U.S. distributors such as New Line. It has also taken on an increasing number of domestically produced films, such as *Song for a Raggy Boy* and *Adam and Paul*. Finally, half a century after Kevin Anderson's experience with filmmaking, the group has tentatively returned to production through an alliance with Stone Ridge Productions. *Peaches*—the first feature from that company—was partially funded by Abbey Films, which also distributed it.

WHELAN, DES. One of a handful of Irish technical crew members with an international reputation, Des Whelan began his career as rostrum camera trainee at the Gunther Wulf animation studio at Ardmore in the late 1970s. After four years there, he retrained as a clapper loader, traditionally the first step to becoming a cinematographer. In four more years he graduated to focus puller, and in 1987 he was given his first opportunity to work as a camera operator on the **Radio Telefís Éireann (RTÉ)** drama series *Troubles*. From that point on, Whelan has secured work on virtually ever major production shot in Ireland including *My Left Foot*, *The Field*, *The Playboys*, and *Into the West*. More recently he has worked as camera operator on **John**

Boorman's *Tailor of Panama* (2001), **John Moore**'s *Flight of the Phoenix* (2004), and Tim Burton's *Charlie and the Chocolate Factory* (2005), among other films. He is also much sought after for commercial shoots, and he has taught at the National Film School.

WHEN BRENDAN MET TRUDY **(2000).** Directed by Kieran J. Walsh and written by **Roddy Doyle**, the film is a comic pastiche and homage to a range of classic films. In the opening scene protagonist Brendan (**Peter McDonald**) is lying face down in the gutter as it rains, deliberately evoking one of the character's favorite films, *Sunset Boulevard* (1950). Other intertextual references include Jean-Luc Godard's *A Bout de Souffle* (1959), as the character slowly acquires Jean-Paul Belmondo's mannerisms, clothes, and—in case the audience does not fully appreciate the intertextual link—posters for said film. The ending even pays homage to the close of *The Searchers* (1956) when John Wayne holds his hand in a certain pose (itself an homage to an older Western actor), framed against the homestead entrance.

Unlike characters in the Hollywood narratives, however, McDonald plays someone who is a poor teacher at the start and does not get any better. But his mundane existence is enlivened when he encounters Trudy (**Flora Montgomery**), who may or may not be a militantly radical feminist. Although the film plays with gender and race stereotypes, it is rarely more than a light romantic comedy that has been criticized, along with *About Adam*, for failing to realistically evoke an Irish milieu. But such quibbles simply ask the film to accomplish what it never set out to do.

WHEN THE SKY FALLS **(1999).** *See VERONICA GUERIN.*

WIDOWS' PEAK **(1993).** Directed by John Irvin, from an original story and screenplay by Hugh Leonard, a well-known playwright and columnist, this stereotypical Irish woman's story has a major all-star cast including Mia Farrow, Joan Plowright, and Natasha Richardson alongside **Adrian Dunbar** and Jim Broadbent. Set in the 1920s on a hill overlooking the picturesque village of Kilshannon, the Widows' Peak community, (mostly, as the name implies, made up of widows) is led by the rich and well-heeled Mrs. Doyle Counihan (Joan

Plowright), who excels in knowing everyone's business and who seeks to influence the lives of a poor and unbelievably shy spinster, Miss O'Hare (Mia Farrow). She is challenged for this role by a rich new interloper, Edwina Broome, who locks horns with the self-appointed leader of the community. The often tongue-in-cheek narrative lacks flair and fails to bring the ribald story alive at times. Nevertheless, the Irish landscape and environment are used effectively, and the characterization is strong in this period drama.

***WILLY REILLY AND HIS COLLEEN BAWN* (1920).** Derived from an 1855 novel of the same name by William Carleton (rather than Dion Boucicault's 1860 play *The Colleen Bawn*), *Willy Reilly* was the last of the **Film Company of Ireland**'s major features. Directed by John McDonagh, the film is set in the 18th century in the context of the operation of the Penal Laws, a legal code designed to place Irish **Catholics** in a subordinate position relative to their Protestant counterparts. The eponymous Willy Reilly plays a disenfranchised Catholic who falls in love with Helen (the Colleen Bawn), daughter of Squire Folliard, a local Protestant landowner whom Reilly rescues from a local bandit. Helen, however, is engaged to notorious Catholic hunter Sir Robert Whitecraft. But when Whitecraft's sectarianism becomes violent, leading to the destruction of O'Reilly's home, he is arrested, and the major obstacle to O'Reilly and Helen's relationship is removed.

Although the film nominally suggests that the distinction between Catholic and Protestant is largely illusory, *Willy O'Reilly and His Colleen Bawn* isn't an entirely ecumenical film. The Catholic O'Reilly is clearly constructed as a thrusting agent of change, in stark contrast to the Folliards, who are portrayed largely as passive victims of circumstance. In this respect, director McDonagh's own overt nationalist politics (his brother Thomas was executed for his part in the 1916 Easter Rising), clearly show through. Indeed, one could argue that rather than preaching ecumenism, the film demonstrates the inevitability of the decline of the Protestant order associated with unionism and its replacement with a Catholic nationalism.

***WINGS OF THE MORNING* (1937).** Directed by Harold Schuster, this was the first Technicolor film made in the British Isles and was filmed partly in Killarney, County Kerry. The film tells the story of an Irish Spanish gypsy girl, Maria, who escapes to Ireland during the Spanish Civil War and meets Kerry Gilfallen (an early star role for Henry Fonda). While its overly contrived story line and cross-dressing escapades are amusing, the film is interesting primarily for its evocative displaying of the Kerry landscape during the singing of the internationally famous Irish tenor Count John McCormack, which induced some nostalgia in a broad Irish diaspora and helped affirm the **touristic** pleasures of the island.

WOMEN AND FILM. During the recent study of international film, feminist discourse has had a primary role in critiquing existing patriarchal aesthetics and methods of production and in creating a framework for more progressive strategies. Irish critics have adapted the feminist praxis of **Pat Murphy**, primarily as writer and director, as a role model for such a strategy toward filmmaking. Her oeuvre traces the evolution of the feminist study of film in Ireland, from the radical avant-garde polemic of *Maeve*, to the linking of republican and feminist melodramatic discourses in *Anne Devlin*, to what some describe as the postfeminist aesthetic in her period drama *Nora*. Northern politics and engagement with the "troubles" are very well served from a feminist perspective by Anne Crilly's *Mother Ireland* and Margo Harkin's *Hush-a-Bye Baby*, which came out of the **Derry Film and Video Co-Operative**.

However, the extent to which such strategies can be deployed has been limited by the fact that, as in many other national film industries, men tend to dominate within the Irish production process, from directors to crew members, with women often working in backroom production roles. This generalization belies a growing involvement of women of late in all areas of the process, and a healthier gender balance should be achieved in the future. The list of female directors who have shaped the current trajectory of the filmic output in Ireland includes (in no particular order) Orla Walsh, **Mary McGuckian**, Liz Gill with *Gold in the Streets* and *Goldfish Memory*, Kirsten Sheridan with *Disco Pigs*, Trish McAdam with *Snakes and Ladders*, Aisling Walsh with *Song for a Raggy Boy*, and Sue Clayton with *The Disappearance of Finbar*. Nonetheless—for the time being—the vast majority of recent Irish films have been directed by men. This dominance is also reflected among Irish producers: Although one could cite female producers of note such as Katy McGuinness, Martha O'Neill, Juanita Wilson (of Metropolitan Films), and **Lelia Doolan**, they are vastly outnumbered by their male counterparts.

Given this, it ironic that Ireland is unusual in that certain crew grades usually considered male preserves in film in other nations are relatively gender balanced in Ireland. Production management, the job of running a set on a day-to-day basis, has long been open to women in Ireland, and one woman in particular—Mary Alleguen—is arguably the best-regarded production manager in the country, a status reflected in her appointment in the mid-1990s to the **Irish Film Board**. Of course filmmaking remains a very labor-intensive group activity, and the production crew are essential in this process. **Josie MacAvin**'s outstanding work over her long career has been highlighted as exemplary within this dictionary. One could also cite figures like Nuala Moiselle and Ros Hubbard in casting, **Emer Reynolds** in editing, and Eimer Ni Mhaoldomhnaigh in costumes.

A large number of fine actresses have appeared in Irish film over the years. Notable examples of their work include the internationally renowned performance of **Maureen O'Hara** in *The Quiet Man* and more contemporary commanding and Oscar-winning work from **Brenda Fricker**. However, although we have tried to recognize many of the major Irish actresses working within the last few decades, such as **Brid Brennan, Orla Brady, Eva Birthistle**, and **Elaine Cassidy**, it is interesting to note that Irish actresses in recent years have not made the transition to the international stardom achieved by figures like Colin Farrell, Pierce Brosnan, and Liam Neeson. The reasons for this are not clear, and, of course, it is a fact that in a global film culture obsessed with youthful appearance, actresses are often condemned to a shorter "shelf life" than their male counterparts. Nonetheless, the absence of a prominent figure within the ranks of Irish actresses is significant; to the extent that the attachment of a star name to a project can aid its funding and therefore its production, this lack places some limits on what projects can and cannot get made in Ireland. Certainly it is notable that makers of films set in Ireland, especially those with a larger budget, often resort to casting American or British actresses in Irish roles in an attempt to render the project saleable. Indeed certain non-Irish actresses have

374 • WOODS, MARK

become associated with Irish roles: Helen Mirren in *Cal* and *Some Mother's Son*, Julie Walters in *Titanic Town* and *Mickybo and Me*, and Brenda Blethyn in *On the Nose* and *Night Train*. Then there is also the phenomenon of the "parachuting" of A-list actresses into such roles: Julia Roberts in *Michael Collins*, Cate Blanchett in *Veronica Guerin*, and Meryl Streep in *Dancing at Lughnasa*.

WOODS, MARK. He became the new chief executive of the **Irish Film Board** in 2003 after the 10-year tenure of **Rod Stoneman**. He is a Dublin-born law graduate who moved to Los Angeles, where he worked for *Variety* before relocating to Australia with them for 6 years. He subsequently took over as head of international acquisitions and local content organization for Showtime, an Australian film and television network, where he championed the distribution of independent local content production. During his time there the company invested in 29 local films, including *Rabbit-Proof Fence* (2002) and *Innocence* (2000). In total, Woods spent 12 years abroad before returning to Ireland to head the Film Board. In various interviews he affirmed that the conditions that determine a successful film will never change and that, consequently, filmmaking would always be about strong passionate stories that audiences can identify with.

Despite this, Woods came in for criticism from some elements of the Irish filmmaking community who argued that he increasingly stressed supporting projects with commercial prospects, to the detriment of more "difficult" work. The decision to award €1.5 million to *Breakfast on Pluto*, which despite its far from mainstream source material might be considered commercial simply because it was directed by **Neil Jordan**, was cited as an example of this approach. Perhaps as a consequence, Woods's tenure at the board was relatively brief, and in April 2005 he announced that he was returning to Australia to take up a position in the audiovisual sector there.

***WORDS UPON THE WINDOW PANE* (1994).** The screenplay for this film directed by **Mary McGuckian** is based on a play by Irish poet and playwright William Butler Yeats that was first performed in 1930. The play demonstrates Yeats's interest in the occult—he was a founder of the Dublin Hermetic Society and later a member of the London Lodge of Theosophists—and his use of symbolism, which shows the strong influence of the Japanese Noh tradition. The story tells of a London medium invited by the Dublin Spiritualist Society to conduct a series of séances that unexpectedly result in contact with the spirit of Jonathan Swift. The medium and her hostess become possessed by the jealous ghost, reenacting scenes of violent confrontation that occurred in the very same house centuries before. Most critics unfortunately find the film adaptation overly confusing at times in spite of a very provocative backstory. The film stars Geraldine Chaplin, Geraldine James, and **John Lynch**.

WORLD 2000 ENTERTAINMENT. Established by Dubliner Morgan O'Sullivan, World 2000 has been characterized as making productions to order for American studios and TV stations. Born in 1945, as a teenager O'Sullivan attended Presentation College, Bray (near **Ardmore Studios**), where he ran film shows on Saturday nights. He was simultaneously employed as a child actor on radio by **Radio Telefís Éireann (RTÉ)**. On leaving school he joined the **Peter Hunt** Studio, which in addition to recording music serviced the sound needs of non-RTÉ film productions in Ireland. Consequently O'Sullivan worked with **Louis Marcus** and on the **Gael Linn** newsreel with Colm O'Leary.

In 1966 the 21-year-old O'Sullivan and his wife moved to Australia, where he took up a position as a presenter with the local radio and television station. This was followed by work with the Australian Broadcasting Commission in Sydney, and then for commercial television. In 1969 he returned to Ireland and RTÉ. O'Sullivan remained with RTÉ until 1984, presenting a series of radio shows, but he used his time there to establish links with Hollywood. In 1970, he traveled to Los Angeles to make a documentary on the making of *Hawaii 5-0*, and as a result met Irish-born LA-based TV director Michael O'Herlihy (brother of **Dan O'Herlihy**).

Eight years later O'Herlihy came to Ardmore to direct O'Sullivan's first film as a producer, the Frederick Forsyth–scripted *Cry of the Innocent*. With this film O'Sullivan's Tara Productions became the first non-U.S. company to presell a film to any American television network, in this case NBC for its *Movie of the Week*. This also led indirectly to a relationship with Mary Tyler Moore Enterprises. Two years after leaving RTÉ to run Tara Productions full time, he put together a package with Mary Tyler Moore Enterprises and NadCorp to buy Ardmore Studios out of liquidation, and for a period O'Sullivan was the managing director of the studio.

From 1990 to 1992 O'Sullivan lived in Los Angeles developing relationships with Hollywood studios and production companies. Having completed this groundwork, he returned to Ireland and in 1994 formed World 2000 Entertainment Ltd. with a view to developing, producing, and distributing feature and television entertainment for the global market. O'Sullivan quickly pulled off the remarkable coup of "stealing" Mel Gibson's *Braveheart* from its Scottish production base and bringing the $70 million movie to Ireland.

Since then, although O'Sullivan's stated ambitions include developing original material, World 2000 has for the most part continued to operate as a local production partner for foreign (mainly U.S.) productions that use Ireland as a double for other locations. These have included the largest productions shot in Ireland in the past decade such as *King Arthur*, *Veronica Guerin* (both Disney/Jerry Bruckheimer productions), *Reign of Fire*, and *The Count of Monte Cristo* (both Spyglass Entertainment productions). An ongoing relationship with Hallmark Entertainment has also led to World 2000 bringing productions of *Animal Farm*, *David Copperfield*, and adaptations of two Irish novels—*Durango* and *The Blackwater Lightship*—to Ireland.

Bibliography

CONTENTS

INTRODUCTION

Like the Irish film industry itself, writing on the field has really come into its own only in the past two decades. Prior to 1987, with the exception of Liam O'Leary's broad-ranging 1945 publication *Invitation to the Film*, there was virtually nothing in book form on Irish cinema, although a number of journal articles and pamphlets, with varying degrees of comprehensiveness, had been published. However, in 1987, three authors—Kevin Rockett, Luke Gibbons, and John Hill—almost single-handedly created the field of Irish film studies with the publication of *Cinema and Ireland*. Divided into three nearly self-contained sections relating to the interests of the different authors, the book addressed the political economy of Irish cinema, the representation of Northern Irish political violence, and the romanticization of Ireland through Hollywood cinema. Arguably many of the books that followed were effectively footnotes—albeit often very useful footnotes—to this founding text.

The effect of *Cinema and Ireland*, however, was to valorize the work of what would later become known as the "first wave" of Irish filmmakers—those who, in difficult financial conditions, managed to produce culturally specific filmic texts, exploring aspects of Irish society and culture rarely touched by overseas films shot in Ireland.

As the number of academics working in the area increased over the years, more contemporary general studies emerged that dealt with the growing number of "second wave" films. These include Lance Pettitt's broad review of film and television in *Screening Ireland*, Martin McLoone's well-honed *Irish Film: The Emergence of a Contemporary Cinema* with its definitive reading of *Butcher Boy*, for example, and Ruth Barton's student-accessible *Irish National Cinema* with its extensive overview of a large number of new Irish films.

While the academic output continued to grow over recent decades, important links and comparisons were made with British film and television in particular by well-established writers, including Rockett, Hill, Gibbons, and McLoone, who ensured that Irish film analysis would be placed in the context of a broader international framework. Furthermore, international conferences, in America especially, ensured that that diasporic dimension of the study of Irish film continued to grow, as evidenced in readers like MacKillop's. In Ireland as elsewhere, strong connections have been forged particularly with literary studies; many ostensibly literary readers frequently include original work on film adaptations. In Ireland recently, research links between various universities have led to a number of graduate seminars and publications of edited books. Young film academics have entered new avenues of investigation and extended the range of study, which is always a healthy sign. In particular new genre, narrative, and gender studies have enabled Irish film study to move beyond what some perceive as a self-enclosed ghetto of national film study into more mainstream and universal aesthetical concerns.

The broad disciplinary areas of cultural studies and identity politics have also been very active in Ireland, as elsewhere, with a growth in studies of race, class, and of course gender issues, feeding off graduate research in women's studies.

The "troubles" and the forming of a historical identity have remained a major category of film and cultural analysis, as evidenced by the large number of studies in this area, while more recently the contested notion of definable Irish identity continues to attract academic interest. Coupled with this is the less-developed area of political economic study, which is concerned with how the often volatile public sphere directly affects which films get made, as well as their reception. The evolution of the Irish film industry can be seen through the history of censorship and the changing responsibility of the state, which act as a barometer of national identity. Studies like Rockett's, O'Brien's, and Flynn's effectively flesh out these complex and historical contextual issues within Irish film.

At the level of textual analysis, a growing number of studies of directors like Sheridan, Jordan, and others; a number of fascinating book-length studies of individual films; and biographies ensure that researchers have lots of material to help them uncover the mosaics of creative production in Ireland. But there is always room for more studies, particularly about audiences and how films are received.

For researchers looking to go beyond secondary sources, the key center for Irish films and film-related documents is unquestionably the Irish Film Archive, which is currently located in the Irish Film Institute in Dublin's Temple Bar. The archive holds some 20,000 pieces of film, and the attached library keeps extensive material on Irish directors, actors, cinemas, and production companies. It also holds a fairly comprehensive stock of "gray literature," official reports on various aspects of Irish film policy since the 1960s. It is not entirely comprehensive, however, and it is worth contacting the archive in advance of a visit to ensure that they have the material you're looking for. It should also be acknowledged that much film and document material from the earlier period of Irish film is still unavailable. The 1942 *Report of the Intern-Departmental Committee on the Film Industry*, a key text discussed in this volume, was, until 2005, considered lost before it turned up in the National Archive. Researchers interested in aspects of Irish film policy should consider looking at files from the Department of the Taoiseach and from the Department of Industry and Commerce, which are held in the National Archive.

Ironically, researchers may have to travel outside Ireland to explore some aspects of Irish film. The United States Library of Congress has been the source of more than one "lost" film from the silent period of Irish cinema, while the British Library Periodicals section at Collinswood in the United Kingdom is a useful source of early (pre-1930) journals and magazines related to Irish cinema.

One final source for researchers interested in the political economy of modern Irish cinema is the Irish Film and Television Network, whose website was originally established as an offshoot of Paradox Films, a local feature film production company, and which is accessible at www.iftn.ie. Although oriented largely toward the industry itself, the site offers general information on production, distribution, and exhibition in Ireland. It also offers a searchable news archive and a filmography. The content of the latter is somewhat patchy—some of the films are discussed in detail, while others have information only on the key production personnel attached. Nonetheless it is much more comprehensive on Irish audiovisual production than international sources such as the Internet Movie Database.

For a wide variety of Irish-themed television and cinema, visit the Irish Film and TV Research Online website at www.tcd.ie/Irishfilm.

GENERAL TEXTBOOKS FOR IRISH FILM STUDIES

Allon, Yoram, Del Cullen, and Hannah Patterson, eds. *Contemporary British and Irish Film Directors: A Wallflower Critical Guide.* London: Wallflower, 2001.

Barton, Ruth. *Irish National Cinema.* London: Routledge, 2004.

Barton, Ruth, and Harvey O'Brien, eds. *Keeping It Real: Irish Film and Television.* London: Wallflower Press, 2004.

Byrne, Terry. *Power in the Eye: An Introduction to Contemporary Irish Film.* Lanham, MD: Scarecrow Press, 1997.

Caughie, John, with Kevin Rockett. *The Companion to British and Irish Cinema.* London: Cassell, 1996.

Flynn, Arthur. *The Story of Irish Film,* Dublin: Currach Press, 2005.

Hill, John. *Cinema and Northern Ireland: Film, Culture and Politics.* London: British Film Institute, 2006.

Hill, John, and Pamela Church Gibson, eds. *The Oxford Companion to World Cinema.* Oxford: Oxford University Press, 1998.

Hill, John, and Martin McLoone. *Big Picture, Small Screen: The Relations between Film and Television.* Luton: John Libby Press, 1996.

Hill, John, Martin McLoone, and Paul Hainsworth, eds. *Border Crossing: Film in Ireland, Britain and Europe.* London: British Film Institute, 1994.

Hjort, Mette, and Scott MacKenzie, eds. *Cinema and Nation.* London: Routledge, 2000.

Horgan, John, Barbara O'Connor, and Helena Sheehan, eds. *Mapping Irish Media*: Critical Explorations. Dublin: UCD Press, 2007.

MacKillop, James, ed. *Contemporary Irish Cinema.* Syracuse, NY: Syracuse University Press, 1999.

McIlroy, Brian. *Irish Cinema: An Illustrated History.* Dublin: Anna Livia Press, 1988.

McLoone, Martin. *Irish Film: The Emergence of a Contemporary Cinema.* London: BFI Press, 2000.

O'Brien, Harvey. *The Real Ireland: The Evolution of Ireland in Documentary Film.* Manchester, UK: Manchester University Press, 2004.

O'Leary, Liam. *Invitation to the Film.* Tralee, Ireland: The Kerryman, 1945.

Pettitt, Lance. *Screening Ireland: Film and Television Representation.* Manchester, UK: Manchester University Press, 2000.

Rockett, Kevin. *Film and Ireland: A Chronicle* [booklet]. London: A Sense of Ireland, 1980.

———. *The Irish Filmography.* Dublin: Red Mountain Press, 1996.

———. "(Mis-)Representing the Irish Urban Landscape." In *Cinema and the City: Film and Urban Societies in a Global Context*, eds. Mark Shiel and Tony Fitzmaurice, pp. 217–228. Oxford: Blackwell, 2001.

———. *Still Irish: A Century of the Irish in Film*. Dun Laoghaire, Ireland: Red Mountain Press, 1995.

———. *Ten Years After: The Irish Film Board 1993–2003*. Dublin: Irish Film Board, 2003.

Rockett, Kevin, Luke Gibbons, and John Hill. *Cinema and Ireland*. London: Routledge, 1988.

Rockett, Kevin, and John Hill, eds. *National Cinema and Beyond*. Dublin: Four Courts Press, 2004.

Slide, Anthony. *The Cinema and Ireland*. Jefferson, NC: McFarland Press, 1988.

Williams, Alan, ed. *Film and Nationalism*. Piscataway, NJ: Rutgers University Press, 2002.

CULTURAL STUDIES AND IRELAND

Ashby, Justine, and Andrew Higson, eds. *British Cinema, Past and Present*. London: Routledge, 2000.

Brady, Ciaran, ed. *Hutchinson Encyclopaedia of Ireland*. Dublin: Helicon Press, 2000.

Buell, Frederick. *National Culture and the New Global System*. Baltimore and London: Johns Hopkins University Press, 2000.

Condon, Denis. "Touristic Work and Pleasure: The Kalem Company of Killarney." In *Film and Film Culture*, vol. 2, pp. 7–16. Waterford, Ireland: Waterford Institute of Technology, 2003.

Corner, John, and Sylvia Harvey, eds. *Enterprise and Heritage: Crossroads of National Culture*. London: Routledge, 1991.

Coulter, Colin, and Steve Coleman, eds. *The End of Irish History: Critical Reflections on the Celtic Tiger*. Manchester, UK: Manchester University Press, 2003.

Cronin, Michael. *Across the Lines: Travel, Language, Translation*. Cork: Cork University Press, 2000.

Cullingford, Elizabeth Butler. *Ireland's Others: Ethnicity and Gender in Irish Literature and Popular Culture*. Cork: Cork University Press (in association with Field Day), 2001.

———. "Re-reading the Past: *Michael Collins* and Contemporary Popular Culture." In *Ireland in the New Century,* ed. Robert J. Savage Jr. Dublin: Four Courts Press. 2003.

Deane, Seamus, ed. *The Field Day Anthology of Irish Writing*, 3 volumes. Derry: Field Day Publications, 1991.

Dunne, Joseph, Attracta Ingram, and Frank Litton, eds. *Questioning Ireland.* Dublin: Institute of Public Administration, 2000.

Eagleton, Terry. *The Truth about the Irish.* New York: St. Martin's Press, 2001.

Foster, Allan. *The Movie Traveller: A Film Fan's Travel Guide to the UK and Ireland.* Edinburgh: Polygon, Edinburgh University Press. 2000.

Gibbons, Luke. "Engendering the State: Narrative, Allegory and Michael Collins." *Eire-Ireland* 31, 3–4 (1996): 261–269.

———. *Transformations in Irish Culture.* Cork: Cork University Press, 1997.

Graham, Brian, ed. *In Search of Ireland: A Cultural Geography.* London: Routledge, 1997.

Hogson, Andrew. *Waving the Flag: Constructing a National Cinema in Britain.* Oxford: Clarendon Press, 1995.

Horgan, John. *Irish Media: A Critical History since 1922.* London: Routledge, 2001.

Industry Strategic Review Group. *The Strategic Development of the Irish Film and Television Industry 2000–2010.* 1999. www.iftn.ie/strategyreport/.

Kearney, Richard, ed. *Across the Frontiers: Ireland in the 1990s.* Dublin: Wolfhound Press, 1988.

———. "Modern Irish Cinemas: Re: Viewing Traditions." In *Irish Literature and Culture*, ed. Michael Kenneally, pp. 144–157. Bucks, UK: Colin Smythe, 1991.

Kirby, Peadar, Luke Gibbons, and Michael Cronin, eds. *Reinventing Ireland: Culture, Society and Global Economy.* London: Pluto Press, 2002.

MacLaughlin, Jim. *Travellers and Ireland: Whose Country, Whose History?* Cork: Cork University Press, 1995.

McCarty, Conor, ed. *Modernisation: Crisis and Culture in Ireland 1969–1992.* Dublin: Four Courts Press, 2000.

McCormack, W. J., ed. *The Blackwell Companion to Modern Irish Culture.* Oxford: Blackwell Press, 1999.

Moran, Albert, ed. *Film Policy: International, National and Regional Perspectives.* London: Routledge, 1996.

O'Leary, Liam. *A Seat among the Stars*, 1984. Belfast: The Universities Press.

O'Mahony, Patrick, and Gerard Delanty. *Rethinking Irish Identity: Nationalism, Identity and Ideology.* London: Macmillan Press, 2000.

Sheehan, Helena. *The Continuing Story of Irish Television Drama: Tracking the Tiger.* Dublin: Four Courts Press, 2004.

Staiger, Janet. "A Neo-Marxist Approach: World Film Trade and Global Culture Flows." In *Film and Nationalism*, ed. Alan Williams, pp. 230–248. Piscataway, NJ: Rutgers University Press, 2002.

Tovey, Hilary, and Perry Share. *A Sociology of Ireland.* Dublin: Gill and Macmillan, 2000.

Vandevelde, Karen, ed. *New Voices in Irish Criticism 3*. Dublin: Four Courts Press, 2002.

Williams, Raymond. *The Country and the City*. London: Hogarth Press, 1985.

HISTORY AND THE "TROUBLES"

Brady, Ciaran, ed. *Interpreting Irish History: The Debate on Historical Revisionism*. Dublin: Irish Academic Press, 1994.

Cathcart, Rex. *The Most Contrary Region: The BBC in Northern Ireland 1924–1984*. Belfast: The Blackstaff Press, 1984.

Coogan, Tim Pat. *Ireland in the Twentieth Century*. London: Hutchinson, 2003.

Crawdus, Gary. "The Screenwriting of Irish History: Neil Jordan's *Michael Collins*," *Cineaste* 11, 4 (May 1997): 14–23.

Curtis, Liz. *Ireland: The Propaganda War*. London: Pluto Press, 1984.

Ferguson, Bob. *Television on History: Representations of Ireland*. London: Comedia, 1985.

Ferriter, Declan. *The Transformation of Ireland: 1900–2000*. London: Profile Books, 2004.

Haslam, Richard. "Irish Film: Screening the Republic." In *Writing in the Irish Republic: Literature, Culture, Politics 1949–1999*, ed. Ray Ryan, pp.130–146. London: Macmillan Press, 2000.

Hill, John. *British Cinema in the 1980s*. Oxford: Oxford University Press, 1990.

Kirkland, Richard. "Gender, Nation, Excess: Reading *Hush-a-Bye Baby*." In *Ireland in Proximity: History, Gender, Space*, ed. Scott Brewster, Virginia Crossman, Fiona Becket, and David Alderson, pp. 109–122. London: Routledge, 1999.

Lloyd, David. *Ireland after History (Critical Conditions: Field Day Essays)*. Cork: Cork University Press, 1999.

McBride, Lawrence, ed. *Images, Icons and the Irish Nationalist Imagination*. Dublin: Four Courts Press, 1999.

McIlroy, Brian. *Shooting to Kill: Filmmaking and the "Troubles" in Northern Ireland*. Trowbridge, UK: Flickbooks, 1999.

Miller, David. *Don't Mention the War: Northern Ireland, Propaganda and the Media*. London: Pluto Press, 1994.

O'Mahony, Patrick, and Gerard Delanty. *Rethinking Irish History: Nationalism, Identity and Ideology*. London: Macmillan Press, 1998.

Roberts, Graham, and Philip Taylor, eds. *The Historian, Television and Television History*. Luton, UK: Luton Press, 2001.

Rockett, Kevin. "Irish Cinema: Notes on Some Nationalist Fictions." *Screen* 20, 3–4 (1978/9): 115–123.

———. "Irish Cinema: The National in the International." *Cineaste* 24, 2–1 (1999): 23–25.

Rolston, Bill, and David Miller, eds. *War and Words: A Northern Ireland Media Reader*. Belfast: Beyond the Pale, 1996.

Schlesinger, Phillip, Phillip Elliott, and Graham Murdock. *Televising Terrorism*. London: Comedia, 1983.

IRISH IDENTITY

Abercrombie, Nicholas. *Audiences: A Sociological Theory of Performance and Imagination*. London and Thousand Oaks, CA: Sage, 1998.

Anderson, Benedict. *Imagined Communities: Reflections on the Origins and Spread of Nationalism*. London: Verso, 1983.

Ashcroft, Bill, Gareth Griffiths, and Helen Tiffin, eds. *The Post-Colonial Studies Reader*. London: Routledge, 1995.

Bhabha, Homi K., ed. *Nation and Narration*. London: Routledge, 1990.

Blandina, Ruth, and M. Quinn. *Public Policy and the Arts*. Ashgate Publishers, 1998.

Brereton, Pat. "Nature Tourism and Irish Film." *Irish Studies Review* 14, 4 (2006): 407–420.

Brown, Terence. *Ireland: A Social and Cultural History, 1922–1985*. London: Fontana Press, 1985.

Byron, Reginald. *Irish America*. Oxford: Oxford University Press, 1999.

Carby, Hazel V. "What Is This 'Black' in the Irish Popular Culture?" *European Journal of Cultural Studies* 4, 3 (August 2001): 325–349.

Connolly, Claire. *Theorising Ireland: Readers in Cultural Criticism*. London: Palgrave Macmillan, 2003.

Cullen, Fintan. *Visual Politics: The Representation of Ireland 1750–1930*. Cork: Cork University Press, 1997.

Curran, Joseph M. *Hibernian Green on the Silver Screen: The Irish and American Movies*. Westport, CT: Greenwood Press, 1989.

Dalsimer, Adele M., ed. *Visualising Ireland: National Identity and the Pictorial Tradition*. London: Faber and Faber. 1993.

Duddy, Thomas. *A History of Irish Thought*. London: Routledge, 2002.

Flynn, Arthur. *The Story of Irish Film*. Dublin: Curragh Press, 2005.

Foster, Roy F. *The Irish Story: Telling Tales and Making It Up in Ireland*. London: Allen Lane/Penguin Press, 2001.

———, ed. *The Oxford History of Ireland*. Oxford: Oxford University Press, 2001.

Geraghty, Christine. "Cinema as a Social Space: Understanding Cinema-Going in Britain, 1947–63." *Framework: The Journal of Cinema and Media* 42 (Summer 2000). www.frameworkonline.com/42cg.htm.

Gibbons, Luke. "The Cracked Looking Glass of Cinema: James Joyce, John Huston and the Memory of *The Dead*," *Yale Journal of Criticism* 15, 1 (Spring 2002): 142.

————. *Field Day Essays. Critical Conditions—Transformations in Irish Culture*. Cork: Cork University Press, 1996.

Graham, Colin. *Deconstructing Ireland: Identity, Theory, Culture*. Edinburgh: Edinburgh University Press, 2001.

Hill, John. "Contemporary British Cinema. Industry, Policy, Identity." *Cineaste* 26, 4 (November 2001).

Kearney, Richard. *Across the Frontiers: Ireland in the 1990s*. Dublin: Wolfhound Press, 1988.

————, ed. *Migration: The Irish at Home and Abroad*. Dublin: Wolfhound Press, 1990.

————. *Postnationalist Ireland: Politics, Culture, Philosophy*. London: Routledge, 1997.

————. *Transitions: Narratives in Modern Irish Culture*. Dublin: Wolfhound Press, 1988.

Kelly, Mary, and Barbara O'Connor. *Media Audiences in Ireland*. Dublin: UCD Press, 1997.

Kenneally, Michael, ed. *Irish Literature and Culture*. Bucks, UK: Colin Smith Press, 1992.

Kiberd, Declan. *Inventing Ireland*. London: Vintage, 1996.

Lalor, Brian. *The Encyclopedia of Ireland*. Dublin: Gill and Macmillan, 2003.

Lothe, Jacob. *Narrative in Fiction and Film: An Introduction*. Oxford: Oxford University Press, 2000.

McBride, Ian. *History and Memory in Modern Ireland*. Cambridge: Cambridge University Press, 2001.

McCarthy, Conor. *Modernisation, Crisis and Culture in Ireland*. Dublin: Four Courts Press, 2000.

McLoone, Martin. *TV and Irish Society: 21 Years of Irish TV*. Dublin: RTE Press. 1984

Morash, Chris. *Twentieth-Century Irish Drama*. Manchester, UK: Manchester University Press, 2002.

Negra, Diane. *The Irish in US: Irishness, Performativity and Popular Culture*. Durham and London: Duke University Press, 2006.

Norden, Martin F. *The Cinema of Isolation: A History of Physical Disability in the Movies*. Piscataway, NJ: Rutgers University Press, 1994.

O'Regan, Tom. *Australian National Cinema*. London: Routledge, 1996.

O'Toole, Fintan. *Black Hole, Green Card: The Disappearance of Ireland.* Dublin: New Island Books, 1994.

———. *The Ex-Isle of Erin: Images of Global Ireland.* Dublin: New Ireland Books, 1997.

———. *A Mass for Jessie James: A Journey through 1980s Ireland.* Dublin: Raven Arts Press, 1990.

Peillon, Michael, and Eamon Slater, eds. *Encounters with Modern Ireland.* Dublin: Institute of Public Administration, 1998.

Peillon, Michael, and Mary Corcoran, eds. *Place and Non-Place: The Reconfiguration of Ireland.* Dublin: Institute of Public Administration, 2004.

Porter, Joy. "The North American Indians in the Irish." *Irish Studies Review* 11, 3 (December 2003): 263–272.

Ross, S. J., ed. *Ireland: Movies and American Society.* Oxford: Blackwell Press, 2002.

Savage, Robert J., Jr., ed. *Ireland in the New Century.* Dublin: Four Courts Press, 2003.

———. *Irish Television: The Political and Social Origins.* Cork: Cork University Press, 1996.

Smyth, Gerry. *Space and Irish Cultural Imagination.* London: Palgrave Macmillan, 2001.

Soila, Tytti, Astrid Soderbergh Widding, and Gunnar Iverson. *Nordic National Cinemas.* London: Routledge, 1998.

Thomas, Nicholas, ed. *International, Dictionary of Films and Film-Makers—1: Films* London: St. James Press, 1990.

GENDER

Barton, Ruth. "Feisty Colleens and Faithful Sons: Gender in Irish Cinema." *Cineaste* (Contemporary Irish Cinema Supplement) 24, 2–3 (1999): 40–45.

Bradley, Anthony, and Maryann Gialanella Valiulis, eds. *Gender and Sexuality in Modern Ireland.* Amherst: University of Massachusetts Press, 1997.

Brewster, Scott, Virginia Crossman, Fiona Becket, and David Alderson, eds. *Ireland in Proximity: History, Gender, Space.* London: Routledge, 1999.

Connell, R. W. *Gender and Power: Society, the Person and Sexual Politics.* Stanford, CA: Stanford University Press, 1987.

———. "Politics of Changing Men." *Australian Humanities Review* (June–August 2001). www.lib.latrobe.edu.au/AHR/archive/Issue-Dec-1996/connell .html.

Craig, Steve, ed. *Men, Masculinity and the Media.* London: Sage, 1992.

Farley, Fidelma. "Interrogating Myths of Maternity in Irish Cinema: Margo Harkin's Hush-A-Bye Baby." *Irish University Review: A Journal of Irish Studies* 29, 2 (Autumn/Winter 1999).

——. "Neil Jordan." In *50 Contemporary Film Makers*, ed. Yvonne Tasker. London: Routledge, 2002.

McCabe, Martin. "The Irish Male in Cinema." *The Irish Review*, 1993.

McCarthy, Gerry. "Feature Reviews." *Film West*, 43 (Spring 2002).

Monk, Claire. "Men in the 90s." In *British Cinema of the 90s,* ed. Robert Murphy. London: British Film Institute, 2000.

O'Leary, Alan. "The Gendered Space of Cinema and Nation in *Elizabeth* and *Michael Collins.*" *Studies in European Cinema* (Bristol) 1, 2 (September 2004): 117–128.

Pettitt, Lance. "Pigs and Provos, Prostitutes and Prejudice: Gay Representation in Irish Film: 1984–1955." In *Sex, Nation and Dissent in Irish Writing*, ed. Eibhear Wash, pp. 252–284. Cork: Cork University Press, 1997.

POLITICAL ECONOMY

Arts Council. *Annual Report 1983*. Dublin: Arts Council, 1984.

——. *Annual Report 1984*. Dublin: Arts Council, 1985.

Boland, Gerard. Speech. Dáil Éireann, vol. 98, 17 October, 1945.

Bruton, John. Speech. Dáil Éireann, vol. 357, 20 March, 1985, p. 37.

Connolly, Neil, and Maretta Dillon. *Developing Cultural Cinema in Ireland.* Dublin: Arts Council, 2001.

Coopers and Lybrand. *Report on the Indigenous Audiovisual Production Industry*. Dublin: Coopers and Lybrand, 1992.

Dwyer, Michael. "10 Days That Shook the Irish Film Industry." *Film West* 30 (Autumn 1997).

Film Industry Committee. *Report of the Film Industry Committee*. Dublin: Stationery Office, 1968.

Film Industry Strategic Review Group. *The Strategic Development of the Irish Film and Television Industry 2000–2010*. Dublin: Stationery Office, 1999.

Film Makers Ireland. *Independent Television Production Sector Report*. Dublin: FMI, 1992.

Flynn, Roderick. "Raiders of the Lost Archives: The Report of the Inter-Departmental Committee on the Film Industry 1942." *Irish Communications Review* 10 (2007): 30–40.

——. *Cinema and State: Irish Film Policy since 1922*. London: Irish Academic Press, 2008.

Government of Ireland. Broadcasting Act. Dublin: Government Publications, 1960.

——. Irish Film Board Act. Dublin: Government Publications, 1980.

Indecon. *A Strategy for Success Based on Economic Realities*. Dublin: Indecon, 1995.

Inter-Departmental Committee on the Film Industry. *Report of the Inter-Departmental Committee on the Film Industry*, 1942 (unpublished—available in National Archives at R 303/GB/18).

Irish Film Board. Annual Report and Accounts 1993. Dublin: Irish Film Board, 1995.

Magennis, William. Speech. Dáil Éireann, vol. 3, 10 May 1923, p. 762.

Marcus, Louis. Keynote Address to Irish Film Board, Day of Debate, 12 April 2003, Unpublished.

National Archive Document 323/272. "Irish Finance Film Corporation Enq. re. State Aid to Film Production in Other Countries." 1967.

O'Higgins, Kevin. Speech. Dáil Éireann, vol. 3, 3 May, 1923, pp. 586–587.

PriceWaterhouseCoopers. *Review of Section 481 of the Taxes Consolidation Act 1997*. Dublin: PriceWaterhouseCoopers, 2003.

Reynolds, Albert. Speech. Dáil Éireann, vol. 334, 18 May, 1982, p. 1316.

Special Working Group on the Film Production Industry. *Report to the Taoiseach, Mr. Albert Reynolds, T. D., 24 Nollaig, 1992*. Dublin: Stationery Office, 1992.

Stoneman, Rod. "Sins of Commission." *Screen* 33, 2 (Summer 1992): 127–144.

——. "Sins of Commission II." *Screen* 46, 2 (Summer 2005): 247–264.

——. "Under the Shadow of Hollywood: The Industrial versus the Artisanal." *The Irish Review* 24 (Autumn 1999): 96–103.

EXHIBITIONS AND AUDIENCES

Connolly, Neil, and M. Dillon. *Developing Cultural Cinema in Ireland*. Dublin: Arts Council, Irish Film Board, and Enterprise Ireland, 2001.

Keenan, Jim. *Dublin Cinemas: A Pictorial Selection*. Dublin: Picture House Publications, 2005.

McBride, Stephanie, and Roddy Flynn. *Here's Looking at You, Kid!* Dublin: Wolfhound Press. 1996.

Restrictive Practices Commission. *Report of Enquiry into the Supply and Distribution of Cinema Films*. Dublin: Stationery Office, 1977.

CENSORSHIP

Carty, Ciaran. *Confessions of a Sewer Rat: A Personal History of Censorship and the Irish Cinema*. Dublin: New Island Books, 1995.
"Irish 'Accept and Want' Censorship." *Irish Times*, 18 February 1965, p. 1.
O'Drisceoil, Donal. *Censorship in Ireland 1939–1945: Neutrality, Politics and Society*. Cork: Cork University Press, 1996.
Rockett, Kevin. *Irish Film Censorship*. Dublin: Four Courts Press. 2004.

INDIVIDUAL FILMS

Barry, Kevin. *The Dead*. Cork: Cork University Press, 2001.
Barsam, Richard. *The Vision of Robert Flaherty: The Artist as Myth and Film-maker*. Bloomington and Indianapolis: Indiana University Press, 1988.
Cronin, Michael. *The Barry Town Trilogy*. Cork: Cork University Press, 2006.
Devlin, Ann. *Ourselves Alone*. London: Faber, 1986.
Duane, Paul. *The Making of Rocky Road* (Documentary). Newly restored DVD, 2004.
Farley, Fidelma. *Anne Devlin*. Trowbridge, UK: Flicks Books, 2000.
——. *This Other Eden*. Cork: Cork University Press, 2001.
FitzPatrick Dean, Joan. *Dancing at Lughnasa*. Cork: Cork University Press, 2003.
Gibbons, Luke. *The Quiet Man*. Cork: Cork University Press, 2002.
Herr, Cheryl. *The Field*. Cork: Cork University Press 2002.
Jordan, Neil . *The Crying Game: An Original Screenplay*. London: Vintage, 1993.
——. *Michael Collins: Film Diary and Screenplay*. London: Vantage, 1996.
Keane, John B. *The Field*. Dublin: Mercier Press, 1991.
MacCabe, Colin. *The Butcher Boy*. Cork: Cork University Press, 2006.
Maddox, Brenda. *Nora: A Biography of Nora Joyce*. London: Hamilton, 1988.
Levy, Emanuel. "*About Adam* Review." *Variety Online*, posted February 24, 2000.
McBride, Stephanie. *Felicia's Journey*. Cork: Cork University Press, 2007.
McGuinness, Frank. *Dancing at Lughnasa*. London: Faber, 1998.
McNamee, Eoin. *Resurrection Man*. London: Picador, 1995.
McPherson, Conor. *I Went Down: The Shooting Script*. London: Nick Hern Books, 1997.
Meaney, Geraldine. *Nora*. Cork: Cork University Press, 2004.
Messenger, John. "Islanders Who Read." *Anthropology Today* 2, 4 (April 1988): 17–19.

Mooney, T., and Stephen Eustace. *BattleGround: The Making of Saving Private Ryan*. Wexford: Milestone L. Press, 1998.

Mullen, Pat. *Man of Aran*. London: Faber and Faber, 1934.

Norris, Margot. *Ulysses*. Cork: Cork University Press, 2004.

Pettitt, Lance. *December Bride*. Cork: Cork University Press, 2001.

Power, Paul. "The Fine Art of Surfacing." *Film West* 30 (August 1997): 16–19.

Roche, B. *Trojan Eddie: A Screenplay*. London: Methuen, 1997.

Scarlata, Jessica. "Reading of *The Butcher Boy*." In *Literature and Film: A Guide to the Theory and Practice of Film Adaptation*, eds. Robert Stam and Alessandra Raengo, pp. 233–251. Oxford: Blackwell Press, 2005.

Sheeran, P. F. *The Informer*. Cork: Cork University Press, 2002.

Sheridan, Jim. *In America DVD, Director's Commentary*. 20th Century Fox HomeEntertainment, 2004.

Vaughan, Dai. *Odd Man Out*. London: BFI Press, 1995.

Walsh, Maurice. *The Quiet Man and Other Stories*. Belfast: Appletree Press, 1992.

DIRECTORS AND WRITERS

Barsam, Richard. *The Vision of Robert Flaherty: The Artist as Myth and Film-maker*. Indiana: Indiana University Press, 1988.

Barton, Ruth. *Jim Sheridan: Framing the Nation*. Dublin: The Liffey Press, 2002.

Boorman, John. *Adventures of a Suburban Boy*. London: Faber and Faber, 2003.

Browne, Vincent. "Cathal Black Interview." *Film West* 24 (Spring 1996): 18–22.

Brownlow, Kevin. *David Lean: A Biography*. London: Faber and Faber, 1998.

"Death of General Emmet Dalton." *Irish Times*, 6 March 1978.

Huston, John. *An Open Book*. London: Macmillan, 1981.

Marcus, Louis. "Mourning an Artist—and a Genre." *Irish Times*, November 4 1994, p. 15.

McBride, Joseph. *Searching for John Ford*. New York: Faber and Faber, 2001.

McCarthy, Dermot. *Roddy Doyle: Raining on the Parade*. Dublin: The Liffey Press, 2003.

O'Leary, Liam. *Rex Ingram: Master of the Silent Cinema*. Dublin: The Academy Press, 1980.

Quinn, Robert. *Cinegael Paradiso* [Television Documentary]. Dublin: Distinguished Features, 2004.

Rockett, Emer, and Kevin Rockett. *Neil Jordan: Exploring Boundaries*. Dublin: The Liffey Press, 2003.

"Thaddeus O'Sullivan Interview," *Film Ireland* 74 (February/March 2000).

Thomson, David. *A Biographical Dictionary of Film* (3rd ed.). London: Andre Deutsch, 1994.

"Tiernan MacBride Dies, Aged 63." *Irish Times*, 19 July 1995, p. 5.

Woods, Gerald C. *Conor MacPherson: Imagining Mischief*. Dublin: The Liffey Press, 2003.

Woodworth, Paddy. "A Solid Grasp of a Histrionic Industry." *Irish Times*, 10 April 1993, p. 10.

Robbins, Christopher. *The Empress of Ireland*. London: Scriber Press, 2004.

ACTORS

Academy of Motion Pictures Arts and Sciences. Citation on the awarding of an Honorary Oscar to Peter O'Toole. 2003. Posted at http://awardsdatabase.oscars.org/ampas_awards/DisplayMain.jsp?curTime=1174923011921, accessed 26 March 2007.

Barton, Ruth. *Acting Irish in Hollywood: From Fitzgerald to Farrell*. Dublin: Irish Academic Press, 2006.

Bryan, Phillip. *Noel Purcell a Biography*. Dublin: Poolbeg Press, 1992.

Byrne, Gabriel. *Pictures in My Head*. Dublin: Wolfhound Press, 1994.

Carrick, Peter. *Pierce Brosnan*. London: Robert Hale, 2000.

Freedland, Michael. *Peter O'Toole: A Biography*. London: W. H. Allen, 1983.

Miller, Ingrid. *Liam Neeson: The First Biography*. London: Hodder and Stoughton, 1995.

O'Connor, Aine. *Leading Hollywood*. Dublin: Wolfhound Press, 1996.

O'Hara, Maureen, with John Nicoletti. *'Tis Herself: A Memoir*. Simon and Schuster, 2004.

Ryan, Philip B. *Noel Purcell: A Biography*. Dublin: Poolbeg, 1992.

———. *Jimmy O'Dea: The Pride of the Coombe*. Dublin: Poolbeg, 1990.

Smith, Gus. *Richard Harris: Actor by Accident*. London: Robert Hale, 1990.

Toibin, Niall. *Smile and Be a Villain*. Dublin: Town House, 1995.

Wapshott, Nicholas. *Peter O'Toole: A Biography*. London: New English Library, 1984.

Witchel, Alex. "On Stage, and Off." *New York Times*, 29 May 1992, p. C2.

About the Authors

Roderick Flynn was born in Ireland and received his secondary and third-level education in Dublin. He has a bachelor's degree in history and politics from University College Dublin and a master's in film and television studies from Dublin City University (DCU). In 1998 he completed a doctorate on Irish telecommunications policy, also at DCU. He began lecturing in 1995 and became a permanent member of the faculty at the School of Communications, DCU, in 1999. Since then he has chaired the master's program in film and television studies at the university. He has published extensively on various aspects of Irish media and communications policy and is a noted commentator on these issues. He broadcasts a weekly radio show on Irish, European, and American independent cinema. His policy history, *Cinema and State: Irish Film Policy since 1922*, will be published in 2008.

Patrick Brereton was born in Ireland and after receiving his third-level education lived in the United Kingdom for over a decade. He has a bachelor's degree in English and history from University College Dublin and a master's in film and television from the University of Westminster. In 2001 he completed his doctoral dissertation, *Hollywood Utopia: Ecology in Contemporary American Cinema*, at the University of Luton (2004). He has also published *Media Education* (2001) and several papers on film and new media in various journals. He is a guest editor for *Convergence*, a journal of new media studies. Since moving back to Ireland in 2000 he has worked in the School of Communications, Dublin City University, where he is a senior lecturer and where he chairs the degree in multimedia. He teaches various courses including the Masters in Film and Television Studies.